THE MASS
THROUGH THE EYES OF
CHRIST

Other works by Elizabeth Wang also published by Radiant Light:

Teachings-in-Prayer Volume One: Spiritual Training.
Teachings-in-Prayer Volume Two: Spiritual Nourishment.
Teachings-in-Prayer Volume Three: Spiritual Work.
Teachings-in-Prayer Volume Four: Spiritual Life.
Teachings-in-Prayer Volume Five: Spiritual Peace.
"My Priests are Sacred."
How to Pray (Part One: Foundations)
How to Pray Part Two: Liturgy and Morals.
Falling in Love: A Spiritual Autobiography.
Radiant Light: How the Work Began.
"Speak about Hope."
"Speak about Holiness."
What is Jesus like?
What is Mary like?
The Majesty of the Mass.
The Beauty of the Rosary.
The Glory of the Holy Trinity.
The Wonder of the Christian Story.
Prayer Postcards: Hope and encouragement.
An Invitation from Christ: prayer card.
A message from the Father: prayer card.
For Prisoners and those in Darkness: prayer card.
The Holy Sacrifice of the Mass: Mass Poster.
Radiant Light Conference Video 1999.
Radiant Light Conference Video 2000.
The Christian Story Video.

Radiant Light *books, paintings and posters are available to buy in person or by mail-order or to order on-line from:*
St Pauls (By Westminster Cathedral)
Morpeth Terrace, Victoria, London SW1P 1EP, UK.
Tel: 020-7828-5582; Fax: 020-7828-3329
email: bookshop@stpauls.org.uk. Website: www.stpauls.org.uk
Visit the Radiant Light web-site for an updated catalogue:
www.radiantlight.org.uk

THE MASS
THROUGH THE EYES OF
CHRIST

Written and illustrated by
Elizabeth Wang

This book is published by **Radiant Light**
25 Rothamsted Avenue
Harpenden, Herts., AL5 2DN, UK.

First published September 2002

'C.C.C.' refers to the *'Catechism of the Catholic Church'*,
Geoffrey Chapman, London 1994, copyright © 1994
Geoffrey Chapman - Libreria Editrice Vaticana

Scripture quotations have been taken from the Jerusalem Bible
published and copyright 1966, 1967 and 1968
by Darton, Longman and Todd Ltd
and Doubleday & Co. Inc.

ISBN 1-902960-39-4

From the Letter to the Hebrews.

" ... through the blood of Jesus we have the right to enter the sanctuary, by a new way which he has opened for us, a living opening through the curtain, that is to say, his body. And we have the *supreme high priest* over all *the house of God.* So as we go in, let us be sincere in heart and filled with faith, our minds sprinkled and free from any trace of bad conscience and our bodies washed with pure water. Let us keep firm in the hope we profess, because the one who made the promise is faithful. Let us be concerned for each other, to stir a response in love and good works. Do not stay away from the meetings of the community, as some do, but encourage each other to go; the more so as you see the Day drawing near." (Heb 10:19-25)

The Holy Eucharist
in the Catechism of the Catholic Church.

"Jesus said: I am the living bread that came down from heaven ... he who eats my flesh and drinks my blood has eternal life ... abides in me, and I in Him." (Jn 6:51-56) 1406

"Christ is ... really and mysteriously made present." 1357

"In the most blessed sacrament of the Eucharist 'the body and blood, together with the soul and divinity, of our Lord Jesus Christ and, therefore, the whole Christ is truly, really, and substantially contained.'" 1374

"'By the consecration of the bread and wine there takes place a change of the whole substance of the bread into the substance of the body of Christ our Lord and of the whole substance of the wine into the substance of his blood. [This change is called] transubstantiation.'" 1376

"'It is a substantial presence by which Christ, God and man, makes himself wholly and entirely present'" *1374*

"In the Eucharist Christ gives us the very body which he gave up for us on the Cross, the very blood which he 'poured out for many for the forgiveness of sins'." *1365*

"Christ's sacrifice present on the altar makes it possible for all generations to be united with his offering." *1368*

"In the liturgy of the Mass we express our faith in the real presence of Christ under the species of bread and wine by ... genuflecting or bowing deeply as a sign of adoration of the Lord. 'The Catholic Church ... still offers to the sacrament of the Eucharist the cult of adoration, not only during the Mass, but also outside of it, reserving the consecrated hosts with the utmost care, exposing them to the solemn veneration of the faithful, and carrying them in procession'." *1378*

"The Sacrifice of Christ" on Calvary *"and the sacrifice of the Eucharist are one single sacrifice: 'The victim is one and the same: the same now offers through the ministry of priests, who then offered himself on the cross; only the manner of offering is different.' '... in this divine sacrifice which is celebrated in the Mass, the same Christ who offered himself once in a bloody manner on the altar of the cross is contained and is offered in an unbloody manner'."* *1367*

"The Eucharist is also the sacrifice of the Church" ... which is *"the Body of Christ ... With him, she herself is offered whole and entire* *1368*

"The lives of the faithful, their praise, sufferings, prayer and work, are united with those of Christ ... and so acquire a new value." *1368*

"In the Eucharist the Church is as it were at the foot of the cross with Mary, united with the offering and intercession of Christ." *1370*

Frontispiece
"PIERCED TO THE HEART"

Only because of Christ's Passion, Death, Resurrection and Ascension can we now live in hope of reaching the Father, and coming to Heaven. OIL-M:216B. *("So it is proof of God's own love for us, that Christ died for us while we were still sinners." Rm 5:8).*

CONTENTS

PART THREE: THE HOLY SACRIFICE OF THE MASS

LIST OF ILLUSTRATIONS
arranged throughout the book in groups of six.

LIST OF ILLUSTRATIONS, Continued

LIST OF ILLUSTRATIONS, Continued

Group six: The Mass, continued.

Group seven: Mission.

Group eight: Perseverance.

INTRODUCTION

ANOTHER BOOK ABOUT THE MASS.

Only to please Christ have I dared to put pen to paper yet again, on the subject of the Mass. The reason for my trepidation is that Christ has asked me to fulfil a new task. My main work in the past few years has been to encourage people I meet to practise their Catholic Faith. I've been sharing the good news about Christ's infinitely-tender love for each one of us - no matter how weak we are. Following Christ's precise instructions, I've given talks, and published books and paintings to do with Christ and prayer and the sacraments. But now He has requested a book with a different emphasis. Christ has asked me to put together most of the teachings which I've received from Him in prayer about how we should pray and act at Mass.

This book contains a great deal about Christ's love for us; yet it also includes details about how priests should act at Mass, as well as servers, other helpers, and members of the congregation. This is not a collection of private opinions - though I do believe in the truth of what Christ has shown me - but a collection of specific 'teachings' given to me, unasked and undeserved.

Everything within these pages was taught to me by Christ Himself, usually during prayer. I am simply passing on what I have seen and learned 'through the eyes of Christ' whenever He has chosen to teach me about the Catholic Faith - and especially about the Holy Eucharist which is the 'source and summit' of our lives.

'TEACHINGS' IN PRAYER.

Christ has been teaching me in prayer for over forty years, at first intermittently and now daily. He has taught me in different ways, sometimes in a swift wordless 'implanting' of knowledge, sometimes by means of an image given interiorly and accompanied by a wordless explanation, and sometimes in a soundless but real conversation. In the early years, His teachings were brief but profound explanations of, for example, the glory of the Holy Trinity, the importance of prayer, and the meaning of the 'communion of Saints'. Only in recent years has Christ instructed me, in detail, about problems within the Church.

In every age, there are problems, because we are all sinful and imperfect. Yet Christ has shown me on many occasions the particular sins which tarnish the Church in our age. He sees that many Catholics not only disobey His Commandments but openly mock the teachings of the Church and lead others to do the same. He says that few of us have given Him our hearts, entirely, and few make sacrifices for His sake and for the sake of the Gospel. He has made special mention of the incomplete or distorted versions of Church teaching sometimes offered today to children and to new 'converts'. He frequently mentions the decline in reverent behaviour towards Himself in the Blessed Sacrament. And now He has shocked me by asking me to speak and write about these subjects.

In all my adult life as a Catholic I have tried to share my faith, doing so by sharing my delight in the authoritative and coherent teachings of the Church, and my gratitude for the Holy Eucharist - with no desire to examine or comment on the lives and actions of other people. My general attitude has been that of a grateful convert, ashamed of her own failings but thrilled to have been received into full communion. And I've supposed that most 'cradle Catholics' are as grateful as myself for the Mass and the other sacraments, and for the sure teachings of the Church.

Until I became involved in local Ecumenism after many years in the Church, it never occurred to me to comment on how the Sacred Mysteries are celebrated. It became necessary then, occasionally, when it was my duty as a Catholic representative, to question some unorthodox innovation being proposed or enacted. But I was reluctant to speak out. Furthermore, until recently, I have had no official role in Catechetics. I have had no ambition to do anything more at Mass, moreover, than to pray with sincerity and fervour. And now it's solely to obey a direct request from Christ that I've written about the Holy Eucharist, and about the way in which it is celebrated today.

A DAUNTING TASK.

At every Mass, for decades, I've been awe-struck, whatever the style of a particular celebration and whether my own life and soul, at a particular time, have been full of darkness or light. This awe arises simply through my belief that what the Church teaches is indeed true. Jesus Christ our God is really and substantially Present with us, in His sacramental Presence, on the altar and in the tabernacle! So I hope it is plain that Christ has chosen me to write and speak about the Mass simply as a believing Catholic, not as someone from a special faction or with a peculiar point of view.

I know I am not a good person. Christ just wanted someone who would abandon her own plans in order to accept an unexpected and frankly daunting task. I've had nothing to gain from undertaking it except the knowledge that I'm being obedient to Christ - with His promise that it will help the Church.

Many people will be helped by the 'teachings', Christ has shown me; and others will shun them. My only concern, He says, must be to reproduce them, in obedience to His wishes, and then to leave the results in His hands.

A GOOD CARPENTER.

Christ has told me plainly, though with His usual affection, that He is using me as a good Carpenter uses a rusty implement: one which is flawed, but designed for a particular purpose, and which is ready-to-hand, neither lost nor broken.

He has explained that He is offering people in the Church, through me, His observations, instructions and comments about things which - He has also said - some people have neglected to mention. He wants to see change not in the structure of the Sacred Liturgy but in the current lukewarm attitude in the Church toward sacred things and sacred places. And it's because He has first place in my life, as my Lord and Saviour, and has made His wishes very plain, that I've been determined to obey Him. In sharing His teachings with priests and even certain Bishops I've been frightened, at first, and even tactless, I'm sorry to say. But Christ has told me what He has told others before me: "Stand up and tell them all I command you. Do not be dismayed by their presence" (Jr 1:17).

"WRITE DOWN EVERYTHING".

When I was planning the first draft of this book, and when I had finished copying most of Christ's instructions, I asked Him if I should include His teachings on a particular subject. And He told me: "Write down everything, Lizzie: everything! That is why I have trained you." He meant that He has trained me in obedience.

Year after year He has been making plain His wishes, and explaining my work, as well as giving me frequent demonstrations of His wisdom and love. As well as sending me to the Clergy, to explain His wishes, He has Providentially arranged for my writings to be examined by a theologian. So now I'm content to trust in Christ, grateful for His patience and kindness, and grateful for His assurance that this book, with all its flaws, and my clumsy descriptions of sacred matters, is His gift to His Church. More accurately, it is a gift to those of His own 'children' in the Church who are willing to believe that He has taught me, and will listen to what He is saying through me.

Christ wants to remind us all about the holiness of the Mass, the glory of His sacramental Presence amongst us, and the love with which we should approach Him at the altar and at the tabernacle. He is urging us all to live in a state of grace. That's why He has given me a great many teachings not only about our participation in the Mass, but also about our preparation, and about the way we should live our lives when the Mass has ended.

RENEWAL AND REFORM.

As I write about these things I risk giving the impression that Christ is hard to please, which is nonsense. He is thrilled by our least efforts to honour Him. He delights in seeing us trust in His love for us. Yet He has asked me to share not just the good news about His love, but also the sad news that He sees, today, the very things He once saw in His Passion, in Gethsemane and on the Cross. Back then, He looked 'ahead' and saw the sins and failings of people in future centuries, including our own. I've had to describe these things, in obedience to Him, despite the 'plank' in my own eye, to help to fulfil His tremendous plans for renewal and reform in the Church.

Christ wants us all to realise that our 'full participation' in the Mass is achieved not solely through well-rehearsed physical and vocal involvement. Our hearts should be full of gratitude towards Him for His saving sacrifice. Our participation should be wholehearted and immensely reverent. Yet Christ frequently sees a different 'picture'.

He has explained to me that He sees widespread irreverence, many sacrilegious Communions, and new attempts to make our worship in church banal, entertaining or self-centred rather than God-centred and holy. He sees that many of His people worship in clean, well-lit, vigorously re-ordered sanctuaries, but that in many of them the praise of God is 'diluted' by the attention nowadays being focused upon the participants. Such celebrations might radiate joy, but show little sense of awe and humility because many Catholics are entirely ignorant of the awesome nature of the Holy Trinity.

LITTLE SIGN OF RESPECT.

Christ has told me that many Catholics have little understanding of the purpose of the Mass, or of its holiness. Many make no preparation for Mass, show little sign of respect or interest, and approach the altar and tabernacle with none of the gratitude and awe with which Christ deserves to be greeted. Few people pause to pray after receiving Christ in Holy Communion. Many idly chatter in the pews, or rush out of church, ready to forget Christ for a further week or more. Some of the people who organise our worship even promote or allow things - Christ has told me - which give Him no honour or glory but only distract people from the Sacred Mysteries, or focus attention upon individuals rather than the Lord. Some of these novelties are unseemly, or wholly unfitting for inclusion in a sacred Christian rite. Furthermore, there has developed a routine acceptance in some Catholic churches of huge irreverence and noisiness, as the whole of Heaven looks down upon the extraordinary sight. If the Saints and Angels could be shocked, Christ has told me, they would be shocked by what takes place.

In many places which have well-rehearsed choirs and servers, spotless garments and well-ironed altar linen, the heart of the worship is spoiled, as Heaven sees what Christ sees from the tabernacle. He sees that Angels are disturbed in their adoration, devout visitors are amazed to see children run riot, and many of those who take part in the Sacred Liturgy are not awed and prayerful, but bored or incomprehending. Furthermore, many of our Catholic churches have been despoiled of all visual reminders of the Holy Trinity, the Communion of Saints, the Passion of

Christ, the Heaven to which God calls us, and the holy Angels who guard us during our journey. So when people gather for prayer who have had poor or minimal instruction about the Mass, their hearts and minds are not easily lifted 'up' towards God. They are scarcely aware of the majesty of God in Heaven, and 'blind' to the holiness of Christ Who is sacramentally Present. They remain unmoved by the words of the Mass which describe - and make present, by God's power - the sacrifice which Christ offered for our sakes on Calvary. And the solution, Christ tells me, is neither the provision of further novelties, nor attempts to make the Mass more entertaining.

Christ has shown me that our initial duty is to adopt a new attitude in catechesis. We should first consider the nature of God, and the Will of God, before we consider our human nature and our needs. Newcomers to the Church, as well as Catholic children, deserve to have consistently orthodox teaching about the holiness of God, and about our duties towards Him 'as obedient children' (I Pet 1:15). We need priests and Bishops brave enough to insist upon orthodox teaching in Catholic institutions, and orthodox Catholic textbooks. They should be brave enough to ask us to repent of our grave sins before we receive Holy Communion, and brave enough to insist upon reverent behaviour in our churches. We need leaders willing to call a halt to the iconoclasm of the past thirty years. We need a general return to the 'obedience of faith' (Rom 1:5), since Christ has told me that disobedience lies at the heart of the current liturgical crisis.

WIDESPREAD DISOBEDIENCE.

Christ has explained to me that the spirit of disobedience is so widespread that many Catholics routinely disobey the sure teachings of the Church, and contradict her articles of faith. They fail to teach those truths to the children or adults in their care, and blithely criticise or jettison those disciplinary practises or customs which they find irksome or not to their taste. At the same time, He sees that many Catholics who try to remain obedient to His wishes - as expressed in the teachings of the Pope and the other Bishops - are described as having a 'rigid piety'. They are even told that they are 'fostering disunity' if they speak the truth about current irreverence and disobedience in Church life, and about the distorted versions of truth sometimes put forward in Catholic groups and Catholic publications today. Yet Christ prizes the virtue of obedience.

Christ obviously doesn't want us to practise blind obedience that would send us rushing to do anything in order to please people in authority. Yet He has shown me that when adult Catholics see themselves as too 'mature' to act in obedience to the teachings of His Church, Adam's sin is repeated, so to speak, since it was through disobedience that Mankind became alienated from God. Christ has shown me that whenever there arises a spirit of disobedience in the Church, faith grows cold, and further problems follow.

LACK OF FERVOUR.

Where there is a lack of faith in God, there follows a lack of reverence for His holiness and majesty. Then there can develop a casual attitude towards everything sacred, a cynical attitude towards the Pope and the other Bishops who teach with Christ's authority, and a lack of enthusiasm for a life of prayer. People eventually lack willingness to make the sacrifices necessary for Priesthood, for the religious life, or for faithful family life.

Eventually there develops a lack of fervour in handing on the full teaching of the Catholic Faith. There arises a man-centred rather than a God-centred style of catechesis with much stress on Resurrection but little mention of the Cross. Then some Catholics even begin to imagine that dissent and contradiction are 'healthy'. Some believe that the Church and her Saints before the mid-twentieth century held 'primitive' views on earthly life, sin and sanctity. Then at last there arises - amongst Catholics! - a changed attitude towards the solemn worship of God in the Mass. A forgetfulness of God's majesty causes a blithe unconcern about how unfit we are for Heaven, and a near-total neglect of penance and Reconciliation. There's also a greater emphasis on the 'family meal' aspect of the Mass than upon the saving sacrifice which makes possible the 'Holy Communion' we rightly treasure. So we gradually lose the sense of being present at the Sacred Mysteries of the Church, on the threshold of Heaven. Peculiar innovations are permitted when an effort to 'build community' begins to take precedence over our first duty which is to praise God worthily.

These are some of the sad things which Christ has shown me about the decline in recent years; and that's why He is calling us back to obedience. He wants us all to know that just as it was through His loving obedience to the Father's Will that we were redeemed, it is through loving obedience that we, in our turn, can give glory to God the Father. We all need to show ourselves willing to listen to the Spirit Who has been given to us, show our gratitude that Christ died for our sakes, demonstrate love for His Church - and also act bravely to teach the truth about the holiness of the Mass. We need to approach the altar and the tabernacle with awe and reverence as well as 'community spirit'.

THE GREAT COMMANDMENTS.

It is sometimes said that when there are enormous tragedies in the world, such as famine and poverty, incurable diseases and horrible injustices of many kinds, Christ surely can't be concerned with our Liturgical problems. It's through the Sacred Liturgy, however, that we are reconciled with God, delivered from our sins, and made ready to enter Heaven when we die, so the celebration of the sacraments, and our approach to them, can hardly be seen as 'minor' matters.

It's the Lord Who has told us that there are two great Commandments, the first being that we love Him with all our heart and mind and soul and strength, and the second, that we love our neighbour. And while there are thousands of Catholics, and other Christians, urging us all to obey the second Commandment, there are far fewer - He has told me - who are concerned about the first. Hence the extraordinary task Christ has given me: to have to describe the entire Mass from His 'point-of-view'. He has explained that by means of His teachings of the past few years He wants to 'steer' us all towards the sort of devout, reverent and glad celebration of the Sacred Mysteries which is worthy of the Most Holy Trinity, and beneficial for ourselves and for the world.

A CLEARER UNDERSTANDING.

I've had to include some teachings from the Lord in which He reminds us not to equate the Holy Sacrifice of the Mass with a non-Catholic Communion Service. Such a Service is highly praiseworthy for those non-Catholic Christians who devoutly commemorate Christ's Paschal Work in this way. It's a cause for sadness, nevertheless, that some Christians aren't yet aware that the Catholic Church celebrates a 'living memorial' of Christ's Paschal Work, and that Christ is really and substantially Present with us, after the Consecration of the elements by a validly-ordained priest. That's part of the 'good news' that Christ wants everyone to hear. He has explained that we practise what can only be called a 'false Ecumenism' if we never speak the plain truth to fellow-Christians about Catholic teaching, and if we ignore - for a false peace - every subject by which we are divided.

THE OVERALL PLAN.

When I had finally gathered together all the appropriate teachings for this book but had not yet sorted them into different categories, I wondered whether to keep them all in chronological order, to show out Christ's method of teaching. I yearned to show how wise He's been in introducing various aspects of Eucharistic doctrine. First, He taught me through simple images and analogies, and then in greater depth. In between, He wove various teachings about sin and virtue, and catechesis, and a hundred other subjects. Yet I guessed that people who might hope to examine His teachings on one special aspect of the Holy Eucharist might find it difficult to 'trawl' through the whole book. That's why I've sorted the teaching into groups, and have arranged them in a special sequence.

My overall aim has been first to set the scene, and then to work through the Mass, finally sharing necessary details which Christ has explained to me about present-day concerns. Within each group, however, the teachings remain in chronological order; so something of Christ's teaching method can still be discerned.

Another problem is that I've frequently had to put, side by side, a teaching on some very minor matter, with a paragraph on some crucial part of Christian doctrine. I couldn't see how to avoid this, without losing entirely the chronological sequence. Furthermore, there's some imbalance in the numbers of teachings given on various subjects. For example: there are few about the bidding prayers, compared with the great number of teachings about Holy Communion. This simply reflects Christ's desire to offer more powerful instructions and reminders about one subject rather than another. There's very little can go wrong when good-hearted people offer sincere petitions to God, together, about matters of urgent concern - apart from the microphone failing, or the reader being over-shy, or speaking too fast; and Christ is delighted to see us turn to the Father in trusting intercession. When Christ regularly sees people being careless or disrespectful, however, or in a state of mortal sin, as they approach Him for Holy Communion, the problems are more serious. He has spoken to me many times on this subject.

CHRIST OUR GOD.

Christ has explained to me that there has been so much emphasis on His humanity in recent years that He wants to remind us all of His Divinity. So although the 'teachings' I'm about to share are clothed sometimes in my inadequate phrases and sometimes in language 'borrowed' from the Church, they are Christ's teachings, not my personal opinions. They are His reminders to us all that He is all-holy as well as all-compassionate. He is at work through the sacraments of His Church, to make us holy. He is Really - substantially - Present during the Holy Sacrifice of the Mass, and in the tabernacle; and He asks us all to approach Him with reverence, awe and contrition as well as trust in His infinite love for us.

Whatever problems Christ has revealed to me, He has helped me by explaining that the Mass is 'like a great jewel at the heart of the Faith'. He said: "Nothing can diminish the brilliance of this jewel"; and that's something encouraging to have heard. Every Mass is a sublime and holy offering to God, even where there is misunderstanding or carelessness, or poverty or irreverence, or a nervous or inaudible priest or an unresponsive congregation. Nothing need mar the joy of those who realise how privileged they are to be able to participate in the Holy Mysteries of Christ's Church (T:2782). Christ invites us all to trust in Him, and to treasure His friendship. If we surrender to Christ, we shall be led by Him in the Spirit, to the Father: first, through prayer and the sacraments, and at last through death, at our 'homecoming' to Heaven where we will share His glory.

THE GLORY OF GOD.

Some of that glory is indicated in the paintings which are scattered throughout the text. The numerous images found in this book, except the frontispiece, have been given to me by Christ in prayer, to make clearer some of His soundless 'teachings', and to provide a further means of sharing good news with other people. This news is that He is alive and active. He loves us, and He is still powerfully at work in His Church today. There is no need for despair. He is leading us towards a new 'flowering' of the Catholic Faith after recent turmoil and opposition. He is urging us to persevere, no matter what the cost - nor how frequently we stumble, through our weaknesses.

It's because I want children as well as adults to glimpse something of God's goodness and glory that I have just completed the 'true story' – a book for children about the Mass – mentioned at the foot of page 268. I hope that this will be published in 2003. Meanwhile, I thank God for having given us the good news which everyone deserves to hear, that if we trust in Christ and remain faithful we can hope to arrive safely in Heaven one day, to share His incomparable joy at the heart of the Holy Trinity.

Elizabeth Wang
28 March 2002: Holy Thursday
(The day of the 'Last Supper': the first Mass).

ABBREVIATIONS

In the main text:-

T:535 - indicates the number of the 'teaching-in-prayer' upon which a particular section is based.

P.U.T: 25 - indicates the number of a previously unpublished 'teaching'.

G.H.T. - indicates a handful of paragraphs which have been adapted from passages previously published in The Glory of the Holy Trinity, by the same author.

In the picture-captions:-

OIL-S:535 - indicates that the illustration is a reproduction of a small (S) oil-painting. The number of the oil painting corresponds with the number of the teaching-in-prayer which it illustrates.

Some of the prayer-paintings are medium (M) or large (L).

Water-colour versions of many of these images are found in other books by the same author. Such illustrations are labelled (for example) WC:535.

1.   UNION WITH GOD

THE HOLY TRINITY

The soul, a 'Kingdom'.

Each baptised person who is in a state of grace can say, of his own soul: "My soul is a 'Kingdom'! Here live the holy Three: the Three Divine Persons, one God, Who reign in the glory of the Divine light." Christ reigns there, in that interior universe, no matter what images or shadows might appear in our souls, in prayer, to dim our faith in His presence. (T:29)

A wonderful invitation.

God the Holy Trinity, the Creator of all that exists, is actively inviting us to share His life - and to become holy as He is holy.

The Father calls us. The Spirit 'propels' us so that we reach out to the Father. Jesus unites to Himself each loving and contrite person who has become a member of His Church and who can therefore make one offering with Him from the altar during the Holy Sacrifice of the Mass.

Through Christ's awesome sacrifice, we can be brought into the life and light of the one and only God: the perfect and holy Trinity. (T:37)

Our Most Holy God.

We would all be astonished, were we to see the true glory of the worship in which we take part, as we celebrate the sacraments. The infinite glory of God would blind us, were we to see it now. This all-holy God - surrounded by the vast gathering of Saints and Angels in Heaven - is the 'object' of our worship, as we celebrate the Holy Mysteries. He delights in the least movement towards Himself of a contrite soul. Yet He is so glorious in His majesty that we should tremble with awe in the midst of our joy. (T:42A) *(See illustration 48)*

The purpose of life.

Christ wants us to see how privileged we are to have received life and love, and a thousand gifts, from Heaven. Yet our life's purpose is not self-glorification but self-giving. The life of each of us should be a sacrifice in praise of God: in freely-offered obedience and service. (T:42B)

During our journey.

Each of the Three Divine Persons is at work to help us. Because of Their infinite love for us, They are active within our lives on earth. We cannot 'see' the end of our journey, but it is Jesus Who holds each 'child of God' throughout this pilgrimage. It is His Spirit Who fills our hearts as we move with Jesus gently towards the Father, Who is nevertheless ever-present in our lives, and ever-welcoming as we turn to Him in prayer. (T:56)

Humanity, in God's embrace.

The greater is our love for the Church, for the Sacred Scriptures, and for the Holy Eucharist, the greater is our delight in pondering the marvellous things which God has done for us. We begin to burn with the desire to share more widely and more boldly the Good News about God's love for us all and His forgiveness of our sins; and we burn with the desire to see God loved. As we grow in faith, we're glad to share what we've learned, to help to deliver other people from sin, hopelessness and isolation.

It's as though God the Father is hidden far above, in glory; yet His love for Mankind is so great that He has reached out from on high to send powerful help towards a sinful world. It's as though, through His plan of salvation - through His self-revelation - He has enfolded humanity in an 'embrace of God'.

The Word and the Holy Spirit are like two arms from God the Father. For century upon century the living God has been calling out to us all, through His Church, urging us to come out of darkness, and to enter His glorious light. (T:1439) G.H.T.

Christ awaits us.

We hear in the words of the Mass that God has "no need of our praise", since nothing we say can either cause or augment the infinite, perpetual bliss which is of the essence of the life of the Holy Trinity, in Eternity. Yet we should never doubt that our praises are worthwhile. It is our duty to honour God. Our hearts and minds were made for worship; and so we are fulfilled and helped to some degree whenever we pray. Our praise is also worthwhile because Christ our Lord is at the heart of the Godhead. He is true man as well as true God, and He is now at the heart of Heaven; and since we are His true brothers and sisters, we touch His heart very deeply by our loving praises.

Christ is made happy by our veneration, and by our praise of the Father: praise which we offer through Christ, in the Holy Spirit. Christ awaits us, at the heart of Heaven's triple glory; and He longs with all His heart for us to join Him. This is His plan for Mankind. This is what would cause Him tremendous delight: to see a great crowd of the faithful loving Him and longing to meet Him. He wants to see us all pouring like a river into the Godhead, into the heart of the Most Holy Trinity. (T:1476) G.H.T.

Distinct but united.

If we picture a blazing fire, we have an image of the marvellous life and 'work' of the Holy Trinity. God is like a living fire which is composed of three great flames, each of which is distinct; yet the three make one fire, or one light, which is the Godhead.

Wherever the Holy Spirit is at work, the Father and the Son are at work. Wherever the Father is at work, He is at work with both the Son and the Holy Spirit; and we know that wherever the Son is at work, the Father and the Holy Spirit, also, are active.

We can think of God as being like a fire which is forever unchanging, calm, inextinguishable, indefinable, and un-containable: like a fire which has no source. Neither lamp, candle nor tinder caused this fire to shine. This 'fire' - these flames - exists of itself, and represents our God, Who is Three-in-One, and has neither beginning nor end. (T:1913) G.H.T.

The burning love of God.

None of us knows what Heaven looks like. None of us has seen the Father's face. We cannot imagine the 'white-hot' love we shall meet in Heaven. But there, at the heart of the Three-in-One Whom we have worshipped in our earthly 'darkness', we can find answers to some of our questions, as well as the fulfilment for which we were made.

The Divine love at the heart of the Godhead - the pure, 'white-hot,' perfect love which God is - causes Christ to come amongst us at each celebration of the Mass, and to remain amongst us through His sacramental Presence in the tabernacle. This white-hot love makes each sanctuary of our churches resemble a furnace: an area now full of the fire of love which is blazing fiercely, as it pours out graces from the Godhead. (T:2143) G.H.T.

Our 'homeland'.

At every second of our earthly life, we are on a journey: a spiritual journey. Though always held 'in' God, and sustained by Him, we are in some manner either moving closer towards Him or turning away from His face; so we must do all we can to remain in His love, and to show love towards our neighbour.

God the Father delights in our longing to know Him, and draws us further into His life the more generously we co-operate with His graces. The Father delights in our faith, and in our gratitude for His gifts: for life and faith and every blessing - and in our gratitude for Christ, His Son, Whom He sent down to earth to die for us.

If we give our consent, we eventually find ourselves drawn into God's heart, by God's power. We are swept towards Him as if towards the heart of a whirlpool, or as if in a whirlwind of love, or a storm of rejoicing. True friends of God who are living in God are as if soaring within His being, in everyday life and in prayer. They are at peace in His love, and are united with Him in every act, thought and intention.

God the Holy Trinity is the 'heart' from which we were born. In Him, we can dwell in friendship. He is the 'homeland' in which we can move in freedom. He is the infinite torrent of light and joy in which we can soar, in prayer. He is the goal of our yearning hearts. He is the destination at which, through our life 'in Christ' and our union with Christ, we already arrive. He is the love in which we are held, safely. He is the breath which we breathe, in His embrace. He is the 'playground' for us, His children. It's as if, in silent prayer, we search enraptured, in the vast, soaring heights of His infinite love, in safety. (T:2169) G.H.T.

Intimacy with God.

The life of the Holy Trinity is ours to share, through our Baptism, and even ours to enjoy in a known and blissful manner. If we persevere in love, and nourish our 'life in Christ' through the sacraments, and prove our love for Christ by loving our neighbour, and grow close to Christ in prayer, then we can be drawn by Christ, even in this life - in prayer - into the heart of the Godhead. Then at last we realise that the Three Who are so powerful and majestic are at the same time gentle, sweet, consoling, palpably 'present' to the soul, and infinitely kind and patient.

Through Christ we can be drawn into real intimacy with the Holy Trinity: one God, yet Three Persons, to Whom we offer our lives, in willing service. And when the 'nights' of darkness have ended, we can find the joy, glory and fulfilment for which we have been yearning. We learn that joy and glory are the 'climate' which is enjoyed by everyone who lives 'in' God, in true union. (T:2221)

In mutual love.

We can say that God is wholly 'occupied' with love. The Three Divine Persons - The Holy Trinity - are 'occupied' in a ceaseless, unbroken, and blissful mutual giving and receiving of perfect love, 'in' joy and glory. And whoever consents to God's love and action is drawn into the heart of the Godhead. It is as though, in prayer, we are leaping, joyfully - even now, in earthly life - into the bliss and glory of the Divine life of the Holy Trinity: the one eternal God Who can be our eternal delight and joy. (Also T:2221) G.H.T.

The Holy Trinity at work.

The Three Divine Persons are Three-in-One: one and active. Father, Son and Holy Spirit work as one, to draw frail creatures into Their blissful embrace, and to share Their Divine life forever. Truly, the Father is the origin of all life, light and love. His loving Son, having the same infinite love, generosity and compassion, could not have failed to come out from the Father's heart, to save us; and the Holy Spirit is the Person and the power by Whom sinful people can be transformed and lifted up to Heaven. Yet the

Three Divine Persons are one, and work as one: always active in the great, holy work of love in Eternity, in the eternal 'dance' and delight of Heaven. (T:2731) G.H.T.

Three Persons: one love.

While we still remain in earthly life, we can find God, no matter where we are. We can reach Him in a deserted part of the world or on the crowded pavements, in the dark void of our wounded heart or in the sunlight of our moments of fulfilment. He is never absent from us, but is always prompting us to pray. He always gazes lovingly upon us, ready to share His life and love with us, if only we'll open the 'door' of our souls.

Perhaps we like to chatter - friend to friend - with Christ our Saviour. Perhaps we delight in offering reverent words of praise, or whispered endearments, to our Father in Heaven. Perhaps we call out, frequently, for the help of the Holy Spirit. Yet none of us, in pondering the glory of God's inner life, must forget the unity of the Godhead.

When we pray to one Divine Person we pray to the one, Triune God: whether we pray to the Father, the Son, or the Holy Spirit. There are not three Gods, but only one, in Whom are Three Divine Persons Who are distinct but united. Whenever we speak to Christ in prayer, therefore, we address at the same time the Father and the Holy Spirit. And when we speak to the Father we also address Christ and the Spirit. And when we speak to the Holy Spirit we address, at the same time, the Father, and Christ His Son. Three Persons hear us: Three Divine Persons Who are gazing upon us with infinite love and compassion. So we have good reason to be faithful to the patterns of prayer which are treasured in the Church.

Although we can pray to the Father or to the Son or to the Holy Spirit, it was Christ the Son Who taught us to pray to the Father in His (Christ's) name, in the power of the Holy Spirit. And so

Christ's Church, for centuries, has formed and developed our patterns of Christian prayer in accordance with Christ's wishes. (T:4237) G.H.T.

In perpetual exaltation.

God the Holy Trinity is alive and active. The Godhead can be pictured as being like a great river of love and light and glory. It's as if it flows in a great circle in Eternity in perpetual exultation and delight. The Three Divine Persons hold within Their life and love all who have become Their children, who have persevered in love, and have been made worthy to enter Their embrace forever. Happy souls who have left behind the transient joys of earth have found, in the interior of the Godhead, a place of unending delight: a place of unmatched sweetness and unparalleled beauty.

There, at God's heart, are vistas greater and more astounding than can be seen in a thousand universes. God's love is like balm to a wounded heart. His pure light delights those who have loved truth and beauty.

Even during life on earth, however, we can enter this 'world' and this embrace, if we love God and live in a state of grace, and take part in the Holy Sacrifice. In meeting Christ, we meet the Father and the Holy Spirit. Even if nothing is seen, felt, touched or heard, we are thoroughly 'in touch' with God. (T:4315) G.H.T.

Intimate union.

We in the Church are God's adopted children; and we can learn to approach Him with reverence and love, aware of the wondrous invitation He holds out to us as He asks us to enter the heart of the Holy Trinity.

After our necessary purifications we find that we are upheld within the life of the Three Divine Persons. It's as if we can gaze around us in awe, in our prayer, while still enveloped in the huge 'cloud' which veils the mystery and beauty of the Godhead. As we reach intimate union with God, in the heights of contemplation, however, we shall know our souls to be wholly encompassed by the presence, love and power of the Three Divine Persons; and we shall no longer be afraid, but safe, and wholly at peace, and joyful. (T:4727)

Adoration and self-offering.

This is pure worship: to be at rest with the Three Divine Persons, in and through Christ. In being held by the all-holy, some of us are content to gaze, to adore, to wait, and to offer our whole heart and self in love and adoration. Others yearn both to stay at God's heart forever, yet also to run 'outside' to make His love known.

Truly, whenever we celebrate the Sacred Mysteries of the Church, we can say: "This is pure worship." As we join in the praises offered by the Church in and through Christ, in solemn phrases and reverent gestures, we honour the Holy Trinity and also mirror the worship of the Heavenly company. (Also T:4727).

THE FATHER

The source of all joy.

We who belong to Christ should know something about the glory and splendour of the Father from Whom Christ came, at His Incarnation. The Father is the source of all joy. He exists beyond time and space. He is free and sovereign, yet is united in love and bliss with the Word and the Holy Spirit, Who are equal to Him in majesty and holiness.

The Father is the sublime 'heart' of the Holy Trinity. He is the source of all beauty, and is glorious beyond our imaginings. He is the Father of all that is created. He holds within His embrace the Saints and holy Angels who worship and adore Him. And He also holds, in His 'heart', those faithful souls who have been 'freed', through death, to live with Him eternally, yet who are undergoing their necessary purifications. (T:55B)

Over-flowing love.

The marvel of the Christian faith is that we need no longer rely on our limited observations - about the world and its creatures, and about the universe with its laws and its beauty - to know what God is 'like'. From love, He has revealed Himself to Mankind, most fully through His own Son, Jesus Christ, in Whom is found 'the fullness of Divinity'. In this way, we have been given overwhelming confirmation that the Father's love is warm, overflowing, generous and tender. He is always longing to pour out His gifts upon His children on earth.

From His perpetual newness and youth and beauty the Father gives us good things, good news, and spiritual joy: gifts which delight us. The greatest gift has been our renewed friendship with Him, through Christ our Redeemer who was given to us through His Holy Mother Mary. (T:1244) G.H.T.

A precious child.

We are sometimes tempted to imagine that God is 'absent', when the truth is that He is very close indeed, and is lovingly holding us in existence. And if we have been made adopted children of God, through Christ, we have a sure hope of Heaven, if we remain faithful to the end. Throughout our journey towards the Kingdom we should remain confident in prayer.

Every sincere prayer which we offer through Christ to the Father, in the Spirit, is greeted with delight. The Father delights in the humility with which we approach Him, and in the trust which we demonstrate by our prayers. His love for us can be pictured as being like the tender embrace of a good father for his little child. Whenever we pray with real trust and humility we are very close to Heaven's 'border'. It's as though Heaven lies just above our heads: a place of light and sweetness and love.

It's as though our Heavenly Father, Who is one with the Son and the Spirit, is always waiting at the edge of Heaven: waiting to listen to our prayers. The littlest prayer, and the briefest whisper to God, is welcomed, heard, valued and rewarded. It's as though the Father is lovingly and tenderly stroking the neck of His own dear child, as He reaches out to caress a precious supplicant who trusts in Him and confides every need.

As God's children, we have the sure knowledge that He loves us at every moment. We can turn to Him whenever we please, in trusting prayer: certain of being heard and answered. (T:1396) G.H.T. *(See illustration 16)*

His full attention.

Some people wonder - "See how many people exist! How can I be important to God? How can He hear me?" But if we think about the perpetual 'now' in which He lives we can realise that each of us - created by our loving God - remains wholly within His loving gaze at every moment of our existence.

We who live in time find it necessary to 'move' our attention from one person to another; but God neither 'moves' from moment to moment nor moves His attention from one person to another, since He is not imprisoned in time. He is the Creator of all that exists. He lives in the eternal 'now'; and He sees, therefore, all that He has ever made or ever shall make. He sees everything and everyone in the 'now' of His being; and He sees it all-at-once, by which we mean that He doesn't see or 'learn' anything little by little, as we do in our everyday life.

Our Father knows all things. He knows all people. He knows

them wholly. Nothing is hidden from His sight. Seeing and knowing are like a single perpetual act in the perpetual 'now' of His Divine and holy existence; and therefore He sees, knows and loves everyone who is praying to Him, during every single moment of each person's prayer. That is why, whenever we turn to Him, we can be certain of having His full, loving attention. (T:1766)

Something to offer.

What a wonderful thing it is, that we who are members of Christ's Church no longer have 'empty' hands in prayer, when we long to offer something good to our Heavenly Father from within our poor lives. Jesus Christ is the Father's gift to us; yet we who pray in Christ's name and offer His Holy Sacrifice have the joy of knowing that Christ's perfect sacrifice is our gift to the Father! (T:2152).

The refiner's fire.

There is no love to match the Father's love: no tenderness or sweetness on earth as tender and sweet as His love towards us. Yet we can say that His pure love is like a raging fire: like the 'refiner's fire' of Holy Scripture. It is so radiantly pure and powerful that to meet Him unprepared would be to be frightened and harmed by such contact. Only after our purification and transformation do we 'taste' and enjoy Divine sweetness.

If we bear in mind God's immense glory, and the frailty of sinful human beings, we can see that God revealed Himself to His Chosen People in the only possible way. He revealed Himself little by little, through gentle words and invitations, then also through signs and wonders and warnings. Thus, He taught us all about the astonishing juxtaposition, in Himself, of tenderness and majesty.

At last, God wonderfully chose to come amongst us, to teach us about Himself. He did so 'when the appointed time came', at a particular place, through Christ His Son, Who is true God: the Son of the Father. Christ is God-made-man. He is love incarnate: love embodied and so made visible, for our joy and our salvation. (T:3319) G.H.T.

Glorious and majestic.

Whenever we pray: "Glory to God in the highest," we are praying to the Father Who is glorious and majestic. It's as if He is 'on high' in the fiery radiance of Heaven, surrounded by the Saints and holy Angels - in their thousands. It's to this glorious Father - the only God - that our worship is directed at Mass.

Some of us have been slow to realise that great reverence is appropriate as we join the assembly to take part in the Sacred Mysteries. Yet it pleases God when we make new efforts to honour Him, and when we encourage other people to be reverent before Him (T:4562)

THE HOLY SPIRIT

The Spirit at work.

We should realise that the Holy Spirit is doing powerful and glorious work as Christ offers his Holy Sacrifice to the Father.

During the Mass, the Three Divine Persons are 'at work' - joyful, loving and active. Our Saviour is Present - by His Spirit's power - in the Blessed Sacrament; and as Christ makes His eternal offering from the altar, the Holy Spirit is present, accepting the offering in the love of the Father. (T:1481)

Through the Holy Spirit.

God is the powerful and majestic Lord of all things; and He is also love. Love is His nature. To share love is His eternal purpose; and so the Father cannot fail to reward His friends for their struggles to please Him and to be fit for Heaven. He loves to reach out to a contrite heart, from Heaven's splendour, after that soul's fierce purification. Then God reveals how great is the height and depth of the loving union which has been brought about between Himself and the soul, through Christ, and through the prayers of the Blessed Virgin Mary. It is through the loving 'touch' of the Holy Spirit - as if by an outstretched hand - that the Father brings light and joy to a soul in prayer He demonstrates His love, shares His life to a greater degree, teaches that soul about His nature, and invites her to rest more frequently with Him, in contemplation: to rest with God, within her own soul, as if within a tabernacle or a tent.

Whoever meets God in such a true union and communion has been brought by the Holy Spirit close to the furnace of love which is shining at the heart of Divine life. That soul begins to fathom God's nature: to glimpse Divine love in its beauty and perfection. And that Divine love consists of gentleness and peace as well as power and glory. (T:1941) G.H.T. *(See illustration 9)*

Warm and effective love.

The Holy Spirit is alive and active; and He yearns for us all to realise that Divine love is the source of all true love, and the cause of true spiritual joy. Divine love is the light which illumines the souls of God's children. It is the blissful burning which wounds the heart of all who love truth, goodness and beauty. It is the sweet love which binds together all true friends. Divine love is unchanging yet alive, warm and effective. It is the treasure which is found by all who enjoy true Christian married love in earthly life, yet also the eternal prize of all who deny themselves to remain celibate and faithful in God's service. It is also the fire at the heart

1. REACHING OUT IN LOVE.

It's as if the Father in Heaven screens His face on considering the torments which His Son will undergo on earth. He reaches out in love to His Son. And that reaching-out-in-love is the Holy Spirit: the Third Divine Person. OIL-S:3889. *("The Spirit of the Lord Yahweh has been given to me, for Yahweh has anointed me. He has sent me to bring good news to the poor, to bind up hearts that are broken." Is 61:1).*

2. ETERNALLY BEGOTTEN OF THE FATHER.

The Son Who has been born of Mary is eternally begotten of the Father. He springs forth eternally from the white-hot love of the Father's heart, in the power of the Holy Spirit, in the oneness of love of the Godhead. OIL-S:3198. *("The Word was made flesh, he lived among us, and we saw his glory, the glory that is his as the only Son of the Father, full of grace and truth." Jn 1:14).*

3. A WORTHY MOTHER OF A DIVINE SON.

In her holiness and purity the Blessed Virgin Mary was a worthy mother of her Divine son, Jesus.   At her consent, she was made fruitful for the sake of the whole world. OIL-M:1349A. *("Of all women you are the most blessed, and blessed is the fruit of your womb." Lk 1:42).*

4. A TORRENTIAL FLOOD, FOR ALL AGES.

Christ's Precious Blood poured out from His body on the Cross, in a torrential flood, for all ages, so that we can bathe therein. OIL-M:832A. *("He loves us and has washed away our sins with his blood, and made us a line of kings, priests to serve his God and Father; to him, then, be glory and power for ever and ever." Rev 1:5).*

5. A CORNER OF THE KINGDOM.

The Church which Christ has founded is like a Kingdom of light, of which a little corner can be seen on earth.   The rest of the Kingdom stretches up beyond earthly life to where it is populated by the Saints and the Holy Angels, and the Holy Souls of Purgatory.   OIL-M:1332. *("I tell you most solemnly, unless a man is born through water and the Spirit, he cannot enter the Kingdom of God." Jn 3:5).*

6. OUT FROM THE FATHER'S HEART.

Christ came out from the Father's heart, to search us out, and to draw back into the Father's embrace all who are willing to follow in His Way. OIL-S:1197. *("He has let us know the mystery of his purpose ... that he would bring everything together under Christ, as head, everything in the heavens and everything on earth." Ep 1:9-10).*

of every sort of true, loving communion, whether between frail people in earthly life, or between an individual soul and her Creator. (Also T:1941) G.H.T.

The Spirit: true God, almighty and tender.

Truly, God lives within our souls, in His purity and dazzling splendour, if we are living in a 'state of grace'. Here are Three Persons yet one God; so we must believe not only in Christ's power, and in the Father's power, but also in the almighty power of the Holy Spirit.

The Father loves to hear the prayers we offer in Jesus' name; and Christ loves to hear our trusting prayers; yet we're wise also to turn to the Holy Spirit for help in difficult times. He is true God; and therefore He is holy, adorable, majestic and infinitely kind. He is equal to Christ and the Father, in His perfection. By His power, the Holy Spirit can give us what we ask of Him. He can give us purity, courage and peace, as we surrender our lives to Christ once more, in order to reach the Father: as we yearn to be brought 'safe to his glorious presence, innocent and happy'. (T:1978) G.H.T.

In His purity and fervour.

The Holy Spirit is infinite love: one of Three Divine Persons Who eternally love and are loved in Heaven. The Holy Spirit is like a burning fire in His purity and fervour: always longing to give joy. The Spirit Who was given to the infant Church at Pentecost is a love so generous and tender that He reaches 'outwards' from the Godhead in a ceaseless mission of love, to embrace, guide, console and teach all who will open their hearts at His touch. The Holy Spirit is always gathering in, purifying, and setting souls alight with His love. Yet He is always one with the source of all love, the Father, and with His Son, the eternal Word. (T:3899) G.H.T.

The gifts of the Spirit.

We should have faith in the power of the Holy Spirit. He can do so much in our lives, if we believe that He is at work guiding the Church and enlightening us, God's children. We should believe in His gifts and ask Him for them. We can ask for an increase, even praying every day for greater faith, hope and love, as well as for other gifts. We can be certain that whenever we call out for help, He helps us.

We should act as though we really believe in the Divinity of the Holy Spirit: praising and adoring Him as one of Three Divine Persons. He is equal in wisdom and majesty to the Father and the Son.

We can show our love for the Holy Spirit by trying to follow His inspirations, by speaking to Him and about Him with reverence, by telling Him of our love, by adoring Him, and by loving and adoring the Father and the Son Who are one with Him in the unity of the Godhead (T:4531)

The Spirit, in our hearts.

Truly, the Holy Spirit praises the Father, within us, in our individual prayers at home. He acts powerfully within and through our souls to send, as it were, a great breath of praise and joy Heavenwards, when our hearts are weak and exhausted.

This is what happens, also, at the Mass. It is 'in Christ' and through His Spirit that we reach out to the Father at every Mass. And so we are right to trust that the Spirit is powerfully at work in all our prayers, all because of our union with Christ, through our incorporation in Him and in His Church through Baptism. (T:4737)

THE SON

Beautiful and holy.

Jesus Christ is God-made-man, Who once lived and died on earth, then rose from the grave in triumph, and ascended to Heaven's glory. He is awesome and powerful, yet also beautiful and holy. He is alive, today; and He longs to bring us peace and perpetual joy. His Divine radiance pours upon us all, from Heaven, though we would be dazzled by it, were we to see it while we still live in the 'twilight' of our present sinfulness. Yet if we pray with sincerity and contrition, we allow Him to shine that light within our souls, so that we can see ourselves as we really are, and repent, and allow Him to change us. He is not distant, but close-by; and His love for us is inexhaustible, and very tender. (T:10)

In every sort of grief.

Christ loves us, each one of us; and He wants us to put our trust in Him. He is 'waiting' for us in every circumstance, longing for us to turn to Him. He is waiting to touch us in every sort of grief, remorse or loneliness - whether we have brought them upon ourselves or have suffered at the hands of other people. Yet He asks us to fulfil our duties towards Him before anything else. We must love Him and our neighbour, and keep His Commandments, no matter what the cost. (T:18)

Immeasurable love.

Christ loves each one of us just as we are now, even before we are perfect. He loves us in our weakness; yet He longs to see us delivered from sin, and made happy and at peace. (T:43)

Our need of Christ.

We should be grateful that we are no longer struggling to make a spiritual journey on our own. We need Christ, Who is our wise guide, our sure 'way,' and our powerful Intercessor. (T:56)

Christ, amongst us.

We should never doubt that Christ is Really Present during the Holy Sacrifice of the Mass. He is Present on the altar at every Mass, even when we are half-hearted in prayer, or the priest is rushing through the celebration. Yet Christ loves to be amongst people who love Him. And as we prepare to receive Christ in Holy Communion, thousands of Saints and holy Angels bow low in reverence for Christ's Precious Blood which is here on the altar. They are awed by Christ's astounding love. (T:613)

Aware of Christ's Presence.

Although the altar is the focal point, as we worship, we should always glance towards the tabernacle as we enter the church. Christ is Really Present there. His holy Angels surround Him, standing silently in adoration. (T:928)

Eternally our High Priest.

Christ is God-made-man. He really died on the Cross then rose up from the grave to a new and glorious life. He can never die again. He is now in Heaven, ready to welcome us. He endured torment on earth because of His longing to save us. He is eternally the High Priest and Mediator for His earthly brothers and sisters; and we are very precious to Him. In the depth of our prayer, and even in the apparent tragedy of the moment of our death, Christ is ready to welcome us, His true friends, to the heart of the Holy Trinity. (T:1039C) G.H.T.

Out from the Father's 'heart'.

The joys of Heaven are no fantasy held out as a means of pacifying weary or rebellious people. They are a continuation and an 'expansion', to an astonishing degree, of the joys which have already been tasted on earth by those who have surrendered their lives to God, not in fear but in love. No earthly joys can compare with the joy, peace and bliss which are found in Heaven. The Father is infinitely good. He is also powerful and majestic and beautiful. He is like a vast and infinitely-holy fire of love into which we can be led, by the Spirit, through our life in Christ, to experience the love and fulfilment for which we have been yearning.

Christ shares the Father's Divine nature; and Christ is so loving and generous that He longs to save us. It's as if He came out, at His Incarnation, from the 'heart' of the Father, to bring us hope and salvation, rather as a man might soar out from the brilliance of a huge planet in order to rescue small creatures who are lost in space. We can picture Christ as having come 'outwards' from the Father in order to reach us, and to reach many other people who are far away, and in danger. At our consent Christ takes hold of us, and draws us back into the Divine embrace. (T:1197) *(See illustration 6)*

True God and true man.

It's because Christ is both God and man that He can reconcile us - men, women and children - with our Creator. Our hearts should be ever-thankful that we are being drawn into Eternal Life and joy through our Baptism, and through many wonderful actions of the Holy Spirit, much of Whose work is secret.

The grace of Christ flows vigorously into our hearts through our trust in Him, and through our moments of sincere and reverent prayer. Through our reception of the Sacred Host - Christ Himself - in Holy Communion we allow our souls to be drawn into

Christ's own communion with the Father in the bliss of the Spirit. Christ's grace is then at work in our souls in power and glory. (Also T:1197) G.H.T.

Divine Light, embodied.

Christ can be pictured as being like an 'image' beamed down to earth from a window in Heaven. The unseen, almighty Father is pure, mysterious and powerful, a furnace of inextinguishable love. And Christ our Lord came out from the Father's glory, sharing the same glorious Divine nature. By the power of the Holy Spirit, two thousand years ago, Christ took flesh from Mary. Sharing our human nature, Christ has given 'shape' to Divine light.

No impurity exists in Christ, Who is true God, on fire with Divine love. When we hear Christ speak, we are listening to the eternal Word of the Father. When we see Christ touch and console and heal, we see the Father's love for us all, poured out from the heart of the Godhead. And if we picture the glory of Christ, after His death and Resurrection, we picture the Father's glory. And we shall share it one day if we have been changed through Christ's transforming love, and if we have remained faithful to the end. (T:1244) G.H.T.

Here in our world.

Christ is Really Present in our churches, in a sacramental manner. He truly enters our world, from Heaven, in the Most Holy Sacrament of His Body and Blood, at the Consecration; and He is truly with us, from Heaven, in His continued Presence, after Mass, in the tabernacle. (T:1304)

Stripped of all glory.

Every blessing we receive through the Church today, and every sacrament and every word of wisdom, comes to us because Christ our God once lived on earth and died for us because He loves us.

It was as if He was once carried on a wave of Divine grace and power - the power of the Holy Spirit - as He came out from the Father's 'heart', leaped through the 'bars of Heaven', and left behind His glory to live on earth amongst people like ourselves.

Christ is a Divine Person of immense majesty, now united with frail humanity by the extraordinary union of His Divine and human natures. Since the time when He became incarnate in the womb of the Blessed Virgin Mary, He has possessed a real human nature whilst possessing, as ever, the fullness of Divinity. As He grew to maturity in Nazareth, He wasn't someone partly Divine and partly human; nor was He a Divine Person merely disguised as a man; nor was He simply the greatest of the prophets, a man wholly 'open' to Divine influence.

Christ is true God and also true man, and shall ever remain so, in Heaven, where He has lived in His glorified body since His Resurrection and Ascension. So we must humble ourselves before Christ, the Divine Person Who has come down to us in such intimacy. He was made the same as us in fragile flesh, and - like each one of us - born of a woman! What a weight and a burden Christ bore in His humanity. What amazing love: that made Him come down to earth so that He might call out to the Father on our behalf, praying for help and for salvation. He is side by side with us in our intercessions and supremely during the Holy Mass. (T:1320) G.H.T.

Ascension to glory.

Truly, our faith is a wondrous gift. Through it, we know that by the Father's Will, foreknowledge, plan, consent and justice, Christ suffered and died on the Cross, for our sakes. Then He leapt up to His Father in glory by the power and light of the Holy Spirit; and it's as if Christ now draws in His wake those of us who are willing to recognise Him, to thank Him for what He has endured because of our sins, and to follow in His way to Heaven. He wants to banish, in the end, all our darkness and suffering, and to bring us up high to the glory of Heaven: to the Father's embrace. (T:1351) G.H.T.

Christ's powerful help.

Whatever sort of life we lead, Christ's powerful help is ours. He cannot leave us alone, even if we sometimes imagine that He is far away from us. Only the thinnest of 'veils' hides Him from our sight.

Christ's whole desire is to reach out to us, to draw us into His light, and to lead us towards the invisible Father. The Holy Spirit guides us in the freely-made acts and efforts by which we reach out to Christ in daily life.

The Holy Trinity is powerfully at work in our lives: at work in our souls, and in our everyday life, when we love God wholeheartedly, and share His life, and co-operate with His Will and actions. As we pray to the Father, we can be sure that Jesus Christ is drawing us up to the heart of the Father; and the Holy Spirit 'presents' us to the Father as a holy offering.

This pattern of co-operation with the work of the Holy Trinity should be the pattern of our whole life's work and our whole life's prayer. This 'pattern' can be woven by everyone who lives in and for God. It consists of the 'interweaving' of all our prayers, thoughts and actions with God's Divine and unending work of love! (T:1469) G.H.T.

At Heaven's 'door'.

Even now, day by day, with thousands of our spiritual brothers and sisters upon earth, we are being drawn closer to Heaven. Yet it's only through the work of salvation which Christ accomplished on earth long ago that we can live in hope of reaching Heaven. So the Church thanks Him for what He has done for us all through His Passion, Death and Resurrection, and also for His Ascension into Heaven.

Christ's work on earth was successful. Only because of Him has the 'door' to Heaven opened; and if we are Christ's true followers today, He has a message for us to share. He is longing to save us all. He is longing to see us, His real brothers and sisters, enter the glory which He now enjoys.

Only because of His return to the Father - making a Way, opening a pathway - has Christ given hope to us who love Him and who follow Him on the pathway to Heaven. This pathway was made ready through His Passion and His triumph. (T:1588) G.H.T.

Christ's act of self-surrender.

If we open our hearts, we can let Christ lead us to the heart of the mystery which is the Mass. The Holy Sacrifice which is offered from the altar before us is the same offering - or sacrifice - as that which Christ offered, long ago, on the Cross. It is the same, although it is not now being offered in pain, and in fleshly blood-loss and dying. It is the same, in that it 'consists' of the very Christ Who surrendered Himself to the Father's Will on Calvary, being Present here, now, and making that same perfect act of self-surrender to the Father. The Redeemer Who died for us on Calvary is now glorious and unchanging. He therefore remains, always, the spotless Victim and High Priest through Whose perfect offering we can be saved! (T:1740A)

Christ's great love for us all.

We cannot deny how great is Christ's love for us all, when we realise that He has gone to such lengths to reach out to us. We, today, are not denied Redemption just because we couldn't live in Christ's earthly life-time, or because we couldn't stand on Calvary and associate ourselves with Christ's sacrifice then. How marvellous it is that we can unite ourselves with Christ and with His once-for-all sacrifice, at the Holy Sacrifice of the Mass. We unite ourselves with a perfect offering. It's because He, the Divine

Son, is perfect, that we can rely on the prayers which He offers on our behalf. (Also T:1740A)

Our holy Saviour.

We should recognise how fortunate we are to have the consolation of knowing that Christ is Really Present with us in the Blessed Sacrament. We are right to genuflect before the tabernacle, where He awaits us. Two holy Angels - like spears of light - are guarding the tabernacle, so greatly do they venerate Christ, as they stand in silent adoration. So holy is Christ, and so precious is the sanctuary, that His holy Angels never leave Him. (T:1874)

From His infinite love.

We make great progress in the spiritual life when we really know, believe and delight in the knowledge that God is love. From love, God created us. From love, He gradually revealed Himself to His Chosen People. From love, He revealed Himself most fully in Him Who was conceived by the Holy Spirit of the Virgin Mary: Jesus Christ. St. Paul tells us: "In his body lives the fullness of divinity" (Col 2:9). From love, Christ founded a Church for us to join, giving us the sacraments in which we receive a great out-pouring of His graces, for our transformation. From love, Christ is Really Present in the Blessed Sacrament of His Sacred Body and Blood, and gives Himself to us in Holy Communion. Christ is true God: the same God Who in Old Testament times spoke with Elijah and with Moses and the Prophets. That's why we are sometimes so powerfully affected by our union with Christ in Holy Communion. (T:1978) G.H.T.

Reparation for our sins.

God our Father loves us all dearly, whatever our state; yet when we have given our lives to Him He is utterly delighted by our longing to serve Him well. He is ever-loving: ever-willing to make us worthy of His service and, by the merits of Christ His Son, to make us worthy of entering Heaven. Yet only by Christ's sacrifice on the Cross, and through His Divine power, has a way been made in which we can follow. This way had been closed, because of Mankind's sinful disobedience soon after the dawn of man's life on earth. By Christ's perfect obedience to the Father's Will, reparation has been made for Mankind's sins. We are all in Christ's debt, therefore, even people who don't yet know about Him, or who refuse to believe in Him.

Christ the God-man was born on earth for this: to love, to heal, to teach and to set an example, but supremely to die. He knew that after His death He would rise from the dead, and thus would rise up from the darkness of a sinful world to pierce Heaven's light - and He succeeded. He has made it possible for us to follow Him: to soar swiftly through the narrow way which opens out into the breadth of Heaven's light, and so to reach the Father. (T:2003) G.H.T.

No other way.

Christ has told us that there is no other way into Heaven but His way: a way made by Him at His Resurrection when He returned in glory to the Father. Christ's way is now open to all who believe in Him and have been baptised into His life. These believers feed on Him in the Holy Eucharist in order to live a new life in Him and to keep His commandments. They welcome the presence of His Holy Spirit into their hearts and lives. It's through Christ's merits, therefore, that we speak with confidence to our Heavenly Father, rely on Christ's help in intercession, stand beside Christ in prayer, and offer Christ's Precious Blood as our gift. We must live in the hope that since we love Christ we'll rise upwards, one day, like Him. We should yearn to be clothed in white, as if in the 'wedding garment' which Christ described as being the suitable clothing for the King's banquet. (Also T:2003) G.H.T.

A hearth for the homesick.

In our dark times we wonder: "What is God's love really like?"

And it's at such times that Christ wants us to remember that we can trust in Him. We can discover that the love of God, known in and through Jesus Christ, can satisfy every human need. That has been the message given through the Saints in every age.

Divine love, for the weary soul, is like a birth into joy, or a gift from father to child, or a reward for devotion, or warmth for a bruised heart, or peace for the mind. It is like a loaf for the hungry, a hearth for the homesick, a warm coat for the exile, soft arms for the lonely, an endearment amidst pain, a whisper of kindness - and a promise of Heaven, where that love in its fullness brings both healing and bliss. (T:2006)

Christ here, in glory.

Through Christ's sacramental Presence in our church, each trusting soul can be sure of receiving courage and comfort. We can think about His Real Presence in the following way. Just as people will stand by a bonfire at a special celebration, to delight in its beauty and to warm themselves by its glow, in the same way we can all draw near to the tabernacle, to believe in Christ's love, and to delight in Christ's glory, even when we can't yet see it. (T:2479)

A 'Mount Tabor' experience.

If we pay a visit to our church for a time of private prayer, we can be content to kneel or sit silently in Christ's Presence. This isn't idleness, but true prayer. We should rejoice that we can spend a quiet time with Christ, with no interruptions. If we love Him we like to be close to Him, just like Saint Peter, who was so thrilled to be with Christ during the Transfiguration that he wanted to stay there on the mountainside.

We can look upon our closeness to Christ in our private prayer, or in our thanksgiving at Mass, as being a 'Mount Tabor' experience of our own. We can stay with Christ joyfully for a little while; and then we can picture ourselves as 'descending' obediently to the 'valley' below: to our everyday work and conversations. (Also T:2479)

An astounding privilege.

Christ's sacramental Presence is so astounding a privilege that it would not be wrong of us to fall prostrate before Him, in gratitude and joy, if it were appropriate to do so. (T:2741)

An everlasting union.

It is through Christ and His Church that each of us can enter a true and everlasting union with the Father, by the Spirit's transforming power, and so become a friend of God. (T:2957)

Worthy of our reverence.

Christ is infinitely loving and tender towards us all; yet none of us should forget that He is worthy of immense reverence, love, devotion and worship. He wants everyone to understand such things about worship; and so He wants to see these things taught, if people don't yet know about them.

It's only right that we genuflect to the tabernacle, as we take our places in church, or when we enter the building. And genuflexions to Christ should not be rushed, but reverent. The Sign of the Cross should be made with dignity, and should be used reverently and unselfconsciously on every appropriate occasion. (T:3064)

Touched by our gratitude.

Christ is man, as well as God; and He loves to see evidence of our love for Him. He is deeply touched by our gratitude for His Real Presence in the Blessed Sacrament. (T:3076)

Delighted by our greeting.

Christ delights in seeing us greet Him. He loves to see us turn towards the tabernacle with a bow, or a genuflection. And when people choose to make the sign of the Cross Christ is honoured by such devotion. (T:3355)

In the tabernacle.

Christ's sacramental Presence is as 'real' as if He were walking amongst us, just as He walked amongst the Apostles in Galilee, though He is Present with us in a different manner. (T:3810)

In His Presence.

Christ delights in the love shown by all who come before Him in admiration and trust. He knows that His true friends recognise and welcome His Presence in church. They never treat a church as if it were a worldly place. They know that in stepping over the threshold, they have arrived at the 'edge' of Heaven.

We don't usually see Christ in prayer, or see His glory shine out from the tabernacle, but we know that He is now the triumphant Redeemer Who reigns in Heaven in glory, which is the glory, also, of the Father and of the Holy Spirit. So although it's true that we are adopted children of God - temples of the Holy Spirit - and don't need to take off our shoes in God's presence, as Moses did, we should nevertheless approach Christ with profound love and reverence. Whenever we honour the sacramental Presence of Christ - the living God Who is one with the Father and the Holy Spirit - we can be joyful and at peace. We can shake off, for a while, some of the turmoil of everyday life in the world. By our glad yet reverent bearing in God's 'house of prayer' we can encourage other people to be reverent and so to practice the ways of Heaven. If we love God, we long to enter the 'City' of the living God, to be close to Him eternally. By adoring Christ in church, as if in Heaven's ante-chamber, we can prepare for the moment of death. (T:3915) G.H.T.

In a house of prayer.

Those who welcome and acknowledge the sacramental Presence of Christ our God in the tabernacle are made joyful by the knowledge; yet they recognise that they owe reverence and worship to Him. They do essential tasks in church, talk quietly where necessary, but generally act as if in a house of prayer. They return to prayer as quickly as possible - unless they are leaving the building; and by their example they encourage other people to be reverent and prayerful. (T:3916)

Straight after Mass.

If we really believed in Christ's Real Presence we would never sit chatting loudly in church straight after Mass as if in a cinema or café, ignoring the presence of Christ - and His holy Angels.

We must never forget that Christ now lives in majesty and glory - which is the glory, also, of the Father and of the Holy Spirit; and Christ is Really Present in the tabernacle that we see before us.

We cannot see Christ; but it is Christ our God - the living God, Who is One with the Father and the Holy Spirit - Who is Present in the tabernacle. It is plain, therefore, that someone who routinely chatters loudly in church must be grossly ignorant of the Presence of Christ, or does not believe in it, or is spiritually so blind or insensitive that he barely remembers that Presence, and remains oblivious to those who are praying. (Also T:3916)

Christ's love for us.

Christ's Presence is Real. This means that our living Saviour is very close to us. It's as though Christ is calling out from the tabernacle, to say to each person present: "I love you!" And so He deserves a greeting or some other loving response. (T:3952)

A King, in His palace.

When we enter the church, or turn our attention to Christ, it's as if He leans from the tabernacle like a King leaning from His palace window, His arms open wide, to give a lovely greeting. He is pleased by our devotion. He is one with the Father and the Holy Spirit: one God, always kind, just, tranquil and reliable; and we should try to imitate Him - by relying on His graces. (T:4456)

A worthy place.

It is Christ our God Who has told us, of Himself, that He is Really Present amongst us in the Blessed Sacrament. It 'follows', therefore, that where Christ is sacramentally Present, we must provide a fitting place for the Sacred Species, we must honour and adore Him Who is Present, and we must teach others to offer praise worthy of our God. We must ensure that we all act with love and reverence in His Presence, and make a fitting preparation to receive Him in Holy Communion. (T:4538)

Through an open heart.

Whoever spends a lot of time close to Christ and His Mother begins to resemble them. Christ wants us to realise that if we persevere in prayer and draw closer to Him and to His holy Mother, and spend time before the Blessed Sacrament, we are able to absorb something of Christ's peace, charity, sweetness, beauty and radiance. It's as if this peace passes through an 'open heart'. (T:4583)

The peace of Christ.

There are times and occasions in everyday life when we need not use words, when we speak to Christ in prayer. It is enough simply to be there with Him, where He is Present in the Blessed Sacrament, and where He 'radiates' towards us His pure holy love and His incomparable peace. (Also T:4583)

2. SETTING THE SCENE

SALVATION

Only through Christ.

Through Christ's sacrifice of Calvary it has been made possible for us to enter Heaven, after our preparation. And that is the very sacrifice which is re-presented, for our benefit, in the Mass. (T:323)

An admirable state.

It is through our true friendship with Christ - in an active and fruitful union - that we are wholly enclosed within God's life and love. And since God is our salvation, we who live wholly 'in' God are now saved, which is to say that we shall be saved at death, if we have continued to live 'in' God in this blessed and admirable state to the very end. If we have remained in a state of grace, in friendship with God, we can hope to enter glory when we die - in the beauty of Heaven. (T:2538)

Persevering to the end.

We really need Christ, Whom we can receive in the Holy Eucharist. We cannot drift into Heaven by accident. Only by a free decision, and through determinedly holding fast to Christ in faithfulness and love, can we hope to persevere to the end, to find eternal salvation at the Father's heart, in Heaven. (T:2772)

Christ's saving sacrifice.

The Three Divine Persons are 'at work' to save and sanctify us through the sacraments, today. They do so supremely through the Holy Sacrifice of the Mass, at which Christ's saving sacrifice of Calvary is re-presented and at which we receive Christ Himself as our spiritual food. We are doing something powerfully fruitful and effective whenever we come together in this way, as the 'Body of Christ'. We know, by faith, in a way beyond human understanding, that the Father contains and sustains all things; and our understanding of this can be increased through prayer. If He 'contains' everything that is, He 'contains' the risen Christ. And in the risen Christ we can now find Christ's Passion, Death, Resurrection and Ascension, which is the work of our salvation: the Paschal Work. It's as if everyone who is incorporated into Christ can therefore touch and be changed by the saving events of Christ's life, and so can hope to achieve salvation. (T:2772) G.H.T.

Held 'in Christ'.

To belong to Christ, Who lives at the Father's 'heart,' is to be changed by His work and also to be 'held' by Him close to the Father. So whoever ignores Christ cannot be close to the Father. It's true that everyone on earth is in the Father's care in earthly life. Yet whoever refuses to meet or to know Christ, Mankind's Saviour, is in danger because he refuses to allow Christ to change, sanctify and save him. If, when he dies, he is not 'held' in Christ as if in the Father's heart, he falls away into the Abyss.

That's the reason why Christ continually reminds us through His Church that only in Christ have we a sure hope of remaining 'in' the Father after our death, and in His tender love, saved by Christ the Redeemer in Whom we have put our trust. (Also T:2772) G.H.T.

Love for God.

We can cling to Christ on the Cross, so to speak, through our faithful participation in the Mass. We can also cling to Him during His return to the Father - since the Mystery of the Resurrection is also celebrated during the Mass. If we do this, it's as if we are practising what we should do when we die. How can we not be saved if we cling wholeheartedly to Christ in that manner, freed from sin, reconciled, burning with love for God our Father, and longing to see Him? (T:3022)

A perpetual Easter.

Heaven is like a perpetual Easter, full of glory, beauty and joy; yet we need to be made fit to enter such beauty and holiness. Christ longs to see each of us develop a real friendship with Him which brings joy to us, and fulfilment, as well as holiness. We grow closer to Him, the more we know and relish the truth about Him: including the truth that He is truly God and man. (T:4444)

THE PASCHAL MYSTERY

The Great Praise.

By our union with Christ at Mass, in His sacrificial prayer, we celebrate His Resurrection and Ascension. We join in the joyful praise which Christ offers to the Father. Christ holds us firmly in His prayer - and in His peace - while the holy Angels dance in the Great Praise which is being offered in unison by all who worship the Father 'through Christ' and in the Spirit. (T:355)

A marvel of Divine love.

Every Mass is a marvel of Divine love; and we who take part are privileged beyond our greatest imaginings. Only God Who is all-loving and all-holy could have devised a memorial celebration which is so many things all at once: a reminder of His gradual Revelation of Himself to the Chosen People; a re-enactment of what Christ did for us before He was betrayed and sent to His death; a living memorial of Christ's Death and Resurrection and Ascension; a foretaste of the feasting which Christ's friends enjoy in Heaven; a spiritual communion with those dear friends of Christ's who have already left earthly life to enter the safety of Purgatory or the glory of Heaven; and a real Communion with the living Lord Himself, with Jesus. (T:535) G.H.T.

Through the power of the Spirit.

The miracle at the heart of the Mass is achieved through the power of the Holy Spirit, as He works through the words of Christ which are spoken by our priest over unleavened bread and a cup of wine. Bread and wine are changed to become Christ's own Sacred Body and Blood, Soul and Divinity. Christ our Lord is present 'whole and entire', in a sacramental manner; and through our regular participation in the Holy Sacrifice of the Mass, we allow Christ to draw us steadily towards Heaven: towards the heart of the Holy Trinity.

It's as though Christ holds out His arms in utter surrender to the Father and offers the Holy Sacrifice on our behalf. We who love Christ and who cling to Him, not just in everyday life but also in the Sacred Liturgy, are like jewels on Christ's robe as we make the offering with Him. By our loving union of ourselves with Christ, as He prays in our presence, we give honour to Christ. Furthermore, by our self-offering with Christ we make a unique adornment of Christ's perfect praise of the Father's glory. (Also T:535) G.H.T. *(See illustration 30)*

Our privileged place.

Christ asks us to remember that God the Holy Trinity is one God

Who is endless in love, infinitely great and majestic; united, pure, perfect, simple, and unchanging. Christ wants us to remember that each of the Three Divine Persons is 'at work' in the Holy Sacrifice of the Mass.

Christ, Who is God-made-man, is Really Present amongst us after the Consecration. He is our High Priest - and also the Victim on our altar. Only through, with and 'in' Christ can we offer perfect praise and homage to the Father, in the Spirit.

Christ proved His love for His Father by loving His Will, even when faithfulness to the mission on which the Father had sent Him led to betrayal, humiliation, desertion, and death on a Cross. The love which Christ demonstrated on Calvary is the very love with which the Son loved the Father before the world began. It is also the very love which is being offered by Christ to the Father through the Holy Sacrifice of the Mass, at which the offering of Calvary is re-presented; and we are privileged to be able to take part in that offering.

At every Mass, we are present at an awesome and holy celebration and commemoration. Even in the darkest church, and amongst sad or very sinful people, Christ is Present with His holy Angels, in glory.

The Holy Sacrifice of the Mass is the 'work' of Christ, and of the Father, in the power of the Holy Spirit. (T:572) G.H.T.

Christ's unending triumph.

We should ponder with awe and wonder the great event at the end of Christ's time on earth. We celebrate His Ascension at every offering of the Holy Sacrifice, as we also celebrate His Death and Resurrection. During the last days of His life on earth, Christ parted from His holy Mother, who joyfully surrendered Him to the glory which lay ahead; and when He ascended into Heaven He was greeted as though by a roar of joy, and a great swell of triumph. The hosts of Heaven witnessed His return to the Father in bliss, when He took His place on high. So we should rejoice that, at the Holy Mass, we are present to Christ's unending triumph and to Heaven's eternal joy!

Heaven is even now filled with joy, glory and triumphant sounds when - during the Holy Mass - we offer Christ to the Father, in praise, thanksgiving and intercession. (T:903)

On our behalf.

We need to remember how completely dependent we are on Jesus. He is Present amongst us, at the Consecration. He stands before us, as if facing away from us, in order to gaze upwards to the Father and to speak with Him on our behalf; and we really need Christ, our Mediator. No praise - no prayer - can be deemed worthy of the Father, or ascend to Him, unless that praise is extended through Christ as if it were flowing upwards through His out-stretched arms, during the Holy Sacrifice. (T:1033)

For all Eternity.

We should hope for Heaven. During the Mass we celebrate not only Christ's Passion, Death and Resurrection, but also His glorious Ascension, when He entered Heaven; and we who believe in Him and remain faithful can hope to follow the way opened by Him, to enjoy His love and His presence for all Eternity. (T:1102)

At the Last Supper.

We must never cease to be grateful for what Christ has done for us: for what He did at the 'Last Supper', and for what He did by His Crucifixion and Death.

Christ was determined to endure His sufferings, and to give His life in order to save us; yet what courage He needed for His preparations! Even as He sat with His Apostles, and held up the cup of wine, and gave thanks, and changed the wine - even as He spoke about that "cup of My Blood" - it was as though He could see before Him a deep pit into which He was going descend, to be crucified. This 'pit of suffering' was constantly before Him, as He dealt calmly with His friends, and established the pattern of the Sacred Banquet through which - here, today - we can meet Him and also remember His Passion. (T: 1650)

Of infinite worth.

Christ wants us all to remember that we have no more fruitful way of praying than by offering the Holy Sacrifice. As the priest offers the Holy Sacrifice at the altar, he offers the very same sacrifice as that which Christ once offered to the Father from the Cross; so we can be sure that the sacrifice of the altar is of infinite worth, and bears the fruit of the Sacrifice of Calvary. It makes possible, for sinners in this era, a forgiveness no less certain than that which was 'won' by the same sacrifice when Christ offered His life on the Cross. (T:1740A)

God's plan of salvation.

In all sorts of ways, Christ is urging us, through His Church, to realise the meaning and purpose of His Passion, Death, Resurrection and Ascension: His whole Paschal Work, to which we are made present through the Holy Sacrifice of the Mass.

The entire plan of salvation effected by God - by Father, Son and Holy Spirit - has sprung from God's love for us. Truly, Christ the Son died to save us. So we pray in Christ's name to the Father during the Mass, to say, of Christ's sacrifice, "Father, accept this offering from your whole family. Grant us your peace in this life, save us from final damnation, and count us among those you have chosen." We can be confident that the Son of God, Who poured out His blood on Calvary to save us, will give us every help and encouragement to remain faithful to Him until death. (T:3889) G.H.T.

To a sinful world.

It is the Will of God that we know about His great plan of salvation. We will become more grateful to God for His mercy if we realise how much He has done for us. Then we shall be more likely to persevere in loving service of Him and of our neighbour, and be more determined to prepare for life in Heaven.

We can increase our understanding of the infinite love which caused God to reach out from Heaven to save us if we picture to ourselves the Son of God, in Heaven, before He descended to earth to save us. He was full of love for sinful people on earth. Mankind was alienated from the Father, and had no hope of Heaven. Some people were contrite. Some made good but inadequate gestures of love for God and submission to His Holy Will, for example, by fasting, prayer and alms-giving, and by offering animal sacrifices. Yet those things alone could not take away their sins. So let us picture the Son in His goodness and humility. He is about to be sent 'down' to earth by the Father, by the Spirit's power, in order to help and save sinners and live amongst them. He is going to live as we live, yet without sinning; and He is willing to accept the sufferings which are inevitable if He is going to live a life of love and truth-speaking in a sinful world: a life of faithfulness to the Father's Will in every circumstance. (Also T:3889) *(See illustration 1)*

Shedding His blood.

Let us now picture Jesus Christ, that incarnate Son, when He has been born of Mary, His Virgin Mother. He grows to maturity, then preaches and teaches the Good News about the Father's love for us all, and about repentance and the forgiveness of our sins. As He teaches, heals, rebukes and consoles, He accepts the sort of opposition which is inevitable when someone holy and single-minded speaks the truth at all times. He is even willing to accept death - a cruel death - if it should occur.

By His patient acceptance of the sufferings of earthly life, Christ will demonstrate to Mankind how love conquers fear: true love for God the Father, and love for His Will, which is that all people live in love together as children of one Father. Yet something even more marvellous will ensue. Christ knows that the Father won't allow Him - His only Son - to remain in the grave, but will lift Him up again by the power of the Holy Spirit. And when the Son lays down His life, and the Father raises His Son from the grave, They will demonstrate to Mankind that darkness cannot conquer· light.

Furthermore, when the Son pours out His blood in death, He will be shedding it out of love for Mankind. This is because if He were sinful, and didn't love, He would hate and revile and even kill those who opposed Him. He would shed their blood rather than be humiliated and defeated. Yet as the Son pours out His blood on the Cross, He will be shedding it for love of His Father. If He didn't love His Father and His Father's eternal 'law' of love He wouldn't endure suffering in order to speak the truth, to do good, and to do His duty to the bitter end. Therefore, when the Son eventually sheds His blood, out of love for God and man, in total self-giving, He will know that His freely-accepted death can be seen as the last and most perfect blood-sacrifice for sin. By pouring out His blood - as is inevitable, in a sinful world - He will make a new covenant: a new agreement between Mankind and God the Father.

Since the Son will be amongst sinners and will number amongst them through having been made man - though without sin - He will pray heart-felt prayers for their salvation; and He will do so even when they are crucifying Him. And since the Father always grants the prayers of His Son, it is plain that the Son, when He sheds His blood on the Cross, will seal by that blood a new covenant between the human beings for whom He prays - whom He will represent as their spokesman - and the Father in Heaven. A covenant which has been sealed in the blood of the only Son of God, and not in the blood of an animal, will be a covenant so powerful that nothing shall ever break it. (Also T:3889).

A perfect sacrifice.

Truly, a marvellous plan was fulfilled nearly two thousand years ago, to benefit people of that time, and to benefit sinful people of every era, including our own. God's whole plan of salvation has stemmed from love. No blood-sacrifice was necessary as if to placate an angry tyrant. God is wholly love and light. A blood sacrifice was freely offered, by the loving, incarnate Son, Jesus, in His own body, with the 'consent' or Will of the Father, in the love of the Holy Spirit.

Christ went like a pure, innocent lamb to the slaughter - like the spotless lambs then being offered in the Temple sacrifices. And ever since Christ rose from the dead, and ascended to Heaven to await us in glory, His disciples in each age have told the good news about what Christ has done for us by His once-for-all, perfect loving sacrifice and His Resurrection from the dead. Christ has won forgiveness for our sins, and has made salvation possible for everyone; and so Christ teaches through His Church, in every age, that people who are grateful to Him and who recognise their sinfulness will want to change. They will be willing to die to themselves, as the Son has done.

All who are willing to repent and to believe, and therefore to receive the Holy Spirit as they undergo the mystical death and rising in the waters of Baptism, will thus be reconciled with the Father. They can share the Son's Divine life through eating the spiritual food which is His Eucharistic Body and Blood; and therefore they hope to come to Heaven, one day, through the Son, in the Spirit, to live in bliss forever, close to the Father's heart. (Also T:3889) G.H.T.

OUR WEAKNESS

Worthy of the Father.

We need to remember that no lips can speak praise which is worthy of the Father unless that praise is offered through Jesus Christ, His Son. That's why we always praise the Father in Christ's name. When mere words are addressed to the Godhead by a frail creature, with merely human power, those words are like dry leaves which are swept away, as if in a mighty gale, by the powerful currents in the furnace of Divine glory.

Truly, we need Christ Our Divine Redeemer. As we approach the Father in the prayer of union it is Christ alone who, by His purity and power, can hold each willing soul in the overwhelming radiance, purity and power of the life of the Godhead. Christ is God: pure, holy and powerful. No-one but Christ is strong enough to 'stand' before the Father to bring us close to Him, and to 'shield' us, as we are praying, from the 'fire' of the Father's love. (T:2551)

Prayer 'in Christ'.

Whenever we pray in the name of Jesus it's as though Jesus is standing beside a bedraggled person who is in desperate need: a sinner who, by himself, is unworthy to approach the glorious Father-King of Heaven to ask for help. Although everyone on earth is free to cry out loudly to Heaven for help, no-one can be sure that his prayers 'reach' Heaven unless he is praying 'in Christ'. (T:2696)

To enter Heaven.

We must remain firm in our conviction that Christ is our help and salvation. We cannot leap up to glory and joy by merely human power. Only through Divine grace and power can we avoid the horror of living 'outside' God, and come to enjoy Christ's embrace during earthly life, and enter Heaven in the end. (T:2842)

A home in our hearts.

Christ wants us all to be faithful to prayer and to the sacraments. We can have utter confidence in His love for us; however, it is not easy to be saved. Christ sees that few of us are reaching out to our Heavenly Father with sincerity and contrition. Few of us reach out and find Christ, Who alone can bring us to the Father's heart; and few of us hold onto Him for a life-time.

Goodwill is not enough - though it is 'fertile ground' in which the seed of faith can be planted. Divine life and power are necessary to bring a human being from spiritual death to Eternal Life: and we need to remember that true life has begun only where the Holy Spirit has made a home in human hearts. (T:3242)

Group prayer.

As Christians, we are members of the Mystical Body of Christ. We need the Church, which became our 'home' at our Baptism; and so we should value not just private prayer but also group prayer, whether with families, friends, colleagues or visitors. And it is when we gather together at Mass that we are gathered for the best possible 'group prayer', when the group consists of the whole Church: the Communion of Saints.

The 'focal point' must be Almighty God to Whom the Holy Sacrifice is being offered, though we should be gratefully aware that we worship with our spiritual family, and indeed there are designated times at which we acknowledge their presence.

(T: 4018)

In the bond of love.

No human being can find words eloquent enough to praise the Holy Trinity in a manner which is worthy of the Divine glory. No words of ours are adequate to express thanks to the Three Divine Persons for Their goodness to us. If we belong to Christ, however, we know that He 'belongs' to us. We can count on His love; and in our bond of love with Him we have Him as our perfect Word of praise of the Father's glory, our perfect sacrifice to offer: the one Who is like ourselves, though 'he is without sin' (T:4299) G.H.T.

Worthy praise.

God is so great and we are so weak and sinful that we need the Divine life and power of Christ amongst us if our prayers are to 'reach' Heaven as worthy praise of the Almighty Father. (T:4465)

OUR DIGNITY

In a state of grace.

We who have been called to take part in Christ's holy worship at Mass should rejoice in our majesty and dignity as God's children. Christ wants us to realise that if we are in a state of grace, we reflect God's own majesty and dignity as we stand together before the altar, glorious, and very close to our glorious Saviour. It's as though our frailty is clothed in gold. (T:317)

Ablaze with Divine light.

We should rejoice in our union with Christ our Redeemer, and in our membership of His family through the Holy Catholic Church.

Christ is united with His Church as He offers His Sacrifice. Truly, He stands amongst us, during the Holy Mass, praying to the Father on our behalf; and the church is full of worshippers, both Heavenly and earthly. The church is ablaze with Divine light. Christ is surrounded by His holy Angels and watched by the Saints of Heaven, as we all unite ourselves to His sacred and perfect offering. (T:1815)

Sincere praise.

Even if we see ourselves as weak and insignificant, we can be sure that our prayers are valuable and worthwhile. A few words of sincere praise freely offered to God by a mere creature are more glorious and precious, and give Him more delight, than even the sight of the magnificent beauties of nature: the beauty of all the glorious skies, and the other wonders of His Creation. (T:2565)

FAITH

A powerful Presence.

We should believe in the marvel of Christ's powerful Presence on the altar in His Sacred Body and Precious Blood. He is alive! He is with us; and He pours His Divine light and wisdom upon all who are gathered about Him. (T:430)

Christ's perfect prayer.

We should look towards the altar, during the Holy Sacrifice of the Mass. That is where our Saviour - powerful and prayerful - offers His sacrifice to the Father; and the Father delights in our faith and confidence when we turn our hearts towards Him and ask: "Listen to Jesus' prayer!" He delights in seeing us purify our intentions. We can leave behind our selfish ambitions and unite our prayers with Christ's prayer to the Father. It is a perfect prayer; and because we belong to Christ we are entitled to offer it as our very own. (T:1419A)

Strength to resist evil.

We must be strong in faith. The very sacrifice which Christ offered on Calvary is 'held up' and offered today, on the holy altar. We can be sure, therefore, that just as men in battle were strengthened as they looked upon Moses, who held up his arms in obedience to God, to help them, so we who look upon Christ or who cling to His Cross, in faith, during current battles against evil, will find new strength. Then we'll be able to resist the evil forces which make a waste-land of friendships, commercial transactions, civic society and religious practice.

It is through the Holy Mass where the sacrifice of Christ is re-presented that we can find Christ most surely. As He holds up his arms, interceding, we can cling to Him, there before the altar. We too can hope for victory amidst our trials. We can endure the assaults of evil, in our day. We can remain upright in virtue. We can persevere to the end, if we remain 'in Christ', entrusting ourselves to our Heavenly Father. (T:1613)

A living faith.

To achieve salvation it is necessary that we have faith, and that our faith be active. (T:2772)

Free will.

For faith to grow, we must put it into action. Many more of us could find real joy in Christ. Belief is a gift; yet it is a matter of the will, at the same time. Each of us consents to believe - to trust in Christ - or else withholds that consent and so remains at a distance from our Saviour. (T:2932)

Faith in Christ's plan.

It's important that we realise, and explain to other people, that the Mass is not one social event amongst many; rather, it's an astonishing meeting which has been arranged by Christ our God Who once lived on earth amongst us.

When Christ had died for us all, had risen from the dead, and had ascended into Heaven - having promised His beloved followers that they would be able to join Him later on - what more wonderful thing could He have done for them than to have given them a unique gift? He has given a way of offering thanks for Him, to God the Father, a way which consists of Christ being there amongst His followers, thanking the Father with them, on their behalf, and also giving Himself to them as their spiritual food. (T:4894).

From Christ's point-of-view.

Christ wants to see us believing in His love for us, and being grateful for His gift of the Holy Eucharist; and so He invites us to look at everything, for a moment, as if from His point-of-view.

Christ asks us to reflect upon His astonishing arrangement: that in every age He brings His troops of Angels with Him, as He comes down to be sacramentally Present with His friends on earth while His friends, the Saints of Heaven and the Holy Souls, worship close by. He has arranged this so that His friends on earth can be drawn towards Heaven to receive a foretaste of the glorious life ahead. So Christ wants us all to consider what He sees from His home in glory. We can consider the manner in which He'll be greeted by those who really believe in Him.

People who love Christ will have made efforts to build a church or shrine which is worthy of His majesty - though of course, He is equally 'at home' in a poor little house or a prison cell. Furthermore, if Christ's friends are both delighted and awestruck by His Presence, they will wait attentively and prayerfully together, longing for Him to be with them at the Consecration. They will have provided a beautiful sanctuary and altar for Him, with symbols of His sovereignty and Divinity. They will show out their faith and love by their gestures of reverence and admiration; and He will be delighted by the efforts they've made to be worthy to receive Him. He will be touched by their contrition and trust, as they provide bread and wine for the sacrifice, and, with their priest, await His arrival. (Also T:4894)

Real trust in God.

The whole of the Christian life consists of trusting in God. If we trust, we believe in God's Son Jesus, Who was sent to save us. We give up sin, with God's help, and do good. We trust God enough to follow the way which God opens before us, in whatever vocation He offers us; and we rely on Him in dark times; and we believe in the promised glory. (T:5004).

OUR INTENTION

The glory of God.

We should always remember that we are present to the glory of the Holy Trinity each time we turn to God in prayer - even if He is hidden from our sight at present. (T:67)

Our heart and minds.

With confidence, we should unite our hearts and minds to the Church's intentions during the Mass. In his prayers, in the Sacred Liturgy, the priest calls out on behalf of Christ's Body the Church, gathered together; and Christ comes to us, His own People, who belong to that Body. Christ is really Present amongst us - though

His tremendous glory is usually veiled from earthly eyes. (T:112 and 113)

By our union with Christ.

We should unite our poor prayers to Christ's perfect prayer and sacrifice. By our union with Christ, we truly pray His prayer to the Father, offer His Holy Sacrifice for our sins, and entrust everything to the Father's love, in the love and power of the Holy Spirit. (T:349)

Saintly witnesses.

We should purify our worship by examining our hearts, and by asking ourselves if we are worthy of being present at this awesome event. The Mass is immensely holy. By our pure worship 'in Christ', humanity is wed to its all-holy God, witnessed by the Holy Ones: the Saints and the holy Angels. (T:678)

Christ our Mediator.

Before the Mass begins we should unite our hearts to Christ and to His intentions. His prayer includes all our needs. He adores and praises the Father on our behalf. He thanks the Father. He offers reparation for our sins; and He pleads for our spiritual and bodily needs. (T:844)

In union with Christ.

Our 'outlook' in prayer should change, as we move through the Mass. If we are prayerful and attentive at each moment, we move swiftly from repentance - at the beginning of Mass - to worship; then we can unite ourselves wholly with the sacrifice which Christ is about to offer to the Father from our altar. We can unite all our loving and contrite thoughts, and the loving acts and the sufferings of our everyday lives, to Christ's act and words and offering.

As we turn to the Father in prayer, we offer Christ as our praise, our thanksgiving and our plea. Thus, all our intentions are included in Christ's prayer; and when our offerings are united to Christ's offering, they are perfect, and are accepted by the Father. (T:921)

The same sacrifice.

During the Holy Sacrifice, it's as though a 'chasm' lies before us, as we remember and reflect upon Christ's marvellous self-offering. Christ was crucified for our sins long ago, in a past age; but by our presence at Holy Mass, where Christ is gloriously and Really Present, it's as though we are gazing into that past age, to look at Christ on the Cross; yet at the same time we are gazing upon that same sacrifice of Christ as it is offered from our altar.

Through the Holy Sacrifice of the Mass, we are given an opportunity to show sorrow for the sufferings which our sins brought upon Christ, to thank Christ for His now-finished sufferings on our behalf, to thank Our Lady for her steadfast devotion, and to offer our own lives to God, grateful for our Redemption. (T:1052)

More closely united.

During the Mass, we are made a part of Christ's one Holy Sacrifice for sin. By our mere presence at this sacrifice we are united more closely to one another in the assembly, and to all who belong to Christ today, and to all those faithful members of the Church who have died 'in Christ' and who, in their different centuries, have been present to the same sacrifice. (Also T:1052)

At great cost to ourselves.

We are more truly united to Christ's perfect offering, the more closely our hearts are fixed on Him, not by fervent emotion but by a true entwining of our wills with His. Our wills are one with

Christ's Will whenever we imitate Christ by being determined to love and serve the Father even to 'crucifixion', that is, at the cost of our own lives. (Also T:1052)

Ever-closer union.

We should strive for ever-closer union with Christ. Someone who lives in close union with Him, united in heart and love and sacrifice, offers the perfection of Christ's praise as her own, both within her own soul and in the Holy Sacrifice of the Mass; and this is true even if she is not yet perfect. (T:1077A)

The essence of our worship.

We should remember the essence of our worship. Each time we offer Christ in the Holy Sacrifice, and offer ourselves in union with Him, for the Father's glory, we 'touch' the Father. Christ our Mediator is our way to the Father, and our means of sure contact. (T:1143)

For the sake of the Gospel.

The best way of participating in the Mass is by wholeheartedly uniting our intentions with Christ's intentions, in one sacrificial prayer. The person who is willing - out of love for Christ - to accept the Cross in the whole of his life, is most closely united to Christ's offering. He accepts all sorts of humiliations for the sake of the Gospel, crucifying selfish desires, and even reasonable desires, also, for the sake of the Kingdom. Christ's prayers and the prayers of such a person are truly one. (T:1209)

At the foot of the Cross.

Before Mass, and during the Mass, we should try to become worthy of our task: the task of remaining near the foot of the Cross, as Christ offers His Holy Sacrifice for sinners. (T:1633)

Helping other people.

Our prayers will be more sincere and confident if we understand the reason why our sincere participation in the Mass benefits not just ourselves, but also the people we love. Whenever we pray with our spiritual brothers and sisters, united in one intention - which is to offer prayer through Christ, to the Father - it's as if we are 'touching' Heaven. It's as though we are all bound together, with Christ, in a single body; and our prayer is successful.

Through the merits of Christ's sacrifice, we are truly in touch with the Father. In this one great prayer, Christ is pleading in our midst for all that will make us most joyful eternally. We can be sure that as we reach up to Heaven, united with Christ in prayer, all the people in our hearts - all our precious friends and relations - are lifted up too, as if held in our midst. How can they fail to benefit, when we pray sincere prayers for them, in Christ's Presence? (T:1685)

Heart-to-heart.

It's best to prepare ourselves for Mass by prayer in church; and it's also best to make a good thanksgiving there, after Holy Communion. We can pray as if 'heart-to-heart' with Christ. We can pray frankly and well, and unselfconsciously, in a public place, unworried by others, if we look within our souls and gaze straight towards Christ; or we can direct our soul's gaze straight towards Him in the Blessed Sacrament - in the tabernacle - as if there were not a single person nearby.

We are right to leave prayer, to turn and help our neighbour, when someone is in need of help; but when we are free to pray, we should try to pray calmly and intently, ignoring all distractions and giving Christ our whole attention. (T:1698A and T:1698B)

The 'heart' of the Mass.

Truly, something momentous is happening during the Mass. The priest offers the Holy Sacrifice in which Christ Himself pleads for us all, in order to save us. We, Christ's People, unite our hearts to Christ's prayer: to Christ's self-offering; and we show our hearts' intentions by saying 'Amen'. This is the heart of the Liturgy. This is how we offer perfect thanks and praise to God the Father. We offer an atoning sacrifice for the living and the departed.

It is plain, therefore, that the 'heart' remains the same, century by century. This great act of sacrifice is effective in every circumstance. It is effective because it is Christ's great act. It is effective whether the language in which it is 'clothed' is familiar to those who worship or unknown. It is effective because it is offered through the priest by Christ our God and Saviour.

We are right to join in the congregational prayers, where it is possible. Our heart's union with Christ is what 'counts' above all, however, for a prayerful and sincere participation by us, the laity, in the Holy Sacrifice of the Mass. (T:1804)

Honesty in prayer.

To live as true followers of Christ, and to participate well in the Holy Sacrifice of the Mass, we need to be faithful to prayer; and we must be reconciled with Christ our Saviour. All of those shameful things which we try to hide from His sight in private prayer, or which we are reluctant to 'reveal' to Him in Confession, will be revealed later on. Everything will be unveiled at death, when we shall see clearly both His Divine beauty and our own imperfection. No sinful thought, bad motive, unconfessed sin or foolish yearning can be 'hidden' from Him forever. (T:2034)

In humility and peace.

It's worth being 'painfully' honest and trusting in every moment of prayer. These efforts can help us to enter Heaven just as peacefully as we now 'enter' prayer. What a marvel it is, when Christ's friends can enter either prayer, or Heaven, in a humble and peaceful way, undismayed by the radiant light of His glory. If we work ruthlessly to discard everything which is unworthy of His Divine majesty, we will grow accustomed to His light, in prayer; and we shall have more hope of being able to delight in His radiance when, at death, we leave behind earthly darkness. (Also T:2034)

A closer resemblance.

If we want to share most fully in Christ's offering to the Father we should realise that there's an intimate connection between our offering of the Holy Sacrifice and our way of acting in 'ordinary' life. The more truly are our thoughts and acts - outside the church - conformed to Christ's wishes, thereby resembling Christ's thoughts and acts, the more easily and sincerely can we unite our hearts with His intentions during the Mass. And the reverse of this is also important. Whenever we are sincere in uniting our heart's intentions to Christ's, during the Mass, we are more likely to go out into our daily activities determined to think and act in ways which will please Him. (T:2087)

Striving to be holy.

We are right to take part in the Mass with careful attention to how we speak; and we are right to make reverent gestures; yet the truest worship begins in the heart. If we turn our hearts and minds to God our Father, in love, to offer the Holy Sacrifice in union with Christ, we can be sure that this is the best sort of 'active participation' which Christ and His Church want to encourage.

We must do more than pay strict attention to externals during the Mass - though it's important that the Mass is ordered and conducted according to the rubrics. Someone to whom the Mass is really important will offer his heart and life to the Father. He will strive to be holy, with a living faith and a lively charity. He will be willing to sacrifice everything which is unworthy of 'a child of God'; and he will be united in a sacrificial union with Christ, in penance, and in love for Christ and for his neighbour. (T:3206)

Of one mind with Christ.

It's the simple truth that we offer Christ's sacrifice to the Father most perfectly when our heart's desires are the same as the desires of Christ's heart.

We're doing what God and His Church ask of us whenever we unite our works and sufferings to Christ's offering; yet when we can truly say that our desires are the same as Christ's, we are truly one with His unique offering; and those desires should include a burning desire that every person see the truth about Christ. We should want everyone to realise that He is our only Saviour: that He founded a Church which He invites everyone to enter, and that He asks everyone to believe in His teachings, to receive the sacraments, to give up sin, and to live in holiness and peace, loving God and serving one's neighbour.

Christ sees how small is the number of Catholics who believe and profess the truth that Christ's Church is for everyone, and that all who belong to it have sacred duties and obligations as well as immense gifts and privileges.

If we really want to offer the Holy Sacrifice most worthily we will be praying, with Christ, that the Church will continue to preach and to grow, and to share, from its fullness, all "the means of salvation". We will pray for the other desires of Christ's heart, also mentioned in the Mass, thereby bringing special help to the Clergy, comfort to the Faithful Departed, glory to the almighty Father and honour to His Saints in Heaven. (T:3684)

An eternal offering.

If we love God, we should be thrilled and comforted to know that, by our sincere intention at Mass, we can praise God in a manner worthy of His holiness and majesty. There is no greater act of worship on earth than the Mass; and the reason why the praise which is offered in the Mass is so powerful and exalted is that it is Christ's own praise, offered from our midst.

At every Mass we participate more fully than at any other time in the eternal act of praise and love which takes place within the Godhead: within the 'heart' of God. It is during the Mass that we can leap most surely into Christ's perpetual loving prayer to the Father, in the Spirit, which takes place in Eternity. If we look back for a moment to Christ's life on earth, and to the reason why Christ instituted the Holy Eucharist, we'll see that when He was doing His Father's Will on earth, whatever the cost, Christ was living out in the flesh, for our sakes, the very self-giving love which He has shown towards the Father from all Eternity. (T:4270) G.H.T.

One great act of love.

The Mass provides us with a tremendous opportunity to increase our love for God, and to increase our union with God. Christ showed out His love for the Father by loving His Father's Will even when this led Him through an unjust trial, to the Cross. So whoever makes himself one with Christ today in the living memorial of the Cross, by sincere participation in the Mass, is also one with Christ in His eternal self-offering in the inner life of the Holy Trinity.

Everything God does is one great act of love. We can picture God's love for God, in Eternity: the unending love of Three Divine Persons, which caused Christ to descend to earth to draw other people into the life and love of the Godhead. That same love is now made ours to offer to the Father through the Holy

Eucharist. As we gather with our priest, by whose hands we offer Christ's sacrifice to the Father, in the Spirit, we offer a love and homage worthy of the Father. We increase our union with Him Who is love's origin and source; and we have a foretaste of Heaven's joy. (Also T:4270) G.H.T. *(See illustration 26)*

PREPARATION

Access to the Father.

We must keep in mind the intrinsic perfection of our worship at Mass, no matter how drab or noisy our surroundings.

By Christ's sacrifice, we 'break through' to the Father! United with Christ in one prayer before Heaven, we can 'touch' the Father Who is the summit of our life, the goal of our struggle, and the focus of all our worship. (T:1288)

A careless preparation.

By a careless preparation for Mass before we set out for the church, we are more likely to have distractions; and we lessen the likelihood of an instant and joyful union with Christ in Holy Communion. (T:1338)

Christ's plan for us.

Few of us can say that we never arrive late for Mass, or that we are never exhausted from rushing. Our carelessness in planning our journey to the church, and our avoidable lateness, are more silly than wicked. But they are silly, because we deprive ourselves of some of the blessings which Christ longs to pour upon us through our devotion to Him, and through every moment of the glorious worship of the Church.

We should never forget the ultimate purpose of all Christ's dealings with us. He wants to give us joy! He calls us, and others, to the whole of Mass and to prayer, so that we can be blessed and made happy - happy both now and in Eternity - and not simply so that we might fulfil our real duty of joining in the offering of the Holy Sacrifice to the Father. (T:1462)

A radical change.

If we look carefully at our lives, we see that no 'area' should remain hidden away from Christ, if we accept His friendship. A radical change is needed if someone wants to offer Christ a new 'wineskin' into which He can pour the new 'wine' which is the life of grace.

If we consider the true meaning of a radical commitment to Christ, and to His Holy Will, we'll see that He wants to be welcomed and made 'at home' in every single area of our lives. We need to make a thorough examination of our former ways of life.

A new way of life 'in Christ' won't last if an attempt is made to superimpose it on a life which is still given up to immorality, immodesty, carelessness in duty, or uncharity. Nor will our 'life-in-Christ' flourish if, from presumption and pride, we foolishly cling to dangerous habits or 'places', or to dangerous companions.

It's a wonderful thing we do when we freely turn to Christ. Yet if we are sincere in asking Him to share our lives we need to examine - in His light - our places of work and leisure, and our regular habits and attitudes, as well as our companions, tasks, hobbies and duties, our manner of speaking, and even our clothing. Nothing in earthly life can be seen as 'neutral'. Everything that we touch, choose, share or seek will either help or hinder us in our journey to Heaven, and will help or hinder those who look to us for an example. (T:1777)

In joyful prayer.

Everyone who is willing to co-operate with the Father's plans, and to obey His wishes, and to make a good preparation for the Mass, could be lifted high in joyful prayer, especially in Holy Communion. Such is the Father's plan for everyone; yet He sees that few of us are willing to co-operate with Him in all things.

Some of us need to prepare for Mass by putting things 'right' with God, by confessing our sins. Some of us have been careless in our efforts to allow enough time to travel to church. We should all set out in good time, with a good intention, having made an effort to be worthy of praying with the Saints of Heaven who also take part. Many of us forget the presence of the Saints - and of the holy Angels - as the whole Church is united in offering the Holy Sacrifice to the Father. (T:2647)

Reluctant attendance.

We need to ask ourselves if anyone would guess, from the reluctant way in which we drag ourselves to church, that we are on our way to meet the living God: to meet Christ, 'through whom all things were made'. This is Christ Who sacrificed His life out of love for us all, yet Who is risen and alive, and Really Present amongst us today. If a member of another Faith were to look inside our church to see how we behave there, would anything lead him to believe that we are in the presence of the all-holy one: Creator and Judge of all Mankind? (P.U.T:1)

Infinite heights of glory.

It makes a tremendous difference to our worship if we remind ourselves of the majesty of God. He lives in infinite heights of glory which tower for all Eternity above the depths of the Abyss which separates the Godhead from Mankind. He is reaching out to us, in love, through Christ; and we are sometimes bored or ungrateful!

Yet we who live 'in Christ' and share His life need not fear to approach the Father. We can claim, with truth, that we belong to Him: true children of the Father of light. We can know Him, meet Him, converse with Him and adore Him. At every moment of the day we can live contentedly in His love. (T:2669)

Christ's sufferings.

We must do all we can to encourage one another to show reverence and gratitude towards our Saviour Who is Really Present in our church. It's as if Christ's sufferings on the Cross are made greater through every act of irreverence He witnesses today, whether tiny or appalling things, which He hears and sees from the altar or the tabernacle. During His life on earth, He suffered grievous heartache because of the sin and irreverence of our day, which He could already see. (T:2676)

Insufficient instruction.

Few of us in the Church today have been given sufficient instruction on how to pray well, or how to be spiritually one with Christ in His sacrificial prayer, which is the most important aspect of the Eucharistic celebration.

A disproportionate amount of time is spent by Catholics in learning how to stand, walk, recite, carry, collect or process in one part of the church or another. These things are important; yet they are rarely conducive to intimate union with Christ if the people involved are not prayerful as well. If we do these things for the sake of Christ, however, we can achieve an admirable state: our exterior conduct matching our inner disposition. (T:2847).

Setting a good example.

It is a wonderful thing when people make time to pray in church for a few minutes before the Mass begins. It is especially helpful when willing priests set a good example to their flocks in this matter - and when they also spend some time in prayer, visible to their people, after the celebration. (T: 3063)

Clothed in holiness.

At our liturgical celebrations we praise the Father in an especially-close union with the Court of Heaven; and so the Lord likes to see our souls properly prepared, adorned and purified in readiness.

As the priest clothes himself in the chasuble, so ought we to prepare for solemn worship. If we turn our attention to God, we allow God to clothe us in holiness. (T:3274)

Holy water.

By using holy water as we enter the church, and by making the sign of the Cross, we demonstrate our faith in God and our trust in His Church which powerfully helps us through holy customs, symbolic gestures and sacramentals. By prayer and the use of holy water we can help to purify our hearts and minds and drive away evil spirits. (P.U.T: 2)

Willing to listen.

If we open our eyes and ears at Mass, and pray sincerely, we'll become more aware of the eternal truths about Eternal Life. What we need to know is plainly heard, here in church, in the words of the Mass: words about Heaven and damnation, salvation and sin, glory and weakness, the life of grace and our selfish desires - and about the Saints and Angels whom we shall see if we enter Heaven. Everything we need to know is plainly put before us in Scripture and the Tradition, through the authoritative teaching of the Church, even though in Catholic education and catechesis the 'picture' of faith which is offered is sometimes incomplete. (T:5072)

CROSSING THE THRESHOLD

Christ's welcome.

As we enter the church for Mass we can be sure that, from the tabernacle, Christ welcomes each of us, individually, with great joy and delight. (T:73)

Acts of faith.

We can increase our faith by making fervent acts of faith in Christ's Real Presence with us, and in His love for us. An act of faith is when we express our Christian faith with conviction: for example, by saying: "I believe that You are Present - but increase my faith, Lord." Or we can use other prayers.

We should look with faith upon the Holy Mysteries. Here before us, during the Holy Sacrifice, is majesty, glory, and salvation. Christ is alive in the love and life of the Father, united in the Spirit. The Holy Trinity is 'at work' to save us and to make us happy and holy. (T:191 and 219)

Over the threshold.

We should enter the church with reverence, not chatting and laughing, heedless of what we are doing. Christ loves to see us cheerful; but when we cross the threshold we should remember that we are entering a 'house of prayer'; so we should enter quietly. The holy Angels are present in the church. They bow low, in solemn reverence before Christ, Who is Really Present in the tabernacle. (T:809)

A glad welcome.

We should greet Christ in the Blessed Sacrament. He is Really Present in our church; and as we welcome Him, He welcomes us. (T:1055)

With awe and wonder.

We should approach the sanctuary with awe and wonder, and revere the holy altar from which Christ's Holy Sacrifice is going to be offered. (T:1064)

Angels on guard.

The Church is not empty when we arrive, before the Mass begins. Christ is Present in the tabernacle; and many holy Angels stand guard, and worship Christ, even amidst the cold and darkness. Like blades of glimmering light, they also cluster about the altar where the Holy Sacrifice is to be offered. (T:1068)

Christ our High Priest.

We should greet Christ as we enter the church. Truly, He is Present. He awaits us at the tabernacle, and He delights in our greeting. He is robed as a priest; and He is praying to the Father on our behalf. A golden halo encircles Christ's head; and He holds His arms outstretched towards Heaven in fervent intercession. (T:1539)

In the hall-way.

Each of us should treasure Christ's Real Presence in the tabernacle. Whenever we come here to speak to Him we can think of the tabernacle as being like a place of meeting such as people find when they are travelling - or even like a meeting-place in their own homes. Of course, we can speak to Christ our God at any time, and everywhere. But when we come to the tabernacle to enjoy the blessings of His Real Presence, it's as though we have entered the little 'space' between earth and Heaven. It is as though we have stepped into the little space which links one railway carriage with another, or into the hatch through which people enter a space-craft.

More than anything, however, this place of meeting resembles a hall-way at the front of a brilliantly-lit house. We who approach the tabernacle with faith are like people who yearn to be present at a joyful party. And in order to find Christ, the Host, we go to the 'hall-way': a place which looks so wonderful to those of us who, until we reach Heaven, seem to stand 'outside' the 'house' of Heaven, in the darkness. (T:2035)

Close to Heaven.

As we approach the tabernacle - which is like a 'hall-way' to Heaven, a hall-way where Christ our Host is waiting to welcome us - we can be sure that He delights in our approach, since it is He Who has invited us to come to his Home, which is Heaven.

We can all remember how we have felt before joining friends for an earthly party. We have prepared for the celebration in all sorts of ways. We have longed to go in. We have listened - as we approached the house - for the sound of familiar voices. We have been happy to draw closer to our friends, as we have approached the doorway of our host's house. We have enjoyed emerging from darkness into the radiant light which is streaming from the windows and the front door; and we have heard snatches of music which delighted us. We can approach the tabernacle with the same sort of glee! (Also T:2035)

A place at table.

Christ wants us, His faithful 'children', to be as confident and carefree as the children of any good father. There are several reasons why we can feel secure; and the main reasons are that we have a sure place at table, which means a sure place at His eternal 'Banquet' in Heaven, provided we remain faithful. Also, we have a sure place at the celebration of the Mass, where, in receiving Christ as our Heavenly food, by receiving the sacrament of His Sacred Body and Blood, we are anticipating the 'Feast' of Heaven.

If our days are full of turmoil and struggle, it should comfort us to know that, if we are reconciled to God and faithful to Him, in His Church, we have a right to be here before the holy altar. (T:2461)

An expression of love.

We touch Christ's heart deeply when we enter the church and when we also glance towards the tabernacle, to express delight at His Presence, and to offer a simple expression of love for Him. (T:2609)

Meeting the living God.

Christ is delighted when we enter the church and kneel down to pray, to prepare for the Mass. It's quite right that people greet one another - but not to chatter for long minutes, as people chatter in a cinema when they're waiting for a film to start. We should all realise that the Mass is not an entertainment, but a meeting with our living God: with the Son of God Who comes to our altar for the offering of the Holy Sacrifice.

Few of us would think about going to an important 'worldly' event without also thinking about what to wear, what to do and say, and what sort of gift to take - or how to express our thanks, when it's time to go home. When we attend church, therefore, for something as important as the Mass, a good preparation is essential if we want to pray worthily before the Father, amidst the Saints and the holy Angels. (T:2697)

THE SIGN OF THE CROSS

Protection against evil.

When we make the sign of the Cross, it's as though we are fastened to Christ by it: wrapped up safely with Him. It protects us from evil. It is a true badge of our Faith. It is a real 'work', because it is an act of faith in the Holy Trinity; and it honours almighty God immensely. (T:60)

A prayer to the Holy Trinity.

The sign of the Cross is used at Mass both to begin and to end our prayers. It is a sign of our life 'in Christ', and is a devout and holy prayer to the Three Persons of the Most Holy Trinity. It is like a firm rope which binds us to Them in every task or every danger. (T:75)

A powerful help.

Wherever we are, we can make the sign of the Cross in any threatening darkness of soul, or in bodily danger. It draws graces upon us, through our faith, and Christ's power. (T:82)

Remembering our Baptism.

The sign of the Cross is a powerful prayer to the Holy Trinity; and we use it not only in private prayer at home, but also on entering the church, and at different times of the Mass. Through it, we honour God, remember our Baptism, place ourselves in God's presence, and deter the Evil One. (Also T:82)

United with the Saints.

When we make the sign of the Cross, as is customary, the Saints do the same; and this is because they love to join us in our worship. (T:627)

Pleasing our Guardian Angels.

When we make the sign of the Cross with reverence - or any other faith-prompted and loving act, done for God's honour and glory - we delight our Guardian Angels who are at our side as usual and who witness everything we do. (T:4510)

THE HOLY ANGELS

Gathered about us.

Our prayers should be fervent, as we pray amidst the holy Angels. The Angels are pure spirits, who are unseen but real; and they are gathered about us, united with us in prayer, as we prepare our hearts for the Holy Sacrifice. (T:541)

Reverent gestures.

The holy Angels - huge and radiant - stand in rows beside us as we pray. They are like a Heavenly guard, who encourage devout souls to be even more devout. They imitate our reverent gestures, join in our prayers, and make the sign of the Cross, just as we do at the end of our prayers, in honour of the Most Holy Trinity. (T:994B)

Guarding the priest.

The holy Angel who guards the priest is especially glorious - in

7. THE FATHER'S LOVE.

God the Father's love for us all is infinitely-great, and unchanging. It is as fervent as the love which a bridegroom has for his bride, and a King for his subjects, and a mother for the infant on her lap. OIL-S:2550 *("As tenderly as a father treats his children, so Yahweh treats those who fear him." Ps 103:13).*

8. AT A BAPTISM.

The newly-baptised person is a 'new creature' who has been delivered from sin and made a member of the Church. He is an adopted child of God who can learn to call God "Father". He can be certain that every sincere prayer is heard and answered. OIL-M:876. *(" ... proclaim the Good News to all creation. He who believes and is baptised will be saved; he who does not believe will be condemned." Mk 16:15-16).*

9. THROUGH THE TOUCH OF THE HOLY SPIRIT.

The Divine fire of the Holy Spirit, which transformed the soul at Baptism, gives special strength to the soul in Confirmation. The confirmed person has been clothed in Heavenly gifts, so that he can defend and spread the faith and speak boldly about Christ. OIL-S:1941. *("But when the Spirit of truth comes he will lead you to the complete truth." Jn 16:13).*

10. SHELTERED BY HIS GLORY.

We are made full members of the Church through Baptism, Confirmation and the Holy Eucharist. And as we gather to offer worthy praise to the Father through Christ, in the Spirit, it's as if our weaknesses are blotted out by the glory of Christ, our Priest and sacrifice. OIL-M:1269. *("These remained faithful to the teaching of the apostles, to the brotherhood, to the breaking of bread and to the prayers." Ac 2:42).*

11. IN THE FIRE OF DIVINE LOVE.

The Fire of Divine love surrounds and inspires us as we praise and thank the Father in and through Jesus Christ, in the Spirit, at every Mass. It is almighty God, our Creator, Who has called us, made us His own children, and gathered us together to join in the Liturgy of Heaven. OIL-M:1534. *("You are our Lord and our God, you are worthy of glory and honour and power, because you made all the universe." Rev 4:11).*

12. A TORRENT OF GRACES.

During the Sacred Liturgy, it's as though we are on the brink of Heaven's worship. The whole Church of earth, Heaven and Purgatory is united with the Holy Angels in praise of the Holy Trinity. At every Mass, we await a marvellous out-pouring of graces from the heart of God. OIL-L:442A. *("Before the world was made, he chose us, chose us in Christ, to be holy and spotless, and to live through love in his presence." Ep 1:4).*

keeping with the special dignity which Christ has conferred upon our priest. (T:1005)

Pleased to hear our praises.

Our Guardian Angels, in particular, are pleased to hear us praise and honour the Holy Trinity. (T:1060B)

The Angels' delight.

We must never forget that we pray amongst the holy Angels. They applaud with joy every grateful prayer we offer before the tabernacle: for example, whenever we say to Christ - in the Blessed Sacrament - "Thank you for being here." (T:1083)

Encircling the altar.

The holy Angels, on high, encircle the holy altar. They gaze towards it, ready to adore Christ our God when He appears before us, when He is made Present through the words of the priest and the Spirit's power, at the Consecration. (T:1596)

Solemn and dignified.

We should imitate the dignity of the holy Angels, if we want to serve Christ well. As they worship with us, in the church, they are solemn and dignified. On slim wings, they soar above us, bowing their heads, as they adore Christ our Saviour. (T:1671)

Everyday courtesy.

Christ loves to reward those of us who offer acts of faith and loving prayers to Him, and who remember to greet His holy Angels. The Angels are ranged above the altar steps like spears of light. Truly, they stand guard, day and night, praying in the sanctuary; and it's only courteous of us to acknowledge their presence. (T:1856)

Angelic companions.

We should treasure our Heavenly friends, the Saints - and also treasure our Angelic companions. Truly, we are worshipping with the holy Angels. They stand in long rows, bowing down in adoration at the elevation of the Sacred Host - Christ's Sacred Body.

The priest's own guardian Angel follows behind the priest, as he moves about the sanctuary. And when Christ comes to each of us in Holy Communion, His holy Angels stand close to us - one on each side. We who believe in Christ and in His Heavenly companions can encourage one another to worship Him with tremendous love and reverence. (T:1939)

Angels to guard us.

The holy Angels are pure spirits, who serve God in many ways. They are at work in the world to guard both the Church and the world from evil; and we are wise to ask for their assistance. (T:2802)

Before the Mass begins.

Our sanctuary is full of holy Angels, before, during and after the Mass. (T:2894)

Angels of higher rank.

Our greeting to the holy Angels should never be omitted. We should be aware of how privileged we are to be amongst them. Furthermore, we ought to realise that the Angels who guard a church which belongs to a religious order are even more magnificent, and of higher rank, than those on guard in a parish church. This is because the Lord shows honour, in this way, to the religious who worship there: each of whom has dedicated himself wholly to Christ by solemn vows. (T:2978)

By our dignified behaviour.

Our church is full of holy Angels who are worshipping Christ in the Blessed Sacrament; and it is Christ's wish that we acknowledge their presence, by our dignified behaviour. We can encourage everyone to greet them, and to act reverently in their presence; and we can also greet and honour the Saints who are so close to us and whose shrines adorn our churches - especially our Mother Mary. (T:3064)

Entering the church.

Christ is pleased when we greet the holy Angels each time we enter a church and approach the sanctuary. (T:3230)

Created by God.

Very few of us regularly express gratitude for the love and work of the holy Angels. Christ loves them dearly; and He brought them into existence not only for the glory of God the Father, but so that they could eventually help human beings.

There's something else Christ wants us to consider: something helpful. As we stand on the earth's surface, most of us are unaware of the teeming life which is there beneath our feet, in many metres of soil and other strata which are 'home' to all sorts of large creatures and little organisms. Christ wants us to realise that most of us are just as unaware that 'above' and around us - in a spiritual manner - the air is teeming with life: the life of the holy Angels in their hundreds of thousands, who were all created by God. (T: 4103)

Angels in the sanctuary.

At the Consecration, hundreds of holy Angels fill our sanctuary, adoring Christ Who is now Present on the altar. (T:4245)

Joining in our praise.

As we sing the Acclamation at Mass, after the Consecration, we are singing together as Jesus is Really Present before us under the appearance of bread and wine; and the Saints and holy Angels are present too, joining in the praise and homage which we are offering to our Saviour. (T:4771)

---

3. THE HOLY SACRIFICE OF THE MASS

SORROW-FOR-SIN

Penitent and forgiven.

At the beginning of the Mass, as we stand together and confess our sinfulness, we have good reason to give thanks to God if we are weak, penitent, forgiven, and peaceful. If the opposite is true - if our hearts are so full of earthly joys that we rarely give thanks to God Who is the source of all good things - we leave little place for Him in our self-sufficiency; and so He doesn't dwell in us as He dwells in the hearts of those who call to Him from their emptiness. (T:120)

Spiritual poverty.

We should rejoice in our spiritual poverty. All poverty, inadequacy, shame and broken-heartedness can be used as a marvellous 'stepping-stone' to the God of compassion and tenderness: Christ the Crucified. (Also T:120)

Serious sin.

It's important that we attend Mass, no matter what spiritual state we're in; but it's a wonderful thing to attend Mass in a state of grace. If we have led holy and innocent lives, or if we have been purified of serious sin through the sacrament of Reconciliation, we have honoured and delighted Christ, and we've given joy to our Guardian Angels. (T:905)

The spiritual life.

We ought never to worry about our little imperfections, as we turn to God our Father in sincere prayer. At every stage of the spiritual life - and even before we have reached the summit of the 'holy mountain' of sanctity - Christ's perfect praise is ours to offer to the Father, at every step throughout the climb. This praise is offered when we unite ourselves, heart and soul, with the Holy Sacrifice. (T:1003)

In Christ's embrace.

We can think of our small faults and failings as being like little bits of dust on our feet, if we have just walked barefooted along a dusty road. In confessing these little faults at the beginning of Mass, in prayer before Christ, it's as though we pause to brush away the dust from our feet, seated in His embrace; and as we do this, Christ looks on with tremendous love and admiration. (T:1118)

With a new purity.

We should remember the tremendous value of a sincere act of contrition, by which we can be sure of purifying our souls. The effect of contrition is as immediate and powerful as if silt were suddenly made to fall to the bottom of a pool of water, so that the water sparkles with a new purity and brightness. (T:1149)

On our behalf.

We should be grateful for the priest who serves the local Church, and for his priestly power of intercession. Wonderful Divine gifts are drawn upon us by his mediation, as he does Christ's work in our midst during the Sacred Liturgy. As the priest recites certain words about forgiveness, during the Mass, solemnly addressing the Father on our behalf, he draws down upon us - as if drawing down a silky white veil from Heaven - the grace and light which Christ has won for us through His Holy Sacrifice. (T:1387)

Clothed in white.

It's important to be in a state of grace, which is to be leading a Christian life free from grave sin. If we have committed grave sins the Church asks us to confess them in the sacrament of Penance, and to be reconciled, before receiving Holy Communion. When we are forgiven, and free from grave sin, we can be at peace before God, just like those who have never committed grave sin. Then we can understand and delight in our status as people who through God's mercy are faith-filled, repentant, reconciled and forgiven. With the whole Church we'll be able to pray powerful prayers to the Father in the name of Jesus.

As we pray, in a state of grace, our prayer is worthy of being heard. Because of Christ's sacrifice on our behalf, on the Cross, and the blood which He shed for us, we are now washed in His Precious Blood. It's as if - through that 'washing' - we are now clothed in white garments. We have been prepared and made fit to pray in His name on earth, and eventually to enter Heaven. (T:1414)

Acts of penance.

God our Father wants us to give our hearts and souls to Him in the sort of steady self-offering which is achieved by penance. He sees how rare, today, are penance and surrender. Only by acts of penance can we prepare our souls to be clothed, fully, in the forgiveness which God holds out to us all at every moment. Only by acts of penance can we co-operate with the work of purification and sanctification which God is accomplishing within our souls at each stage of the spiritual journey. (T:1617)

Wonderful news.

If we are wholehearted in our love for Christ, we'll want to share the good news about forgiveness: the wonderful news that everyone who wants to receive forgiveness from God can receive it! The forgiving love of Christ our God pours out ceaselessly towards us all. His forgiveness shines towards each of our souls just as surely as when a beam of torchlight shines into a dark cavern as a rescuer searches for someone who needs his help. Everyone who wants to receive Divine light and grace has the duty, therefore, and the simple need, of clearing away the sins which - like huge rocks from a roof-fall - block that light and grace and keep Christ from the soul's 'centre'.

We can accomplish a great deal, by our courage. All can be made bright, within our souls, after our Reconciliation. A true clearing-away of sins can be achieved through the means which Christ Himself has established within His Church: through the sacrament of confession, of Reconciliation. Through a 'clearing-away' of sins in this manner, we permit Christ to pour His light and joy within our hearts. (T:1618)

A wise choice.

Whenever the Holy Sacrifice is offered today, we are free to choose whether to draw close to Christ, or whether to stay some distance away. We should understand, however, that although Christ invites us to exercise our free-will, some choices are immensely wise, and others are foolish. For example, a Catholic who chooses to obey Christ's wishes, and to take part in the Holy Sacrifice of the Mass, where circumstances allow, and to receive Christ in Holy Communion, is acting very wisely - unless that person is not in a state of grace. If he is unable to take Communion because of serious sin he can choose to change his life and to receive Christ's forgiveness. And then he can approach Christ in true friendship.

Whoever postpones a necessary Reconciliation risks an eternal loss of friendship with Christ, or - at the very least - postpones a much-needed and eventual purification, and must enter Purgatory before finally entering Heaven. (T:1620)

Unending, unconditional love.

Whatever our present problems, we should always remember that Christ's love for us doesn't depend upon our state-of-soul! He is not 'put off' by our frailty or foolishness; yet He tremendously admires us when we are penitent, and when we approach Him in humility and trust! (Also T:1620)

Children of God.

We need to make sincere efforts to co-operate with Christ's graces, in order to be holy. It is the Will of the Father that we who receive Christ in Holy Communion - men, women, and children too - should strive to be worthy of Christ's Presence. It is the Will of the Father that we who are called the 'children of God' be pure, which means: devoted to Christ entirely, loving His Will, determined to fulfil His wishes, contrite, faithful, chaste and obedient, and longing to give Him glory.

Truly, we have been made 'children of God' by our Baptism; but only if we lead pure and holy lives are we worthy of our title. (T:1734C)

Making excuses.

If we want to honour God, we must try to be faithful in attending the Holy Sacrifice of the Mass, even if we're tempted to make excuses for not attending, or even if we feel unworthy of being present because we know that we're not perfect or that we're not reconciled to Christ and not 'in Communion'. The reason why we should attend is that God, by His Divine and redeeming work, by Christ's offering and through the Spirit's power, can bring about wonderful changes in our lives. He achieves things which none of us can achieve unaided. He can even draw us - sometimes as if inch by inch - from the mire of sin which has entrapped us. (T:1747)

Sinful and disobedient.

Even if we are determined sinners we can still benefit from attendance at the Holy Sacrifice. But if we are grievously sinful people who carelessly stay away we are not only grievously sinful but are also disloyal. We add disobedience to our present offences against Christ. (Also T:1747)

Blind and shameless.

We should never try to persuade ourselves that our unconfessed, serious sins don't matter. When a defiant and determined sinner stands in church, his soul befouled by his sins, and 'clothed' in the shameless rags of impenitence, he can still be certain that Christ loves him unceasingly, with the deepest tenderness. Christ understands that this precious person wants to be united with the whole Church in prayer. But Christ looks on with deep pity whenever such a person - who has not repented of his grave sins - thinks himself fit to offer pure praise to the Father, amidst penitent friends. Truly, Christ's love is endless; yet He sees how blind we are - or how shameless - if we are living in mortal sin. We are not clothed for Christ's feast. It's as if we have refused to wear the white garments of grace and forgiveness.

Everyone who takes part in the Sacred Liturgy steps into the light which is shining down from Heaven, as all Heaven looks on. That's why we're extraordinarily blind - or arrogant - if we've done serious wrong, and haven't yet repented, and still think ourselves ready to receive Christ, and step up to approach Him for Holy Communion. (T:1770)

Wearing white garments.

We should be determined to live grace-filled lives; and we'll be helped if we remember that Christ our Saviour is Really Present with us, at Mass. We can imagine that He is standing at the centre of a little pool of light, on the surface of the dark globe of the earth. In truth, He is the source of the light. His radiance is streaming all around Him; and it streams powerfully upwards, all the way to Heaven. He is surrounded by people who are wearing white garments; but one person is clothed in rumpled dirty garments which are wholly inappropriate for the celebratory life of the holy company; and the gloomy clothing represents that person's serious and unrepented sins.

The Mass is like a beacon of praise of the Father, a beacon which was only established through Christ, by His sacrifice: a sacrifice once offered on the Cross and now offered from the altar. Within Christ's holy Church, this beacon of prayer burns unceasingly. It is fierce and bright, because it burns with Christ's power and light. This praise streams upwards through the darkness to reach as far as Heaven; and those who are truly united to Christ as He praises the Father are the reconciled. We should all consider, therefore, before the Mass begins, how best to prepare for the glory which will surround us at Mass as we step forward to praise our Creator. (Also T:1770)

To be made clean.

Christ wants us all to realise that since it is only through Him that Divine light shines so powerfully here on earth, in our midst, during the Mass, we have a duty to make efforts to be worthy of His friendship. Who can celebrate new life worthily in the presence of Christ if he will not first, and by his free act, become a member of the Church, which shines like a lamp amidst earthly darkness? Who can hope to soar up to Heaven one day if he has refused to stand within this Divine and holy light to be made 'clean' by the priests, who are doing Christ's work, as they forgive sins, in the sacrament of Reconciliation?

It is Christ Who wants us all to change. If we are blind and shameless He can help us to recognise our sins, and repent. If we confess our sins, and are reconciled, it's as if we are clothed in the 'white garments' of the forgiven; and we can stand in the light of Christ with joy, to enjoy His Presence, and to offer His Holy Sacrifice in a worthy manner. (Also T:1770)

True sorrow-for-sin.

We should increase our determination to conquer all our little failings. If we consider our thoughts and actions, as if through Christ's eyes, we'll see how few of these things are worthy of Him; and so we need to strive for perfection. Christ delights in our trust, as we freely 'open' our souls to His gaze; but if we are really sorry, we'll be willing to change our less-than-perfect attitudes and actions.

True sorrow-for-sin is productive. It produces within the soul a determination to overcome every failing, for Christ's sake, so enabling us to travel further along our path towards Heaven. We should reject utterly, therefore, all that is unworthy of Christ: not only sin, but everything which is even slightly imperfect, self-seeking or foolish. (T:1821)

Ignorant and unrepentant.

It's important that we sincerely repent of our sins at the beginning of every Mass. If we don't do so we're like a person who visits a friend during a rain-storm but who insists on tramping through her house in his muddy outer garments - oblivious to the damage he is doing to the carpet and to the bad example he's giving by his selfish attitude. Christ does not condemn us, on seeing such behaviour; but He pities all who are ignorant and unrepentant; and He perpetually invites us to turn to Him for help, and to change our lives. (T:2302)

No 'locked doors'.

If we are well-established in the spiritual life we wisely seek the graces which are lavished upon us through the wonderful sacraments of the Church. Our examination of conscience should reveal no 'locked doors' or dark areas: no secret areas of the sort which would make us refuse Christ entry. If we shut out Christ, we're shutting out the only one who can make our souls beautiful and radiant and pure. (T:2428)

Criticism of priests.

Christ wants us all to put our trust in Him, and to give up sin: whether rebellion or lack of charity. He is especially delighted to see us repent sincerely of those thoughts and words by which some of us have criticised His priests or the Sacred Priesthood.

We should believe the words of Sacred Scripture, through which we hear Christ say that He counts as done to Himself whatever is done to others. This is true about His priests, also. Whoever hurts or insults Christ's priests hurts or insults Christ - no matter what the failings of the Clergy. (T:2612)

Real contrition.

If we approach Christ with real contrition it's as if we open the 'door' of our soul to show truth to Him Who is Truth. We allow Him to come close, to explain things to us, and also to console us. By sincere and contrite prayer we allow God to purify us, as His Holy Spirit works within our souls. (T:2608 and 2643)

Reconciled and forgiven.

Christ sees that much of the spiritual gloom and decay in the Church today is caused because very many Catholics don't believe that they are sinners, even though they do wrong in God's sight. Others know that they do wrong, yet won't repent. Others do wrong, and are contrite, yet won't go to be reconciled.

Only a few Catholics live like simple children of God: still somewhat sinful, and living amidst other sinners, yet taking every care to avoid serious sin, and living in an admirable way: reconciled to God, fully in communion with His Church, enjoying His friendship, and at peace in His love. (T:2683)

The simple truth.

We should be glad to admit that we are sinful people. It's when we're not afraid to say so that we're included with the many people who benefit from Christ's prayer during the offering of the Holy Sacrifice. (T:2885)

Degrees of glory.

We don't usually know much about our spiritual state, or the state-of-soul of the people who surround us, but we should long for holiness. The souls of some of those who enter a church to pray are full of glory. Others possess God's glory to a lesser degree. Some, however, even in a state of grace, don't 'shine' as they might, because they are burdened with little sins and much self-love; or they are cluttered with the detritus of great sins which have been forgiven but for which little or no reparation has been made. Other people, who are not in a state of grace, have no light in them at all.

Though it cannot usually be seen, Christ's glory shines out from the souls of those who are entirely dedicated to Him and who are wholly innocent souls, or else penitent souls who have completed their purification. (T:3277)

One fire of praise.

Whenever Christ's true friends are gathered together it's as if there are many 'lights' of glory meeting and intermingling, so beginning to make one light, or one 'flame' of praise before the Father. This is the case in Heaven, where the thousands and thousands of glorious Saints live and celebrate together: each distinct, perfected and joyful - yet all forming, together, one raging, blissful, loving fire of praise which burns, inextinguishable, forever, before and within the Godhead, in honour of the Holy Trinity.

It follows that someone who attends Mass, even with his soul shrouded in darkness, has done well to recognise his membership of God's family and his need of God's graces. Yet if he has not cast off his grievous sins he is not 'on fire' in the one 'fire' of praise which rises up from that community. (Also T:3277)

Christ's prayers, ours.

It is part of the power and the wonder of each person's participation in the Mass that since we are one with Christ as He prays amongst us, if we participate sincerely, in a state of grace, His prayers are ours. And since His prayers on behalf of His contrite and trusting brothers and sisters are infallibly granted by the Father - for example, "Make us worthy to share Eternal Life" - we have good reason to hope that we shall indeed receive the Eternal Life and the other blessings for which we pray, if we remain faithful until death.

Regular attendance at Mass is essential, however, unless through no fault of our own we are kept away: perhaps by care of the sick, or by our own illness, or because of imprisonment or other things. Each of us remains in need of Christ's powerful intercession for as long as we live in earthly life. (T:3328)

A love-letter to God.

We must never be embarrassed that we have to confess our faults over and over again. Each act of contrition is like a love-letter to God. (T:3560)

Holding out His arms.

Whenever we speak to Christ with contrition about our sinfulness, it's as though He's holding out His arms to us, saying: "Well done! ... How wonderful that you have come to Me in trust and contrition yet again." (T:4440)

Ready to enter Heaven.

We're always wise to make a good confession. It is always worthwhile, when we look within our hearts in order to gauge our spiritual state, to ask ourselves: "Am I ready to enter Heaven?" By asking that simple question, we immediately begin to see in what ways we have failed to do good, or what things we have done which are unworthy of a child of the Kingdom.

Whoever teaches the Faith can invite people to ask themselves the same question: Are they ready to enter Heaven? Wouldn't it be wise to cast off their sins and bad habits in preparation for the purity and holiness of the Godhead? (T:4723)

THE GLORIA

Praying with the Angels.

We should be glad to know that the Angels are praying with us. They pray the 'Gloria' with us, just as we pray the "Holy, Holy, Holy Lord" with them. (T:986)

The whole Church.

Whenever we offer heart-felt praise together, during the Mass, as we adore the Most Holy Trinity, we can be certain that we in the Church on earth are united with many other members of the

Church who also praise God: with our brothers and sisters in Heaven and Purgatory - and with all the holy Angels. (P.U.T:3)

HOLY SCRIPTURE

Eternal wisdom.

It is Christ's eternal wisdom that we receive through the Scriptures. As we listen to Holy Scripture in the course of the Liturgy we receive wisdom from Heaven, not merely-human reflections of people in past ages. (T:10)

Listening with care.

We should listen carefully to the readings from Holy Scripture, thus allowing Christ our God to speak to our hearts. (T:569)

The Holy Gospel.

We should listen carefully as a member of the Clergy reads a passage from the Holy Gospel during the Mass. When these words are read out to us, Christ comes close to us all; and He teaches everyone who is attentive. (T:888B) *(See illustration 17)*

Light and wisdom.

It's important to keep a balanced view of the Holy Scriptures which we revere. Our faith is vivified and increased as we listen to God's Word and make prayerful reflections. It's a marvel, and a cause for thanksgiving, that Christ's light and wisdom are always 'pouring' through the text of Holy Scripture; yet we should never forget that He - the Divine and living Saviour - is the source of this wisdom. The book which contains Christ's words about Himself is extremely precious, yet it remains a book. As an object, it is to be revered and not idolised. As a source of grace and truth it is to be used and understood conjointly with the living, Sacred Tradition of the Church, and the Teaching Office of the Church; in other words, it is to be understood with the 'mind' of the Church. (T:1635)

Reluctant to hear.

We mustn't be afraid to encounter truth, as we listen to the Word of God. To listen with faith and trust is to be dazzled, at times, by shafts of light from Heaven, or to be disturbed by what we hear. Some of us listen timidly, if we are reluctant to hear, and reluctant to make the changes which the Lord of the Gospels invites us to make. Some of us, if we understand little about Christ's purposes, and don't want to know His Will for our lives, are tempted to dispute the plain meaning of many passages of Holy Scripture.

We must remain watchful - to see if 'the doors' of our hearts are 'open' to God, or if they are tightly shut, to keep out His light and truth. (Also T:1635)

With courage and reverence.

We benefit immensely whenever we 'risk' the implications of standing in the full glare of Christ's brilliant light and wisdom, received through the Holy Scriptures. If we learn to approach the texts bravely and reverently we recognise in Holy Scripture - and see illuminated ever more clearly - the very truths which are being held by the Church in her constant teaching and Tradition. We see, confirmed, the truth that Christ's purposes are magnificent and unchanging, and that He invites us to obey Him, and to co-operate with His plans. Truly, we meet Christ, as we listen to Holy Scripture, or listen to the homily. (Also T:1635)

The Father's Will.

It's important that we listen carefully to the readings during the

Mass, and to the homily. In Holy Scripture, wisdom is offered both to the simple and to the wise.

It is the Lord Who encourages us. The good spiritual nourishment which we receive from the Church, through the readings from Holy Scripture and in the homilies, is directly Willed by the Father in Heaven. (T:1730)

Unwise changes.

It is the Will of Christ, shown through His Church, that a priest in certain circumstances may substitute one Scripture reading for another, where this seems to be appropriate for special groups of persons present, or for special occasions. Yet a priest is not exercising this sort of prudent and wise judgement if he bans the reading-out of certain portions of Scripture in order to appease sections of his congregation - for example, to appease extreme feminists who are enraged to hear St. Paul's request that a wife submit to her husband because he is 'head of the household'. (P.U.T:4)

Ready for death.

If we are sincerely trying to lead good lives we should allow the Gospel readings to make us more thoughtful, but not anxious. We might hear, for example, something about Eternal Life, in the reading from Holy Scripture; and immediately, we might wonder if we are sufficiently prepared to 'face' death and judgement. Our great cause for hope, however - the main thing in which to rejoice - is the knowledge that we have definitely put our trust in Christ, not once, but many times. He wants us to be at peace, and to remain hopeful, if we have confessed our sins, and if our whole desire and aim, each day, is to love and serve Him. (T:1892)

Through prayer.

We should revere the Holy Scriptures, and pay attention to the readings, by which our hearts, souls and minds are taught and fed; yet we will understand better what we hear in church if we have already come to know Christ in prayer: even in apparent darkness and silence. If we know Him, we more rapidly and easily understand what we hear of His words and actions in the Scripture stories. (T:2746)

Lips, forehead and heart.

Converts especially need to be told the significance of the crosses we trace on our forehead, lips, and breast at the beginning of the Gospel reading, at Mass. But each of us will benefit if we make these signs with a living faith: with a real desire to understand the Gospel with our minds, then to speak out, sharing the truth with other people, and also to treasure the Word of God in our hearts. (T:3552)

THE HOMILY

False teaching.

We should beware of the advice given by those persons in the Church who carelessly or deliberately lead us astray by false teaching, or by their example of disobedience. They endanger our souls; and those who wish to be faithful to Christ must take care not to be influenced by such preachers or teachers. (T:1155)

Light and wisdom.

We should remain eternally grateful for the Catholic Faith which is God's gift to us, and which we have accepted: glad that we have walked forward, willingly, to share in the light and wisdom which fill Christ's Church. It's as if Christ's light streams through the whole Church, and particularly through the ministry of the Holy

Father, who sits in Saint Peter's place, and through the bishops and Clergy who are in communion with him. All of them, together, preach and teach the very same faith. The holy light of truth pours upon all who willingly 'walk' into that light by listening to the teachings of the Church; and its source is in Jesus Christ our Lord.

By their preaching, our Clergy can nourish the souls of the faithful. They can so clearly illumine the Way we follow that other people are encouraged to walk into the 'light' which streams from the Church, and to emerge from their present 'gloom' of uncertain doctrine and confused behaviour. (T:1212)

The teaching of the Church.

We should listen to the homily with open hearts, and not sit in judgement on the deacon, priest or bishop who is preaching. Yet if we want to know whose preaching in church gives us the best nourishment for our souls, we have only to reflect on whose words most closely embody the teaching of the Church. We become spiritually stronger and more healthy when we listen to Christ's faithful and authoritative teachers. (T:1532)

Basic principles.

We should be able to rely on the Pope, and on the Bishops who are in communion with him, to help us to see more clearly what is right and wrong in everyday life. For example, when we hear in the News about new ways of creating human beings, the Clergy can help us to look at the basic principles which underpin all of the Church's teachings - about the dignity of the human person, the humanity of even the smallest human embryo, and related matters.

If we are faithful to the teachings of the Church, we can speak and discern God's Will more easily in every field of human exploration. (T:2025B)

By our behaviour.

We should expect to hear, from the Clergy, the whole truth about God's Will for us, and about our need of Him. They shouldn't be afraid to speak about right and wrong, indeed, they have a duty to do so.

Some of us believe in the life of grace but risk the loss of joy, by our behaviour. We risk the loss of Divine light and friendship for all Eternity if we persist in our carelessness or in our serious and deliberate sins; and it is the duty of the Clergy to remind us, at appropriate times, of the true and sure teachings of the Church which some timid parents and teachers rarely mention. (T:2028)

"He who does not believe".

Everyone in the Church - including the Clergy - should hope and pray that many other people will come to recognise Christ's one, true Church, and will be eager to embrace the truths which she offers to the whole world. Christ said that He has come to give us life; yet He has said that "He who does not believe will be condemned."

Christ invites everyone to believe in the truths which He teaches through His Church; truths which all 'fit' together. He is not unjust in asking that we believe them all, since no truth is less true than other truths, although some truths, we can say, are more - or less - important than others according to their 'place' in His scheme of salvation. (T:2066A)

Precious truths.

Through their homilies, the Clergy can urge us to make time to think, study and pray, if we are reluctant to accept the truths which are taught by the Church with Christ's authority. If we 'judge' those truths just as we examine and judge the goods on sale in a shop, we are making a sad mistake.

Christ wants us to realise that if we examine those truths one by one, and reverently, in order to understand them, our attitude is admirable; but we are foolish or ignorant if we accept some truths and reject others, judging them according to our private evaluation instead of accepting these truths as precious gifts which are being offered through Christ and His Church by our Heavenly Father. (Also T:2066A)

A Catholic clergyman.

It is God's Will that nothing less than Truth be offered to us during the homily at Mass; and the truths of our Faith should be conveyed in the homily by an ordained minister of the Catholic Church. It is not God's Will that Christian leaders who are not in full communion with the Catholic Church preach during the Sacred Liturgy. The giving of the homily is a liturgical act, not to be undertaken by someone who has not been trained and ordained in the Catholic Church for that sacred duty. (T:2423)

Our duty and privilege.

The Clergy have a duty to believe and proclaim that membership of Christ's Church involves the duty and privilege of regular attendance at the Holy Sacrifice of the Mass. (T:2570)

Necessary reminders.

Christ wants those in authority in the Church to give reminders to His people about things forgotten by many Catholics today: about modesty, about reverence in Church, and about faithfulness to His Holy Will - to His laws - in marriage. He sees that few of those whose duty it is to teach such things to us actually do so. (T:2577)

Speaking the truth with love.

Christ tells us, through Holy Scripture, that we should always 'speak the truth with love;' and so it is entirely wrong for the

Clergy to mention by name, uncharitably, a particular film star or politician, just to make a point about foolish or immoral life-styles or foolish ways of thinking. Nor should any Clergyman - who should be a model of holiness for us all - use the pulpit as a place from which to launch an attack, even a veiled attack, upon any group or individual who has annoyed him. That is contrary to our Christian way of life, in which we try to explain difficult or problematic things to fellow Christians with patience and charity. (P.U.T:5)

Faith and morals.

In some places, because of rebellion, few people respect the beliefs and advice of our priests. Yet there are failings amongst priests as well as failings amongst the laity. For example, some priests fail to give clear reminders about God's Will: about discipline and duty, and also about things to do with faith and morals. (T:2589)

Half-truths.

No priest should preach anything in his homilies which betrays the sure teachings of the Church. Souls are led into danger wherever a Gospel of half-truths is preached, with serious omissions. Each priest who is lazy, cowardly or proud or faithless leads astray some of those 'people of God' who might have been led closer to Heaven. (T:2724)

Polluted water.

Where a careless or faithless priest offers a distorted version of the Faith, or expresses his doubt or disbelief in certain teachings of the Church, he is like a father who offers polluted water to the members of his family. (T:2725)

Widespread disrespect.

As our priests prepare their homilies Christ wants them to bear several things in mind. Although the Church can never be defeated, since it is Christ's Church, it's a Church in which a disaster has occurred. For example, Christ sees that within the Church thousands of priests and religious have left their work and calling. Mass attendance is 'down'. Few parents welcome, in their own family, a vocation to the Priesthood or to religious life. There is widespread disrespect for Christ in the Blessed Sacrament. There is widespread criticism and even scorn for reliable Church teachings. The Faith has almost been lost, for two generations, in some parts of the world. And although there are several reasons why the Catholic Faith flourishes in one place and declines in another, one thing is certain, which Christ wants us all to know: that where the Faith is not taught in its fullness, with joy and conviction, it cannot flourish as He wishes. (T:3004)

Failure in catechesis.

Christ is 'at work' today, through His Holy Spirit, inviting the Clergy to see the plain truth about a wide-spread failure in evangelisation and catechesis. He asks them to consider what He sees: that several plain truths about faith and morals are widely un-taught today in schools and in parish groups.

Many Catholics who think of themselves as 'faithful' nevertheless believe that some sure and authoritative Church teachings are 'old fashioned' or wrong.

Some Catholic writers are a bad influence on other people through their loud dissent.

Many Catholics are ashamed of their Catholic culture, if not of the Faith itself.

The Saints are no longer routinely held up as role models, since their emphasis on sin, repentance and penance is deemed by some Catholics to be unhealthy.

There is a too-casual attitude to Church laws and customs. Catholics are wrongly labelled as 'Pharisees' if they ask why the rubrics are ignored at Mass, or why children are allowed to continue their riotous behaviour. It was Christ who praised people who are "faithful in little things."

Harm is caused by a careless attitude to many aspects of Christian life, and a blithe attitude towards sinful things which can endanger one's faith. The number of 'mixed' marriages has led some people, of weak faith, to a casual attitude to Catholic beliefs and instructions. (Also T:3004)

Our need of holiness.

Christ watches some of His priests as they speak with pity or even scorn about Catholics who speak truthfully about sin and virtue, Heaven and Hell, and holiness and spiritual danger. Christ wants to remind such men about some of the things which He sees today: for example, some teachers and priests are afraid, in case they 'drive people away,' to speak the plain truths which are desperately needed by sinful people. Yet Christ Himself has shown us, through the way He spoke frankly about our need to eat His flesh and drink His Blood, that we must speak the truth, then allow people to accept or reject it.

People in the Church today - and outside it - rightly hear comforting words about God's love for Mankind; yet there is comparatively little said about His immense and awesome holiness, or about the sufferings Christ bore for us, or about our debt to Christ, and our need of holiness.

Much is rightly heard from preachers and teachers about how those who love justice must criticise the unjust and so must protest about nuclear warfare, unjust governments, poverty and homelessness. Yet comparatively little is said about the need for each of us to be reconciled to God, about fighting our personal inclinations to sin, about shunning immoral practises such as contraception, about recognising our neglect of prayer and our irreverence in church, about resolving to be regular in Mass attendance, and about professing the Faith to other people rather than denying it.

There is much worthwhile encouragement to love one's neighbour; yet there is little, in comparison, about loving God through praising Him with reverence, honouring His Will, and being obedient to His Church.

The Faithful are taught to be concerned about civic and social problems yet receive less advice on supernatural matters such as penance, reparation, temptation, spiritual dangers, recognition of spiritual enemies, and on regular and reverent prayer, combined with true devotion to God and trust in an army of supernatural friends and protectors. (Also T:3004)

False ecumenism.

True Ecumenism should have a sure place in the heart and life of every Catholic. But when, in the cause of Ecumenism, there are special guests present at a Mass, the Clergy must beware of watering-down the Faith.

Where 'false Ecumenism' is practised, some Catholics have such a fear of upsetting other Christians that they are afraid to mention sure truths about the Papacy, about the moral law, about Christ's founding of a single, visible holy Church which exists today, and about Our Blessed Lady's eminence.

Although an admirable sensitivity to language has arisen, the demands of false ecumenism and other reasons have caused language to be changed to such a degree that God's truths are hard to see. For example, by the exclusive use - by some Catholics - of 'Community' for Church, 'pastor' for priest, 'falling short' for sin, 'table' for altar, and even 'bread and wine' for the Holy Eucharist which is Christ's Sacred Body and Blood. (Also T:3004)

The Cross.

It is plainly essential that whoever preaches a Gospel of love should include words about kindness, forgiveness and affection, trust, respect, sharing and acceptance. Yet it is not Christ's Gospel if it leaves out truths about the hard road and the Cross, or if it fails to encourage enquirers to put God first in their lives, whatever the cost, and to love their neighbours most perfectly, for God's sake, by working and praying for their salvation.

Priests should encourage us all in personal holiness: inviting us to pay as much attention to the First great Commandment as to the Second. (Also T:3004)

Sin and Reconciliation.

Christ wants to encourage all of His Bishops and priests to say to all who will listen: "Believe in God! Repent of your sins. Abandon sin, by Christ's power. Be reconciled to Christ and His Church. Practise the Catholic Faith. Remain on the spiritual path: faithful to prayer, to the Mass and the other sacraments, and to the love of your neighbour - all the while growing in the hope of Heaven." (Also T:3004)

Fervour and conviction.

Christ delights in hearing a faithful priest speak frequently, and with gratitude, about Christ's Presence at Mass in the Holy Eucharist. As the priest gestures towards the holy altar and speaks with simplicity, faith, fervour and conviction, Christ delights in hearing us taught plain truths: about the human condition, about our need of Christ's friendship and graces, about our hope of salvation, about the graces we receive in the Blessed Sacrament, about the power of prayer, and about how we should all try to lead the sort of lives that true children of God should follow.

A preacher has more need of faith, hope and love than great

learning - though learning is important too. Christ can give eloquence and fervour to weak, hesitant speakers, whereas a clever and articulate priest brings little benefit to the souls of his parishioners if he lacks faith, hope and love. (T:3013)

Deadly weapons.

It is supremely important that the Clergy know the truths of the Faith, and believe them. To foster doubts, when preaching about the Catholic Faith, is to send deadly weapons through the air towards living targets, to destroy their faith. (T:3016)

A liturgical act.

Only the designated Minister should preach the homily after the Gospel. It is a Liturgical act which our Catholic Bishop, priest or deacon should accomplish when required. The homily at Mass is not something to be 'pushed' aside so that other people can share their opinions, even if on worthy subjects. It is not for Catholic laity, or non-Catholics, even if they are ministers in their own communities. (T:3064)

Life-saving words.

The Clergy must be brave in proclaiming truth. It is true that people who speak truth won't always be popular. We all have a duty, however, to 'save life' - in the moral order - by giving a warning if possible: to save someone who is in danger of losing Eternal Life in Christ. (T:3125)

In the shadows.

Any priest or teacher in the Catholic Church who deals in half-truths or evasions of truth, or disobedience to revealed truth, is like a person who, instead of leading confused and lost people into the light, remains with them in the shadows. Every ordained priest, whose duty is to preach the Good News and to bring people towards God, who neglects truth or refuses to speak truth to his people, is not fulfilling God's plan for his life. (T:3167)

Into the light.

It is the simple truth: that a priest is like a well-trained physician who should imitate Christ, the great Physician. A qualified and capable doctor who encounters needy people attempts to draw them into the light so that he can show concern, remove dead tissue, apply his ointments, or re-set damaged limbs. We would all be astonished if a qualified and capable doctor, instead of doing such things, were to move into the half-light where sick and injured people are waiting, only to say: "Stay where you are. There's really no need for you to have your rotten teeth removed, your gums cleaned, your sores healed, your diseases banished, or your clothes washed. Don't disturb yourselves."

That's what happens whenever priests fail in their duty, and, through neglecting to speak the truth, fail to rescue 'injured' children of God from their sinful ways, their moral dilemmas, their uncertainty about matters of faith, or from their arrogance or pessimism or despair. (Also T:3167)

Dangerous fashions.

Christ asks the Clergy to realise that they are not fulfilling His plan if they offer us strange teachings, or promote inadequate or dangerous fashions in spirituality. Those preachers who won't teach clearly the truths of the Catholic Faith are shutting up the Kingdom of Heaven in the faces of their hearers, and also lessening the likelihood that they themselves will ever enter. (Also T:3167)

Confusion and rebellion.

Christ sees that some of His preachers today encourage one another in their faithless or distorted ideas; and their aim is to increase the number of 'converts' to their way of thinking. They are not being true to their calling if, when they preach to like-minded Catholics, they re-inforce or 're-infect' one another with confusion and rebellion. Furthermore, they are drawing into spiritual danger those simple and trusting people who look to them for guidance about the truths of the Faith. (Also T:3167)

A malady of soul.

The Clergy endanger the souls of their hearers, as well as their own souls, if they try to mould opinion today by contradicting or casting doubt upon sure truths of the Faith.

Someone who has only a small cut on his hand can give entry to a life-destroying disease. And so, in the Church, a person who looks rebelliously at one Church teaching of comparatively minor importance can easily give entry to a malady of soul in which he rebels against major teachings and seriously endangers his spiritual health - and then the health of other people. (T:4165)

Lamentable ignorance.

Christ longs for us to know the crucial connection between the Cross and the altar; and that's why good preaching and teaching are essential. He sees a lamentable ignorance in the souls and minds of many of His own 'children' - in both adults and children in the Church.

Many of us know almost nothing about the sacrifice which He made in coming to earth, as man, to die for us. Few of us realise that the Mass is a true re-presentation of the unique sacrifice which Christ, the God-man, offered for our sakes on Calvary. And so Christ is delighted whenever, through fervent and truthful explanations, those who love Him bring truth, comfort and encouragement to His people. (T:4307)

In a war-zone.

Some preachers provide elements of Catholic teaching whilst neglecting to ensure that the basics have been understood and accepted.

Some preachers treat as mature and knowledgeable some of their flock who have never heard clear teaching on important issues of faith and morals, and who have great need of Reconciliation, and other sacraments. Every such preacher is like a man who blithely gives a talk on first-aid and hygiene whilst scarcely looking at his audience - and who doesn't notice that many of them have shattered limbs and punctured lungs: evidence of having lived in a war-zone.

These people need more than first-aid. Many of them are so sick that they don't realise what a terrible state they are in. Yet others are appalled by their own specific injuries or addictions; and they need much more than just false reassurance about their state of health. They know they need help from a kind but firm 'physician' who will insist that they abandon their life-threatening habits. (T:4308)

'Chains' of truths.

Every good preacher should be able to explain, of the truths of the Faith, that everything 'fits'. None of these truths can be denied. Each truth 'hangs' upon another truth. All of these little 'pieces' fit together in and from God, whether these 'chains' of interlinked truths are about the Mass and the substantial Presence of Christ in the Blessed Sacrament, or about the Church and Christian Mission, or about marriage and procreation.

In each of these topics, as in others, there is a 'chain' of truths which must be unbroken; for whoever carelessly or deliberately 'uncouples' such links risks losing sight of God, Who is Truth.

Whoever believes the truth proclaimed by the Church about the meaning and purpose of marriage, for example, will 'see' such a chain of truth. As the true 'purposes' are recognised and accepted, the enquirer can recognise the truth about total self-giving and commitment, which leads to truths about faithfulness or sin in marriage, about the education of children, about the joys and duties of spouses, about the life of the wider family and therefore of society. All these truths are interlinked; and if one link is wrenched out and cast aside, the chain is broken. (T:4538)

About sin and sanctity.

Whoever is disconcerted to hear strange things preached in the homily and is not sure if the preacher is orthodox should take note of what the preacher chooses repeatedly to leave out as he speaks about the life of faith.

We are wrong to judge consciences; yet we're right to be concerned if a priest who supposedly preaches Good News with sincerity rarely mentions Christ, sin, sanctity, conversion, Church, truth, sacraments or Heaven. If he speaks mostly, for example, in terms of psychology, it is possible that he has not much faith in Christ or much love for the Church. And though we mustn't sit in judgement on him, we may chose to seek advice elsewhere. (T:4782)

Reserved to Catholic Clergy.

It is the simple truth that it is not fitting that a Catholic lay-person or a non-Catholic, even a minister, be invited to preach the homily during a Mass in the Cathedral (or a Mass in any Catholic church) since the homily is part of the Sacred Liturgy: reserved for Catholic Clergy. (T:4856)

A call to holiness.

It's important that priests keep in mind their prime duties, one of which is "to sanctify the Christian people" - as they heard on the day of their Ordination. So as they reflect on their own homilies, they might ask themselves if their words are helping to consolidate and illumine our faith, or to weaken or destroy it. They might ask themselves: is the effect of my words to cause people to rely on Christ and to abandon sin, or to persuade them that their persistence in sin need be of little concern to them?

Since the Lord tells us through Holy Scripture that His love is everlasting, yet also says that we shall be judged on our behaviour, wise priests speak about the love of God for each one of us, yet call and inspire us to strive for holiness. God is holy, and He wants us all to realise that we must be holy if we would share His eternal joy. (T:4870)

Without apology.

Christ wants every priest, teacher and parent to know how thrilled He is whenever He sees someone set out, simply and clearly, the sure teachings of the Church, without apology or embarrassment. It is unusual, today, for the whole truth to be told about Christian marriage: about joy and fulfilment, yet also about sin and disobedience. Many married Catholics disbelieve or ignore the Church's teachings about the evils of contraception, abortion and other matters. Reminders are necessary, for the sake of the eternal welfare of wives and husbands, as well as for the good of the whole family and society. (T:4946)

Glorious truths.

Christ is full of delight whenever He hears His priests, and other people, speak with gratitude about the Sacred Priesthood, and when He hears us speak not only of the loving service He asks His priests to undertake, but also about the power and authority which He gives to the Clergy. Furthermore, Christ is always thrilled to hear people share the glorious truths about the Eucharistic Sacrifice and about His Real Presence amongst us in the Holy

Sacrifice of the Mass. (T:4948)

Spiritual darkness.

Christ wants to see His priests offering hope and consolation, as they preach the good news about His infinite love for us all; yet He relies on them, also, to speak the truth about our need of repentance and about how important it is that we make a deliberate effort, with God's grace, to give up sin.

Christ on the Cross, His heart aching, could see all of those sins by which people through the ages have plunged into spiritual darkness, wrecked family life, harmed other people, damaged the Church, insulted God, and shut the 'doors' of their hearts to Divine grace and salvation. (T:4960)

With joy and conviction.

Christ is overjoyed to hear someone speak gladly and with conviction about His sacramental Presence on the altar and in the tabernacle. He longs for us all to believe that He is Really Present: risen and alive, 'whole and entire', glorious and joyful, and that He is as close to us as He was to His Apostles during His short life on earth. (T:5006 and 7)

Away from the cliff-edge.

Preachers and teachers bear a great responsibility. Since Christ came to earth, it's as though a great light has shone upon our lives, so that we can see clearly - but not so that we can choose our own path. The light shines so that we can see the 'cliff-edge' clearly as well as our own souls and lives. We are wise to set out on the safe path which leads away from the cliff-edge, which is separation from God.

Since it is the Church which can give us the right direction at each moment, so that we can follow the way of Christ, Christ asks all

His preachers and teachers to say with conviction: "Respond to God's love. Don't hear the Gospel message without acting upon it. Turn away from evil and take the road to Heaven." (T:5023)

Purposeful treatment.

There are kind-hearted priests who are reluctant to speak about sin. They don't realise that they can be kind and gentle even as they speak the truths that many of us need to hear.

A good surgeon is kind and gentle when he gives his patient the sad news that the patient's condition is serious and requires purposeful treatment. And whoever speaks the truth about sin and repentance has some good news to offer: that with real sorrow for sin and a 'firm purpose of amendment' each of us can enjoy God's forgiveness and have a sure hope of Heaven.

It is seen as un-Christian today, even amongst Christians, to speak the truth about right and wrong, for fear of sounding judgmental; yet Jesus' first message in the Gospel was "Repent, for the Kingdom of Heaven is close at hand." He said this because He wants to lead people to joy; and we all deserve to know what we should repent of so that we can enjoy life in His Kingdom.

Priests today should be like Christ, inviting us to repent of our sins, and not acting solely as counsellors or comforters, without truth-speaking about the serious sins which entrap some of those they speak with. They have the right and the duty to ask people to give up their sinful practises and to purify their sinful relationships. (T:5041)

Prepared to be unpopular.

Christ wants His priests to realise what a great example for priests is St. John Vianney - Patron Saint of parish priests. The Curé of Ars was fearless and frank, as well as kind to people in need and to sinners. He was prepared to be unpopular; and he suffered a lot.

But he trusted in God even in the awareness of his own weaknesses; and God blessed his work tremendously.

It's unfortunate that many people in the Church who long to see God's Will done in everything are called 'Pharisees' - even when they don't despise anyone, but want to offer the truth that saves, and to be obedient as Jesus was obedient. It was Christ who spoke with gladness about people who can be trusted in 'little things'; and about how they can be trusted with greater responsibilities. (Also T:5041)

About sin and virtue.

Christ sees that there are priests in the Church who rarely or never speak against grave sinfulness, even though the Holy Father, the Pope, who preaches the truths about God's immense love for each precious individual, also speaks in season and out of season about sin and virtue, in the face of much scorn. We lay-persons need to be reminded - just as much as priests - that we should hold fast to the truths of the Catholic Faith, no matter what the cost.

Christ asks us to remember that Saint Thomas More was prepared to die in defence of the Papacy, though most of the English Bishops of his time obeyed a tyrannical King instead. Saint Joan of Arc was faithful to the mission given to her by Christ, and faithful to her Saintly friends in Heaven, even when fellow Catholics tried and condemned her unjustly.

Christ wants us to see that in our day, also, there are martyrs for truth. Saint Maria Goretti died for the truth about chastity; and Saint Charles Lwanga and companions died rather than commit immoral acts. Others suffer rather than use immoral means to prevent conception. Others bravely refuse to undergo an abortion. Priests have a duty, therefore, to encourage their parishioners to persevere in holiness, whatever the cost, and not to accept the foolish opinions put out in our society on serious moral issues, about which the Church already teaches the truth. (Also T:5041)

THE CREED

Precious acts of faith.

We give joy to Heaven by our sincere prayers; and so we should rejoice if we can say the 'Creed' with joy, and with total conviction. It is not simply a 'recitation', but a powerful act of faith - made in the 'darkness' which is life on earth; and it is powerfully rewarded. (T:1544)

A cry of delight.

We are united ever more surely to the Saints, whenever we do anything good; and so whenever we pray a sincere prayer to God the Saints are overjoyed to hear our acts of faith in Christ and in His goodness. For example: whenever we proclaim - as in the Creed - that the Father truly sent His Son to save us, such an act of faith is like a cry of delight to the Father from a dark and distant world.

Our little acts of faith are precious. They rise up to Heaven like beams of light, piercing the darkness of unbelief which surrounds us. (Also T:1544)

From a darkened world.

We must look upon prayer as being a very worthwhile activity, and not be worried because we are sometimes a bit hurried or absent-minded. It's our sincerity of heart which is important; and we should believe that God our Father is pleased whenever we pray 'the Creed' sincerely. He is far above us; yet it's as if the door to Heaven is opened to us because we offer our prayers in the name of Christ.

By offering a sincere act of faith to our Heavenly Father - faith in His existence and in His goodness, and in His son, Jesus, Who came to earth to save us - we send up to Heaven a triumphant cry. It is a cry of hope, love, fervour and determination and defiance of evil - from a darkened world. We call out as if from a dark, pitted landscape, a filthy battlefield where, here and there, a voice arises. It's as if each faithful friend of Christ - a 'warrior', a soldier of Christ who believes in Christ his Saviour and in the power of prayer - calls out to his friends: "Our cause is worth fighting for, as we fight against sin! Our hero is worthy dying for, in our 'dying' to self, daily, in order to serve him." (T:1570B) *(See illustration 18)*

Speaking the truth.

As we pray the Creed, God delights in hearing us voice the truths of the Faith with gladness and sincerity. (T:2702)

THE BIDDING PRAYERS

From Christ's heart.

We should be tremendously grateful that we have been united to Jesus Christ, through our Baptism, and that we can therefore unite all our prayers to His perfect prayer. No matter how worthy our prayers might seem to be - no matter how eloquent or heart-stirring - we cannot be certain that they 'reach' the Father unless they are 'channelled' to Him through Christ our Mediator.

If we reflect upon the meaning of prayer, and the attitude of Christ to His Father, we'll see that every good thought and desire which streams to the Father from Christ's heart is acceptable. We can be sure that the prayers which we offer through Christ are worthy of being heard if they can be described as closely expressing the desires of His heart, or worthy of gracing His lips as He prayed on

Calvary, or worthy of being presented to the Father by our priest - through Christ - at the Holy Sacrifice of the Mass. (T:1033)

Unworthy requests.

If we consider Christ's truthfulness and holiness, and His desires for our salvation, we can understand why any prayer which is unfit to be uttered by Christ's lips cannot be offered to the Father in Christ's name. We cannot pray 'in the name of Christ' for a foolish or an evil thing to be done. God is good and holy, and in all His answers to prayer He brings about good or overcomes evil. (Also T:1033)

Accurate expressions of faith.

The celebrant of a particular Mass is responsible for the wording of the Bidding prayers. He can delegate this work by offering it to Catholics who are faithful and who can accurately express their faith in writing. If he is not vigilant, however, the entire congregation sometimes is asked to pray for peculiar intentions; or they hear unorthodox statements about human life and the Church; or the writer seems not to have decided whom we address, as petitions are prefaced by first 'God' then 'Jesus', then perhaps 'Father' - or by no name at all. Such confusion is not necessary - nor is it appropriate for what is part of the Sacred Liturgy. (P.U.T: 6)

The Faithful Departed.

It is a source of comfort for many Catholics, to hear the name of a beloved friend or relation read out loud in church, on the anniversary of the death. The Faithful Departed who are mentioned at such a time are being solemnly commemorated during the Sacred Liturgy. They deserve our prayers. They deserve to be remembered. They belong to the 'Communion of Saints', and are very close to us. These are some of the reasons why their names should be read out clearly by someone able to pronounce them. If a child cannot do this, for example, at a special Mass in which children are involved as readers, the priest or some responsible person should read the names and thus ensure that those Holy Souls benefit from everyone's prayer. (P.U.T: 7)

By every fervent prayer.

Christ wants us to believe that every sincere prayer we pray is effective. We don't always see the results; but if we want to understand what we achieve by our intercessions we can picture a scene in an adventure story. Here, an explorer makes camp in the middle of a jungle because his friend is sick; and then he holds aside the vines which surround them both, in order to let the moonlight shine down upon the friend who, until then, has been lying in darkness. By every fervent prayer which we offer, in Christ's Name, for a needy friend - or for a stranger - we are doing something even more powerful and effective. By our prayer, it's as though we are parting and holding aside the 'strands' of darkness, to allow Heaven's light to touch the needy person. It's as if that needy person's body and soul are irradiated by Divine love, because of our charitable act. (T:2066B)

THE GIFTS

Taking bread and wine to the altar.

When God our Father gives us a great gift - His own Son - in the Holy Sacrifice of the Mass, He doesn't suddenly lavish this gift upon us like a rich man who suddenly reaches out to help a beggar. Because God loves us, He grants us the dignity of being able to contribute to the Holy Sacrifice. We are His own children: no longer poor, helpless persons who can do nothing but accept favours. That is why God has arranged, through His Church, that we can contribute the very gifts which He is willing to change into the Sacred Body and Precious Blood of His beloved Son, Christ.

God is so generous and tactful that, before the Consecration, He allows us to speak truthfully about our bread and wine being "the work of human hands" - even though we can only offer those gifts of bread and wine because He has generously caused things to grow and has allowed us to harvest them. (T:2616)

Our whole lives.

When we see the gifts of bread and wine being taken to the altar, that's the time to offer our whole lives to God, in a heart-felt prayer. If we offer Him our devotion, our service, our joys and sufferings, our dreams and our failures - everything - we freely unite ourselves with the whole Church and with Christ our Head. We unite ourselves with the perfect offering which Christ will soon offer to God our Father, through the priest, from the altar.

We can also 'hold up' to God, to be helped and sanctified, all those precious people in our hearts: people close to us and far away, some faithful and some estranged from God. Christ prays for them, as we open our hearts to reveal our love for them, our trust in Christ's prayer, and their need of His graces. (P.U.T:8)

"HOLY, HOLY, HOLY LORD"

At the brink of Heaven.

We should think about what we say, when we pray "Holy, Holy, Holy Lord ... Blessed is He who comes in the Name of the Lord."

It's as if Christ stands at the brink of Heaven, contemplating the world to which He came in His infancy, listening to us as we cry out with the holy Angels in adoration and love, and ready to come amongst us once more, to give us joy, to pray for us, and to delight in our love. (T:763)

THE EUCHARISTIC PRAYER AND THE CONSECRATION

Jesus, our thanksgiving.

Christ wants us to understand that when He comes to our midst, at the Consecration, He is someone Whose worship is of infinite value; and we who welcome Him are His own brothers and sisters; so when He makes His infinitely-worthy offering to the Father we can join our prayers to His, with confidence.

If we want to praise the Father, here is Jesus, praising Him for us! If we want to thank the Father, Jesus is our means of thanksgiving: our offering. We want to offer reparation for our sins; and here is Jesus, our sacrifice! And we want to plead and intercede with the Father; and since Jesus pleads with us, His Church, and for us, the Father cannot refuse to grant Jesus' prayers. That is why we can be confident that the prayers offered by the priest from the altar, for the growth and welfare of the Church, and for mercy to be shown to the Faithful Departed, are heard and granted. (T:921)

The same yesterday, today, and forever.

We should always be thankful for the sure knowledge that the Saviour Who comes to us in the sanctuary and in Holy Communion is always the same. No matter how weak or foolish we are, He is the same 'yesterday, today, and forever'; and so we can count on His love and forgiveness. (T:934)

Whatever state we're in.

We should believe in Christ's love for us. He comes to us gladly and joyfully, at the Consecration. This is always true, no matter what we might feel, at a particular moment, and whatever state of soul or mind we're in at present. (T:952)

Amongst friends.

It's the simple truth - something to warm our hearts - that Christ delights in being here, at Mass, with people who love Him. He is man as well as God; and He loves to be with His friends. (T:972)

The Precious Blood of God.

We should ponder the great love which Christ has shown for us. When He, the Son of God, died on the Cross, His Precious Blood poured out from His breast, for sinners. It poured out as a sacrifice for sin; and that same sacrifice is now offered from the altar, where bread and wine are changed, at the Consecration, into Christ's Sacred Body and Precious Blood. (T:1157)

A closer resemblance.

At the Consecration, Christ is Really Present amongst us in power and glory. Christ our Lord and God, our Saviour, guide, lover and friend is Really Present, worthy of our loyalty and worship. So we should unite our intentions to His, whenever we pray, aiming to be of one heart and mind with Him.

Since we belong to Him we should resemble Him, praying sincere and reverent prayers, in His name, to the invisible Father in Heaven. Christ's prayer is powerful because of the sacrifice which He offers on our behalf and that's why our prayers, when united with His, are always powerful and effective. (T:1363)

To pay our debt.

Straight after the Consecration, we can look up, to adore Christ; and as we gaze upon the Sacred Host, it's as if Christ Himself is calling out to us, saying: "This is My Body!" Truly, He is here before us. We are present to the one holy sacrifice which He offered on Calvary; and He is Really Present with us - here on the altar - pleading on our behalf to the Father.

If we look towards Christ with love, we'll be like those of His friends who looked up and saw Him hanging on the Cross as His Precious Blood was poured out for us all. We touch His heart by our repentance and devotion.

Christ has demonstrated for us the true meaning of love, by giving Himself up for us, wholly. Not content with giving us words of love, from Heaven, by speaking through the Prophets, Christ our God chose to become man, and to live amongst us. He gave up His Body for us, giving it not in ploughing fields like a family man who proves his love by toil, giving it not in sexual love, but giving it wholly, most perfectly, in sacrifice, allowing others to take His life. He did this for us, to pay our debt. That's how much He loves us! This should be a cause for joy and not for sadness. (T:1375)

Our generosity.

When we welcome Christ at the Consecration, we delight Him by our love; and we also allow His joy and wisdom to pierce the 'opening' of our heart. Each of our generous acts towards Him brings blessings upon our own souls. (T:1461)

Sincere acts of faith.

We can increase our faith if we make sincere acts of faith in Christ's Presence before us, here at the Holy Sacrifice. Truly, He is risen and glorious. Robed as a priest, He stands before us, after the Consecration. (T:1468C)

In chasms of loneliness.

We should have faith in Christ's Presence amongst us. He is Really Present with every community of the faithful, wherever the Blessed Sacrament is present - even with those of the faithful who are scattered throughout the world, hidden away, physically isolated, as if in deep chasms of loneliness. Christ is with them, in their obscurity. (T:1501) *(See illustration 44)*

Veiled from our sight.

When the priest holds up the Sacred Host for veneration it's as though a thin white veil is hiding Christ from our gaze; but we mustn't imagine that Christ veils Himself from our eyes during the Mass because of our unworthiness. Jesus is Present before us, loving us, even though He is 'hidden' in this Holy Sacrament. He is hidden, however, until we meet Him when we die and - after sufficient preparation - gaze upon Him in His unveiled glory. (T:1509)

Christ's hidden glory.

God the Father's concern for us is so great that when Christ is with us at the Consecration, His glory and power are veiled, lest we be afraid of meeting 'God-with-us.' All the glory which is Christ's in Heaven, as Son of God, yet which is hidden from us during our earthly exile, is offered to the Father today, from our altar: offered in our presence, through the power of the Holy Spirit! (Also T:1509)

The same Person.

If we really believed in the Church's teaching on the Holy Eucharist, we would be overwhelmed with gratitude for Christ's Presence with us. He was shown out, in His first 'Epiphany', as a true and living human child. Yet His Presence has not been restricted to His earthly home in a long-ago time. He is Present with us today, after the Consecration, although in a different manner: in a sacramental Presence.

We should be awed and grateful that we can say - of the Sacred Host, after the Consecration - that this is God-with-us, veiled! His Presence is 'Real'. He is shown out to us daily, truly: He Who was born of Mary, He Who is the Son of God, yet Who is also true and living man. The manner of His being-with-us is different, but we can be sure that the Person is the same: in Bethlehem, and in the sanctuary! (T:1530B)

On fire with love.

We must never doubt Christ's love for us. He is 'on fire' with love, eager to join His People. He delights in coming to us in our churches and in our tabernacles. He comes to the altar from Heaven, with Divine light and love and power, at every Consecration. (T:1531)

True devotion.

Christ treasures our faithfulness and devotion. He is deeply touched when we adore Him at the Consecration, and revere Him in His Precious Blood. (T:1595)

The once-for-all sacrifice.

Our hearts should be full of gratitude to the Father for Christ's birth and death - and for His work of Redemption. Christ's Precious Blood is offered from the altar, in these Holy Mysteries. Truly, His sacrifice of the Cross is re-presented before us.

It's as though we are separated by time from the day of His Crucifixion, as if by a huge crevasse in the floor of the sanctuary; and there within its depths, in the gloom, Christ is hanging on the

Cross, fulfilling His total self-giving. We who attend the Holy Sacrifice of the Mass are like people who are standing at the edge of that crevasse, since we are present as Christ offers that once-for-all sacrifice, through His priest, from our altar.

We shouldn't remain cast down, however, made gloomy by thoughts of sin and sacrifice. We can look upwards and be joyful. Christ is risen; and He is with us now. His eternal dwelling-place is in the bliss of Heaven; and we should live in joyful hope that we will one day join Christ in Heaven's glory. (T:1637)

Of infinite worth.

We should remember the reason why the prayers of Christ's Church on earth are heard, and why His holy Church is sustained on her journey to Heaven: it is only through the merits of our Saviour, Who is Present amongst us. Here in the sanctuary He is praying His Divine prayer, making His infinitely-worthy offering to the Father on our behalf; and as He offers infinitely-worthy reparation for sin, His sacrifice is accepted.

We shouldn't allow ourselves to be pulled down, in sorrow for Christ's sufferings on Calvary: sufferings through which we were redeemed. The sacrifice which He now offers from the altar, during the Holy Mass, is offered in glory. Christ is now risen and triumphant as He offers His sacrificial prayer to the Father before the awed and adoring gaze of the whole court of Heaven. His Saints and His holy Angels play their part, as these Holy Mysteries are celebrated. The glory of Heaven shines around this holy company, as they gaze upon Christ, their Lord and King, Who is now Present in our midst. (T:1693)

Overshadowing the altar.

We should be overwhelmed with wonder and gratitude when we think about the power given to the priest at his Ordination. At the altar, the priest can call out to the Father, praying in Christ's name, and asking: "Send your Holy Spirit" - to consecrate the bread and wine set before him. Above the altar, it's as though a great veil is being pushed aside; and yet that 'veil' itself is a powerful force, and a movement. It's like an arm reaching from Heaven, or like a gigantic wing, the tip of which just brushes the altar. The Holy Spirit is at work in the Consecration, with Divine power.

At a mere 'touch' of the Spirit, these inanimate materials of bread and wine are changed into the Sacred Body and Blood of Christ: the Divine Son Who is our living Saviour. All who are present should pray with great reverence as the Holy Spirit overshadows the altar. (T:1839)

In a different manner.

We should rejoice and be thankful that Christ's true glory - with the fullness of the Godhead - is 'contained' in the Sacred Host which we see upon the altar after the Consecration.

We need not imagine that since we don't see Christ's human bodily features we are less close to Him now than were His contemporaries, in earthly life. During His life on earth, Christ was Really Present with His friends and relations: though with His glory veiled. He is Really Present today - His glory veiled - amongst us His people, although Present in a different manner. (T:2120)

Christ, in Heaven.

Christ lives in Heaven, eternally; and He is made Really Present amongst us, after the Consecration, while He still inhabits Heaven. He has not moved; rather, it's as though the 'edge' of Heaven extends over the altar; and each of us who receives the Sacred Host or the Precious Blood truly receives Christ whole and entire: His Body, Blood, Soul and Divinity. Bread and wine have been marvellously changed, as the Church has always taught.

(T:3047)

The joy of the Angels.

The holy Angels are pure, bright and holy spirits who are thrilled by Christ's Presence amongst us. They delight in serving Him; and they are clustered about the altar during the Holy Sacrifice of the Mass. (T:3092)

Radiant with Heaven's light.

Truly, Christ is worthy of adoration. He is holy: radiant with Heaven's light; and His sacrifice is holy. (T:3101)

Awesome properties.

We can picture the Sacred Body and Blood of Christ, here on the altar, as being surrounded by a white cloud, which represents the holiness of Christ. He is here amongst us in the Blessed Sacrament; and all who approach Christ in prayer or approach to receive Him in Holy Communion should be aware of His awesome holiness.

People on earth are rightly in awe of even a small source of radioactivity: aware of the power of a radioactive substance drastically to change other substances. We treat it with the respect and reverence due to its awesome properties - even making special preparations before we handle it. God's holiness should be approached in the same manner. (T:3980C)

Sacraments of initiation.

Christ wants us to remind one another that the Baptism of a child or adult should eventually lead to the reception of Christ's Sacred Body and Blood in the Holy Eucharist, and also to Confirmation. (T:4108)

The words of Consecration.

We should remember that Christ is with us, sacramentally, from the moment when Christ's words of consecration are spoken by the priest.

In the midst of our every heartache, loss, puzzlement or separation, we can be sure that Jesus is here; and He is with us from love. It's as if He loves us so much that He cannot bear to leave us alone. (T:4472)

Christ, our meeting-point.

Through His Eucharistic Presence - His Presence in the Blessed Sacrament, after the Consecration - Christ can be seen as the point of meeting or convergence of all who love Him. We can picture the place where Christ is sacramentally Present as being a 'place' where four arrowheads meet; and within each arrow-shape are assembled all the people who belong to a particular group.

Wherever Christ is, it's as if, at that meeting-point, we find joined together, first, everyone who lives in Heaven. Secondly, we find all the Holy Souls of Purgatory. And with them we find, thirdly, all who in earthly life have gathered together before their Eucharistic Lord. We also find, fourthly, the people who are physically absent, perhaps abroad or ill at home, but who in earthly life are still 'one spirit' with us in Christ.

Truly, it is in the Holy Eucharist - 'in' the Eucharistic Christ - that we can meet all those people who are precious to us and who also live 'in Christ': some living, and some now departed. It is through and with Christ that we can express our love and concern for them, and know that in this blessed 'Communion of Saints' we are really in touch, really communicating, and really offering effective prayers for their joy and welfare. (T:4488)

Shameful irreverence.

Christ is so often greeted at Mass today by a shameful irreverence that He is encouraging us to make special efforts to remedy this evil. (T:4758)

Amidst thunderclouds and fire.

We should never forget that Our Lord Jesus Christ, Who is sacramentally Present on the altar, is the very love of God made visible to Mankind. He is also the glory of God. In His Divine nature, He is Divine fire and warmth, as well as love and peace.

God spoke to Moses on Mount Sinai amidst thunderclouds and fire; and Christ Who is Present with us in the Holy Eucharist is no less Divine and holy than when - with the Father and the Holy Spirit - He led the Chosen People through the wilderness and taught them His eternal laws. (T:4981)

THE ACCLAMATION

A cry of wonder.

Christ comes to us in joy and glory, at the Consecration; and so He is glad to be welcomed to the altar by His friends. He is risen from the dead, and is radiant with Heaven's glory; and though He is Present in sacramental form, under the appearance of bread and wine, our faith in His Real Presence should cause us to cry out in wonder at the Acclamation, overwhelmed at Christ's goodness in being amongst us in this special manner. (T:550)

A fire of love.

When we are at Mass, and we sing "Christ has died, Christ is

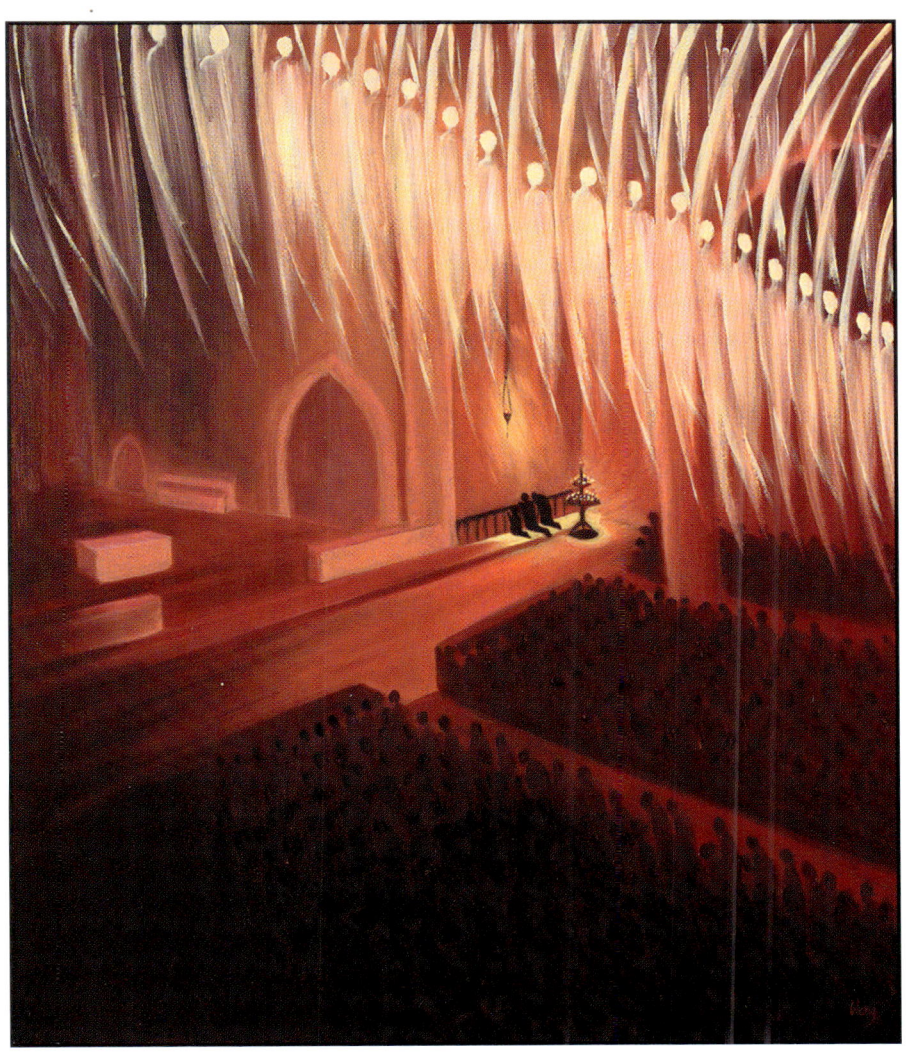

13. IN THE PRESENCE OF THE ARCHANGELS.

When we enter the church for Mass, we join the Angels and Archangels who wait with reverence and awe for the Holy Mysteries to be celebrated. Heaven and earth are united in worship, to the glory of God and the good of souls. OIL-M:860. *("But you have come to Mount Zion and to the city of the living God, the heavenly Jerusalem, and to innumerable angels in festal gathering, and to the assembly of the firstborn who are enrolled in heaven." Heb 12:22-23).*

14. THE ALTAR OF SACRIFICE.

Our Catholic churches have been consecrated as holy places for a 'Holy People'. We long to be more worthy to approach the altar, and therefore we prepare ourselves by prayer, penance, and acts of love. OIL-M:1630. (*""Come no nearer" he said "Take off your shoes, for the place on which you stand is holy ground."" Ex 3:5*).

15. THE DAZZLING PURITY OF CHRIST.

When the Mass begins, we can glance within our hearts, and repent of our sins; but we shouldn't be despondent. Though our souls appear shadowy before the dazzling purity of Christ, we are on our way towards Heaven. OIL-M:771B. *("If we say we have no sin in us, we are deceiving ourselves ... but if we acknowledge our sins, then God who is faithful and just will forgive our sins and purify us."* 1 Jn 1:8-9).

16. THE LITTLEST PRAYER.

God the Father is endlessly forgiving. The littlest prayer of ours, in trust or contrition, is rewarded with infinite kindness. It's as if a father is stroking the neck of his precious child. (OIL-M:1396). *("Lord God, you who are always merciful and tender-hearted, slow to anger, always loving, always loyal, turn to me and pity me." Ps 86: 15-16).*

17. CHRIST, THE WORD OF GOD.

It is Christ the Word of God who speaks to us through Sacred Scripture as well as through the Sacred Tradition of the Church, and through the Church's teaching authority. When we listen carefully we hear those truths we need to know if we are to live as God's children in a sinful world. OIL-M:888B. *("All scripture is inspired by God and can profitably be used for teaching, for refuting error, for guiding people's lives and teaching them to be holy." 2 Tm 3:16).*

18. A CRY OF FAITH, FROM A DARKENED WORLD.

Whenever we pray the Creed sincerely, we cry out to Heaven, full of joy at Christ's triumph. Every act of faith in God is like a cry of hope and determination from a darkened world. OIL-M:1570B. *("Keep as your pattern the sound teaching you have heard from me, in the faith and love that are in Christ Jesus. You have been trusted to look after something precious." 2 Tm 1:13-14).*

risen, Christ will come again", we are right to believe these things and to proclaim them out loud. Truly, Christ our Saviour is true God, Who came from Heaven long ago, to save us, and Who is with us now, today.

It's as if a fire of love blazes within the sanctuary: the Divine fire of the Godhead. God the Father reached down to us, two thousand years ago, to give His Son to live amongst us. And He now 'gives' His Son to us at every Mass.

The effect of that fire, as it reaches out towards us, is almost to engulf us all in its embrace. It's as if a great dam which has been holding back a great ocean is now disintegrating, as great torrents of living water shoot forth, to pour into our sanctuary.

How much more reverently would we all worship, were we to see, briefly, the power and majesty of God. How much more reverent and humble would be our conduct and worship in church, if we really believed that God is all-holy and glorious, and truly 'God-with-us': if we could see those flames reaching out into the church. (T:4779)

THE GREAT OFFERING

A perfect offering.

We can be certain that, because of Christ's immense love, and the immense power of His intercession, the sinfulness of those present has no power to mar the perfection of His offering. (T:107)

Self-giving love.

Those who are most like Christ in self-giving love, in everyday life, are more easily drawn to the Father in prayer than those who don't resemble Christ so closely. (T:366)

Jewels on His robe.

By our full and sincere participation in the Mass, both in joy and solemnity, we allow Christ to draw us steadily towards Heaven. He is here before us, robed in priestly garments; and it's as if people like ourselves who love Him and make the offering with Him are jewels on His robe. (T:535) *(See illustration 30)*

Pleading for our salvation.

We should never forget what Christ is doing for us as He offers His Holy Sacrifice to the Father. As He reaches up in love to the Father in a sacrificial offering of Himself on our behalf, He is pleading for our salvation. (T:690)

On our behalf.

When He was on the Cross, Christ gave up His life for us; and here in the Mass, He prays and praises on our behalf. It's as if He joins in the words of the priest and stands with arms outstretched to the Father, saying: "All glory and honour is yours, Almighty Father, for ever and ever. " (T:839)

From our altar.

For much of our lives, we might seem to be in spiritual darkness; yet we needn't worry about being small and powerless. Christ's arms reach out to the glory which we cannot see. From the tabernacle, and from our altar, He prays the eternal prayer to which all our prayers are united through His merits and our union with Him. (T:928)

Our common humanity.

We should be confident that our prayers are heard. Christ's perfect prayer is heard by the Father because it arises from Christ's union of Himself, the Divine Word, with Christ's own holy humanity. Christ's perfect prayer arises from a Divine Person: from the Divine Person Who now has both a Divine and a human nature. It's because we belong to Christ in a union of faith and love that our prayers are heard. Through that union - in our common humanity with Christ - our prayers and Christ's prayers are 'heard' as one prayer: a prayer of infinite worth, worthy of the infinitely-holy Father. (T:954)

Present to the same sacrifice.

We should have faith in the power of Christ to help us; and we should remember that the whole Church is involved in our sacrificial offering. Here at Mass, it's as though we are gazing downwards through layer upon layer of past centuries, through row upon row of spectators from past generations. These are our spiritual brothers and sisters, who are standing together, reverent and prayerful; and they are looking at the hill, and at the Cross on which Christ has been crucified. They look upon His sacrifice: an act of love which He offered to save us. We, too, are present to that sacrifice, whenever we attend the Holy Mass.

In every era of the Church's history, Christ is Present before us, His People, proving His love for us, atoning for sin by His offering, and setting an example of self-giving. Yet He is risen and glorious! His soul is now joyful. His heart is on fire with praise: ablaze with fervour. Christ offers now - through His priest, from the altar - His own infinite thanksgiving, His perfect reparation for our sins, His great plea for the holy desires of our own hearts, and His perfect prayer for the needs of His Church. (T:1470) *(See illustration 25)*

Human suffering.

Christ invites us to think about the meaning of 'mediation' so that we'll understand that His fervent prayer from the Cross for sinful men and women was wholly sincere. This was because He, the Son of God, had become man; and so He knew Himself to be wholly 'involved' with the plight of His human brothers and sisters. No-one could have pleaded more fervently or more successfully to the Father, for mercy to be shown towards us, than the God-man: Jesus Christ our Redeemer.

His prayer for sinners surpassed - in power, fervour, and effectiveness - all the prayers which had ever been offered from upon earth by other people. This was because Christ held out to the Father His Divine love combined with His human cry from the depths of the 'pit' which is human estrangement and human suffering. He offers that same prayer, on our behalf, during each celebration of the Mass. (T:1661)

Weak and sinful.

We should never doubt the value of sincere prayer. Our prayers, and our efforts to increase our union with Christ, are very worthwhile. As we offer the Holy Sacrifice with Christ to the Father, it's as if we can cry out to the Father, within our souls, saying: "I have nothing to boast about. I am weak and sinful. I have nothing but Jesus Who is my prayer and my offering". We can be certain that the Father is looking upon us with infinite love, delighting in our trust and humility. (T:2148)

The supreme homage.

Whenever we assist at the offering of the Holy Sacrifice, we offer it to the Father; and we are offering the perfect Victim, Whose surrender to the Father's Will is the supreme homage. That's why we can be sure that we are offering an infinitely-worthy prayer to the Father: one which is worthy of His infinite love and holiness. (T:2230B)

A sincere intention.

We should be of one heart and mind with Christ during the Holy Sacrifice of the Mass. We honour the Father through Christ's perfect offering, and through our sincere intention to be united with Christ in prayer and sacrifice.

We unite our offering with Christ and the priest as he prays: "All glory and honour is Yours, Almighty Father, for ever and ever." In this way we honour the Father through our worship just as Christ honoured Him from the Cross. That's how privileged we are, as we take a worthy and fruitful part in the Holy Sacrifice of the Mass. (T:2342)

We shall be like Him.

When we make Christ's praise our own, in delight and thanksgiving, and offer Christ our perfect Word to the Father, it's as if we do what the Father already does, as He utters His Word for all Eternity, in Eternity. Thus, we already begin to fulfil what Holy Scripture tells us, about life in glory: "We shall be like Him." (T:2813)

THE GREAT "AMEN"

Effective, for our salvation.

We should add a sincere and fervent "Amen" to Christ's self-offering: to the offering of Calvary and altar. In that way, we make Christ's offering our own. We make it effective, for our own salvation. (T:548)

A moment's pause.

At the summit of our celebration, the priest prays: "All glory and honour is yours, almighty Father, for ever and ever", and we respond, "Amen." It's unfortunate that at this marvellous moment of the Mass many priests, with barely a pause for breath, rush to invite the congregation to pray the "Our Father". That's indeed what we should do next. Yet if there is not even a momentary pause it's as though we're being asked to drag ourselves swiftly away from the glorious offering which we've just made through Christ. It's as if we all rush ahead in vocal prayer, whilst the thousands of Angels, with all the Saints, are still rapt with admiration and awe before God as they echo our great "Amen". (T:4776)

Our oneness with Christ.

As we unite our voices and hearts in sincere praise of the Father by offering the sacrifice of Christ from our altar, we are one with Christ in the eternal offering of love which He makes to the Father, in the Spirit, in Heaven, watched by the Saints and holy Angels. By our "Amen" we signify our oneness with Christ in His holy and perfect offering. (T:4884)

No greater act of worship.

There is no greater act of worship on earth than the Mass; and the reason why the praise which is offered in the Mass is so powerful and exalted is that it is Christ's own praise, offered from our midst. At every Mass we participate more fully than at any other time in the eternal act of praise and love which takes place within the Godhead, within the 'heart' of the Holy Trinity.

It's as though the Mass is the 'moment' at which we can leap most surely into Christ's perpetual loving prayer to the Father, in the Spirit, which takes place in Eternity. And if we look back for a moment to Christ's life on earth, and to the reason why Christ instituted the Holy Eucharist, we'll see that when He was doing His Father's Will on earth, whatever the cost, Christ was living out in the flesh, for our sakes, the very self-giving love which He has shown towards the Father from all Eternity.

Christ's love is now made ours to offer to the Father through the

Holy Eucharist. As we gather with the priest, by whose hands we offer Christ's sacrifice to the Father, in the Spirit, we offer a love and homage worthy of the almighty Father. We increase our union with our Heavenly Father Who is love's origin and source; and we have a foretaste of Heaven's joy. (Also T:4884)

THE "OUR FATHER"

Praying with sincerity.

We should try to mean what we say, when we pray the "Our Father" together, especially as we pray: "Thy Kingdom come." We should hope with all our hearts to see God's Will fulfilled in our lives and to see His Kingdom spread throughout the whole world. (T:109)

A close connection.

Christ wants us to treasure the prayer which He has given to us: the "Our Father". When He taught His disciples this prayer, long ago, He had in mind both the future Eucharist, and the earthly needs of all who would follow Him. It's a prayer which He composed for sinful people like ourselves to recite; yet He wants us to understand that we can picture Him saying this prayer, today, as He stands amongst us during the Mass. He is praying it on our behalf. He wants us to be happy to know that as He prays with us, we are all praying to the Father for the same wonderful things to be achieved.

Christ invites us to picture our joint prayer in the following way. As we all say "Our Father, Who art in Heaven," Christ is gazing towards His Heavenly Father; and we, adopted of children of God, can join Christ in saying: "Hallowed be thy name." With Christ, Whose praise is of infinite worth, we offer ourselves to the

Father, to bring Him honour and glory. With Christ, we pray: "Thy Kingdom come" - longing to see the Father loved and praised everywhere, at all times: to see Him acknowledged by all people as sovereign, pure, holy, wise, powerful, loving and compassionate, and worthy of adoration. Then we say, with Christ, "Thy Will be done!" We all want to see the Father's Will greeted with delight by every creature: to see it fulfilled in every aspect, simply because it is His Will, and is therefore admirable and holy. We pray, with Christ, that the Father's Will shall be done "on earth as it is in Heaven." We ask for His Holy Will to be achieved in the Church, in our lives, and in the lives of our brothers and sisters - both living and departed - and in the hearts of people everywhere.

Then we think about our needs; and we pray with Christ, Who prays on our behalf, as we ask: "Give us this day our daily bread," by which we mean: everything we need for true life, on earth and in Heaven. Christ speaks as true man, amongst His family; and so He prays with sincerity and charity and power that the Father will give us the food of earth for our strength, the 'food' of consolation and wisdom for our hearts and minds, through the Holy Spirit, and also the 'food' of Christ's glorious Body and Blood for our souls and bodies, in Holy Communion.

As we remember our weaknesses - both physical and spiritual - we pray: "And forgive us our trespasses;" and Christ asks the Father to forgive our sins. Christ is our brother and our Redeemer, and therefore our Mediator between earth and Heaven; and so we are confident that His prayer is heard. Then we ask the Father to forgive us "as we forgive those who trespass against us". Here, Christ holds up His wounded hands: priestly hands, once nailed to the Cross. During His Passion, He set an example to us, His own human family. He said, of His tormentors: "Father, forgive them; they don't know what they are doing." Even today Christ is interceding for sinners: for us, as He asks the Father to send the Spirit to our hearts, so that by His power we can act as true children of God should act, by forgiving our enemies.

Next, we pray: "and lead us not into temptation" - knowing that the Father hears us. He Who heard Christ's prayer, offered from the depth of the 'pit' in Christ's Passion, and lifted up Christ from death to life in glory, now hears our prayers, as we call out from the depth of our 'pit'. We struggle against temptation, though we yearn for true life with God. We pray that God will keep us from sin, and make us holy - and will "deliver us from evil." Christ is here, praying for us to be protected from the evil one who tries to devour us; and the Father hears His beloved Son.

Through the merits of Christ's Passion, the marvel of the Father's mercy, and the power of the Holy Spirit, we can be brought eventually to the Kingdom on high, to where the gentle Mother of Christ, with all the other Saints and the holy Angels, all wrapped in bliss, praise the three-fold glory. (T:1926)

"LAMB OF GOD ... HAVE MERCY ON US"

Joining in our praise.

As we sing at Mass, after the Consecration, asking for mercy and peace, we are addressing Jesus Who is Really Present before us - under the appearance of bread and wine; and the Saints and holy Angels are present too, joining in the homage we offer to our Saviour. (T:4771)

HOLY COMMUNION

In a state of grace.

We should receive Holy Communion in a state of grace. The life of grace is like a beautiful garment: like a long, golden cloak.

Each person who wears such a cloak has had his sins forgiven, is reconciled to the Father, and so is fit to approach the altar, to meet Christ the King. (T:33)

Sharing His glory.

Christ is alive. He can never die again. He lives in perpetual joy and glory in Heaven - and He loves to share His glory with loving souls who receive Him in Holy Communion. We who receive His grace and Presence are made holy and glorious through His holiness. (T:49)

Our dignity and splendour.

We should remember our dignity. We are awe-inspiring, in our glory, when Christ is Really Present within our souls, in Holy Communion. We ought almost to bow down to others, for their glory in Jesus Christ. Each has a special dignity and a spiritual splendour which are unseen in other human beings. We are right to honour Christ 'in' one another. (Also T:49, and T:71)

Honest conversation.

It's important to be honest when we speak to Our Lord in Holy Communion. Through our beautifully-composed prayers He is given praise and honour, in public; and these can be useful in private. But we should never 'hide' behind them. We should never use flowery words as a substitute for the honest conversation through which we learn to confide in Him. It's by opening our hearts to Him and showing Him our true thoughts and desires that we permit Him to help us. (T:86)

Refreshment for our souls.

We should be ever-grateful for the marvel of Christ's Presence in the Mass, and for Holy Communion. Christ's Presence within us is as vital and refreshing for our souls as is pure water for our bodies. (T:116)

An honoured guest.

We should put our trust in Christ. His love for us is tremendous. He is so good that when He enters a frail but repentant soul in Holy Communion He treats that sinful person as an honoured guest. (T:135)

At peace before Heaven.

If we put our trust in Christ we can rest with Him in Holy Communion, together before Heaven, as we offer sincere praise to the Father in Christ's name; and in receiving Christ we are brought very close to the Saints and Angels who serve Him in Heaven.

In Holy Communion we can rest with Christ, giving silent glory to the Father, in the peace of the Holy Spirit - even amidst our distractions. (T:150)

More and more clearly.

It's important to be faithful in going to Holy Communion. Christ fills us with His light in this intimate meeting; and it's through His life, light and gifts that we grow in holiness and wisdom, and begin to see and judge the things of life more and more clearly. (T:175)

True union with God.

We ought to long for Holy Communion, through which Christ can give us a joy which is unknown elsewhere. Nothing can compare with the peaceful joy of a true union with Him, our infinitely-loving God and Saviour. (T:188)

Not yet united.

Those other Christians who are not 'in full communion' of faith
and worship with the Catholic Church are not usually permitted to
share in the Holy Eucharist. They can please Christ by their
patience, and by their respect for this teaching. If they ignore it,
and receive Communion, it's as if they try to take a handful of
glory. If they wish, they should instead turn to Christ in sincere
prayer to ask Him to bring them into the full unity of His holy
family: His holy People. (T:366)

Like a child.

It's important that we learn how to pray like little children, in
peace and unselfconsciousness. It's best to avoid complicated
prayers.

We can pray in Christ's name, in Holy Communion, asking for
the things we really need; or, in our weariness, we can pray a very
simple prayer. In Christ's Presence, we can turn to the Father
above, giving Him our whole attention, and saying: "Father, I sit
here for Your glory."

Later on, if we are faithful to Christ, and to prayer, we learn to
recognise each special invitation from Christ, and to respond to it.
When He offers us His prayer of silence, we accept it, because we
find that we can rest in Christ, within our souls. Whenever we
pray 'in Christ', we are stepping into Eternity, truly joining the
Saints and holy Angels in the glory of their unceasing praise and
worship. (T:383)

From within our hearts.

Instead of day-dreaming or looking around us, we should spend
time in prayer, in Holy Communion. We can offer Christ's glory
to the Father in Holy Communion, from within our own hearts, as
we say: "Here is Jesus Whose praise and glory I offer to You,

Father, because He is mine, and I am His." (T:444)

Glory to the Father.

It is a privilege and a cause for joy that even in our weakness we can give glory to the Father, in Holy Communion, and at the same time allow Christ to transform us by His grace.

We should remember that to receive Christ in Holy Communion is to be brought close to Heaven, close to that Holy Country where light shines perpetually. The veil which separates Heaven and earth is very thin. (T:447)

Christ, our 'everything'.

There's no need to be anxious, in our weakness. We can pray well even though we have nothing good of our 'own' to offer. Because of our faith in Christ, which brought us here to receive Christ, we can be confident that Christ is the 'All' that we have now, the 'Everything' of goodness, Really Present here, Whom we can offer to the Father for His glory. (T:477)

After our purification.

If we are in a state of grace, we mustn't be preoccupied by our sense of unworthiness. It is through our humility - after our purification - that Christ delights in leading us into the heart of the Holy Trinity, in prayer. (Also T:477)

In Christ's silent praise.

We can rest peacefully with Christ in Holy Communion, in a wordless silence, if it seems that Christ invites us to rest in His own silent praise of the Father; and we can let Christ guide us gently 'back' to attentive silence whenever our hearts and minds wander away in day-dreaming or distractions. (T:500)

Heaven starts now.

We should pray for an increase of faith, so that we'll really believe that Heaven 'starts' now. Whatever our feelings, Heaven is here, with Christ, whenever He comes to us in Holy Communion. (T:509)

A pillar of light.

When Christ comes to us in Holy Communion, and when we pray with Him, in Him, and through Him, He prays in us; and He makes our prayer and His truly one. He is like a pillar of light before Heaven, offering His prayers and His sacrifice to the Father. (T:517)

No anxious thoughts.

We are right to offer thanks and homage to Christ, in Holy Communion, but we should also put our trust in Him. There is no need for anxious thoughts about past sins which have been blotted out entirely through Reconciliation, love and penance.

We should remember how much Christ loves us, as He comes to us joyfully, with His holy Angels. (T:560)

In a fitting manner.

We should welcome Christ in a fitting manner when He comes to dwell in our hearts in Holy Communion. He loves us; and if we welcome Him properly, we allow Him to share His Divine joy with us - even here in earthly life. (T:574)

Honoured by our Angels.

Christ wants us to remember that we each have a Guardian Angel who stands beside us as we receive Christ in Holy Communion. Each one holds in honour the soul made radiant with Christ's

Presence. (T:600)

Christ's own Kingdom.

Christ deserves a worthy welcome, in Holy Communion. He is Really Present in each of our souls, as if in His own little Kingdom.

During our 'exile' on earth, it's as if we can provide a 'home' for Christ when we welcome Him with pure hearts and true love, in Holy Communion. Here, in our hearts, He can dwell and be loved: united in mind and heart and intention with each person who loves Him above all. (T:620 and T:650)

God praises God, through God.

We can rest in Christ, in Holy Communion, knowing that as He praises the Father, through the Holy Spirit, from within our souls, something extraordinary is happening: an astonishing privilege. God praises God, through God, within us! (T:684)

Confident prayers.

We mustn't be afraid to ask the Father for good things. We can pray with Christ in Holy Communion. We can turn to the Father, with Christ, praying confidently for the salvation of the living, and for consolation for the Faithful Departed - and for perseverance and salvation for ourselves. (T:756)

A swift ascent.

We mustn't be afraid to leave behind our thoughts and words whenever we are sure that Christ is 'calling' us to ascend swiftly to the Father in prayer, in Holy Communion. We shouldn't linger unnecessarily, speaking endlessly about our needs and desires. We can trust in Christ's prayer which is being offered within our souls, and by which everything needful will be said to the Father.

(T:852)

Shedding our burdens.

It's best to 'clear the ground' for honest prayer, in Holy Communion. Christ wants to lighten our burdens; and He can do so more easily if we first speak to Him about the things which are distressing us, but then turn our minds away from our problems to give Him our full attention.

If we are honest with Christ, and trust Him, and place our burdens at His feet, we free ourselves to move onward with Him in a light-hearted prayer of praise. (T:864) *(See illustration 32)*

An overburdened heart.

We can honour Christ, and also be happier, if we have cleared and scoured our souls in honour of Him, the holy Saviour Who wants to enter our souls in Holy Communion. If our possessions are too important to us, they are cluttering and filling the 'cavern' of our soul, just as boxes and rubbish clutter an untidy attic. It's as though - within our soul in Holy Communion - Christ cannot stand upright in worship! Although, in His great love, He has come to the soul, His influence upon us is severely limited; and His praise cannot 'stream up' to the Father from within such a selfishly-overburdened heart. (T:865)

An unfit dwelling-place.

We should beware of being anxious about possessions. A heart which is consumed with a longing to possess certain things, or which is consumed with fear of losing 'things' - whether those things be material treasures, ambitions, friendships or supposedly good plans - has little 'room' within itself for anything but its own dreams. Such a heart is an unfit dwelling-place for Christ. Truly, His love is unending, yet such a small, gloomy, untidy soul is unworthy of His Divinity. (Also T:865)

In utter simplicity.

None of us should try to 'make up' for tiredness in prayer by composing elaborate phrases. It's as though Christ is waiting patiently and silently, half-hidden within an anxious soul, as a 'veil' woven of such 'clever' words drifts to and fro in front of Him. He has no need of fancy words of supplication. Though He is touched by the prayers, hymns and litanies which - through His Spirit - He has inspired people to write in honour of His Divinity, He is delighted above all to hear a whisper of truth from a humble heart. He wants to share our sorrows as well as joys. (T:885A)

Not from a sense of duty.

We must remember that Christ doesn't come to a loving soul from a sense of duty. He delights in being with His friends. He loves to come to His little 'Kingdom' - which is the soul of each person who really loves Him and makes Him welcome. (T:900A)

Faith and obedience.

Faith is important. Christ is at work in loving souls in Holy Communion, even if nothing is felt, heard or seen. He works in secret, purifying our souls, as we wait in peaceful prayer, in happy ignorance and obedience. (T:926)

To unknowing prayer.

We can be content with Christ's silent and gracious Presence in Holy Communion, until the moment when the Spirit invites us - by an interior prompting - to rise 'up', interiorly, in prayer. It is when we have been happy to adore Christ without words or desires, except the desire to do His Will, that He sometimes leads our obedient soul, through His Spirit, to 'leap' with Him, upwards, to 'unknowing' contemplation. (T:934)

Simplicity and trust.

We can be like happy children, in Holy Communion, confident about Christ's love for us: happy to stay in His Presence, despite our little faults and miseries. (Also T:934)

Total privacy-of-soul.

We can be certain that our conversation with Christ is entirely private, in the depths of our souls, in Holy Communion. We can confide every hurt or wrong to Him, knowing that not even our Guardian Angel knows what we're saying. (T:944)

Sure of a welcome.

We mustn't think of Christ's love as something which He offers to sinful people with disdain or reluctance. He delights in coming to a soul where He is sure of finding a welcome. For Him, it's like coming to a home. (T:955)

With Christ's own praise.

We can be content to sit in prayer, in our weakness, in Holy Communion, praising the Father with Christ's own praise. We can say "Father, here is Jesus! I sit here for Your glory - as Jesus praises You from within my soul!" (T:1077A)

A sincere greeting.

We needn't think that we must 'impress' Christ in Holy Communion with vigorous and lavish praise. He welcomes a sincere greeting. He accepts our heart's true homage, however quietly it is expressed. (T:1120)

Inevitable distractions.

We shouldn't worry about our busy and distracted thoughts, as we try to peer 'through' them, to pray, in Holy Communion.

We should remember that Christ's Divine nature is unchanging. Everything which we believed and knew of Him yesterday is unchanged. He's just the same today; and therefore His love for us hasn't changed. It never decreases! It's as fervent and as tender as ever; so we mustn't be upset by our numerous distractions in prayer. (T:1125B)

Because He loves us.

We must believe in Christ's love for us. He comes to us in Holy Communion because he loves us, not primarily in order to do good to us.

Within our souls, we can see the debris of various weaknesses and temptations. But in Holy Communion Christ doesn't first of all come to our souls in order to heal, reform, cleanse or protect us - although He does all these things, if we permit His love for us to enter, and to affect our hearts and lives. Above all, He comes to us because of His tender love for us. (T:1155)

In the heart of God.

We should be thrilled that we can receive Christ in Holy Communion. When His grace flows into a pure soul, He draws that soul into His own pure loving communion with the Father, in the bliss of the Holy Spirit. Yet we need never be concerned with whether or not we 'feel' Divine bliss in Holy Communion. Grace is at work in the souls of those of us who love Christ, whatever our feelings; and that grace is powerful. We should rejoice in our privilege of receiving the Son of God in our souls and lives. (T:1199)

Drawn in, by adoption.

We should be awed by the goodness of God, shown towards

ourselves through the gift of the Holy Eucharist. The Communion which we can find in God, 'in Christ', resembles the love of God for God, in God, which is flowing in the heart of God, in Eternity, in utter purity and majesty and simplicity.

This simple and everlasting love in Heaven is a three-fold love of Father, Son and Holy Spirit; and when we touch our Heavenly Father and enter His life, through Jesus, in the Holy Communion which is ours on earth, the love we meet is the very love which fills the whole of Heaven. The Persons are the Divine Persons Who share their life with the Saints and Angels in Heaven, but we are now 'drawn in' by adoption. The moment in which we share Divine life in this marvellous way is the very 'now' of Eternity, since love has no end or beginning. The bliss is the very same bliss as that which is experienced in Heaven - though it is muted here, lest we be destroyed by joy. Because of all these things, therefore, we can truly say: "Heaven is here; I taste Heaven, in Christ!" (Also T:1199) G.H.T.

In His Presence.

We should accept Christ's encouragement, in Holy Communion, and be glad that our near-constant 'immersion' in His company and in the company of His Saints is so beneficial. People who live constantly in the presence of Christ and His Holy Mother - and of all the other Saints - begin to resemble them in light, in warmth, in charity and in beauty.

Christ asks us to consider how earthly things can so easily affect us; then we'll see that Heavenly things, too, can be 'absorbed'. No-one can fail to absorb light, beauty and perfume, who is immersed in them constantly; and this is as true of Heavenly light, beauty and perfume as it is of earthly. That's why we should encourage one another to pray!

Many of us snatch a brief moment with Christ, in prayer, but then run away to immerse ourselves in the world's feverish activities.

We don't always wait to receive the good gifts and influence which we could absorb so easily and gently by staying for a little longer in His Presence. (T:1228A)

Never far away.

We must believe in Christ's love for us. He is never far away from us, even though we are sometimes tempted to imagine, in Holy Communion, that He is sometimes tired of us, or even absent. (T:1232)

Christ's own praise.

We can remember the following words, if we want to praise the Father most perfectly, when we are at peace with Christ after receiving Him in Holy Communion. We can offer Christ's own praise to the Father, praying within our souls: "All glory to the Holy Trinity, in my emptiness, through You, O Christ." (T:1234)

Warm and affectionate.

We must believe in Christ's love. If we think about the sort of warm greeting which we receive from affectionate little children, we can be sure that that's how Christ comes to us, in Holy Communion! He comes to us with a pure and generous affection. He is always warmly welcoming towards us. He is always loving, pure and simple, longing to give joy - willing to be rebuffed - and always thinking of our joy and welfare. (T:1247A)

A gift for God.

Each of us should yearn to be a true channel of grace, so that we can bring Christ's 'living water' to other people. Yet we can 'channel' gifts even to our Heavenly Father. What a gift we make to Him, when, in Holy Communion, we offer Him Christ's Divine life, from within our souls. We can turn to our Father, saying: "I offer You Jesus' glory!" and thus we can give Divine glory to the

Father even from within our frailty and weakness. (T:1274)

A living relationship.

We should realise that Christ has a unique relationship with each person He visits in Holy Communion. Our friendship with Him changes from day to day, even if we ourselves detect no change. He Who is love and life is active. He is at work in our souls. It's as if His light - within us - is spilling over our particular faults and regretted failings. It's as if sunlight is pouring around the dark framework within a stained glass window. Thus His Divine light creates within each one of us a different and beautiful glorious pattern. This is a pattern of sanctity and humility which would not be seen by Christ and His Church, had it not been for our repented and forgiven faults! (T:1288)

Doing God's Will.

To be aware of coming into Christ's radiant Presence in Holy Communion is a great privilege. People who do experience His Presence in this way are those who have no ambitions of their own, who think only of His glory - of doing His Will at all times rather than their own - and who live for Him. Furthermore, such people are effective, for good, in everyday life.

People who are able to plead with Christ most effectively, before the Father, for this generation, are those who suffer wounds and bear burdens patiently in union with Christ. They bear the Cross with Him in this century, and bear it through accepting even the ordinary trials of daily life, including sad experiences and sickness. (T:1322)

Like a blood transfusion.

We should realise what Christ does when He lavishes His gifts upon us. Almost like a blood transfusion by which life or the properties needed for life are given, a great gift is given to us in

Holy Communion, a gift by which the Divine life within us is strengthened. (T:1341)

Equal to Himself.

Christ wants us all to know that His love for us is so profound and true and tender that His gift to us in Holy Communion is His very self; and so He gives to each beloved soul just what is needed for the union of the soul with Himself in an equality of love!

He gives to the soul - as if adorning it with Divine gifts - love, knowledge, Divine life, and beatitude, thus making the soul equal to Himself in love, intimacy, Eternal Life, and bliss. (Also T:1341)

Astonishing changes.

We must remain hopeful that Christ can bring us to perfection, in true holiness. If we believe that the bread and wine which are taken to the altar during the Mass are changed into Christ's Sacred Body and Precious Blood through the words used by the priest, and by the power of the Spirit, we can believe that Christ can change even weak and sinful creatures like ourselves.

During the Consecration, there is no physical evidence of the Spirit's action, yet His Divine power is at work in an action which is silent, swift and invisible. And just as Christ can change bread and wine so astonishingly, through His Spirit, so He can also work astonishing changes in human hearts - if He is 'allowed , by people who want to become more loving. He makes those changes in the same way, in the sense that whenever He's at work through His Spirit, that work is swift and silent, yet powerfully effective. (T:1360)

A very tender love.

We must never forget that Jesus' love for us is real, and very tender. This means that He looks on delightedly whenever we greet Him at the tabernacle or welcome Him in Holy Communion. (T:1448)

Shame and timidity.

We shouldn't let our little faults make us afraid to approach Christ for Holy Communion. His holy Angels surround Him as He stands here in glory; and they love to see Christ's friends approach Him; yet we sometimes let shame and timidity keep us at a distance. (T:1451)

Self-centred thoughts.

It's worthwhile overcoming thoughts of self, as we approach Christ in Holy Communion. He is waiting patiently to welcome us; so we should greet Him as He deserves, and enjoy His Presence. (Also T:1451)

Hidden faults.

We should remember that Christ longs to be welcomed; yet He sees that only a few of us can say "Welcome" to Him with any truth. His Presence is unwelcome, when we see it only as a reminder of grudgingly-done duty, of hidden faults in our daily lives, of secret sins of the past, or of unconfessed longings. If those things darken our hearts, we won't want to be illumined by Christ's Presence.

Whoever doesn't open the 'doorway' of his heart to Christ doesn't let Christ's light shine in. The 'wound' in our hearts which is the open doorway by which Christ can enter is the constant and willingly-accepted knowledge of our own sinfulness. Such knowledge is initially painful; but it's value is recognised by Christians in every age who are willing to accept purification. (T:1461)

Opening our hearts.

We should never fear that our weariness in prayer can deter Christ from helping us or from revealing His love. None of us should imagine that it's our physical frailty that keeps Him from our hearts in Holy Communion. More usually, it is shame or fear which keep Him at a distance, or other things which He alone can see; or perhaps we recite humble words of welcome yet keep our hearts firmly closed against Him.

We can be certain that our struggles against weariness, and our efforts to greet Christ as He deserves, bring many blessings from Heaven upon us: invisible blessings, but real. When we greet Him with a 'throwing-open' of the door of the heart, and with a glad greeting, it's as though we are saying to Him: "Cast Your light within my soul, and enter. All I have is Yours!" It's by the sincere 'opening' of the heart to Christ that His glory can pour into the soul, filling it with every blessing. (T:1465B)

Glory to God.

Our marvellous union with Christ in Holy Communion brings us consolation, with further purification, and a further 'cementing' of our friendship with Christ. It also brings us a means of giving glory to God the Father. It's because of our real communion with Christ, when we have received Him gladly into our hearts, that the Father is glorified from within us!

We can say that God is praised from on earth, in this way, by the glory of His Son, as Christ's glory and light pour upwards from within our souls, and reach as far as Heaven. (Also T:1465B)

A joyful welcome.

We should be joyful, in Holy Communion. This is a time for glory, and for gladness, not reparation; so we shouldn't persist in thinking about self and sin, even though our motives are generous.

By turning away from self, towards Christ, we can give Him a joyful and fitting welcome; and we can enjoy the glory of His holy Presence. (T:1477)

Secret fears.

We shouldn't be afraid to show Christ our heartaches and our secret fears. We honour Him by such trusting prayer; and we also enable Him to enlighten and help us. (T:1478)

Love and loneliness.

It's important to remember Who and What Christ is. Our Saviour is both God and man. The fullness of the Divine nature is found in Christ. All that is lovely in human persons is found in Him, since all loveliness stems from His Divinity. His Person 'contains' every possible facet of love and loveliness. This is why His loving Presence is experienced by His true friends as warmth and beauty. (T:1489)

Lukewarm or fervent.

It's important not to be careless or half-hearted when we receive the sacraments of the Church. Of our free will, we can choose to be luke-warm in our manner of greeting Christ; or we can pray fervently, in Holy Communion. For example, we can actively unite ourselves with Christ's intentions, in prayer, as we offer His glory and His virtues to the Father; though we do this more effectively if we understand more about our 'work' of adoration.

The soul which obediently offers Christ's praise to the Father - because of Christ's Presence within that soul - doesn't merely 'reflect' Christ's glory in the way in which an inanimate mirror lifelessly reflects a light which belongs entirely to a source outside itself. No! A soul which reflects Christ's glory - the Divine glory of our Saviour - is far from being lifeless. The soul is caught up into the life of the living, Holy Trinity: into God's life and action.

Furthermore, that soul shows out whatever is 'found' in the Holy Trinity. It shares in, and shows out, Divine life, love, light, joy, power and wisdom, and all that is good. (T:1521)

Our privileged state.

If we genuinely enjoy Christ's Presence in Holy Communion, we should rejoice in our intimacy with our God and Saviour, and be immensely grateful for our privileged state. It's a cause for thanks if we can see His glory and find that we're able to bear it, just as some can bear that same glory, after death, at the brink of Heaven! (T:1547)

Just as we are.

We mustn't be despondent about our obvious weaknesses. Christ loves us; and we can see the meaning of true friendship, if we think about Christ's Presence with us in Holy Communion. We can cling to these marvellous but simple truths: that He visits us, that we trust Him, that He knows all our faults, yet that He loves us tremendously, just as we are! This doesn't mean that He doesn't want us to become holy. It means that His love is real: it endures through all our sins and troubles and doubts and hesitations. (T:1576B)

Christ's Passion, and Christ's glory.

It's important to welcome Christ in Holy Communion when He comes to our souls in the radiance of Divine glory. This is a Person Who has risen from the grave. He is alive; and He's very near to us. Yet although He wants us to rejoice in His triumph and in our friendship with Him, He wants us to keep two 'views' of Him in mind, as if we possess a double portrait of Him. We can see Him as "Christ Wounded"; and we can also see Him cloaked in glory, as "Christ triumphant."

We will be more thoughtful and steady in all our thoughts and actions if we keep in mind what Christ has done for us in His holy Passion; yet we also need to remember that His present joy and glory are so great as to be beyond our imaginings.

If we remain constantly aware of the purpose of Christ's sufferings, and remain full of wonder at His triumph over death, this will help us to pray the two types of prayer which always balance one another and 'work' together. These types of prayer are: first, sorrow with gratitude, and, secondly, gladness, with hope! (T:1595)

To love and to be loved.

It's very worthwhile to think about our Saviour: about Who He is, and about His two-fold nature. Whenever we welcome Him fervently in Holy Communion, we are honouring our Lord and Creator; but we are also delighting someone Who is truly human. Christ loves to be loved! He feels great delight at the love and affection of every person who loves Him.

If we realise something of the marvel of Christ's holy Incarnation, and believe that He is really human as well as Divine, we'll understand that - just like ourselves - He delights in receiving expressions of love and loyalty and gratitude. He experiences a real and unfeigned delight in seeing evidence of our love for Him. We can remind ourselves of this extraordinary truth, something very encouraging for weak and perhaps timid people: that, by our love, we can give Christ joy, we can make Him happy, we can lighten His heart, we can 'ease' His longing to love and to be loved, and we can satisfy His concern for our welfare. (T:1610)

Through Christ to the Father.

During our life on earth, God our Father guides us in several ways. He illumines our souls through the teaching of the Church, and through the Sacred Tradition, and through Holy Scripture. Yet it is Christ our radiant, living friend and Saviour, sacramentally Present, Who is the principal 'means' by which our Father meets, touches, guides and enlightens us. We meet the Father in Person, wholly, when we meet His Son, Christ, through Christ's Real, 'entire', and holy Presence in Holy Communion. (Also T:1635)

Under various titles.

We should treasure the truth: that everything that 'belongs' to Christ is now ours, through our union with Him. So when we pray, we can meet Christ just as He is today - risen and glorious - but we can also meet Christ in all the important incidents of His life on earth, many centuries ago. It's true that our friendship and our knowledge of Him are based upon faith and not upon clear sight. However, our faith can assure us that He is Present with us in the Eucharist, and that when we meet Him 'in Person', in such intimacy, we are 'touching' every incident of His life.

It's as if we are going back to make real contact with Christ at the time of His Passion. It's as if we can see Him standing before us - at the far side of a little chasm. We are within reach of many incidents of His life: His public ministry, and boyhood and even babyhood. We can rejoice at being able to come so close to every aspect of His life. We are not 'shut off' from contact with His earthly life just because we live on earth many centuries after Him. So it's quite all right for us to pray to Him under any one of various titles. Anyone who prays to the 'Infant Jesus' or to the 'Wounded Christ' is truly approaching Him as He is, since His earthly life is eternally 'available' within His Divine Person, in prayer. (T:1641)

The Blessed Sacrament.

We should treasure not only Christ's Presence in the tabernacle, but also His Presence within our souls in Holy Communion. And we should be thankful for our faith in His Presence, faith which was His gift to us, a faith which leads us to adore Him and to delight in staying in His Presence. We should pity and pray for people who don't benefit from His Presence in the tabernacle. How happy we are, to be able to find Him in the Blessed Sacrament. (T:1666)

In spiritual poverty.

It's true to say - of Christ's Real Presence in the Eucharist - that it has changed the lives of all who know Him. Some of those who genuinely love Christ, however, are so ignorant of the teaching of the Church and live in such spiritual poverty that they are ignorant even of Christ's Presence in this Holy Sacrament. Even some Catholics refuse to believe in His Presence, or refuse to pay towards the Blessed Sacrament - towards Christ - the reverence which is due to His Divinity. Their careless acts and attitudes betray them. (Also T:1666)

Established in humility.

If we serve Christ and love Him we should delight in our union with Him in Holy Communion; and we should believe that we are very close to Him. Yet we need humility, as well as confidence in His love.

Christ invites us to imagine that we can see, in the distance, a vast mountain-range, which represents the God-head. Yet on the plain in the foreground we can see a little figure, alone, who is standing in prayer. What we should understand is that nothing is more certain than our insignificance, when set beside the grandeur and majesty of our Divine and Holy Redeemer! Christ looks upon us with enormous tenderness, yet wants to establish us in humility. (T:1717)

Foolishness and pride.

We can ask ourselves these questions, whenever we are tempted to be proud of our friendship with Christ, or proud of Christ's gifts:

who can do favours for our Lord and God? Who is worthy to serve Him? It's true that we are loved with an everlasting love. Yet which mere human being can be anything except 'one-who-has-received-good' from his Creator? What could be more foolish than for a creature to believe that he has given something more to God than was His 'due'! (Also T:1717)

Unsullied purity.

In striving for humility, we must remember what Christ is like. In Christ, there is no shadow of imperfection. In meeting Christ we meet the clear, patient intelligence of the Divine Person Who knows all truth. He is like a pure child, direct and simple, and is unwilling to co-operate with half-truths, flattery, conversational ploys or false insinuations. That's why every word we address to Him in prayer should be truthful, as we speak about our hopes, fears, problems and desires. And that's why in everyday life we should speak truthful words in every circumstance. How can we claim to be acting and speaking in the name of Christ if we offer flattery or untruth?

He Whom we approach in prayer is Divine, perfect and holy, living in unsullied and glorious purity. Yet if His purity is infinite and perfect, so too is His compassion which pours out ceaselessly upon us, His children. Through that compassion for sinners, Jesus Christ sacrificed Himself to save us: to offer salvation to Mankind. (T:1734A)

Purity and holiness.

We must strive to be faithful to Christ. Great peace and fulfilment are given to people such as ourselves who are incorporated into Christ and who even on earth share His life, through receiving His Sacred Body and Blood.

Christ offers us great gifts. For example, He offers us His own purity and holiness, so that we can be transformed, and made pure and holy. Through His kindness and compassion, we can live in innocence after the forgiveness of our sins. We can allow Christ's pure life and virtues to flow through us, because of our union with Him. We can be indwelt by His Spirit. We can be one with Christ, in the Holy Spirit Who already inspires all our prayers; and it should be a cause for astonishment and wonder that people like ourselves can pray to the Father just as Christ prayed from the Cross, confident of being heard. (T:1734D)

The very same gifts.

We should treasure our union with Christ in Holy Communion. When we receive His Sacred Body, in Holy Communion, He is within our souls as surely as when He appeared to His Apostles, when He re-entered their lives after His Resurrection. It's true that because of human weakness, or sin, or turbulent emotions, we don't always enjoy His gifts. He comes to each soul in Holy Communion, however, with the same gifts as those which were experienced by His close companions on earth. He comes with His gentleness, silence, peace and reassurance. This is the meaning of 'Holy Communion': that He, the Holy One, is Really Present with us, enfolding us in His love. (T:1740B)

Always helpful.

We should be at peace in Christ's Presence. Whether we are tired or alert, distracted or fervent in prayer, we needn't worry about our distractions, when Christ comes to us in Holy Communion. A loving welcome delights Him above all. And since He loves us, we can be sure that His Presence within our souls is always true, glorious and helpful no matter how tired or distracted we are.

If we think about Christ's purpose in coming to us in Holy Communion we'll realise that it's not primarily in order to do good to us, although His Presence will inevitably bring about good, within contrite and generous hearts. But He comes to us because He loves us. His intention is to give us joy, if we will open our hearts to receive it. (T:1800)

A blazing fire.

We shouldn't worry about our tiny little faults. Christ's sacred Presence within our souls, in Holy Communion, is like a blazing fire which burns and destroys all our little failings, and then ascends like a great flame of pure praise, to the Father and to Heaven. (T:1816)

True communion.

The more we live in communion with Christ in every aspect of our lives upon earth, then the briefer will be our soul's 'journey' to Him at death, and the swifter will be our arrival in Heaven. The purification which is needed by most of His friends will be very brief, for us, if we are very close to Him. It could even be unnecessary. (T:1884)

Sincere acts of trust.

We mustn't let ourselves become burdened with shame, in Holy Communion, when we realise just how good Christ is, and how unworthy we are to receive Him. If we have genuinely made a good preparation to receive Him, and are glad and grateful to have received Him, we need only welcome Him, and thank Him. Then we can make sincere acts of trust in His Real Presence, in His love for us, and in His power to help us in everything. It is through such acts that we open our hearts to Him. It is through such acts that we consent to receive the gifts which He then lavishes upon us: His joy and reassurance. (T:1891)

Conversing with Christ.

Everyone who welcomes Christ and trusts Him, and converses truthfully with Him in Holy Communion instead of carelessly waiting for something to 'happen', will benefit immeasurably from

His Presence. (Also T:1891)

Preparing to meet God.

It's good to remember what we have heard in Holy Scripture, about how Elijah covered his face with his cloak as he prepared to meet his God. The Lord Whom we love to welcome in Holy Communion is the very Lord Who spoke with Elijah; and that is why we are sometimes awed, and powerfully affected by our union and Communion.

Even in our new humility, however, we should be confident in our petitions. Truly, Christ our Lord loves us. With the Father and the Holy Spirit He lives within our souls, in beauty and dazzling splendour: Three Persons yet one God. (T:1978)

Christ's glory, ours to offer.

We should consider how marvellous it is that we can praise our Heavenly Father in a worthy manner, since we have Christ's own glory to offer to the Father as our very own praise! When our souls are ablaze with Christ's glory, in Holy Communion, each soul is a living monstrance for the Sacred Host - for Christ's Sacred Body - the sight of which causes the Angels to rejoice. It is because of Christ's sacramental Presence within our souls that His holy Angels bow down beside us, as they adore Him. (T:1993)

The flame of sacrifice.

Our Holy Communion can be more than a consoling experience. It can also be a means of giving glory to the Father. Within our souls, Christ is ours, to offer as our praise of the Father. It's as if Christ, in His own glory, is our 'burnt offering'. Christ is our sacrifice.

Christ is our homage to God our Father, as each of us prays - united with Christ - in Holy Communion. Christ is 'fire' from the

Father: fire given for the work of praise, in contemplation. Christ's own glory is burning within our souls. Christ is the 'burnt offering' on the altar of our hearts. Christ's love is the flame of sacrifice which rises upwards from within our souls as from within the temple; and Christ wants us to understand that this offering of love is the 'heart' of contemplation. (T:2005)

A Heavenly sanctuary.

We need to remember that it is trust which ensures 'access' to our Father, through our meeting with Christ in Holy Communion. It is because of this way of life in Christ, and because of our sincere greeting to Christ in Holy Communion, with sincere thanks, trust, humility, and honesty, that we who are truly His friends have access to the Father, through Him. It's as if we can open the 'door' to the Father's 'heart' in prayer. This is how we come to share in the Father's life even while we are still living on earth. His heart is a Heavenly sanctuary in which we can rest amidst the disturbances of earthly life. (T:2029B)

Trials and sadnesses.

We need never doubt Christ's goodwill, or His ability to help us. He knows and understands all of our problems and weaknesses. He knows our heartaches. That is why He is here, in Holy Communion, to strengthen and to console us; and if we consider the extent of His love, we'll realise that from all Eternity He has foreseen the trials and sadnesses which would arise in the lives of all living people - and this includes ourselves. (T:2065)

Uncreated fire.

We can remind ourselves that in receiving Christ in Holy Communion, we receive our incarnate God; and He brings us very close to the Father. It's as though we are standing at the entrance to Heaven: at a place from which we might glimpse, not yet the face of our Heavenly Father, but something of the uncreated 'fire' which surrounds Him. In revealing something of this fire, Christ shows something of His own nature: the Divine nature which He shares with the Father. He is showing something of His glory and purity: something of the Divinity we long to share as we pray our trusting prayers. (T:2161)

To make us happy.

As friends of Christ, trying to show out His love, we sometimes forget that we should be as happy to receive love as to give it. He wants us to realise, in Holy Communion, that He has come to us in peace and mercy, with infinite tenderness and compassion. No-one visits close friends in order to judge them, but rather, in order to make them happy; and thus it is when Christ visits us, in this special way, in Holy Communion.

We are Christ's friends; and although we shouldn't normally receive Him if we've committed serious sin, and haven't yet been reconciled, He wants us to know that He doesn't visit us in order to sit in judgement on us but to make us happy. (T:2163)

Joy, to His creatures.

We need to remember Who Christ is, as we enjoy His Presence. He is not only the dear brother and friend Who speaks with us and Who helps us to endure earthly trials. He is our God and Saviour Whose eternal plan of salvation has arisen from the 'heart' of a Person Whose overwhelming desire is to give joy - eternal joy - to His creatures. We can be utterly certain, therefore, that since Christ became incarnate for our sake, He most certainly wishes to see us joyful now, here, even before we reach Heaven.

This is why we should look upon our sacramental meeting with Christ as the most wonderful opportunity for Him to offer us a real taste of Heaven's joy, and for us to receive and accept it! (Also T:2163)

A wonderful exchange.

We should treasure every Mass, and the wonderful exchanges of gifts which take place daily.

We are used to thinking about the most obvious exchange - which consists of our offering to God of bread and wine, which He changes for us, by His Spirit's power and the words of Christ, into Christ's Sacred Body and Blood. Yet there's a further 'exchange' for which we should be grateful: we offer Christ, at the hands of the priest, as our own gift of praise, thanksgiving and reparation to the Father, before receiving Christ in Holy Communion as a perfect gift to ourselves from Heaven! (Also T:2163)

Trust and truth.

We can unload our worries onto Christ whenever we pray, but especially in Holy Communion. It's as if His light shines within our souls, as He comes to us in sacramental form; and if we trust Him we can bring every little worry into His Presence. Every thought or memory which disturbs us can be held up and examined in His light; and we can learn from experience how swiftly such acts of trust in Him enable Him to release us from fear.

Trust and truth always lead, in the end, to the greatest joy and peace in prayer, as we rest in silence with Christ before the invisible Father. (T:2175)

A word of love.

Christ is happy to see us simplify our prayers, as we praise the Father with Christ, in Holy Communion. We can speak to the Father about Christ's Presence within our souls; and we can say to the Father: 'Hear Him!' - in other words, "Hear the word of love which Christ speaks to You from within my soul". Truly, Christ is our Word of praise to the Father. (T:2230B)

Our gift to the Father.

When we are here with Christ, before the Father, united with Christ in Holy Communion and resting before the face of Heaven, we can be sure that the Father delights in all the sincere prayers we offer Him. Yet He takes an especial delight in our loving gift when we allow Christ's own praise to ascend to Him - at a time such as this - from within our souls.

As Christ praises the Father in this way, we can offer His praise as our very own gift, as we give this holy gift to the Father saying: "Glory, for Your glory!" (Also T:2230B)

Brighter than the sun.

Because of His great love for us, our Lord and friend Jesus Christ enters our souls peacefully in Holy Communion. How gently He treats us all! His glory is brighter than the sun. This glory entirely surrounds our Divine and holy Redeemer Who is now risen and glorified. Truly, He is worthy of the reverence we show towards Him, as we honour His Presence. Few of us could bear His glory and majesty, did He not 'disguise' Himself - under the appearance of bread - so that we can receive Him peacefully in the Blessed Sacrament. (T:2273)

The work of contemplation.

How glorious a virtue is sincere trust in Christ. Through Christ's invitation to us, and our trust in Him, we have come to share His life; and therefore He lavishes His gifts upon us, according to His Will, even sharing His glory. Christ's own glory is ours to offer as our praise to the Father during the time of Holy Communion and at any time of day; yet it is ours only because of our acceptance of our spiritual poverty and our faith in our Saviour.

Whenever we praise the Father through offering Christ's glory from within our souls we are doing a magnificent work: the work of contemplation. It is a work which is silent, secret and selfless; and it is fruitful for other souls, who benefit even more from our prayer, the more faithfully do we fulfil this vocation. (T 2321A)

Fruitful work.

We can be sure that our intimate union with Christ in prayer is fruitful. Through the union of our soul with the Godhead in this special work of contemplation, our souls are changing. As we wait in silence, 'at work' in the prayer and praise of the Holy Trinity, we allow God to change us in various ways, in and through this very prayer. It is as though we are being irradiated by Christ's glory; and thus, we are being divinised and made ready for Heaven. (Also T:2321A)

Christ's true friends.

Christ loves to come to the souls of His true friends; and there is a special reason why Christ delights so much in our love. He can say to the Father, about every faithful and loving soul, that the torments of His Passion were worthwhile, that His love has not been rejected, that His works are being done in and through that soul - through the Spirit's power - and that the Father's plan for that soul is being fulfilled.

It's as though Christ, Who dwells within such a loving soul, now offers that soul to the Father. It's as though Christ can say to the Father about each faithful soul who is His dwelling-place and His delight: "Father, I have won this soul for you, through My saving work; and I am bringing him to You, to delight Your heart by his faithfulness and love." (T:2483)

Disobedience.

It's important that we realise that we cannot demand to receive Holy Communion whenever we want, simply because we are members of the Church. If we haven't repented of our serious sins, but still step forward to receive Christ in Holy Communion, we are not acting as Christ's true friends act. In our carelessness or disobedience we are unfit for sacramental union with Christ, which is a foretaste of Heaven; and we will gain no spiritual benefit, despite our attempt to seize some benefit from the sacrament. (T:2536)

Unfit for Heaven.

Through coming to His friends in Holy Communion, Christ works a marvellous transformation in human souls and lives. Yet a state of grace is essential for true Communion with Christ. Unless we repent of our sins and are restored to communion with Christ we cannot be transformed by His life and love. In our disobedience, we refuse to allow Him to change us. Whether it's through foolishness or malice, we refuse to be made fit for Heaven. (T:2537)

Left in apparent darkness.

We need to understand the reason why, out of love for us, Christ sometimes leaves us in apparent darkness, even when we sincerely believe that we are in a state of grace, and have just received Him in Holy Communion. Only when we have been made like Christ through regular prayer, and through regularly and devoutly receiving Christ in Holy Communion, can we bear His radiance within our souls: a radiance which then shines out towards the Father in Heaven as from a mirror, to give delight and glory to Heaven. (T:2551)

Reflecting Christ's beauty.

If we co-operate with Christ as He purifies our souls, both in prayer and in everyday life, there will come a time when our souls mirror Christ's beauty and reflect that beauty towards the Father. Then the Father receives from us, as our own gift to Him, infinitely-glorious homage and praise - especially when we have received Christ in Holy Communion.

We should marvel at the fact that we can belong to Christ, that we can feed on Him, that we can share His life and light, and that we can mirror His beauty within our souls. In giving His glory to the Father in this spiritual and holy way we offer praise which is worthy of Heaven. We have praise which is 'powerful' enough to ascend within the furnace of love, in the glory of the Godhead: praise which cannot be swept away but which must always reach the Father's heart. (Also T:2551)

The language of the Blessed.

If we rest in Christ, in loving silence, in a holy and joyful Communion, we can develop an increasing facility for wordless, spiritual and yet 'real' conversation with Him. We can grow used to conversing with Him in this way - in wordless yet real exchanges of information, with loving requests and mutual expressions of delight. Each thought or intention we make seems to leap 'from mind to mind'; and we receive a response from Christ, in the same manner. Truly, when we converse with Him in this way, we are using the language of the Blessed. (T:2552)

Simple holiness.

We should believe that holiness is something simple, which everyone can achieve, in Christ's friendship. It is possible for people with no great learning, and no extraordinary work - as well as for leaders and theologians. (T:2733)

Purified hearts.

No-one should doubt that Christ loves all of His children dearly; yet His especial delight, in what is rightly called a Holy Communion, is to be welcomed into contrite and purified hearts. (T:2748)

The Communion of Saints.

In receiving Christ in Holy Communion, we are united with Him, and with one another, and also with every other Church member of earth, Heaven and Purgatory, which is to say, with all who belong to the glorious Communion of Saints. (T:2782)

'Whole and entire'.

Christ wants us all to know that it's through the Holy Eucharist that we can be changed most profoundly. He is love incarnate, which means love, embodied; and He is Present "whole and entire" in the Blessed Sacrament, as the Catechism says: His Body and Blood and Soul and Divinity. Everyone who receives the Blessed Sacrament and who therefore receives Christ is receiving love; and so it's plain that the more thoroughly we empty our souls of sin and selfishness, the more 'room' there is in our souls, we can say, for Divine love.

We should never forget that sanctity consists of a soul being full of charity - which brings joy to that radiant soul and also to the people who benefit from such overflowing love. (T:3119)

Holiness, radiating outwards.

We must never forget that Christ wants us to remain close to Him, through further Holy Communions, and further visits to the church. His holiness radiates from the tabernacle and the monstrance - from His sacramental Presence - just as surely as when radiation and heat flow out from a powerful source. (T:3172)

The privileges of Heaven.

For some of us, there is a huge 'overlap' between earthly life and Heavenly life, as we enjoy some of the delights and privileges of Heaven even before we arrive there, almost as though we're living in a new 'country' when we haven't yet left the old one.

Every child of God is invited to have a time of 'overlap' - through receiving Christ in Holy Communion. Christ is our foretaste of Heaven's banquet and Heaven's joy; yet how few of us make fervent preparations to receive worthily and devoutly. Christ sees how few of us permit Him to act within our lives to purify us. Few of us, through penance and patience, allow Christ to prepare us for a way of union with Him which can be enjoyed even in this life: a way which brings incomparable joy. (T:3780)

Christ's love for us.

Christ comes to us in love, in Holy Communion, not primarily to change us for the better, but to demonstrate His love for us - though He changes us as well, if we open our hearts in glad welcome. (T:3960)

A marvellous plan.

We must thank and praise God at Mass for His kindness, and for His marvellous plan. How infinitely wise and loving He is: to have arranged to share His Divine life with us, His adopted children, in everyday life, through what appears to be ordinary food, through the Holy Eucharist.

Who but God could have devised such a marvel: that, in eating, we receive God Himself into our very selves, with all His gifts and graces and power, for our transformation? (T:4465)

Perfect praise.

Since God is so great, and we are so frail, it's plain that we really need the Divine power and life of Christ if our poor human prayers are to 'reach' the heart of Heaven as fitting praise and thanksgiving: hence the glory and wonder of the Mass.

The Mass is our means of salvation, as the Paschal Work is re-presented before us; yet it's also our means of offering perfect praise and thanksgiving to the Father, and confident petitions, as we pray in, with and through our Divine Redeemer. Truly, Christ is God-made-man; but, though man, He is still powerful and all-holy. (Also T:4465)

Offering our Communion.

We can give tremendous help to other souls if we 'offer our Communion' for such people in need. We can't see exactly how they are helped; but we can be sure that Christ pours out extra graces upon these people because of His goodness and our generous and trusting act. (T:4810)

Glad to give a blessing.

Christ looks on with delight whenever one of His priests explains clearly to the assembled people that he, the priest, is glad to give a blessing to all those who cannot receive Christ in Holy Communion. (P.U.T:9)

Driving out the Spirit.

It's important that we consider the state of our souls, before we decide to receive Holy Communion. Everyone who is in a state of grace is holy, to some degree, even with many faults. The Holy Spirit, living within us, makes us holy. He is the Spirit of holiness. Yet if we have driven out the Spirit by serious sin we are not holy; though Christ asks us to consider only our own state, and not to judge other people's souls. (T:4874)

Like a shining sun.

If we want to be more like Christ, and to have more love for other people, we can rely on Christ to change us: or, rather, to come to our souls. By His Presence, He can be the very love that we want to show out and give to others.

'God is love', said Saint John, and so each of us can say: "Love is mine! The love I desire to have and to share is truly mine, through my Holy Communion. In receiving Christ, I receive Him Who is love. Love Himself fills my soul like a great, shining sun; and it is mine to give away. It is an unending source of love. I need only show it, live it, and place no obstacles before me that would prevent its 'rays' from falling upon everyone I meet." (T:4949)

Waiting in patience.

We can be sure, if our thoughts are whirling around when we had hoped to be at peace with Christ in Holy Communion, that it's as if He sits very close to us, waiting patiently for us to turn to Him. He doesn't mind our day-dreams, because He understands how weak we are; and He knows that when we have spent especially-busy times in His service, just before Mass, it takes some time for us to regain our usual degree of recollection. (T:5008)

A Divine Person.

Christ wants us all to realise that He is truly the Son of God: a Divine Person Whom we are receiving in sacramental form. He is the Divine Person Who once entered Mary's womb, to take flesh and become man for our sakes. So we should ask ourselves: are we ready, like Mary, to accept the Presence of the all-holy Word? Have we made a worthy preparation for each Holy Communion? (T:5077)

A personal visit.

Truly, this is the reality and joy of Holy Communion, if we are friends of Christ: that in receiving the Sacred Host we receive Jesus Christ. In receiving Him in this manner we have a personal 'visit' from our dear Saviour, just as when He spent time with His Apostles, seated with them, to enjoy their company - and to give joy, and sometimes instruction. (T:5103)

CHRIST'S LIFE

Touching Christ's life.

Our whole attitude to the Mass can flourish further if we know that we can 'touch' Christ, through His Real Presence, in every incident of His earthly life. Whenever we are with Him Who is Really Present in the Blessed Sacrament, we are present to Him as He is, now that He is glorified. But we are present also to the whole of His earthly life which - because He is God as well as man - is forever 'contained' in Him. Through our being present to His entire life we are present to Him even as He offers His sacrifice on Calvary.

The significance of this - for example - is that when we say to Him: "Thank you for dying for me," we can know that we are thanking Him during His dying! Similarly, whenever we are present to Him, here, on His feast-days - for example on the feasts of His Nativity, Baptism or Resurrection - we can 'touch' His life in each Mystery, and therefore we can receive the graces which arose from a particular incident in His earthly life. Thus we are enabled - bit by bit, as the Church's year unfolds - to thank Him for the whole of His life on earth! (T:1641)

The Mysteries of Christ's life.

Our contact with Christ in these Holy Mysteries provides an astonishing opportunity for us to be touched and influenced not just by His Death and Resurrection, but by all of the Mysteries of His earthly life. The Mass should be seen as the normal means by which we can 'touch' every event of His earthly existence, and can therefore 'touch' Him at each past moment of His joys or His sufferings.

The reason why this is possible is because when we meet Christ, we meet the Person Who is not only human but also Divine; and so we can reach 'through' Him - so to speak - to touch other ages, places and people, since everything and everyone who exists is held within His Being. (T:1668)

The act which redeems us.

Our spiritual life can benefit to a huge extent if we realise that whenever we meet Christ in the Holy Sacrifice of the Mass, whenever we see Him in the Blessed Sacrament, and whenever we meet Him in Holy Communion, we touch a Divine Person Who once led an earthly life. We touch, therefore - 'through' and 'in' Him - His entire earthly existence.

Here before the altar we touch the Holy Child Who was born of Mary. We touch Him as He speaks at the Last Supper. We touch the Christ of Calvary and the Cross as He offers His life to the Father. We touch the Victim Whose sacrifice of total self-giving and obedience is the act which redeems us. We touch the Person Whose once-for-all sacrifice - because of His Real Presence and because of the words and actions of His priest - is re-presented here, today.

It is supremely important that we take part in the Mass. It is the 'intersection' where we can be present to Christ's Passion and Death. It is the place, the time - the very moment - at which we can be present to the very act which saves us from eternal damnation. (Also T:1668)

At the intersection.

Each of us would benefit if we attended Mass more frequently, and prayed more fervently. None of us can fail to benefit from sincere participation. It's true that the Father holds in existence everyone and everything which He has created, and that no-one lies outside His care. It's true that anyone who prays to Him in Christ's name enters a special relationship with Him, through the power of the Spirit. Nevertheless, it is only through the Holy Sacrifice of the Mass that we can fully 'enter' Christ's life.

It is true that those of Christ's friends who visit the church in order to adore Him at the tabernacle, outside the time of Mass, are very close to Him; and He delights in their love. It is true that the sick who are unable to be present at the Holy Sacrifice can nevertheless be united to Him in Holy Communion, and can be wonderfully changed and helped. We who attend and take part, however, are especially privileged, and should be especially joyful, since the Mass is the 'intersection' between our human life and Christ's Divine existence.

Whenever we pray before Christ and unite ourselves heart and soul to His Holy Sacrifice, as it is offered through our priest to the Father, we 'touch' and offer Christ's sacrifice of Calvary. (Also T:1668)

An astonishing privilege.

As our understanding of the Mass increases, we can see what an astonishing privilege is ours: that we can be near Christ as He prays to the Father on our behalf! By our presence here, and by our sincere prayers, the sacrifice of Calvary - the one, perfect sacrifice - is re-presented on our altar, and is made fruitful in our lives. We can make our own all of the prayers which Christ prayed on the Cross. We can offer to the Father Christ's one, redeeming sacrifice through which sins are forgiven. We can offer to the Father - through Christ's total and obedient self-offering - perfect praise and thanks. And we can be sure that our own prayers and intercessions are heard, as we unite our personal concerns with the great plea which Christ makes to the Father on behalf of Mankind, as His sacrifice is offered from the altar.

We need to recognise what's at the heart of this mystery, as we ponder the Holy Sacrifice. It is only because of Christ's Real Presence amongst us, during the Mass, that we can place ourselves at the 'intersection' of His life and ours. It is through the Mass that He provides something like a 'doorway' for our salvation. He provides a 'place' so that we can be present, 'in' Him, to every event of His life, even to the Passion through which He redeemed us! (Also T:1668)

Very close to Christ.

We should be ever-grateful for the privilege which is ours through our membership of the Church and our participation in the Sacred Mysteries. It is a cause for gratitude that at every Mass, when Christ is Present before us after the Consecration, He enables us to touch - to be present to - His entire earthly life. It is a life which is still 'in' Him now, since He is 'eternal God'; and all that He possesses never changes. Whenever we are present with Him during the Holy Sacrifice we are present also to His entire life, which 'includes' His Resurrection and Ascension. (T:1757)

In wisdom and humility.

Christ wants us to realise how important it is that we are faithful to prayer throughout our lives, and that we frequently reflect upon the Mysteries of our faith. Then, as the years pass by, we can look forward to the gradual removal of the 'barriers' of heart and mind which hinder our understanding.

It's important for us to be involved in earthly life to the degree appropriate for our individual vocations. Yet the less we are busily preoccupied with earthly joy and fulfilment, the swifter will be our growth in wisdom and humility. Through moving closer to Heaven, we can see and understand more about Christ's life and Mysteries; and when we die, we will be enabled to see and understand, all-at-once, the whole of His earthly life. (Also T:1767)

A SPIRITUAL COMMUNION

Wholly reconciled.

Though we are sometimes unable to receive the Blessed Sacrament because of unavoidable duties towards a sick relation, or because of illness, we can make a Spiritual Communion. By expressing sorrow for our sins, then inviting Christ to enter our hearts, it's as if we move closer to Him. He delights in being welcomed by a loving heart.

It's true that Christ loves everyone; yet He finds a special delight in greeting those who are wholly Reconciled with Him through His Church. (T:752)

THE BLESSING

Another Christ.

We should be grateful for the priest whom Christ has given to us as our 'Christ' and shepherd and teacher. The priest acts for Christ; and we can be sure that whenever the priest makes the Sign of the Cross at the end of the Mass, and calls upon God to bless us, Christ our High Priest also makes that sign above us and gives us His blessing. (T:1166)

A Divine embrace.

We should remember that it's as if our souls are embraced by the Most Holy Trinity, as the priest blesses us in the name of the

Three Divine Persons.

When the priest blesses us "in the Name of the Father, and of the Son, and of the Holy Spirit", we can be sure that the Father is pouring His Heavenly light upon us, through the priest. At the same time, the Divine Son accompanies our souls in the sweet friendship of a real communion, and the Holy Spirit is teaching, uplifting and comforting our hearts. (T:1259) *(See illustration 36)*

The Father's blessing.

We should value every part of the Mass. From the heart of His three-fold glory in the height of Heaven, God the Father Himself blesses us through our Bishop who is our father-in-God - or through our priest. The blessing is lavished upon all who are present; yet we who believe in, welcome and accept this blessing are marvellously rewarded as God enfolds us in His grace and peace. (T:2507)

Showered with gifts.

When the priest blesses us in the name of the Father and of the Son and of the Holy Spirit, he draws down upon us spiritual gifts and delights beyond compare - whether or not we experience those gifts of God.

At every blessing, the Lord showers us with gifts and graces; and those who are familiar with His gifts feel their hearts being suffused with peace and sweetness, and with Heavenly joy.

The Lord's wish is that all the Clergy be aware of what powerful gifts they give whenever they bless anyone in Jesus' name. They are doing far more than offering a pious and comforting gesture. (T:5002)

OUR THANKSGIVING

In silent adoration.

Whenever we remain in church, at the end of Mass, we can take heart from thinking of the holy companions who surround us as we pray. In this darkened, almost empty church, many holy Angels stand motionless - like tall, gleaming spears of light - facing the tabernacle, in silent adoration (T:1580)

Guarded by His holy Angels.

We should treasure Christ's presence within our souls, especially His Real Presence in Holy Communion. He even guards us who 'guard' Him. As we remain in church, praying quietly, when the Mass has ended, His holy Angels are guarding us, and at the same time they are honouring His glorious and holy Presence within our souls. (T:1665)

Holding court amongst the holy Angels.

We shouldn't imagine that we are alone, except for Christ's Presence, when we stay behind for a while after Mass, and pray to Him before the tabernacle. Christ Who is Present here in the Blessed Sacrament is not 'alone' in a darkened and apparently empty church. No! He's holding court amongst His holy Angels.

Just as a great King holds court and celebrates good news as He is seated on a throne before His friends and courtiers, so Christ, Who is King of Heaven, holds court amongst people who love Him. In the radiant light of His glory, He's joyful and generous. Although, to earthly eyes, the church appears sombre and silent, Christ is here in Heavenly beauty and magnificence, sharing His

19. HEART-FELT PETITIONS AND INTERCESSIONS.

At every Mass we pray with and for the whole Church. Yet we bring to God in fervent prayer every hope of our hearts, each person we care for, and each problem and project which concerns us. OIL-M:532. *("... there should be prayers offered for everyone - petitions, intercessions and thanksgiving - and especially for kings and others in authority, so that we may be able to live religious and reverent lives in peace and quiet." 1 Tm 2:1-2).*

20. TAKING GIFTS TO THE ALTAR.

We not only offer bread and wine to God, for the Holy Sacrifice, we offer ourselves as well: our joys, our works, our sufferings and our prayers, our whole lives, as a thank-offering to God. OIL-L:Mass No. 6. *("Think of God's mercy, my brothers, and worship him, I beg you, in a way that is worthy of thinking beings, by offering your living bodies as a holy sacrifice, truly pleasing to God." Rm 12:1).*

21. COME, HOLY SPIRIT.

After the preparation of the gifts, the priest prays on behalf of the whole Church. He asks the Holy Spirit to come down upon the gifts and to change them into the Body and Blood of Christ. We know that the Holy Spirit will do this by His Divine power. OIL-L:157A. *("I have come to bring fire to the earth, and how I wish it were blazing already." Lk 12:49).*

22. PRESENT TO CHRIST'S ENTIRE LIFE.

We can be certain, when the bread is consecrated, that it is changed into the Sacred Body of Christ. He is Present with us in His Body and His Blood, His Soul and His Divinity. He is with us whole and entire; and we are present to His entire life. OIL-M:1330. *("and this will was for us to be made holy by the offering of his body made once and for all by Jesus Christ." Heb 10:10).*

23. CHRIST'S LIFE-BLOOD, OUR SPIRITUAL DRINK.

On the Cross, nearly two thousand years ago, Christ poured out His life-blood for our sakes. And when we receive His Sacred Body and Blood in the Holy Eucharist, we receive Him as our spiritual food and drink. OIL-M:753. *(" ... the blood of Christ, who offered himself as the perfect sacrifice to God through the eternal Spirit, can purify our inner self from dead actions so that we do our service to the living God." Heb 9:14).*

24. AT THE FOOT OF THE CROSS.

The Church teaches us that at every Mass it's as though we stand at the foot of the Cross with Mary, as we unite ourselves with Christ's sacrificial prayer. OIL-M:1271. *("We have been sanctified through the offering of the body of Jesus Christ once for all." Heb 10:10).*

joy with us, because we are His friends, and with the holy Angels who are His courtiers! (T:1890)

In triumph and glory.

What an example of friendship Christ sets us, in that He doesn't overpower us with His glory. For the benefit of each one of us, He comes to our souls in gentleness and peace, in Holy Communion. He allows Himself to be pictured, most often, as the gentle friend and loving Saviour - poorly clad, and barefoot - Who wishes to share our lives. Yet we can believe of Him, at the same time, that He's living in Heaven now in triumph and glory, surrounded by the Saints and holy Angels who are delighted to serve Him. (Also T:1890)

Our silent attention.

Whenever we remain before God in prayer, we can put aside our thoughts about special needs and past problems, and offer our silent attention as a gift, in praise of God's glory. We honour Him by our silent attention. We are doing what the Angels do. God is honoured by the gift of our time, and by our firm faith, and by our longing to give Him glory, even if some people look upon prayer as a fruitless occupation. (T:1899)

AT THE END OF MASS

The path of obedience.

We please Christ by our determination to continue on the path of obedience to His Will until our life's end: for our good, and for the good of the Church, and for the Father's glory. Our life must be a continual sacrifice of praise, as we sacrifice our own ambitions so that God's Will may be done on earth. (T:88)

Sinful people.

We need to remember that God's forgiveness of our sin is total. Indeed, His love for us is so great that He not only pardons and heals sinful people like ourselves. He even permits us to go out into the world to bring His grace to other people. (T:92)

Christ in our hearts.

It's good to revere Christ in our hearts all day long, no matter how frequently or infrequently we receive Him sacramentally. (T:157B)

Turning away.

All who take part in the Mass can ask themselves: "Am I changed by Christ's sacrifice? Do I realise what He has done for me? In the next few days will I remember what Christ has endured for my sake, and remember that He's alive and very close to me, or will I keep turning away from Him?" (T:229)

Reminding our children.

Parents have a duty, at the end of Mass, to remind their lively children that the Church is still a sacred place even when the Mass has ended, and that other people are still praying. The Lord deserves to see us all reverent and prayerful, and our neighbours deserve their much-needed peace and quiet, before going out into the world. (P.U.T:10)

Day and night.

If we treasure the Mass, we needn't be sad when we leave the church when the Mass has ended. We needn't regret not being present at Mass at every moment of the day! We can comfort ourselves with the knowledge that when the Holy Sacrifice has been offered, Christ's offering to the Father, in the Spirit, is eternal.

We should be aware of our marvellous role, as God's children. We are people who pray 'in Christ.' We who are close to Christ can re-join His offering at every moment we choose, wherever we unite ourselves with it, in spirit. Through Christ, our prayer rises to the Father continually. Day and night, somewhere in the world, the Holy Sacrifice is being offered; so neither space nor time can hold us back from real union with Christ's perpetual offering of Himself. (T:230A)

Christ's comfort and joy.

It's a wonderful moment, when we begin to realise how privileged we are. We are weak, sinful people; yet through our union with Christ, we can bring other people His comfort and joy, from within our own words, conversations and actions. (T:231)

Pains and humiliations.

It's important that, with God's help, we try to live in thankfulness and peace, and try to avoid ingratitude and gloom. The choice is ours: we can grumble impatiently about our sufferings, or we can accept them in patience. If we offer to the Father, with Christ, all our pains and humiliations - at any time of day or night - we unite ourselves with the glorious offering which is continually made to the Father from altars throughout the world. (T:384)

In a suitable manner.

When we go out into the world, after Mass, we mustn't forget that we can bring truth and comfort to other people by offering them the truths of the Faith, at appropriate times and in a suitable manner. (T:431)

Reparation for our sins.

We must remember that God is constantly at work in our lives, and that we can co-operate with Him not just at Mass, but all day, every day. After the Mass has finished, and at any time of day, we can offer Christ's sacrifice as reparation for our sins; and we can also offer praise to the Father through Christ, for everything that is good. (T:981)

Inevitable set-backs.

We mustn't be made despondent by setbacks. Each day that we spend in serving Christ and also suffering for love of Christ, in obedience to His Will, means that each of us can be a living sacrifice on this earth, united with Christ's eternal sacrifice. No matter what our circumstances, we can draw grace upon other people and give glory to the Father. (T:1000)

A bonfire of love.

We ought to leave our church after Mass with hearts full of faith so that Christ can act through us. He has placed a 'bonfire' of love in our hearts, in Holy Communion; and that love, and His blessing, can pour upon other people through our prayers, kind acts and conversations. (T:1015)

A channel of grace.

We should leave our church, after the Holy Sacrifice, determined to love Christ, and to love our neighbour. And we must remember that pride has no place in the heart which would channel the grace of Christ to other people. A 'channel' ought to be as smooth as glass, so that nothing 'snags' on rough patches, and no wilful obstruction impedes the flow. These 'rough patches' are the faults which hinder good communication such as tactlessness, impatience, over-sensitivity, timidity and self-satisfaction. (T:1218)

Day after day.

Christ wants us to realise that He is powerfully at work in His

Church to help, comfort and sustain us, day after day. It's as if He sends us out into daily life 'fuelled' by the love and the strength which we have received from Him in the sacraments. And we have many other sources of strength and consolation in the sacramentals and blessings, and customs and devotions which we find within the Church - so many of which we take for granted.

By our reverent use of sacraments and sacramentals we receive a marvellous increase of grace in our souls. Likewise, we grow in grace whenever we praise God, help a neighbour, curb a selfish instinct, repent of our sins, visit a shrine, pray for a departed soul, defend the Catholic Faith, speak with gratitude about Christ and His Church, or assist our priests, who are 'other Christs' amongst us. There is no limit to the ways in which we can please God and open our hearts to His graces; yet He has chosen certain ways by which we can be especially confident of receiving His help. (T:1259A) G.H.T.

In every area of life.

We cannot 'bring' Christ to others, when we go out 'into the world' after Mass, if we are uncharitable and therefore 'un-Christian'. It's important that our behaviour towards others is perpetually kind, thoughtful, patient and charitable, in every 'area' of life, whether at simple meals or at luxurious dinners, and whether we are amongst friends, acquaintances or strangers. If we sometimes fail in charity, we need only repent and begin again, relying not on our own power but on the grace of Christ.

Christ offers us privileged work as we meet other people in various walks of life. It's because we live in union with Him that He sends us out to love and help others in places where He 'cannot' go at present. His grace can penetrate everywhere, but His bodily and visibly-human presence, which is now established in Heaven, can usually only be seen or touched in this world wherever one of His friends can be seen and touched. He wants to see us conveying His joy and comfort, His smile, His graces and His wisdom to other people, as we go 'bodily' to meet them. We go to them in the normal course of events, and according to the state of the world or the various limits which are placed upon our contact with others. And since we are representing Christ, we have one more reason to ensure that we always speak and act with truth, purity and simplicity. (T:1284)

Each moment of the day.

In thinking of how much we long to glorify the Father, we must remember that we aren't limited to the daily offering at the altar. We can make the same prayer at each moment of the day, as we live 'in Christ,' and keep our hearts turned towards the Father in Heaven.

We cannot always be near the altar where the Holy Sacrifice is offered; so it will help us to remember that Christ's intention is always the same; and He pleads before the Father eternally, in Heaven. Since we and Christ are now one in love, by our union with Christ, from Baptism, Christ's prayer most certainly can be ours. We can offer it to the Father in its fullness and Divine power at every moment of our lives, by a little movement of our hearts. (T:1384)

Into full communion.

We must persevere in our efforts to bring other people into full communion with the Catholic Church. We should be more confident! Truly, we draw people towards Christ and towards the Catholic Church by our prayers, and also by our acts of loving-kindness. (T:1566)

The Way of the Saints.

When we go out 'into the world', after Mass, we mustn't forget that we all have a part to play in the Church's mission. We have a duty to help others to understand that Christ leads His friends most surely towards Himself through the Catholic Church. In being admitted to this great assembly we know that we have a place at the heart of Christ's own People who know the sure way to Heaven, the way which sprang from the Saviour and His Apostles, the way long-followed by the Saints. This way is like a fast-flowing river which leads towards the ocean of Christ's love, in Eternity. (T:1615)

Love-in-action.

If we think how faithfully Christ comes to be amongst us, at Mass, we'll see that He gives us a living demonstration of love-in-action, since He's always the same. The depth of His love for us doesn't change according to the circumstances. Even if our church building is damaged or neglected - or our hearts and minds are scarcely reverent or prayerful - Christ is here, bright and joyful, at the Consecration. That's the sort of reliable, loving attitude which Christ wants us to show towards everyone, when we've left the church building to go back to our everyday duties. (T:1673)

Reliable and constant.

If we think about the way in which Christ comes to the altar, at every Consecration, we can realise that He sometimes encounters muted greetings, careless celebrations, lack of interest or even disbelief. Very few of us, in our loving acts and attitudes, during and after Mass, are always fervent, reliable, constant, and grateful for the least evidence of goodness. Very few of us are willing to fulfil our duties at all costs, or to remain undisturbed when we receive little appreciation or thanks. Christ wants us to ask ourselves if we are genuinely striving to be as loving as He is. (Also T:1673)

In perpetual self-offering.

Our spiritual life doesn't end when we leave the church building, after Mass. If we treasure our close union with Christ during the

Holy Mass, we'll realise that the greatest joy in earthly life, and a great blessing, is to be able to remain in that spiritual state - close to Christ, all day long, and every day. To live like this is to live in a state of true sanctity: united to Christ by perpetual self-offering and loving service. (T:1882)

Christ in the world.

We should try to retain some of the gifts we've received when we have given Christ a fitting welcome in Holy Communion. If we treasure the peace and purity He gives us we will consciously strive to remain joyful, serene, and full of charity. Each of us can strive to be a living monstrance wherever we go, as we love and serve our neighbour. (T:1993)

Fellow-Catholics.

We have a duty towards our fellow-Catholics, as well as towards other people, when we are busy after Mass in our everyday lives. As well as showing love for one another in practical ways, we should encourage one another to persevere in the Faith. We can do so by speaking truthfully to one another about good and evil, instead of carelessly keeping silent when a member of our Catholic 'family' is in spiritual danger.

Just as we can never be right to condone wrong-doing, so we ought never to condone wrong-believing. If a fellow-Catholic tells us about his desire to hold onto a belief which is contrary to the sure teaching of the Church - whether about God's nature, the after-life, or morals, for example - we have a duty to act. Wrong belief leads to wrong behaviour; and so we should help such a person, whether by our words or by our prayers.

None of us should listen with apathy to expressions of disbelief or wrong belief from a Catholic brother or sister. Someone who wants to believe in re-incarnation, for example, whilst imagining that he is a faithful Catholic, perhaps doesn't see that he is putting at risk his faith in God's plan for Mankind, the purpose of earthly life, the Resurrection of Jesus, and Judgement, and the Communion of Saints, for example. Unless he believes the truth that we have only one life on earth in which to serve God and our neighbour, he can have no firm grasp of all the interlinked doctrines of the Faith which show us Who God is and how we can best love and serve Him. (T:2351)

Throughout the day.

Our prayers need not end, at the end of Mass, as we leave the church with our hearts full of love and longing, and laden with numerous concerns. Since we are living 'in' Christ, we can unite ourselves at any moment with Christ's eternal offering: with Christ's perfect prayers.

We can be sure, throughout each day, that when our prayers are united in faith and love to Christ's prayers, they are 'carried' all the way to Heaven, and so are fruitful and effective. (T:2579)

To keep the Faith.

We should leave our church, at the end of Mass, with new courage to speak the truth about God's plans for our lives. It pleases God when we give encouragement and consolation to priests, and to other people. We do this whenever we urge them all to keep the Faith once delivered to the Apostles, to pluck up courage to follow where Christ leads, and to share the good news about His great love for us all, and about the forgiveness of sins. (T:2661)

To bring Christ to others.

At the end of Mass, we are sent out not to fulfil our own ambitions but to share Christ's life and peace and light and joy: to bring Him to other people. (T:2782)

A simple, loving intention.

We are one with Christ in prayer and self-offering wherever we unite ourselves to Him in the Mass: one with Him in His one, perpetual offering to the Father of His infinitely-great and holy love. Yet we can be one with Christ, also, in that very same offering, through a simple, loving intention, at any time of the night or day.

Christ's loving act is offered from all Eternity and has continued in Eternity since His Ascension to Heaven. His praise is ours to 'claim' and offer, at every moment of our lives. (T:3021)

An uncertain journey.

Fortified and encouraged by Christ in Holy Communion, we can leave the building, after Mass, determined to work and pray so that other people will seek full membership of the Church. It is possible for someone to achieve salvation who hasn't had an explicit knowledge of Christ our Saviour, or who has been kept from outward dedication to Christ because of a false image of Him, offered perhaps through a distorted culture. Yet God has provided sacraments for all of us, so that we can be transformed, and endure. For a person to walk towards truth and to persevere, without the sacraments, is to be on a risky and uncertain journey.

When we speak with charity, at opportune moments, to share the Good News about Christ and His Church, we are neither judging nor condemning our hearers. Rather, we are sharing our knowledge of the one way which can lead to peace-of-soul, and joy, and a sure hope of salvation. (T:3299)

On all the altars.

If we treasure Christ and the Mass so much that we are sorry when the Mass has ended, there is a prayer we can say, which many of us know, and which Christ is always pleased to hear us offer with sincerity. It includes all that is necessary for perpetual homage to the Father. We can say, at any time of day or night:- "Father: I offer You Jesus' Sacred Body and Precious Blood, present on all the altars of the world, for Your praise and glory, in thanksgiving for every benefit You've ever given me, in reparation for my sins, and begging You for help and salvation for myself, and for everyone in my heart." (T:3781)

With Calvary's offering in mind.

Whoever adores Christ in the Mass, and longs to serve Him and to work with Him, cannot do better than to remain in spirit beside the Cross all day - with Calvary's offering in mind. This is how we can grow ever closer to Christ, making with Him at each moment, one expression of praise to the Father, one cry of thanksgiving, one offering of reparation for sin - through everyday sufferings and trials patiently accepted - and one infinitely-worthy and confident plea for help and salvation.

If we are really united with Christ, which of us can fail to love as Christ loves or to pray as He prays? (Also T:3781)

Their eternal welfare.

As we go out into the world, we should be bold in sharing our Good News. The Lord would like all of us to know that to love people with true charity is far more than to act with merely human kindness, gentleness, selflessness and truthfulness, although these and other things are very important. To have true charity towards other people is to yearn for their eternal welfare, and therefore to be willing to do everything to bring that about: to speak, work, pray, do penance, and act with love so that they find true joy and fulfilment in God, and never lose Him.

The most effective teachers are those who know their subject and who also speak with conviction, from experience. We can speak from first-hand experience about weakness and failure. Yet as we grow close to Christ, we can also speak from experience about the immense and tender love with which the Lord looks upon each one of us, His precious children. (T:4534B)

AWAY FROM HOME

From the tabernacle.

We should look for Christ whenever we travel away from home. Whichever far-away Catholic church we enter - if it is still in use - Christ is Really Present there, in the Blessed Sacrament. From the tabernacle, He welcomes us, individually - with great joy and delight. Yet we must remember the life of grace within us. Christ lives within every 'soul-in-grace'; and so He is greeting us from within our souls, even while we're travelling. We don't leave Him behind! (T:73)

4. THE PARTICIPANTS.

THE WHOLE CHURCH

Gathered together.

We would be amazed if we could see the glory of our worship at Mass, the glory of those people who are gathered together in Heaven, and who worship with us - and the glory of God Himself Whom we honour in these Holy Mysteries. (T:42A) *(See illustration 48)*

By our intercessions.

Even in our frailty and sinfulness, we who are members of the Church can strengthen the Church. By our prayers for one another, the Church is made even stronger. By our intercessions, offered in the name of Christ, it's as if we spiritual brothers and sisters lift one another into the light of God. Divine 'light' on earth is increased by our deeper fellowship, and the 'circle' of love is stronger: one Body, growing stronger.

Through our prayers, we can strengthen fellow-members of the Church in the best way, which is by helping them to grow in faith and in love. (T:83)

From our midst.

If we are deeply aware of our sinfulness, it should comfort us to know that the whole of Heaven is united in prayer with us, at every Mass. Because of Christ's love, and the immense power of His prayer from our altar, the sinfulness of those of us who are present has no power to mar the perfection of His offering.

Christ is interceding for us, His brothers and sisters, as He offers the Holy Sacrifice from our midst. (T:107)

In exalted company.

We must remember the exalted company with whom we worship during the Mass. The Saints and holy Angels are very close to us. It's as if they are looking on with bated breath as we await Christ's marvellous Presence at the Consecration. (T:901)

All joys and blessings shared.

We should try to pray fervently, throughout the Mass. When we do so, other people benefit; and this is because joy is spread amongst Christ's whole 'family', in some measure, by every good act of each member, and by every blessing received from God by each member. All joys and blessings are shared, in a spiritual manner, within Christ's Body, the Church. (T:905)

The Church, like a bride.

We should recognise that we are members of a Holy People - Christ's Body. When we are present, mysteriously, to Christ's Resurrection and Ascension - at the moment of 'offering' of the Holy Sacrifice - Christ is with us. He stands amongst us, His Holy People. And as we prepare for the celebration, we who belong to Him resemble a beautiful bride who is clothed in white: beribboned and wondrous before her God; and Christ lifts His Holy People to the Father in great love and gladness. Like a bride who rejoices in her beloved, Christ's whole Church reaches out joyfully to the Father. (T:1001A)

Even here, today.

It's important to realise that we don't have to wait until Heaven to worship God with the Saints and the holy Angels. Truly, they pray with us at every liturgical celebration. (T:1059)

Our martyred ancestors.

Christ's urgent desire is that we remain faithful to Him, and to His Church. It's supremely important that we remain true to the Catholic Faith, first planted in this country many centuries ago. As Christ looks lovingly upon us all, from Heaven, He sees that many members of the Church in England have turned away from the Catholic Faith which they had received from their martyred ancestors. Some Catholics today neither know nor care that by their faithlessness they are blithely endangering their souls. (T:1087)

An enormous procession.

We should love the Church. This means that we should cherish our brothers and sisters in Christ, whether Clergy or laity, faithful people or apparently faithless. We should be thankful that we are one family: children of God. Or to use different images - members of the great army of believers: and members of Christ's Body.

Christ wants us to realise how privileged we are to be members of the Church, as it wends its way towards Heaven, its praises streaming to the Father and to Christ with a light and a glory unseen elsewhere. Seen from Heaven, the Church is like an enormous procession of bright people which is surging across a vast, dark wilderness of unbelief. The Church holds close together, within herself, thousands upon thousands of people who are just as fortunate as ourselves to have heard and responded to the Good News about God's love, and the forgiveness of sins. (T:1229)

The Communion of Saints.

We can be confident that our prayers, and our 'offering' of our Holy Communion, will benefit other people. It's as if the Saviour Whom we meet in Holy Communion builds bridges between His friends so that we can bring spiritual help to one another. Because we are united to Christ in Holy Communion we are therefore united with everyone else who is united to Him in Holy Communion. We have a special, spiritual kinship. We can take as the literal truth the word which is used to describe Christ's Church: 'The Communion' of Saints. (T:1614)

Spiritual brothers and sisters.

The 'communion' which exists between Christ's friends is not a pious hope, but a reality. By the gift of Divine life to us in Holy Communion, Christ joins together all the faithful people who have received His Sacred Body and Blood.

It's just as though He is pouring His light from Heaven down towards the earth - pouring that light down to each individual faithful soul through a separate little channel. These 'channels' represent each soul's renewed intimacy with Christ in Holy Communion. Yet it's as though each 'channel' has a little doorway in the side, through which that soul can glance towards all the other people who are receiving Christ's light and Presence; and these people can all communicate with one another - spiritually - even though they might be far apart on earth. Only through the 'channel' which is each one's communion with Christ does each one have a 'doorway' through which he can reach out in prayer to touch the souls of his spiritual brothers and sisters. (Also T:1614)

Transcending natural boundaries.

We should learn to treasure the real, spiritual kinship which exists between faithful Christians. Because of our sacramental union with Christ, we are really 'in communion' with one another. This kinship can exist and endure even when we are half a world apart, or when we can neither see nor correspond with one another, or when we differ in age, temperament or state of health, or differ in gender, race, height, intellect, education or language! This knowledge will remind us to look upon the Church as if with Christ's eyes, to see that the 'Communion of Saints' is something marvellous which transcends every natural boundary. (Also T:1614)

In contact with one another.

We can act upon the knowledge that we are united in a marvellous way with other people who are 'in communion'. If we are full of Divine life - received in Holy Communion - we can meet one another in a spiritual yet powerful way, within our life 'in' Jesus our Saviour. By an act of the will, we can reach out spiritually, to touch one another in a moment of prayer. In this way, our hearts' normal human yearnings can be fulfilled. Our desire for contact with the people we cherish can be fulfilled. Such desires can be channelled through Christ.

Christ is 'the way' by which we can stay in contact with one another. Nothing can separate us from those with whom we are spiritually 'in communion' through Him, even when we can rarely speak to them, or even when we appear to be separated when one of us dies. So we should value our spiritual friendships. (Also T:1614)

Indestructible friendship.

The union which exists between one person and another in prayer - through Christ our Redeemer - is closer and more intimate than any friendship which is based solely upon natural gifts and feelings. True spiritual friendship and intimacy is superior to and even more 'real' than physical bonding; and it is indestructible. (Also T:1614)

The Spirit, by His almighty power.

If we ask the Holy Spirit to fill our hearts with His love, here, during the Mass, and to guide us in prayer, He will most certainly do so. He is powerfully at work to help us, both in the liturgical prayer of the Church, and in our hearts. All who unite themselves to Christ's offering, in the Holy Sacrifice of the Mass, are 'embraced' by the Spirit. It is He Who - by His almighty power - draws us all closer to one another, draws each one of us closer to Christ our Saviour, and draws us all nearer to Heaven. (T:1747)

The guests of a great King.

Those of us who are 'converts' should be ever-grateful for our privilege: that Christ has invited us to come into full communion with His Holy Catholic Church. We can think of ourselves as being 'the poor, the crippled and the lame' whom we have heard about in the Holy Scriptures. We were in need of help, and we accepted Christ's invitation to come closer to Him; and we are now the guests of a great King - Christ - at a Heavenly banquet.

We are like the guests whose presence was desired by the King in the parable, the King who wanted to fill the spaces at His table because those whom He had first invited had rejected His invitation. Christ our Saviour offers a feast to Mankind, through His Church; and yet how tragic it is that many people who are members of the Church no longer practise their Faith, and so reject His banquet.

We should never forget how delighted Christ is by the prayers of those who are grateful for His gifts. (T:1788)

Saints, gazing upon us.

We will be helped in our prayer if we understand the meaning of the 'Communion of Saints'. Our friends in Heaven are very close to us. When we call out to them for help, they hear us; and this is true whenever we pray the 'Litany of the Saints', for example, during an Ordination Mass. Dozens of our friends, the Saints, are standing around the sanctuary: but they are present high up, as if leaning over a balcony which runs round the interior of the church. They are all gazing down at the congregation below, and at the people who especially need their help.

The Saints have gathered to pray for us, just as we have requested; and each Saint who is named during the Litany leans forward to pray a fervent prayer. (T:2011)

Endless delight.

To be 'in communion' forever with Christ and His Church is to enjoy forever God's marvellous gifts, and to enjoy His company. Whoever shares in God's own life, in and through Christ, finds true peace, light, warmth, and sweetness. He finds consolation, security, and wisdom, with true fulfilment and endless delight. A further joy is the lived, known and felt bond of perfect friendship and loving communion with everyone else who has loved God and served Him faithfully until death. These people now await or enjoy the perpetual glory and holiness of Heaven. Everyone in Purgatory and Heaven remains 'in communion' with the loved ones they have left behind on earth and who also live 'in Christ'; and they can help one another by their prayers. (T:4310)

Far into Eternity.

Christ wants to remind us that not even death can separate people who are 'in communion' with one another through Him. This knowledge will bring special comfort to those who are dying and who, though longing to see their Lord, are saddened at leaving behind the friends and relations they know and love. They can be comforted to a greater extent, the greater becomes their faith in the invisible but real bond in which Christ holds His children together in one Body. This is a Body which is not confined to earth, but which reaches far into Eternity and which 'contains' as living members the people in Purgatory and Heaven. (Also T:4310)

Like a conference call.

If we are in communion with the Church, and therefore spiritually united with everyone else in the Church through Christ, we can be sure that our links with one another are even stronger than between people who make contact with one another by earthly means, in a conference call.

What human beings can marvellously bring about by technical means, God can bring about in a spiritual manner, though our communion in Christ is not usually 'felt'. It is real, and reliable, however, which is why we give help and encouragement to one another through prayer. And we strive to bring other people to join the Church, and so to be fully 'in communion' with ourselves as well as with God. (T:5019)

In good repair.

Christ wants us to see how important it is that we stay in communion with one another: that we keep the 'lines' open, and keep the transmitting equipment - which is the soul of each member - in good repair. None of us should risk being cut off from the Body of Christ as a whole, or from individuals, through an unforgiving attitude towards others, or through rebellion against God.

To refuse to forgive, or actively to do evil, is very damaging, spiritually. It's as if we sever all 'lines' of communication, and walk away from our friends, and from God Who is the only source of eternal joy. (Also T:5019)

THE SAINTS

Life in God.

We live by faith; and so we cannot yet see God, nor is it usual for us to see the Saints who live 'in' God, in glory. As members of the Church, however, we are in communion with everyone in the Church, which consists of our brothers and sisters in the Church on earth, and the Holy Souls of Purgatory who are being purified after death, and also the Saints in Heaven. So we can be sure that whenever we turn to God in prayer, we are turning to the Saints at the same time; and whenever we address one of our saintly friends in Heaven to ask for prayers, we are turning to God at the same time, since each Saint lives 'in' Him. (T:67) G.H.T.

United in prayer.

At every Mass we join in the eternal praise of God offered by the Saints and the holy Angels. The whole of Heaven is united in prayer with us all, in immeasurable joy. (T:107)

Very close to Heaven.

Through our union with Christ we are brought very close to the vast throng of Saints and holy Angels who worship the Father in Heaven. (T:140 and 156)

With joy and awe.

The Saints are our companions in our worship. We should imitate them, since they greet with joy and wonder Christ's awesome act of self-offering in the Mass. (T:248)

The glory of our worship.

As we pray at Mass, perhaps in drab surroundings, we can be sure that rank upon rank of Heavenly beings are praising God in glory; and the Saints gaze delightedly upon the radiant light which envelops us.

They can see the glory of our worship. It is glorious because it is offered by Christ's Church on earth, which is to say: by Christ the Head, and the Church His Body. (T:364)

The greatest Saint.

We should recognise the dignity and the goodness of the greatest Saint: the Mother of God. We honour Our Blessed Lady at every Mass, in and through Christ; and she, for her part, honours us by her prayers. She loves us all deeply. (T:812)

A simple cry of adoration.

We should believe that we are really in communion with the Saints of Heaven, in prayer, during the Mass. They too reached the Father through and 'in' Christ, and through Christ's merits. We live in a true communion with them all day long, and all year; yet through our union with them, in Christ, the praises which we offer to the Father are 'heard' as a single, united cry of adoration. (T:980)

Christ, thanking His friends.

We must hope for Heaven. We can draw encouragement, during our current struggles, from the knowledge that Christ Himself is thanking those of His friends who have persevered to the end. And we can be confident that this is so, because it happens in our presence, at the offering of the Holy Sacrifice.

Whenever the priest - in the prayer of the Church - utters words of praise to the Father for the lives of the Saints who are now in Heaven, we can be sure that he is speaking on Christ's behalf. Whenever the Holy Sacrifice is offered to the Father from the altar we can remember - particularly on Saints' feast-days or memorials - that Christ Himself, Who is Really Present, is not only praising the Father for His glory, He is also honouring His beloved Saints for their holiness! (T:1362A)

Christ's love for His Mother.

We should understand more clearly how fervently Christ Himself praises and thanks the Father for the lives and virtues of those who have imitated Him, and have done His Will, and have remained faithful until death. For example, we can consider the greatness of the reward which Christ's beloved Mother now receives, after her life of perfect self-giving. It is during the Holy Sacrifice that Christ stands at the altar giving glory to His Father, and also looking up at the Blessed Virgin Mary. He holds out his arms towards her. He is joyfully expressing His love and admiration for His Mother, before the whole company of Saints; and He is doing so in our presence.

Christ's supreme and unique homage and worship - during the Mass, as in Eternity - is directed to the Father in Heaven. But during our celebration Christ honours, in another way, His friends, the Saints: of whom the greatest is His own Mother. Before the whole court of Heaven Christ honours her, praises her, admires her, and thanks her; and she looks at Him with indescribable joy, silently accepting His loving offering. (T:1468A)

A living memorial.

We should be ever-grateful that we can be present at this true and living memorial of Christ's Passion, as His Sacrifice is re-presented before us. What a marvel it is, that we are present as Christ Himself prays amongst us, and prays for all His faithful people, living and departed (T:1470)

With the eyes of faith.

Whether we see three people at Mass, or thirty, or three hundred, we can be sure that thousands of Heavenly friends are taking part. If we look with eyes of faith towards the altar, it's as though the walls around the sanctuary soar upwards towards a brilliantly-lit region - like a plateau - from which Christ's radiant Saints gaze down upon Him as He stands before the altar.

From within our assembly Christ is united with the Father in Heaven. Here amongst us, His arms reaching out to Heaven, Christ looks upward to greet His brothers and sisters, the Saints, and to honour the Father, through the Spirit. He unites Heaven and earth in His praise, during these Holy Mysteries. We should rejoice and be grateful for these blessings. (T:1536)

The Saints' lives and virtues.

Christ wants us to understand the reason why the Saints of Heaven are all united with us and why we can be sure that they take part in every Eucharistic celebration which is conducted by His Church on earth - even though they are no longer 'held' in time.

We know that the Saints are now 'held' in God's Divine life. And we can understand, therefore, that since they live in God, they are living 'in' Christ our Saviour Who even now offers His praise to the Father from amongst us, during the Holy Sacrifice of the Mass. That is the very event through which we praise the Father, from upon earth, for the Saints' lives and virtues! So we are intimately connected with the Saints, through Christ, and through our union with Christ as we pray to our heavenly Father. (T:1870)

Christ's relations.

We should never forget that Christ is full of the most tender love for us; and that's why He wants us to picture how joyful He will be, if He sees us persevere in love, and join Him one day, in Heaven's glory.

Our Incarnate Saviour loves His relations. Just like us, He delights in being close to people who love Him. So He is thrilled both by our presence at Mass, and by His Saints' nearness to Him in Heaven. Furthermore, His heart thrills with joy whenever another of His close friends arrives in Heaven, after earthly struggles. Christ rejoices in His own, fulfilling friendship with each faithful and spiritually-fruitful man, woman and child. (T:2045)

Amongst the Saints.

We should ponder the significance of our place at Mass amongst the holy company of Heaven. If we wish to belong, after death, to the Communion of Saints in Heaven, we are wise to value during our earthly life our worship among the Saints, here, during the Holy Sacrifice of the Mass. (T:2539)

Shared joy.

The whole of Heaven delights to see us worship Christ in the Blessed Sacrament, honour Him for his Passion and Death, and sing "Alleluia" for His triumphant Resurrection. (T:2734)

Gathered together.

We should remember that thousands upon thousands of happy people in Heaven's glory are praising Christ with us. Truly, the whole Church is gathered for this celebration of the Holy Eucharist. All the Saints and Angels stand in wonder before the majesty of Christ: our incarnate God. (T:3216)

In their Heavenly beauty.

We should always remain aware of being members of God's

family. Everyone on earth who is truly 'in communion' with Christ and His Church through being 'alight' with the Holy Spirit, given in Baptism, is therefore 'in communion' with the Saints of Heaven and with the Holy Souls who are being purified. This is true even though we cannot yet see the Saints of Heaven and the Holy Souls. We know this through faith.

The glory of the Saints of Heaven is so great that it's as though, in their Heavenly beauty and transformation, they form a corona or brilliant setting for the dazzling 'jewel' of the Godhead; yet they are 'in communion' with weak, sinful people like ourselves. They live with Christ in glory, yet they are very close to us. They pray for us. They love to hear our prayers and to fulfil our confident requests. Most of all, they love to see us grow in charity: to see us love Christ and, for His sake, show love for our neighbour. (T:3768) G.H.T.

Real friendships.

Christ wants us to remember that, through the sure bond of charity and spiritual communion, we have a means of finding reliable and frequent help amongst earthly troubles. For example, if we ask the Saints for help, in private prayer, and honour them during the Mass, and celebrate the Saints' feast days, and even yearn to be with them in glory, we are nurturing real friendships between the Saints and ourselves. These friendships will be marvellously fulfilled when we reach Heaven. (Also T:3768) G.H.T.

Across a narrow chasm.

When we reach out to the Father in and through Christ, at Mass, we are brought into joyful communion with all who have died in Christ. It's as if those people who have already entered Heaven are here in front of us, just a few feet from the back of the sanctuary, across a narrow chasm which represents the division between earth and Heaven.

Those of our friends and relations who love us, and who share our faith, can be sure of being close to us at every Eucharist, when at last we have died 'in Christ', and when they reach out to the Father, in Whose fatherly care we shall then live. (T:5000)

THE BLESSED VIRGIN MARY

His Mother beside Him.

Christ our God reigns in majesty, triumphant in Heaven. After His sufferings on earth, He now reigns in glory - with the Father and the Holy Spirit - receiving praise and honour beyond our imaginings. Yet His Mother is beside Him, because He loves her dearly. His happiness would hardly be complete if she weren't close by.

Our 'picture' of Heaven is incomplete if we don't realise that Christ and His Mother Mary are together, in Heaven's bliss, for all Eternity, with the other Saints, and the holy Angels.

Christ wants us to know how vivacious His Mother is, in her joy and beauty. She is full of love and happiness, though she once wept and suffered so that God's Word might be revealed to the world. So Christ asks us to love her, and to thank her for giving Him to us through the Spirit's power. He asks us to be loyal to her, ever-grateful for her devotion and for her motherly concern. He asks us to defend her against those who, through ignorance not ill-will, think that they please Him by ignoring His dearest creature. (T:53)

The Saints, in glory.

During every Mass, we should be aware of our companions. Christ's holy Mother is with us; and the other Saints of Heaven are near by, as well, all radiant and tender. (T:559)

The great dignity of Our Lady.

Christ wants us all to know that He loves and honours His holy Mother. Her holiness surpasses that of all other 'mere creatures'.

Her glory in Heaven is dazzling: the glory with which Christ now rewards her for her self-giving love in earthly life.

God the Father once poured His Holy Spirit upon the Virgin Mary, at her consent, to make her fruitful. Thus did Christ take flesh from her, and enter our world. And God worked this marvel so that His grace would always pour out through Christ, and because of Our Lady. (T:735)

The Mother of God.

We are right to use the lovely title: "Mother of God", when we think about our Heavenly Mother, or ask for her prayers. Jesus Christ our Lord and God came from her, took flesh and blood from her, was subject to her and was taught by her. He alone is our Saviour. Yet she who formed Christ in His earthly life can help us now in every circumstance, through her prayers. (T:735)

Praise and gratitude.

Christ asks us to realise that our friendship with His beloved Mother is not an 'optional extra' for His followers. In His sight, no-one who really loves Him can fail to love His Mother Mary.

Someone who really loves Christ is full of praise of God for Mary's Motherhood, and is full of gratitude to her for her joyful consent to her holy task. On the other hand, someone who does not love Mary proves by that stance that he doesn't fully love Christ. If he did fully love Christ he would be grateful to Mary for giving us - by God's grace - so great a Redeemer. (T:741)

Sharing Christ's insight.

Now that Our Blessed Lady is in Heaven with Christ, she shares to an extraordinary degree His insight into human life and hearts. He wants us to know that her gaze is not limited to Heaven. She understands the hearts of all who try to serve Christ her son. And she sees the actions of all who oppose Him. (Also T:941)

Her astounding purity.

Compared with Our Blessed Lady, we who have been conceived in Original Sin are like people disfigured: wounded by sin. Her purity is astounding. (T:745)

The Mother of Jesus.

We should always be grateful to God for the life and virtues of Our Blessed Lady. The Holy Sacrifice we offer is a tremendous act of love, in which Christ is Present amongst us, reaching up to the Father in eternal intercession. Yet this sacrifice has been made possible because Mary consented to be the Mother of Jesus. (T:974)

A living tabernacle.

We should all remember that Christ treasures His Mother; and He is pleased to see us honour her during the Mass as well as at other times and places.

The Blessed Virgin Mary once cradled the infant Christ within her own body - as if she were a living tabernacle for His Sacred Body. Having been prepared by God the Father for such an exalted task, she has never become less holy, or less worthy of honour. (Also T:974)

Close to us.

Our Blessed Lady is very close to us during the Mass, when Heaven 'touches' earth. It's as though she stands at one side, in humility, even though it was through her that Christ the Word - the Divine Son, enfleshed of her flesh - came down to us. (T:977B)

Motherly encouragement.

We should believe that Christ is constantly at work to help us, and that Mary His Mother works with Him for our benefit and salvation. These are further reasons why we should take part in the Holy Sacrifice of the Mass with a fervent and willing heart.

As Christ stands before the Father, His arms outstretched, pleading for His brothers and sisters, and offering His own praise in all its glory, His holy Mother is 'involved'. It is as though - in her motherly way - she is trying to shepherd us forward, urging us to unite ourselves to Christ in His self-offering. It's as though she is encouraging us to join Him as He offers His sacrificial prayer to the Father, from our sanctuary. (T:1088A)

Quietly at one side.

We should imitate Our Blessed Lady's humility, at Mass, and everywhere we go. During the offering of the Holy Sacrifice, it's as if she stands quietly at one side as Christ stands 'centre-stage'; yet all worship which is offered to the Father through Christ has been made possible because of her! (T:1171)

A crucial role.

We should honour and thank Our Lady for her role in the work of Redemption. Mankind has benefited from Christ's sacrifice only because Mary, His holy Mother, consented to conceive Him, and thus played her tremendous part in the sacrificial offering which lay ahead. The co-operation of the Blessed Virgin Mary was essential for His Incarnation. In allowing Christ to take life from her flesh, she made possible His redeeming sacrifice of Cross and altar. (T:1191)

Our Lady's virtues.

Christ wants us to understand the way in which He honours His Mother, during the Holy Sacrifice of the Mass. Whenever the priest praises the Father - during the Liturgy - for Mary's virtues, and thanks the Father for her life and her role, that priest is praying in Christ's name at the altar, where Christ is Really Present. So we can be sure that at every Mass Christ Himself is praising the Father - in the very words which are used by our priest - for His holy Mother's virtues! (T:1468A)

Living and departed.

Consider how close Christ is to His beloved Mother, during the Holy Sacrifice of the Mass. He is here, in our sanctuary; and it's as though she sits at the edge of a cloud, above Him, at the 'edge' of Heaven. She is surrounded by many other faithful people who are now in Heaven; so we should remember that the whole Church is involved in this celebration. All faithful people, living and departed, are united with Christ in praise of the Father. (Also T:1468A)

Guarding the Lady-chapel.

Christ wants us all to know that He delights in seeing us pay honour to His Mother Mary, especially on her feast-days. And He likes to see us pause for prayer by the Lady-chapel where two holy Angels guard the chapel and keep watch in the church. (T:4326)

Christ and Our Lady.

There are three truths we should always keep in mind: first, Christ died for us; secondly, only through Him have we entered the 'light' of prayer and Divine grace; and, thirdly, only through Mary was this made possible, by God's Will and plan.

Whenever we approach God our Father, therefore, we should always acknowledge Christ as our Saviour and His Mother as our Theotokos: our 'God-bearer.' Christ and Our Lady cannot be set apart as if Mary is no longer important. She reigns with Christ in Heaven: a mere creature besides her God. Yet she is truly the Holy Mother of our Saviour the God-man. (T:4649)

Sound teaching.

Whoever believes in Christ, and learns the great truths of the Catholic Faith (about His Incarnation from the Blessed Virgin Mary, and about His acceptance of suffering and death for our sakes), will be more likely to grow in the knowledge and love of God than someone whose faith is not nourished by sound teaching. (Also T:4649)

THE FAITHFUL DEPARTED

Deliverance from Purification.

Because we are members of the Body of Christ, we can turn to Jesus Christ in the Mass, and reach out with confidence, through Him, to the Saints and the Holy Souls. Christ is the 'bridge' between earth and Heaven. Through Him alone can we pass into the holiness of Heaven, whether through prayer, as we reach out to the 'heart' of the Holy Trinity, where we can 'meet' and greet our friends who live in glory, or when we die, and see God face to face.

Christ is the 'bridge' over the Abyss which separates Mankind from the Godhead; and we have a sure hope of crossing that Abyss in safety only because we have found the safe way across, in the company of our brothers and sisters in the Church. (T:81) *(See illustration 45)*

"Through Christ our Lord".

It's because we all belong to Christ that we mustn't be anxious about faithful people who have died and who have gone to Christ. But we should still pray "through Christ our Lord" for their deliverance from purification. We should look upon Christ as the 'channel' through which our thoughts and words can 'flow' to the Faithful Departed, during the Mass and at other times, as we offer our prayers to the Father in the name of Christ.

It should comfort us to know that we cannot harm the Faithful Departed or make them despondent by our regrets, sad memories or resentments. So we can be sure that if we pray sincerely for their souls, only good thoughts and prayers can 'flow' through the Good Christ, when we pray in His name. (Also T:81)

The 'cloud of witnesses'.

We must be firm in our belief that we are not separated from the Faithful Departed. The 'cloud of witnesses' is here, at Mass, at our holy offering. All who have died in Christ are with Him, and are alive. We who are close to Him are close to them, and are welcomed by them at these Holy Mysteries. (T:121)

The veil between Heaven and earth.

We should always remember, with joy, that we are not far away from Christ. The 'veil' between Heaven and earth is very thin. Christ and His Saints, and the Faithful Departed, are very close to us. If we only whisper to them we are heard. (T:127)

The radiance of Christ.

We should continue to pray for departed souls and to rejoice that they are helped and consoled - through Christ's grace - not only by our prayerful words and intentions but also by the intimacy of our union with Christ at each moment of our day; for example, many people benefit whenever we make a fervent Communion.

It's as if Christ's Divine radiance, when pouring within our souls in Holy Communion, is pouring, also, upon the souls of the Faithful Departed whom He encounters in our hearts at that time. It's as if Christ is encountering them anew simply because - by prayer - we cherish them and show our desire for their eternal joy and fulfilment. (T:1211)

Purified, after death.

We should unite our prayers fervently with the prayers of the Church, for the Holy Souls in Purgatory: for faithful souls who are now being purified, after death. It's as if these Holy Souls are wholly immobile, as they await the fulfilment of God's Will. They are motionless, docile and obedient, after all the mental and physical activity of earthly life.

Some of them are very close to Heaven, and so they are very close to God's light; others however, though not estranged from God, are horribly unprepared to look upon His face. It's as if they are suspended in near-darkness. We can help these Holy Souls who, in their purification, are 'waiting' for complete union with God. They are in great need of our prayers. (T:1403)

The merits of Christ's Passion and Death.

We should have confidence in Christ's merits, as we pray with the whole Church, during the Mass, for the souls of the Faithful Departed. It's because of those prayers - united with Christ's prayer - that our friends can eventually emerge from the purifications of Purgatory. (T:1474)

Hidden from earthly eyes.

We must never imagine that our departed friends and relations who have died 'in Christ' no longer pray with us. We can bear in mind the many thousands of Holy Souls who adore Christ during the Holy Sacrifice of the Mass.

When Christ offers His Holy Sacrifice to the Father, through our priest, it's as though a veil parts, at the back of the sanctuary, a veil which usually hides things of the spirit from earthly eyes. And far beyond the space where we are worshipping, beyond the holy Angels who praise Christ within the church, are the thousands of Holy Souls who - just like ourselves - praise the Father through Christ our Mediator and High Priest. (T:1494)

United in prayer.

The Holy Souls in Purgatory who are undergoing a painful purification are nevertheless full of gratitude to God, Who has saved them from all dangers. They are full of light, since the grace of Christ is at work within them; and they are praying even now with the whole Church, which includes ourselves, as we pray during the Holy Mass. The whole Church - on earth, in Heaven, and in Purgatory - joins together to praise the Father through Christ, at the offering of the Holy Sacrifice. (Also T:1494)

No better prayer.

We should offer frequent and fervent prayers for departed souls; but we can't do anything better for them than to unite our prayers for them with the prayer which is offered at the altar. There can be no better prayer offered either for the Faithful Departed, or for the living, than the prayer which Christ prays to the Father as He offers His Holy Sacrifice through the ministry of the priest. (T:2037)

A 'Mass intention'.

Christ's prayer to the Father is never refused, since Christ is His Son; and that's why people who want to be sure that their prayers are granted will unite their intentions with Christ's. People whose beloved friend or relation has died and who long for that person to reach Heaven will arrange for the Holy Sacrifice to be offered for the purification and consolation of that person's soul. This is because it is during the Holy Sacrifice that our Redeemer and Mediator pleads for help and salvation on behalf of sinners: the living and the dead.

Christ is praying for us all. His prayers for His Body, the Church, are powerfully effective for all who unite themselves with Him as He's praying, and especially for everyone who is included in the priest's Mass intention as he stands at the altar. (Also T:2037)

The point of convergence.

We should be awed and grateful to realise that Christ, sacramentally Present, is the point of meeting or convergence where all those who live in Him are joined together. We who are present before the altar at the Consecration, or before the tabernacle, are united 'in Christ' with the Holy Souls of Purgatory, and with those members of the Church who are physically absent, through sickness or travel, yet who are also 'one spirit' with us, in Christ. (T:4488)

Christ, the 'intersection'.

We should have faith that we can 'reach' the Holy Souls through Christ, in the Mass. All who have died in Christ are now 'in' God eternally; and we who turn to God in prayer thereby turn to all who live in Him. We are in communion with them, in and through Christ, though we don't see or hear them.

The living Christ is the intersection where all who live in Him can meet: the living, the Holy Souls, and the Saints of Heaven. Yet it's at the Mass that we can all meet most marvellously.

When Christ our Risen Lord is amongst us as we celebrate His Resurrection it's as though we have found a 'window' through which we can gaze upon the beloved souls who have gone on ahead of us. Day after day, we can meet them in and through the Mass, as well as fostering our communion with them through our private prayer. (T:4512)

Life in Christ.

We must help everyone to believe what the Church has always taught, that all who live 'in Christ' are one, both in this life and after death. The 'Communion of Saints' is a reality; and even death cannot separate Christ's friends from one another. The whole Church - of Heaven, earth and Purgatory - is one and undivided even though, at Mass, we see only the earthly members of the Church. (T:4723)

Helping the Holy Souls.

We must help to boost the flagging faith of people in the Church - those who grow despondent at the thought of being parted from their friends and relations. We must encourage everyone to believe that all who love Christ are indeed 'one' in Christ. Weak and sinful people like ourselves can be 'one' in prayer with other people who offer Mass or attend Mass many miles away on earth. Indeed, God unites - 'in' Christ and in prayer, at every Eucharist - His people on earth and also those friends of Christ who have died and who now live in Him eternally, whether they are being purified in Purgatory or have entered the glory of Heaven.

If we believe this, and are comforted, reflecting on God's power and God's goodness, we should not just 'rest' in our faith, but use it. For example, we can reach out confidently to the Faithful

Departed at every Mass, through Christ. Through Him, we can speak to them, and ask for their prayers. We can offer Masses for the repose of their souls - and we can actively look forward to being re-united one day with the Holy Souls and the Saints. (T:4775)

A crowd of friends.

A great crowd of saintly friends is waiting to greet everyone who dies 'in Christ.' Yet we can already be in communion with them in our prayers - just as truly as people like ourselves on earth are in communion with one another, even with our imperfections. It's true that most of us, while living on earth, don't 'experience' that spiritual communion; but we can know it by faith, and 'live' it, and thank God for it.

Those Christians who never turn to speak to the Holy Souls or to the Saints are ignoring a large part of the Church to which they belong. (Also T:4775)

At every celebration.

We can be comforted by the certain knowledge that people who have died 'in Christ' and who, in dying, have been released from the constraints of time and space, can be united with their earthly friends and relations in and through the Holy Eucharist. Indeed, they can enjoy a real meeting with us at every celebration of the Holy Sacrifice of the Mass. (T:4728)

The bond of charity.

Members of the Church who are in a state of grace can meet most fully in Holy Communion, by which the bond of charity between us all is strengthened, in and through Christ. So it's plainly true - as the Lord wants us to believe - that it's at the Holy Eucharist that we can meet our beloved friends and relatives who have died in Christ. We can be confident that they know about our love for them, and about our prayers for their eternal joy. (T:4994)

THE CLERGY

A call to the Priesthood.

We should honour our priests, and encourage further vocations to the Sacred Priesthood. Christ is delighted when a man responds to His call to the Priesthood; and the whole company of Heaven is joyful, too. Indeed, Christ Himself - as if reaching from Heaven - honours every parent who 'gives' a son to be a priest. (T:1189)

A male-only Priesthood.

Christ asks us to respect His wish that the Church has a male-only Priesthood. He offers an assurance today, to those of us who are Catholic and to those outside the Catholic Church who criticise Catholic teaching: "My Church does not have women as priests. It is not My Will. It is not seemly. It is not necessary."

By these words, Christ commends the clear teaching of the Holy Father and the other Bishops. Yet He also shows His deep concern both for men and for women, since He asks that the work we do and the vocations we follow be appropriate for our gender.

We need to remember that Christ is our Sovereign. He doesn't have to explain or justify His wishes. Since the Catholic Church doesn't have women as priests, because it is not His Will, no further explanation is required. That should be sufficient reason. Yet because He is kind, and wants to increase our understanding, He wants us to realise that, in His sight, it is not appropriate for a woman to attempt to represent Him in that special task and office. It is unfitting for women, for a number of reasons. (T:1285)

Male headship.

Christ wants us to realise that it is not His Will that women exercise a true spiritual headship over men, in either Church or family life; therefore, women must not attempt to preside over the celebration of the Holy Mysteries. It is not His Will that women preach during the Sacred Liturgy, nor that they listen to the sinful thoughts of mens' hearts in private Confession. It is not His Will that women live and travel alone, in dangerous or threatening places, unnecessarily, in efforts to be Fathers to His flock. Christ wants us to understand that since it is not His Will that even women who are vowed religious should be priests, how much less is it His Will that wives and mothers be distracted, by conflicting duties, from their prime responsibility, which is the care of the needy members of their families.

Christ wants us to realise that it is not necessary that women attempt to represent Him through the Ministerial Priesthood, since women already represent and show Him to others in daily life, in many ways. Women who love Christ can be sure that although they cannot represent Christ in exactly the same way as deacon, priest or bishop, they 'show out' Christ through all their good actions. Both within the life of the Church, and elsewhere, they draw graces upon other people through their union with Christ in all their prayers, works, reflections, sufferings and joys. They draw down these graces whether their virtuous acts are evident to other people, or hidden. (Also T:1285)

'Icons of Christ' on earth.

We should treat every human being with tremendous love and respect, yet we owe a special reverence and courtesy towards those men who have been set apart as 'icons' of Christ on earth. This is true even if they seem to be weak and far from saintly. We should never speak carelessly or flippantly to priests about their work. Christ is saying to us all, of these men: "My priests are sacred;" and it's Christ's wish that, in all our dealings with them, we should avoid being careless, worldly or irreverent. (T:131⁷)

The glory due to sanctity.

We should honour every Catholic priest, for his Priesthood. We owe great honour to the glory in which Christ has clothed each one through Ordination. Christ gives to each new priest - as he is truly changed at his Ordination - the glory which is due to sanctity, although each new priest has still to make that sanctity his own. (T:1336B)

With tact, love and wisdom.

It's important that we recognise our different roles within the Church. To understand one aspect of the Priesthood, we can picture each priest in the following way. He sits alone besides a crowded road, as people make their way towards Heaven. And it's because of his 'solitude' in such a distinct and even elevated place that he is free from distractions, and is always ready to listen to those who approach him.

With Christ-like tact, love and wisdom - and by God's Will - each priest listens and judges. This is because Christ gives to him the task of dispensing Justice and Mercy. Christ asks us to picture each priest as having a special place within the Church, as if beside a busy road which represents the Way to Heaven. Thousands of weary pilgrims move forward together; yet here and there, one of them leaves the crowd to approach a priest; and Christ looks on with gladness, as His priests forgive sins, by His power, and listen to the secrets of wounded hearts, their own hearts burning, scorched by faith and grief. True servants of those they serve, those men sit apart, 'enthroned' to do their good work: a work both responsible and awesome. That is why, by God's Will, they have a special dignity and honour in the eyes of God's People. Yet they are elevated, too, for the sake of the people from afar who search for Christ's teachers, and who need to find them, to receive their help.

These priests are fulfilling Christ's wishes if they stay close to their people: if they await the humble ones who wish to be reconciled. Priests witness to Truth, yet leave people free, entirely: free to approach them, or to stay away. By their attitude, priests are proving how deep and sincere is their love for souls. (T:1554)

One to guard the altar.

Our priests have such a privileged role that the Lord has sent His holy Angels to assist them at the altar.

The Angels who serve Christ in the sanctuary are reverent and obedient, awesome and holy. Of the many majestic Angels who are present, one is here to guard the altar and one is here to guard the priest. The priest's own guardian Angel is tall and beautiful. He is as lovely as a shape in firelight because the golden light of Heaven is gleaming upon his head and wings. We are right to revere him, to trust in him, and to ask that he will help the priest. (T:1560)

When faithful priests enter Heaven.

Christ wants us to pray for priests: for those who serve us on earth, and also for those who have died, so that they will swiftly receive the rewards Christ longs to give them.

Christ invites His priests to reflect upon the joys which lie ahead, to find encouragement amidst their trials. It is a wonderful moment, when faithful priests enter Heaven, and walk towards the Father's throne. They walk along a path which is lined with joyful people. Each priest wears a golden chasuble; and each is given a tremendous greeting by their friends, the Saints, since priests enter Heaven in a special way. They are welcomed as "other Christs." Each is accorded special honour and glory at the end of his earthly, priestly service. (T:1584)

Responsibility and power.

We need only consider the sacred Priesthood, if we need a reminder about how much Christ loves us all, in our frailty. It's plain to everyone that He permits men who are frail and inadequate to share His Priesthood; and He is so generous that He clothes them in power and dignity in order to fit them for their awesome role. (T:1621)

Fulfilling their duties.

We must continue to offer thankful prayers for the work and virtues of our priests. We are right to be grateful for their service. As each good priest fulfils his duties, he reflects some aspect of Christ's fatherly care. Whether priests give us wise counsel with watchful care and guidance, or whether they have great responsibility and power, or whether they be called to some obscurer service or to a gentler ministry, our priests - all together - reflect Christ's many ways of helping us. All together, they reflect the fact that Christ our God is our Head, our Teacher, our Saviour, Consoler and Friend. (T:1634)

Scornful words about priests.

If we are aware of having shown disrespect or ingratitude to members of the Clergy, we would do well - in Christ's sight - to consider the cruelty which Christ endured, when He was tormented before His Crucifixion, and then to believe that, in Christ's sight, the cruelties continue. Whenever - for example - someone speaks scornfully about priests, it's as though that scornful person is pressing down a crown of thorns upon Christ's head.

If we have a genuine grievance about a priest's behaviour, we should speak to someone wise who can advise us what to do rather than act in a way which is not just uncharitable but ineffectual. (T:1712)

No greater claim.

Christ wants us to realise the meaning of a priest's exclusive and total dedication to Him. Every celibate Catholic priest belongs to Christ in a very special way - by that promise of celibacy. He is a man set apart, like Christ, for the Father's work. Therefore no earthly friend or relative shall have a claim on his life that is greater than Christ's claim on his life, his loyalty, his heart's devotion, his time or his bodily energy.

A marvellous freedom is purchased by each celibate priest's exclusive dedication to Christ; and it is a two-fold freedom. First, each celibate priest has the freedom to reach out, unhindered, to us, Christ's People. Secondly, he has the freedom to stand apart, as if behind a small fence, in order to preach, and to avoid the danger of anything which would draw him away from total abandonment to Christ's Will. (T:1716)

Christ's special friends.

We should honour every Catholic priest, married or celibate. Yet we should especially revere each celibate priest. Christ counts each of them as another self, since all of that man's desires for married love and for human fatherhood are immolated - if he is faithful - for the sake of Christ and His Kingdom. Therefore Christ cherishes him not only as His priest but also as a special friend. (Also T:1716)

Christ's authority, Christ's touch.

Christ is at work in His Church, both through the Clergy and the laity - even through imperfect people, as we can see plainly when we remember that none of us is perfect. And Christ want us to believe that He is at work in a special way through the ministry of good priests.

Christ is at work, with His authority, as He guides, reassures and teaches us through His priests' guidance of us, and reassurance and teaching. Christ advises us by their good advice and helps us by their good actions. It is Christ Who touches us through their touch in the sacraments. Thus, Christ is at work in His priests to bring strength and consolation wherever a priest speaks and acts as Christ Himself would speak and act. (T:1799)

Christ our Priest.

We are being unwise and uncharitable, if we say that we prefer to see one particular priest offer Mass, rather than another. We should offer fervent prayers of gratitude to God for all the Clergy, and for Christ's sacramental Presence before us on the altar, no matter which priest is celebrating Mass.

It doesn't matter by which of the priests Christ is made Present, at the Consecration. We can be sure - whenever we think about the Holy Sacrifice of the Mass - that it is always Christ Who is 'at work' in the sanctuary. He, our Saviour, is the Priest Who offers this Holy Sacrifice, no matter which of His priests we see holding up the chalice and the Sacred Host. (T:1887)

Manly and tender.

Those among us who encourage men to test their vocation to the Priesthood, or who help to train them, can know what priests should be like, if they remember that Christ is a source of comfort for all who approach Him in humility and trust. Truly, He is God and man: Divine love, embodied, both powerful and tender! All who humbly approach Him can be sure of receiving the good things for which their hearts are yearning. That's why we know that there can be found, in Christ, and in those of His priests who are most truly 'Christ-like', sure help for all sorts of people with all sorts of problems.

The fearful find a firm embrace. The lonely find the truest Friend. The sinful meet the wisest Counsellor. The repentant find the

Priest who removes their burdens. The weak find the kindest Helper. The aged find the considerate Son. The broken-hearted find a caring Father.

Children find a gentle Teacher. Young men can find a worthy Hero. Young women find a loving Brother. Sick people find a tender Companion. The dumb find One Who knows their every thought. The blind receive the comfort of His touch, and the dying surrender to Him as He gently holds them in His arms.

Every priest should strive to be another Christ to his people, relying on Christ's graces. (T:2064)

Special anniversaries.

Christ is glad that we show gratitude and reverence towards our priests, and that we celebrate their special anniversaries, particularly the anniversaries of their Ordinations. (T:2262)

Through His ministers.

Faith is important: faith that God acts through His ministers with almighty power. It's as though God our Father stretches out His hand from Heaven and blesses the water of the font as soon as our priest stretches out his hand over the water and asks in Christ's name for the Father's blessing. Straightaway, that blessing is given to the water in which new believers will be baptised; indeed, whenever our priest says a blessing, our Father in Heaven gives His blessing - with Christ His Son, and with Holy Spirit. (T:2586)

Insults or ill-humour.

Christ wants us to love and honour our priests. It's true to say that Christ counts as done to Himself not just good things done for His priests, but evil things, too. Christ counts as directed towards Himself whatever insult, scorn, blow, ill-humour or lack of reverence is directed towards the 'other Christs' whom He has chosen to lead and serve us. (T:2722)

Configured to Christ.

God the Father is especially delighted when His priests are greeted and assisted in a loving and respectful manner. He knows that they are especially deserving of such honour because they closely resemble Christ through their configuration to Him both in Ordination and in self-sacrifice. (T:2749)

Authority and power.

Christ has provided us with priests and 'shepherds' because He loves us. Through the Priesthood, we have a visible 'other Christ' amongst us, to teach, guide and console us: so great was Christ's desire to provide us with such care within the Church.

No woman can be a priest, an icon of Christ, in this manner.

Each priest is a man who, though learning how to be gentle, tender and compassionate in Christ's service, is endowed with Christ's authority and power (T:2758)

The gift of Priesthood.

We know that Christ instituted the Holy Sacrifice of the Mass at the Last Supper; but Christ's Mother Mary was not present. That would have been inappropriate for more than one reason, but, above all, because He didn't intend her to be a priest, like the Apostles; and it was on that occasion that He conferred the gift of Priesthood upon those chosen men. (T:2792)

The words of the priest.

There's a further reason why we can treasure the Sacred Priesthood, and treasure the prayers said out loud at the altar. If we are sick or weak, or too exhausted to pray, it's as if we can 'lean' on the words of the priest, who is the 'icon' of Christ amongst us. He speaks to the Father on our behalf.

We can give our whole heart to the prayers which our priest prays at the altar. By a swift and sincere intention we can make his prayers our own. (T:2825)

A solemn duty to attend Mass.

Christ wants His priests to remember that they have certain duties. They should remind us that we have a solemn duty to give up sin, to do good, and to attend Mass every Sunday and holy day. They should also remind us that we have a solemn duty, if we have committed serious sins, to confess them. We should be reconciled to Christ and to the Church before we receive Christ in Holy Communion. This is out of respect for Christ, Who is Really Present in the Blessed Sacrament. (T:2948)

Recited without haste.

It is Christ's fervent wish that His priests celebrate every Mass with dignity and reverence. He wants to see especial care taken; and He wants to hear the Eucharistic prayer recited without haste. Indeed, nothing to do with the Sacred Mysteries should be rushed or careless. We celebrate them for the glory of the Father as well as for our sanctification. So they should be conducted throughout with the reverence due to His Divinity, for the glory of the Holy Trinity. (T:3064)

Through Whom the Universe was made.

It's important that priests set an example by speaking gladly about the Mass. They should help us all to recognise the astonishing truth about the Holy Eucharist: that our Lord and God is here amongst us, and that as we gaze at the Sacred Host we can be certain that we are gazing upon the Son of God, sacramentally Present: the very Word through Whom the whole universe and all its wonders were made. (T:3067)

Priests in the world.

Christ invites His priests to remember that they are called to share the hopes and fears of Mankind. Yet He wants them also to remember that in representing Him in a special way for the Church and the world they should be in the world but not 'of it'. (T:3094)

Really amongst us.

Poorly-instructed Catholics need reminding that every priest deserves respect for his office, whatever his attitude or his weaknesses. Indeed, we all need reminding that each priest is a living icon of Christ our High Priest who is really Present amongst us, after the Consecration. So it matters little, in one sense, which priest offers the Holy Sacrifice.

Whether our celebration is loud or gentle, 'modern' or traditional, it is Christ Who offers the Holy Sacrifice at the hands of His priest: Christ Who should be at the centre of our lives. Christ can ease our burdens as we rely on Him each day, when we come to Mass and Holy Communion, grateful for His Eucharistic Presence, and grateful for every priest who gives us joy and hope not primarily by a pleasant personality or by natural gifts but by his priestly work in making Christ Present. (T:3112)

The generosity of priests.

We should relish, as a perpetual cause for joy, the knowledge that Christ reigns in our midst; and this joy is ours because of His goodness - and the generosity of His priests. (Also T:3112)

The greatest work of all.

Christ wishes to remind His priests that the heart of the priestly life is at the altar. Each priest has been called to preach the Gospel and to care for Christ's flock. These great tasks are fulfilled in the greatest work of all in a priest's life, which takes place at the altar.

There, each priest has the privilege of providing, through and in Christ, and through a re-presentation of the work of Calvary, the means of salvation of the people in his care.

Every priest and every lay-person should remember that it is through priests that we can come close to Christ Who is sacramentally Present during the Mass and in the tabernacle. It is through priests that we can unite ourselves to Christ's perfect offering for sin, that we can praise the Father at Mass through Christ, and that we can also receive Christ - 'The living bread from Heaven' - as food for our souls. (T:3118)

At the time of Christ's Transfiguration.

Each priest who now lives a celibate life, for Christ's sake, needs to remain firm in his belief that he has been specially chosen by Christ to live as another Christ. It is Christ Who has invited each one - each individual - to live in perfect imitation of Himself, just as He was at the time of His Transfiguration, when He revealed His glory, on the mountain. Every priest can reflect that, at that moment of extraordinary glory, Christ was utterly devoted to the Father, and was determined to let nothing and no-one distract Him from the task which lay ahead - as He descended amongst the people in order to preach, to suffer, and then to die for love of us all. (T:3122)

A priceless treasure.

Christ wants all of His priests in the Catholic Church to remember that they have been given - unearned - a privileged role and state. Each of them will be asked to 'die' for love of Christ, in one way or another, whether through the little cruelties and problems in everyday life or by bodily death, perhaps in martyrdom. Yet every vocation to the Ministerial Priesthood should be recognised for what it is: a priceless treasure. Each call is a personal gift from Christ, through His Church, to each of the men whom He has chosen and who has been willing to receive that gift. (Also T:3122)

A marvellous 'impersonation'.

We must treasure the gift which Christ has given to His Church in giving us the Sacred Priesthood. It's true to say that each of our priests is an ordinary man. Yet - as we know through the Church's teachings, and by the vestments we see - a priest acts in the person of Christ, our High Priest. Because the man has special power, in the Priesthood, he knows that as he acts in the person of Christ, he makes happen on the altar what Christ, if He were to do the same things, would make happen. The priest says "This is My body", as if he were Christ; and by the Spirit's power the altar bread does indeed become Christ's Body. And when the priest speaks in a similar way about Christ's blood which was once poured out so that our sins can be forgiven, the wine in the chalice becomes Christ's Precious Blood, which Christ once shed for our sakes on the Cross.

The further marvel of the Mass is that the priest who acts in the person of Christ not only makes happen what Christ, if He were doing the same things, would make happen. The priest makes Present the Divine Person in Whose name he acts. In changing the bread and wine into Christ's Body and Blood, the priest makes Christ Present "whole and entire": Christ's Body, Blood, Soul and Divinity. These truths, and these marvellous acts, have been handed on and celebrated for nearly twenty centuries, since Christ first effected those changes at the Last Supper. He, our God and Saviour, is here amongst us at every Mass, Really Present, offering His own praise and His own sacrifice from our altar. (T:3196)

Fiery and infinite holiness.

Every priest and every lay-person should be awestruck when

thinking about the Holy Sacrifice of the Mass. Scripture tells us that in Christ there dwells the fullness of the Godhead, bodily; it follows that the fullness of the Godhead is here, on our altar, and in the tabernacle, through Christ's sacramental Presence.

Though we cannot see the fiery and infinite holiness of God Who comes to our altar we should realise how closely identified each priest is with the Christ Who is now Present through the priest's words and actions and through the Divine power of the Holy Spirit.

Plainly, each priest - and every member of the Church - should be determined to become pure and holy. (T:3432)

Slow to teach truth.

Christ delights in the goodness of those priests who delight in serving Him. Yet He can see which of His priests are slow to teach the truths which they have been ordained to teach, and which of them rarely keep in mind what an astonishing privilege is theirs. Christ asks them to repent of speaking more frequently about their hardships than about the great honour which the Lord has shown them in calling them to share His Priesthood. (T:3937)

To keep the 'fire' burning.

Christ asks us all to realise that, as members of the Church, we can spiritually unite ourselves with Christ and with the whole Church, in the Spirit, at every Mass. And when we praise God for His glory and thank Him for His blessings it's as though there's a blazing fire here before us on the altar: such is the power and fiery fervour of the sacrificial prayer and offering which is made by Christ Who is sacramentally Present on our altar during the Mass.

Our priest is essential, for the offering of the Holy Sacrifice. Day by day, he should be 'at work' at the altar, doing what is essential in his vocation.

25. EVERY GENERATION, YET ONLY ONE SACRIFICE.

The sacrifice of the cross is unique and unrepeatable. Through the celebration of the Holy Eucharist, every generation of believers is made present to this one sacrifice, which is re-presented on the altar and offered to the Father. OIL-M:1470. *("Until the Lord comes, therefore, every time you eat this bread and drink this cup, you are proclaiming his death." 1 Co 11:26).*

26. CHRIST'S ETERNAL SELF-GIVING LOVE.

When we are present to Christ's sacrifice of the altar, we are present to His eternal self-offering. In Eternity, He is united in self-giving love with the Father and the Holy Spirit, in the unity of the Godhead. OIL-S:4270. *("For the sake of the joy which was still in the future, he endured the cross, disregarding the shamefulness of it, and from now on has taken his place at the right of God's throne." Heb 12:2).*

27. THE BANNERS OF GLADNESS.

During the Sacred Liturgy we are one in prayer with the whole Church, which includes the Saints of Heaven.   It's as if bright banners are waving around them in celebration as they praise God, with us, for Christ's triumph over sin. OIL-M:805B. *("From the angel's hand the smoke of the incense went up in the presence of God and with it the prayers of the saints." Rev 8:4).*

28. HOLY SOULS MOVE CLOSER T0 THE LIGHT.

Some who die in the love of Christ still need to be prepared and purified before they can enter the bliss and glory of Heaven. These 'Holy Souls' of Purgatory are assured of their salvation. They accept this purification willingly. And meanwhile, they remain united in prayer with the whole Church. At every Mass we are one with them, and we pray for them. OIL-M:516. *("And we, with our unveiled faces reflecting like mirrors the brightness of the Lord, will grow brighter and brighter ..." 2 Co 3:18).*

29. THROUGH CHRIST, IN THE SPIRIT.

We need Christ, and the salvation which He has won for us. So we pray together at every Mass "through him, with him, in him, in the unity of the Holy Spirit," as we offer Christ's sacrifice and Christ's praise and thanks to our Heavenly Father. CIL-S:811. *("If anyone should sin, we have our advocate with the Father, Jesus Christ, who is just; he is the sacrifice that takes our sins away." 1 Jn 2:1-2).*

30. LIKE JEWELS ON HIS ROBE.

Death could not conquer God's own Son.   Christ rose from the
grave to a new and glorious life.   He has made a way to Heaven in
which His faithful friends can follow.   We share in His Resurrection
through faith, through baptism, and by offering ourselves with
Him in the Mass - as if we are jewels on His robe. OIL-S-535. *("Now
the Church is his body, he is its head. As he is the Beginning, he was
first to be born from the dead." Col 1:18).*

This 'fire' of praise ascends from our altars all over the world. So we can be sure that a 'fire' of praise burns continuously before the Father; and so we can say, about the Mass, and the Sacred Priesthood, "This is the task of each priest: to keep the 'fire' burning: to tend the flame." (T:3938)

Support for priests.

Christ's perfect sacrificial prayer gives infinitely-worthy praise to the Father, in the Spirit. Through the sacrificial offering the Church is helped and souls saved. So if we sincerely believe this, we will value, support and encourage priests in their vocation, and we will pray earnestly for men to hear God's call to be 'Keepers of the flame.'

Every priest who believes these things - about helping the Church and saving souls - will make sincere and perpetual efforts to be prayerful and holy: to become more worthy to live in union with Christ, and more worthy to be 'another Christ' in the sanctuary. (Also T:3938)

Prayers for priests.

Christ looks with special delight upon people who pray fervently for help to be given to the priests at whose hands His Holy Sacrifice is offered. (T:3976)

Gratitude for the Priesthood.

Christ looks with tremendous delight upon people who value the Sacred Priesthood, and who treasure all that we are given in the Church through the ministry of faithful priests. We are given, for example: Christ Himself, through the Church's sacraments and sacramentals, and also authoritative teaching, healing, forgiveness and consolation, with blessings of various kinds, and fatherly concern, and Christ-like loving-kindness. (T:4008)

In innocence and peace.

Christ wants to help us to understand why He instituted the Sacred Priesthood. He invites us to picture a tropical garden, with all sorts of trees and flowers and animals within it, clustered together with no disharmony or brutality. Thus, we have a simple, brief representation of Eden, representing the home on earth of our first parents, before they rebelled and disobeyed God. Then if we reflect on the sad state of the world, and on our sinful nature and on the purpose of Christ's Church, we can see what priests are 'for'. They are to bring people to the state of soul and state of human dignity which God intended that we should enjoy. They are to bring us to a life of grace, freedom and joy, a life in which each person lives in innocence and peace, in known union with God Who made us all from love. (T:4425)

The road to sanctity.

There is a magnificent purpose to our priests' training and sacrifices, their Ordinations and their preaching, their offering of the Holy Sacrifice, and their faithful and loving service as they administer the sacraments. The purpose is to restore joy, by reconciling people with God, in and through Christ, through the forgiveness of sins.

Christ wants everyone to know that even though the Church sometimes invites individual priests to step 'aside,' so to speak, to do unusual tasks in times of special need, the primary purpose of the Priesthood is not with civic affairs or earthly concerns but with our eternal salvation. Each priest has been called to draw people away from sin and to set them on the road to sanctity, in the love of God. (Also T:4425)

To reconcile sinners.

Some people speak as though a priest's primary purpose is to bring about a healthy secular community, to wait at table, and to build a better world, whereas his primary purpose is to bring the hope of salvation to each precious soul, for each one's eternal joy and for the glory of God. God made us all so that we might live, transformed, at His heart, and share His glory. Each priest who works faithfully to reconcile sinners with God will indeed cause sinful people - including ourselves - to live in greater harmony; and so he will help us to love and serve others and to bring about a society which cares for the weak and marginalised. (Also T:4425)

A missionary Church.

There are very many ways in which a priest might join with other people in doing good; yet if he doesn't preach repentance or if he forgets that Christ's Church is a missionary Church, or fails to invite people to seek perfection in holiness, he is not fulfilling his primary task and role as 'another Christ'. Christ's great desire - by His self-less love, His preaching and truth-speaking and His faithfulness even to death - was to reconcile sinners with the Father. (Also T:4425)

Heaven's delight in good priests.

The Saints and holy Angels in Heaven look with delight upon the men who accept the gift and responsibility of the Priesthood. Everyone in Heaven is wise and holy; and each can see the tremendous good which is achieved through the lives of good priests. (T:4607)

Unworthy comments.

Priests have a duty to set an example of reverence and dignity in worship. Where there are people present who rarely attend the sacraments or who are unfamiliar with Christian worship the priest should not be so concerned to 'make things easy' that he introduces and explains every part of a ceremony with jokes, apologies and even flippant comments about Church customs and traditions. Such attempts to 'lighten the atmosphere' and to make himself seem more approachable are undignified, unnecessary, and unworthy of a priest. He has been ordained to offer sacrifice and to sanctify his people, not to act in the sanctuary to entertain strangers, as if at a private party in a worldly venue. (P.U.T:11)

Prolonged levity.

Neither priests nor laity should forget that a consecrated church is a holy place: a house of prayer. Yet even priests sometimes show disrespect, by their attitude and behaviour - and by the way they explain the Sacred Liturgy to newcomers.

A sense of humour is a gift from God: a delightful quality in the Clergy as well as the laity. Yet by prolonged jovial explanations, or by flippancy, or frequent and unnecessary jokes during the Sacred Liturgy, a priest can destroy our sense of being present at an awesome occasion in which God is at work. A sense of awe and reverence takes time to develop in some souls; and it can be quickly destroyed by a priest's worldly or unwise attempts to entertain rather than to lead by example. (P.U.T:12)

Authority to teach.

Every priest has been given power by God to consecrate, forgive, to bless and to console. Each has also been given authority by God, through the Church, to preach truth, to lead, to discipline, and to encourage or to warn. A priest who chooses only to console, and never to warn or lead, neglects the responsibilities given him by God. He neglects them, for example, when by his silence or indecision he allows members of the laity to behave badly in church, as he permits raucous gatherings before Mass, or frivolous eulogies at the end of a Requiem Mass, or blithely allows people to disobey the customs and traditions of the Church. If he acts in this way he encourages in His flock a spirit of disobedience in little things which can lead to disobedience in major things. (P.U.T. 13)

Quiet words of instruction.

If the presiding priest believes that he should intersperse the liturgy with observations and explanations his comments should be calm and dignified, in keeping with the celebration of the Sacred Mysteries, rather than boisterous or jocular. It's true that interjections are necessary on special occasions or where there are special needs; and a conscientious priest is always longing for his parishioners to have a greater understanding of the Liturgy. Yet the whole Liturgy offers a form of catechesis, through the words and phrases used within it. The overall aim of priest and people during the Liturgy should be to give glory to God, through Christ, in the Spirit, in union with the Saints and holy Angels who adore Him in Eternity.

We should 'see' the Liturgy not as a series of explanations which are interrupted by prayers, but as a single act of worship in which there might be occasional quiet words of instruction, or quiet comments about whether the congregation might kneel, stand or sit. (P.U.T:14)

A mighty river of praise.

Christ asks us to look upon the Mass as being like a great river of praise which is flowing towards God. A priest might occasionally call out 'across the waters,' so to speak, with some brief reminder or instruction. Where a priest interrupts the praise vigorously, frequently and lengthily, however, it's as if he's trying to stop the flow of a mighty river in order to make his voice heard. He is not only unwise to attempt this; but by his interruptions he makes that torrent of praise less beautiful and fervent. (T:4889)

A sense of the sacred.

Some of the Clergy seem unaware of the fact that Our Lord is looking on as they habitually act in a casual and jocular manner in the sanctuary. As they do so, they show that they have lost, to some degree, a sense of what is sacred. In Christ's eyes, a priest who sets a poor example, in this way, shows that his spiritual life is more like a pilot light than a powerful flame.

When the Clergy act in a worldly fashion on the very threshold of Heaven, they are not helping people towards sanctity; rather, they are encouraging low expectations: the cultivation only of human virtues such as friendliness and good humour. (T:4999)

Gentle and quiet conversation.

Priests, above all, have the duty to set an example by praying in church with dignity and reverence, by walking about in a calm and unhurried manner, by conversing - where necessary - quietly, and as briefly as possible, and by giving gentle hints or reminders to parishioners that noisy conversations should be conducted outside the church. (P.U.T:15)

At the end of time.

Christ wants us to understand what our priests are 'for'. Their aim and purpose should be to lead willing people towards the joy of Resurrection: not just to a celebration of Christ's Resurrection at Mass, and especially at Easter - but also to each person's own resurrection, at the end of time.

Everything else in a priest's life should pale into insignificance beside that primary role and task of leading people back to God. All private hopes and plans, or ambitious schemes for his church or parish, should count for little, beside that aim. The personal trials, setbacks and handicaps of priests should be seen as unavoidable crosses: things to be borne with grace and dignity, for love of God, so that the Will of God might be fulfilled.

The task of priests is to save souls, and so to bring them to God for their eternal joy in an eternal Easter. (T:5045)

With special affection.

Christ wants His priests to realise that Our Blessed Lady loves to pray for them all. She looks upon each priest with special affection because each is so closely configured to Christ her son. (T:5059)

OUR NEIGHBOUR

Showing honour to our neighbour.

We should honour and love each of our neighbours. Every man, woman and child is precious to God and must never be viewed merely as part of a crowd. (T:66)

Respect for everyone.

Christ wants each one of us to show a profound reverence towards those of our neighbours who have received Him in Holy Communion. Each one is worthy of our love and respect, as is every human being; but we 'owe' that special respect to our spiritual brothers and sisters because of Christ's sacramental Presence within them, which gives them a dignity and splendour unseen in other human beings. Each person who receives Christ bears some measure of His glory, and we are right to honour Him 'in' them. (T:71)

Unique and immortal.

We must look upon every person as being unique, individual and immortal - like ourselves. We ought never to look upon others as a mass of persons of one 'type', or simply a crowd. Each person, young or old, and each one the child of a real mother, is precious to Christ Who made each one of us. He loves us all, more

fervently than any mother, and He never leaves any of us alone.
(T:74)

With goodwill and generosity.

We know that we should honour our Heavenly companions: the
Saints and the holy Angels. We should look upon each of our
earthly companions in just the same way: with love, goodwill and
generosity. (T:164)

Willing to leave our prayer.

Christ wants us to remember that it is He Who binds us together
by His Spirit, as One Body; and so we must be bound by a tender
love for one another, in church as well as in everyday life outside.
Our love for Christ is a pretence, for example, if we're not willing
to leave prayer in order to give loving help to a neighbour. (T:479)

Compassionate and Christ-like.

Christ asks us to remember that it is He Who, by His Spirit, makes
possible every good thing we choose to do. It is Christ Who
prompts and sustains our good efforts to be compassionate and
Christ-like. His very own love within our hearts is what prompts
us to reach out to our neighbour. Each greeting, kind word, or
tender look, or charitable act - from ourselves to our neighbour - is
one of the holy, happy ways in which Christ greets others through
us. (T:651) *(See illustration 41)*

Christ's Presence in our souls.

We should respect everyone on earth; yet we owe a special respect
to those of our spiritual brothers and sisters who have received
Christ in Holy Communion. It is such an awesome and
wonderful thing, that human beings can receive Him in this way,
that the holy Angels bow low at His Presence within our souls.
(T:948)

SICK PERSONS WHO ARE PRESENT

Inattentive and distracted.

If we are weak, ill, or very tired, we can try to join in formal worship to some degree, but we should never be anxious if we are inattentive or distracted. Christ listens with unimaginable love and understanding to all our sincere prayers. He is always 'waiting' in patience throughout our wavering prayers and reflections. (T:79)

Our good intentions.

It doesn't matter if we're so weak or tired that we can't sing, or say all the words of the Mass. It's the heart's intention that 'counts'; and Christ is delighted by our good intentions. He is touched to the heart by the least effort we make to love and serve Him - even as we sit in church loving Him in our exhaustion. (T:821)

Our loving desire to pray.

We needn't worry if we are weary, at Mass. We can be like children who sit beside a devoted parent. Christ prays for all who are too weary to utter a word, or too tired even to think a pious thought. He delights in our loving desires, and in our desire to pray, even when we can scarcely begin. (T:857)

United to Christ's self-offering.

If we are suffering too much to be able to concentrate on the prayers, during the Mass or at home, all our pains can be patiently accepted, and united to Christ's self-offering of Calvary and altar. This is a very acceptable and effective way by which we can join Christ in His redeeming work. (T:945)

Many little sacrifices.

Whenever we are in church, at Mass, but feel too ill to concentrate on the words, we can offer all our earthly pains and sufferings - time and time again - as so many little sacrifices to be united to Christ's Holy Sacrifice of the altar. (T:991)

Simple and child-like hearts.

There's no need for us to worry about the 'quality' of our sincere prayers. We should realise how joyfully Christ comes to the altar, at the moment of Consecration, since He delights in doing the Father's Will, and He delights in being amongst us to offer his Holy Sacrifice on our behalf. Yet His joy is especially great as He comes to join those of His friends with disabilities and special needs whose hearts are simple and child-like. He rejoices to come to people who are called 'weak' because they are obviously in need of practical help, although some of them are really strong people: strong in faith and hope and love. (T:1611A)

Caring friends and relations.

Christ gazes tenderly upon people who arrange for their 'disabled' friends and relations to be together, in His Presence. He is overjoyed to be with these courageous helpers who are trusting and obedient. He sees that they put their trust in Him amidst appalling difficulties, day after day, obedient to the duties which He, their God, has set before them. (Also T:1611A)

Christ's exhausted posture.

People who are sick, in pain, or disabled need have no fear that they lack reverence for God if they remain seated when everyone else kneels to pray at Mass, or if they are too tired to speak the responses.

We worship the Holy Trinity: our loving and compassionate God. Jesus Christ and His Father and the Holy Spirit are well aware of our difficulties. Christ wants us to remember that He was not irreverent in His exhausted posture, during His Passion, as He hung on the Cross, as He clung wholeheartedly in spirit to His Heavenly Father. (T:2419)

Aches and pains.

God is love; and He knows everything. He knows our every ache, pain or cause for concern, with every thought, desire, fear or hope - as well as every 'shadow' or ray of light which passes swiftly through our hearts and minds. Whatever our state of health, we are resting in God's 'heart', and in His care, whether we are at home, or travelling, or taking part in the Mass. (Also T:2419)

Not appropriate for the 'House of God'.

There are several things to be seen today, at Mass, which are not appropriate for the 'House of God': things which set a bad example; for example - disrespect for people in wheelchairs, who are sometimes made to feel a nuisance. It is made difficult for some to receive Holy Communion, when with forethought, things could have been different. (T:2423)

Sitting at Christ's feet.

During the Mass, if we are very weary, we can place ourselves in spirit as if at Christ's feet, as if we were able to sit close beside Him, to 'lean' on Him, in prayer.

Just as we comfort our children not just with words, but also with gestures, so Christ loves to comfort us. We instinctively hold a distressed child, stroking the child's hair and giving comfort by our love - even in silence. And Christ can comfort us in the same way, in the silence of our peaceful Communion. (T:2648)

Absent from the church building.

Christ delights in welcoming back to church, for the Sacred Liturgy, everyone who has been absent through sickness. In being absent from the assembly, and from the church building - from a holy place consecrated for worship - we haven't been absent from Christ Who, with the Father and the Holy Spirit, lives within the souls of His friends. Yet we were absent from the place where Christ reigns through His sacramental Presence; and we shouldn't deny that this is a real deprivation. (T:3326)

Sick people, unwanted.

A space should be provided in church for people in wheelchairs, so that they aren't made to feel a nuisance. Sick people sometimes feel unwanted as ushers search the building, sometimes unhappily, at the last minute, for a place in which to 'put' them. (T:4494)

Taking the Angels' part.

Whoever has a sincere intention to praise God at Mass is united in praise with the other worshippers even if he can't sing or speak, or is sick or just very tired. Such a person can look upon himself as taking the Angels' part of silent attentive adoration. (T:5102)

SICK PERSONS WHO ARE ABSENT

Too ill to come to Mass.

The holy Angels count it an honour to accompany Christ, as He approaches His sick friends, whenever a member of the Clergy, or an Extraordinary Minister of the Eucharist, takes the Blessed Sacrament to those who were too ill to come to Mass. (T:825)

Acting in the name of Christ.

We mustn't underestimate the importance of the good that we can do through sincere and loving personal contact. Some of us bring Christ to others in the Blessed Sacrament; yet all who love and serve Christ can 'convey' Him to others, in one sense, simply through words and gestures.

Whatever we say and do in Christ's name is as though said or done by Him for others! It is through our union with Him and through the good intentions of our hearts that we can act 'in Christ's name' even when the work or the subject of conversation is seen as un-religious, when it's scientific, social, or domestic. We who act in His name are the Church in action, the Church acting for others. So our every word and gesture ought to be 'Christ-like'. (T:1284)

On our behalf.

It's important to remember that we can pray in almost every circumstance. For example, we can turn our hearts towards the altar, for the Holy Sacrifice, even when we are kept at home through sickness. In that case, even from a distance, we can unite our intentions with Christ's intentions. We can do what we usually do in church. For example, we can pray for the Faithful Departed, and we can honour Christ's holy Mother; and we can ask pardon for our sins; and we can praise and thank the Father for everything good, as we offer Christ's prayers as our own.

We should remember Who Christ is! He is our High Priest, and - through our priest - He offers His Holy Sacrifice to the Father, from amongst His People, on behalf of us all, including sick people at home. (T:1468A)

A prayerful intention.

We must reassure those who, for good reasons, are unable to be present at the Holy Sacrifice of the Mass. They can assist, spiritually, at the offering of the Holy Sacrifice. This is easy to do, and very powerful and effective. The sick, and others who cannot be present, are able to do this by their intention: by their sincere and prayerful intention to unite their hearts' prayers with Christ's great prayer, as He offers His sacrifice to the Father, through our priest, from the altar. (T:1857)

Through no fault of their own.

We must offer reassurance to those of our friends or relations who are absent from Mass through no fault of their own. If they cannot be physically present to this redeeming work they still benefit. It's because of their hearts' good desires that they can benefit from the Precious Blood which was once shed for sinners and which is now offered from the altar. (T:2203)

Asking the priest.

If they are kept at home or hospital, the sick should be simple and child-like. They should ask the priest, if they want to receive Holy Communion. Yet they should be ready to welcome God's Will about when and how often they are consoled by Christ in the Blessed Sacrament - if perhaps the priest is busy. (T:2862)

Wonderful graces.

If we are absent from church through sickness, but unite ourselves in spirit with the whole Church the Father delights in giving us the very graces he would have lavished upon us had we been able to take part in the Mass. Our membership of the Church - our living communion with its members - cannot be blocked by mere walls. (T:2867)

A real deprivation.

Even when we cannot go to Mass, we can make Christ's perfect offering our own. We make His perfect praise our own by the union of our hearts with His offering. We can take special delight in doing this at the time when we know that Calvary's sacrifice is being re-presented on the altar at our local church. The Father can be praised and honoured in no more glorious way than by the offering of Christ - at any time.

Yet it's important for us to be with the Body of Christ, the visible Church, if at all possible. To see, hear, touch and celebrate with that Body is the best thing we can do - if God allows it. We mustn't speak as though it doesn't matter whether or not we attend. Sick people who are absent have a genuine spiritual communion with those of Christ's friends who have been able to attend Mass; but we should recognise that it's a real deprivation not to be able to attend.

Sick people who love Christ long to be able to attend Mass, for several reasons, but principally to be spiritually and bodily there with the Body of Christ, the visible Church at its greatest and most holy celebration. (T:4452)

Indecision.

If we are ill, but can't make up our minds what to do, it's best to be simple: to go to Mass if we can, or to come away again if we can't stay, for some reason, or not to go when it would be really foolish. But as we ask the Lord for help, and try to make sensible decisions, we shouldn't worry. (T:4452)

SMALL CONGREGATIONS

Whether a large or small assembly.

Christ wants us to remember that whether our congregation is large or small, we can be made holy through the Mass, and through Christ's work in our souls and lives; and so we are made fit to praise the Father in and through Christ and to intercede for other people . (T:312)

Amongst the holy Angels.

We need never fear that the Lord isn't sufficiently honoured when only a small group of us has gathered in church for the Mass. Many holy Angels surround the priest and the altar, to await Christ's arrival at the Consecration. Christ is always being honoured and adored by the Saints and Angels, even when, in a particular time or place, He seems to have very few friends on earth. (T:790)

A veil across the sanctuary.

It's important for us to remember that we are not alone when we pray; nor do we pray with only a few hundred fellow-parishioners during the Holy Sacrifice of the Mass. No! It's as if a veil is hanging from top to bottom of the sanctuary. The glorious assembly of Christ's faithful people consists of many more people than we can see with our bodily eyes. Thousands of glorious Saints of Heaven are praying behind this 'veil'. They are very close to us. They, too, offer glory to the Father, through Christ His Son, our Redeemer. (T:1878)

5.   INSTRUCTION.

BEING 'IN FULL COMMUNION'

Repentant and reconciled.

Christ's own joy and peace can be ours, in His Body the Church, if we become humble and holy. There is no community more truly joyful than the community of Christ's Church, where its members are gathered before their Heavenly Father, and when each member is repentant, reconciled and fully 'in communion.' (T:1960)

Not a safe path.

Everyone who has been validly baptised has been made a child of God. Yet those baptised persons who are not in full communion with the Catholic Church are like people who are processing together, not along the safe path which Christ has marked out for us, but along a tiny slip-road.   Though it goes in the same direction, it is half-awash with rainwater and littered with puddles. (T:3212)

Unable to share the Eucharist.

It is important that we remain fully 'in communion' with one another, in the one, true Church, rather than 'out of communion'. Catholics who choose to leave the Church suffer devastating spiritual effects.

Christians who are not in full communion with the Catholic Church and who have not recognised the invitation from Christ to become full members of the Catholic Church, and to accept her teachings, have not endangered their souls. But Catholics endanger their souls if they positively choose to leave the Church. (T:4310)

A downward path.

We who are full members of the Catholic Church should beware of those first few steps which can lead us onto a downward path, away from the Body of Christ. For example, if some of us become distanced from one another through a lack of charity, by a quarrel or misunderstanding, we perhaps experience distress; but much worse is the fact that we lose the ability to pray together sincerely and well. This is disastrous as well as significant because the best prayer which Church members pray together is Christ's prayer, in His self-offering in the Mass. This prayer includes intercessions for the whole Church; and members of the Church are duty-bound to unite themselves to that sacrificial prayer and offering, to be made holy and to achieve salvation.

Whenever a person has withdrawn his friendship from fellow-Catholics, or has lessened in loyalty towards the Church which offers the Holy Sacrifice, or has allowed his faith to diminish so that he cannot pray sincerely what the Church prays in the Mass, he has endangered his 'being-in-communion' with Christ's Church. His 'being-in-communion' with Christ in the Holy Eucharist is endangered: Christ Whom he needs for his true joy and fulfilment. (Also T:4310)

Our need of God's grace.

Everyone should recognise the seriousness of being 'out of communion'. Where people ignore one another for days at a time, or refuse to pray together, or despise or harm one another, terrible things can occur. The bond of communion between souls can be strong, palpable and encouraging, and can cause them to meet 'in Christ', in spirit, so that they receive spiritual light and refreshment in joyful prayer. Yet this bond can be damaged or destroyed; and thus they can lose all or some of the benefits of that communion. In ceasing to pray together in charity less glory is given to God, and less benefit received by souls. Whoever neglects or deserts his prayers is less likely to remain fervent in keeping God's commandments, for we all need God's grace to be faithful to His Will and to persevere in faith, hope and love to the end of our lives.

Whoever removes himself from communion and so withdraws from the Body of Christ on earth risks being permanently 'out of communion', also, with his departed friends and relations in Purgatory and Heaven. We can only know and meet them 'in' and through Christ: through prayer, and through the Holy Eucharist. To be 'out of communion' with the Church is, tragically, to be 'out of communion' with the whole Church of earth and Purgatory and Heaven. (T:4310)

The loss of joy.

During our lives on earth, within the communion which is brought about through Christ by the Father's Will, the worst threat is not death, but sin.

Whoever removes himself from the 'communion of Saints' might ultimately be far removed from a known, experienced communion with Christ's Church members and with Christ Himself. If this tragedy occurs, he will lose spiritual peace, joy, contentment and sweetness. He will not have achieved the fulfilling work and prayer which others have enjoyed, or the sweet companionship - unequalled - of those who are linked together in the bond of charity. He won't enjoy the certainty of being loved - though indeed he is loved, even as he keeps on rejecting God's love. (Also T:4310)

A temporary separation.

True communion between souls can be highly valued even by those who remain on earth after their loved ones die 'in Christ'. The apparent separation, though painful, is only temporary. Christ's friends can live out their lives on earth in the hope of enjoying that marvellous communion in an extraordinary way, at the end of time, provided they remain faithful to the end. And, meanwhile, they remain 'in communion' with departed friends through prayer, supremely through the Great Prayer: the Holy Eucharist. (Also T:4310)

The loss of Heaven.

It's important for us to realise that when someone has deliberately and sinfully put himself 'out of communion' with Christ, through rejecting His Church, or through disobeying His Commandments, and has remained defiant and unrepentant to the end, he cannot enter Heaven. This is because if Christ is the 'Door' to Heaven, and that person refuses to meet Christ or speak to Him, then that person is freely choosing not to enter. Nor can such a person enter Purgatory, in which people are held 'in God' and are on the 'way' to God and Heaven.

To be in Purgatory, which is to undergo purification after death, is to be in a beneficial and secure spiritual state. Though painful, that state is to be prized, since only the Faithful can enter it. Those who are resolutely unfaithful - who have not remained faithful to Christ until death - have therefore put themselves 'out of communion' with Christ and with their brothers and sisters in Christ. They have chosen not to be 'in communion' with the Catholic Church; and people who deliberately turn their backs on Christ and His Church and who remain defiant even at death cannot enter Purgatory or Heaven; and they are therefore tragically alienated from God for all Eternity. (Also T:4310)

A state of alienation.

Christ wants us to realise that by our everyday choices we are renewing our friendship with Him, or we are reinforcing our state of alienation; and He longs for us to see how worthwhile it is to know Him, to serve Him, to believe in the teachings of His Church, and to live in charitable communion with Him and with one another. The blessings which are gained in the heights of the spiritual life, in 'full communion', are like so many precious 'pearls' which only a foolish or careless or stubborn person would dismiss as not worth keeping, or would tragically throw away. (Also T:4310)

THE CHURCH'S HIERARCHY

Christ is faithful.

Christ wants us to be confident about following the constant teaching of the Church, and the discipline of the Church, in our era. Christ Himself supports all the good things which are taught in the Church by those whom He has chosen to speak for Him. Christ guides us through the Holy Father - the Pope - and the other Bishops who are united with him. Christ is faithful to His promise that He binds and looses in Heaven whatever they - the present-day Apostles - 'bind and loose' on earth. So we should encourage everyone to see that they can be sure of pleasing Christ when they accept the teaching and discipline of the Church, through a spirit of faith and obedience.

It's best if we aim to be perfectly 'in communion' with our Saviour and with the Church, His Body, instead of damaging that communion by opposing the teaching of the Church or grumbling about discipline. Christ wants us to understand that just as we benefit from obedient submission to Him and to His Will in our prayer, as we 'allow' Him to draw us into a closer union, so we can be greatly helped by submission to Him at every moment of everyday life. (T:1510)

An admirable pattern.

We please Christ by our gratitude for the admirable 'pattern' which He has made through the hierarchy of the Church. It is He Who has arranged that we be taught and guided by our Priest, Bishop and Pope. They are bound together through faith in Christ and in His Will for them. It is also true that the Clergy, if they are courteous, kind and obedient, increase the harmony and unity between themselves which Christ loves to see: and thus they set a good example to us all. (T:3024)

Saint Peter's successor.

Christ longs to see us pray sincere prayers for the Pope. He wants us to treasure the Holy Father, who serves as Saint Peter's successor and as the bond of unity in the Church. His role is essential to the life and health of the Church. The Church is taught and guided by the Catholic Bishops who are in Communion with one another and with the Pope; and we have an illustration of the importance of the Pope if we picture each Bishop in the world as being like a pearl on a long necklace.

In such a 'circle' of pearls the Bishops can be seen as linked together; yet at one point in the circle a gem-stone is found, which represents the Pope.

If any parts of the necklace except the gem are removed the necklace remains whole, even if smaller than before. It remains a perfect necklace, even if bits have been removed from its length. And so it is in the Church.

If two or three Bishops, sad to say, leave the united fellowship of the other Bishops with the Pope, those two or three have not damaged the teaching office of the Church. The 'circle' remains whole.

Even if a large number of Bishops were to break away - without the Pope - to form another necklace or circle, a body apparently large and united, they would not, together, be God's Church. They would no longer be His faithful Bishops, since only those who have remained in union with the Pope - the gemstone - are fulfilling God's plan for the Church, and have the authority, with the Holy Father, to provide authentic, authoritative spiritual leadership on earth. (T:4010)

THE HOLY EUCHARIST

Christ's once-for-all sacrifice.

As we participate with sincere hearts in the Holy Eucharist - also called the Holy Sacrifice of the Mass - at which Christ's once-for-all-sacrifice is made present, we benefit from its power; and through our Holy Communion, we can become more like Christ our Saviour. (T:59)

Into Heaven's worship.

There is a simple way of looking at the Mass, and at our marvellous role, as we pray together, in and through Christ. Through the Holy Mass, and our Holy Communion, Christ calls willing souls into the joy and glory of Heaven's worship, while we're still living upon earth. (T:426)

Christ's eternal praise.

We shouldn't imagine that Christ suddenly begins to praise His Father yet again, as we offer the Holy Sacrifice. His praise never ceases. By our attendance at Mass, we are present to that praise of

Christ which is His perfect, eternal and obedient self-offering. We are present as He offers that praise from upon earth; and He does so because, at Mass, He is sacramentally Present amongst us. (T:548)

Christ's awesome holiness.

In order to pray well at Mass, it's important that we understand Christ's plan for us.

He is now triumphant in Heaven. He is Truth, Love, Beauty, Purity and Power; and the radiant light of His glory is unbearable for those who love secrecy, selfishness, disobedience and darkness. Christ is burning with the Divine life and holiness which He wants to share with us through prayer and the sacraments, to make us holy with His holiness, and wholly transformed. (T:771B) *(See illustration 15)*

The power of prayer 'in Christ'.

We should remember how powerful are our prayers, at Mass. Each time that we are here when Mass is celebrated, and when we offer to the Father Christ our Saviour, and when we are truly united with Christ in our hearts and wills, we give to the Father, through Christ and His perfection, worthy praise and glory and thanks and reparation and intercession. (T:810)

Faith to pierce Heaven.

We should cherish our faith. It is a gift from Christ which is freely-given, undeserved and lavish. Faith pierces Heaven in a way which we who live on earth cannot accomplish by sight, sound, will or humanity. We cannot reach Heaven by relying on natural gifts or powers. Faith is needed for true prayer, and for true life - which is Eternal Life - and for true wisdom. (T:1027)

The purpose of the Mass.

We should always try to gain a deeper understanding of the purpose of the Mass. Christ lived upon earth for only a short time; and when He was crucified for our sins, it was long ago and in a past age. By our presence at Mass, however, it's as though we are gazing into that past age - as if into a chasm before us - whilst today gazing upon the very sacrifice which Christ once made for us, as it is now offered from the altar.

The Mass is a true and holy memorial of Christ's awesome Passion, Death, Resurrection and Ascension. It's because our Divine Saviour is now Really Present in the sanctuary that we can 'touch' every part of His life, touching even the moment of His self-offering as He died on the Cross. It is an offering - a sacrifice - which He now re-presents here, daily, through His priest, at the altar. (T:1052)

Worthy of awe and gratitude.

We should treasure the Holy Mass. There is nothing on earth more magnificent or fruitful, or more worthy of awe and gratitude, than the Holy Sacrifice of the Mass, which is Christ's own action. This marvellous offering is ours to offer. All the glory which Christ has possessed from all ages was offered to the Father, in the one holy sacrifice of the Cross; and that is the very sacrifice which is now being offered on the altar, though offered here in a sacramental manner.

This sacrifice is perfect, powerful, and worthy of the Father; so we need not worry if we cannot find the right words, the right phrase or the right manner in prayer, provided that our intention is true. We can prove our good intention by our reverent thoughts and behaviour, but - more important for us to know - Christ's praise is perfect and glorious. His praise is ours to offer, in and through the Mass, if we are His. (T:1218)

A bridge across the gulf.

We should recognise the tremendous effects which stem from Christ's self-offering. Through the merits of Christ's sacrifice on Calvary, His Divine life can now penetrate every aspect of our humanity. Through His suffering, He broke down the barrier between Divine life and human, bridged the gulf between His Eternal Life and ours, and entered into our suffering. So we who belong to Him are raised up, by His grace, to His glory: made divine-by-grace, divinised. We are His children, by adoption; and the dignity which is ours is extraordinary.

The Holy Sacrifice of the Mass is the very same sacrifice as that once offered by Christ on Calvary, for our sins. And at the summit of our celebration Christ leads us, His children, into the glory of His self-offering. It's as if we are hand-in-hand, united with Christ and with one another before the Father. With and through Christ we are offering perfect homage to the Father, in the Spirit, even from within our frailty in earthly life. (T:1264)

A uniquely horrible crime.

We need to realise the importance of attending Mass, which is a living memorial of Christ's Death and Resurrection. So we need to consider Christ's infinite love and patience, when He hung on the Cross, uncomplaining, in torment, looking up to the invisible Father.

It was as though Christ said, on Calvary: "Father! Out of My infinite love for You, I came to earth to teach and - inevitably - to suffer. Now, out of My infinite love for my brothers and sisters, I accept and offer to You all these torments, in an infinite reparation for all their offences against You. These offences merit their destruction, since sin is a terrible thing, and such rebellion against You causes the Heavens to shudder. And so here, in My sufferings, I willingly bear a punishment which Justice might demand for the sins of all Mankind! And I bear it, above all, for a crime as enormous as this, one which has no equal: the cruelties inflicted upon Myself, Your Son, the Divine and sinless Son of the almighty, holy and Eternal Father." (T:1351)

A willing Victim.

We must always be grateful for Christ's work of salvation: for the Paschal Mystery which we celebrate at every Mass. He bore the pain of His Passion because He loves us. For our sake He stood before His accusers, His arms bound, and His body dreadfully wounded by the scourging. Truly, He suffered and died for us, in His real, normal, human, sensitive and fleshly body; but because of His great love for us, He was a willing Victim. (T:1595)

Of unique worth.

It's important that we pray to the Father in the name of Christ, and that we believe in the unique worth of the Holy Sacrifice. It's true that the Father looks tenderly upon people who believe in a Creator-God and make sincere efforts to praise Him, even if they don't know Christ, are not 'one spirit' with Christ, and therefore don't pray in the name of Christ. However, the glory of Christ's praise is unequalled. And it's Christ's praise that we offer during the Holy Sacrifice of the Mass.

No other praise is worthy of the Father. All other prayers - all of those prayers which are not offered in Christ's name - are frail human offerings. They have not the power of the prayer which Christ the Son of God offers: a prayer to which our prayers are united because, by Baptism, we belong to Him. (T:1597)

The whole of Christ's earthly life.

It delights Our Lord, if we realise how astounding and how valuable is His Real Presence amongst us.

Every aspect of Christ's life - as once lived on earth - is present 'within' Him still. It's because He is man and God that He 'embraces' in His Being, even now, everything that He has ever experienced in His earthly life: and the wonder of our knowing this is being able to realise, first, that everything Christ did in earthly life was wholly good and graceful; and secondly, that the Mysteries of His earthly life are 'available', now, to everyone who is willing to 'gaze' at Him. It's as if we can gaze through a little 'window' which He has provided at a special point of intersection between His life and ours: at the Consecration.

This is good news because, even though nearly two thousand years have passed since Christ lived on earth, none of us is far-distant from His earthly life just because we are captive, for the moment, in time. None of us need envy the Apostles their earthly friendship with Christ, since even now we can be present to Christ - through His Real Presence. We can be present to His instruction of His first disciples, and to the first miracle, indeed, to every event of His life which can stir us to greater devotion or to greater selflessness. We can be sure that whenever Christ is here before us in the Blessed Sacrament - wherever He is Really Present - we are really as close to Him as were His Apostles and His other contemporaries. (T:1668)

Sharing Christ's life.

If we accept the reality of our nature, we can increase our understanding of the wonderful ways in which the Lord helps us. Since we are not wholly spiritual beings, but are body and soul, we are involved - body and soul - in 'touching' His Sacred Body in the Blessed Sacrament. We touch Him, our God, Who became man at the Incarnation.

It's true that we can achieve an extraordinary closeness to Him solely through faith in Him; yet our union with Him is most perfectly fulfilled when our whole being - body and soul - is intertwined with His life in the Mass and in Holy Communion, in a marvellously intimate and fulfilling way. (Also T:1668)

The fullest contact.

If we consider the fact that Christ our God once united Himself intimately and powerfully with humanity by taking flesh from the Blessed Virgin Mary, we'll remember that He lived on earth for only a short space of time. And now He lives in the glory of Heaven: true God and true man, our Redeemer. But we who love Him need not be despondent that we cannot yet join Him there.

Whenever we take part in the Mass, we are uniting our humanity, powerfully and intimately, to the Divine life which is made present to us at the Consecration when Christ our Redeemer is made Present. It is only through the Mass that our earthly life is 'opened', in a concrete way, to His entire life, and we can 'arrive' - so to speak - at an 'intersection' where human life meets a Divine Person. It is through the Mass that Mankind can make the most certain and the fullest-possible contact with its Divine Redeemer! (Also T:1668)

To bring us forgiveness.

We must be thankful for our faith, which causes us to see things clearly: to see our need for repentance, and yet to see, also, what unfailing help we can receive from Christ, and from His holy Mother.

There is no more fruitful way of praying than by offering the Holy Sacrifice; so we should never forget how powerful is Christ's sacrificial prayer. As the priest offers the Holy Sacrifice at the altar, he offers the same sacrifice as that which Christ offered to the Father from the Cross. We can be sure, therefore, that the sacrifice of the altar is of infinite worth, and is as fruitful as the sacrifice of Calvary. It makes possible - for sinners in this era - a forgiveness no less certain than that which was 'won' by the same sacrifice when Christ offered His life on the Cross. (T:1740A)

A truer participation.

It's important that we consider the manner in which the Church leads us towards the 'summit', during the Sacred Liturgy. All that precedes Christ's great act leads us towards the Saviour whose self-offering will follow. By our greeting at the beginning of Mass, our act of contrition, our love of the Word in Holy Scripture, our open-hearted attention to the homily, and our offering of gifts, we achieve a closer union with Christ: a closer incorporation, and therefore a truer participation in His self-offering which follows in His Holy Sacrifice. (T:1804)

Through our prayerful presence.

We should be ever-grateful for the faith which brings us to this sanctuary to assist at the offering of the Holy Sacrifice. It's true that Christ died to save us all. He died in order to make salvation possible for each individual; yet each of us must acknowledge Him and be baptised, and acknowledge His saving sacrifice, if we want to be saved. Those of us who have faith in Him, and in His sacrifice, must offer that saving sacrifice to God for our offences. The usual way of doing this is through our prayerful presence before the altar, at the offering of the Holy Sacrifice of the Mass. (T:1857)

A sacrifice for sinners.

We should never forget this good news: that there is no sin - no matter how terrible - for which atonement cannot be made through Christ's infinitely-worthy sacrifice of Calvary. This is the very sacrifice which is re-presented before us, and which Christ offers to His Father, at the hands of our priest, during the Holy Mass.

Truly, this sacrifice is so powerfully effective that no-one - not even the worst sinner - need imagine that his sin is so great that he cannot be pardoned. Christ, by His death, has atoned for the most cruel and horrible sins; and the offering which Christ made to the Father from the Cross can be 'touched' and offered today, by us sinners, as it is offered from the altar. (T:1934)

Innumerable blessings.

Whoever doubts God's love should remind himself that the Father, through His kindness, gave us Jesus His Son who suffered and died for us. All that God the Father achieves in our lives has been made possible only through the Precious Blood of Jesus. All the spiritual gifts we receive are ours only because of Jesus Christ: through what He has done for us in His terrible Passion.

Truly, we are utterly dependent upon Christ, and upon His grace. He left behind the glory of Heaven to live amongst us. He alone healed the rift between Mankind and the Father: between us sinners and our Creator. Only because Christ hung on the Cross, dying, giving His life for our sakes, can we now seize and enjoy the spiritual things which delight us, and receive innumerable blessings, many of which we take for granted. (T:2146)

The greatest friend.

Christ wants us to recognise and celebrate the many blessings which He gives us through our membership of His Church, as well as the Holy Eucharist. Amongst those blessings are the real friendship which we are offered with the Saints.

Truly, we have Heavenly friends as well as earthly companions. The Saints love to pray with us and for us. Yet we should be grateful, above all, for knowing Christ: the greatest friend, Whose love for each one of us is infinitely compassionate, and unending. (T:2251)

Fire from Heaven.

We should all be grateful to God that He has sent His Son to earth to live amongst us, to die for us, and that He has provided us with a living memorial of Christ's loving work. It's as if a great conflagration lies before us, on the altar, where Christ intercedes for us, during the Holy Sacrifice. Here, we can say, is 'fire from Heaven', as the fire of Christ's infinite love blazes before the Father. Here, Christ makes His eternal offering, and prays His prayer for us. It's as though the whole church interior has been enveloped in flames which illumine everything and everyone within this space, and which burn so fiercely that they reach beyond the roof, as far as Heaven. Such is the power of Christ's love for the Father, and for us, His own People.

We should always remember how fortunate we are, at Mass, to be able to stand within the radiance of this Heavenly light, the source of which is Christ, Really Present in sacramental form. It is very important that we prepare ourselves by prayer - and some, by Reconciliation - to take part in what is a holy and glorious celebration. As 'God's People' we should all try to be worthy of this holy place, worthy of these Sacred Mysteries - and worthy of the Presence of Christ our God. (T:2251)

A living faith.

Christ wants us all to realise that faith is a wonderful, priceless gift; yet it's also a living thing which either flourishes or dies. If we follow faith's obvious demands, we cause it to grow stronger. For example, a person who really believes in God wants to know more about Him. He discovers and admires God's attributes. He delights in His love. He is grateful that Christ was sent from Heaven to save him. He praises the Father for His goodness. He decides to love and serve Jesus Christ his Saviour.

A sincere believer repents of his sins. He is fervent in prayer. He joins the Church which Christ founded. He delights in her teachings: given with Christ's authority. He reveres those who teach him. He yearns to please Christ. He runs eagerly to the holy sacraments through which Christ feeds and helps him. He tries with all his power to love his neighbour, both by prayer and by service, and also by sharing his wonderful news about the forgiveness of sins, about friendship with Christ, and about the hope of Heaven. So Christ want us all to understand that if we are always grumbling about our prayers, our duties, our obligations as Church members, and our priests and bishops, we are plainly making little effort to increase our faith. (T:2573)

Access to the Father.

It is through the Mass that we who belong to Christ are enabled to 'touch' the Father. Through Christ's sacred offering we are able to bridge the chasm between Mankind and the Godhead, and to be one with the Father from whom Mankind was separated after the Fall.

During the Mass, it's as though we are present to Christ on His Cross. Here in our midst, He is reaching out His arm to the Father. So we have a bridge over which we can climb to Heaven, in spirit: to reach the peace and glory which, without Christ, were beyond the reach of sinful human beings, including ourselves. (T:2615)

Faith in Christ's love for us.

We must treasure our faith, and safeguard it. It is the risen Christ Who is really Present amongst us at every Mass; so no earthly trouble or loss can totally extinguish the joy in our hearts, if we firmly believe that Christ is alive. Nothing can conquer us if we also believe that Christ loves us, forgives our sins, feeds, teaches and consoles us, and urges us on toward Heaven where He awaits us, and where He will bring us into the presence of our Eternal Father. (T:2642)

At the foot of the Cross.

Everyone who is present before Christ during the Mass is really present to the very sacrifice which Christ offered long ago from the Cross on Calvary, for our salvation. Today, it's as though we are standing at the foot of the Cross. The Church makes this claim because, here before us, the very same thing happens as happened on Calvary - though not crucifixion, or the shedding of the blood, but Christ praying to the Father, just as when Christ hung on the Cross on Calvary, asking the Father to pardon sinners. Here today, Jesus Christ that Victim and Saviour is Really Present amongst us; and Christ is praying to the Father, here today, asking Him to pardon us sinners. (T:2674)

The events of Christ's life.

If people ask us about the Mass, Christ is pleased to hear us explain that: "The Mass is at the heart of the Faith". If it's appropriate, we should state what it is, and explain its purpose, then lead people step by step through its several parts.

We should say: "The Mass is a memorial of the Passion and Death and Resurrection of Christ," and, "It is like a story" - though not a mere remembrance.

We can say: "During the Mass we are made present in a mysterious way to the most significant events of Christ's life: to His Passion, Death, Resurrection and Ascension. The real summit of the Mass - after Christ's word in Holy Scripture - consists of Christ Himself being Really Present in the Blessed Sacrament, when the change has been effected in the bread and wine, at the Consecration, by the Holy Spirit. Christ's Sacred Body and Blood are made Present; and His sacrifice is offered to the Father from our altar." (T:2782)

Mankind reconciled to the Father.

In explaining the meaning of the Mass, we can say quite truthfully that the Mass is an act of love. God Who created us loves us. He has reached down to us all in our desperate need. He gave His

Son to live amongst us and to die for us. He raised Christ up to a new life in which we can share one day in bliss and glory if we put our trust in Christ, allow Him to transform us by His Spirit, and remain faithful to the end.

The sacrifice of the Cross was the loving act by which Christ reconciled Mankind to the Father, long ago. And today, the sacrifice of Calvary - the same sacrifice - is re-presented on the altar, somewhere in the world, daily, or hourly. The Holy Sacrifice of the Mass is a loving act: Christ's loving act by which supreme homage is offered, in the Spirit, to the Father. By this act, salvation is offered, today, to all who put their trust in Christ, their Redeemer and friend. (Also T:2782)

Evidence of God's love.

The Mass - the Holy Eucharist - is both a sacrament and a sacrifice; and it's all about love: Christ's love for us and for the whole of Mankind.

All gifts from God are given because He loves us; but the Holy Eucharist is the supreme evidence of His love for us, and the holiest event upon earth. (T:2791)

Present to the same sacrifice.

Christ wants us to know that if we use three simple statements, which we can 'expand' later on, we have a simple way of explaining what lies at the heart of the Church. We can explain the institution of the Holy Eucharist, which is also called the Holy Sacrifice of the Mass.

First, we can say that Christ 'leaped' down to earth to take flesh from the Virgin Mary, to live amongst us, and later to die to save us; and then He rose up to a new and glorious life, and then entered Heaven. Secondly, we can share the wonderful news that Christ left behind a means by which we can always be present to that same sacrifice and can offer it to the Father - through our priest - as our supreme act of homage and worship. Thirdly, we participate in the sacrifice by prayer, and by eating the sacrificial offering, which is Christ's Sacred Body and Blood - our spiritual food. (T:2792)

Present, as Christ prays on our behalf.

We can explain, about the heart of the Mass, this astonishing but simple truth: that when we are gathered together before Christ, Who is Really Present after the Consecration, we are present as He prays to the Father on our behalf!

If we are united to Christ, we can offer His perfect homage, worship and sacrifice to the Father as our very own. (T:2804)

In reparation for our sins.

Our willing and devoted participation in the Mass is powerfully effective for our own souls. When we offer Christ's Sacred Body and Blood - His sacrifice - to the Father, it's as though we rightly 'claim' His wounds as our own, and His Passion and Death as our own acts. It's as though we ourselves can say, of Calvary's offering: "Father: in accepting what has happened to me in a sinful world, through the actions of sinful persons, I have borne all possible punishment that someone might ever want to inflict upon another person; and I've borne it in reparation for my sins." We can make that claim today, for ourselves, because of our belief in Christ and our union with Him. We can make that claim because Christ is the Person Who has borne the sufferings of His Passion for our sakes: for each one of us.

Whoever acknowledges Christ and puts his trust in Him, powerfully benefits from the atoning sacrifice which Christ once offered on Calvary and which is now offered from the holy altar. Each person who does this can be confident and joyful, knowing that he can claim as his own the reparation which Christ, the

Innocent, offers to the Father. (T:2834)

The Church's new Catechism.

Whoever needs to know more about the Sacred Liturgy should ask: "What does the Church teach?" Catechists who want to share and explain the teaching and practise of the Church should especially use the new 'Catechism of the Catholic Church' as they teach the faith of the Holy Scriptures. (T:2920)

An elevated point of view.

We can picture our spiritual journey as being like the crossing of a vast ocean; but we don't need a boat, because the Sacred Liturgy is like a huge wave, which can carry us along, if we're willing to leap onto it.

If we allow ourselves to be swept safely towards Heaven little by little, through the means provided by Christ, we have an elevated view point. We see everything and everyone more clearly from the top of that huge ocean wave. We have the security of going in the right direction, at great speed, and with like-minded companions, pondering our journey. We will eventually be deposited on the shores of Heaven, if we allow ourselves to be immersed in the Liturgy for our whole lives - and if we haven't foolishly tried to make our own way land-wards, by our own power. (T:2922)

God praises God.

We are present to an awesome offering, at every Mass. We can be sure that, through Christ's sacrificial offering to the Father, in the Spirit, God praises God in God, in every valid Mass, whether it's celebrated in a great basilica or a little parish church. That's the glorious truth that we should convey as well as we can to enquirers. (T:2924)

No greater story or drama.

Christ wants us all to realise that He is more deserving of love, awe and admiration than are any of the marvels which He has created. What person or drama or story or landscape can move the heart to greater joy and gratitude - in those who hear and believe - than the true story of a Saviour from Heaven, and of the sacrifice which He has offered to save us? This is why He yearns for ignorant or careless souls to be helped to realise what happens in the sanctuary, and to believe, therefore, that He is worthy of their love, and of their prayerful and reverent attention. (T:3067)

A powerful plea for help.

The Mass is the most powerful means of helping other souls. It is the greatest prayer, the one in which Christ the God-man Who is Really Present amongst us offers a powerful plea for help and graces to be given to His earthly brothers and sisters. That's why we should aim to be more closely united to Him as He makes His prayer from our altar. (T:3091)

A living sacrifice.

We should be overwhelmed with gratitude that we can offer Christ's Sacred Body and Blood in the Mass, in reparation for our sins. Truly, Christ is a worthy sacrifice. It's as if He is our 'burnt offering' for sin. Yet His is a living sacrifice because He is Present amongst us now, in the sanctuary, living and glorious. We can say that the 'fire' of His sacrifice is the glory of the Holy Spirit by Whose power Christ has been made Present. (T:3301)

Asking for salvation.

It's an admirable thing to have a Mass offered for someone's salvation - and to arrange this out of love for a person who is still alive, in earthly life, but who never prays. If we do such a thing, Christ admires our faith: the faith that Christ's offering in the Mass is the greatest and most powerful plea to the Father that can be offered from upon earth. (T:3434)

An effective sacrifice.

If we arrange to have a Mass offered to help another soul - a person living or departed - this delights God our Father, since so few people are fully aware of the power of the Mass.

So few of us pray the Mass with a sincere belief that it is the sacrifice of the Cross re-presented and is therefore effective for the salvation of men, women and children today. It is truly effective for those who take part, and for those for whom it is offered and who don't refuse God's graces.

It's very important that we try to share the wonder of the Mass through books and pictures and speech, and also through our example, and through our prayer. (Also T:3434)

The heart of the Mass.

If we are speaking about the Mass to young teenagers, or to newcomers, we please Christ if we explain the Mass in its simplicity, as simply as a child. This means brushing away the long explanations we could give of one aspect of the Mass or another, in order to mention the 'heart' of the Mass: the sacrificial offering.

Christ wants us to explain that the Mass is a memorial of His saving work on Calvary - and of His Resurrection and Ascension. It is a living memorial, not a mere remembrance, because Christ our living Lord is Really Present amongst us, sacramentally. Indeed, He remains amongst us in the Blessed Sacrament of the tabernacle.

We should go on to say that only through the goodness of God is it possible that we who couldn't be with Christ as He died on the

Cross can be with Him now, as He offers that same sacrifice at the hands of our priest. If we say this, when we explain the Mass, people who are ashamed of their sins will be given more hope than if they are only told that the Mass is a community celebration or a sacred meal.

We should say that if we receive Christ our God devotedly in Holy Communion we can be made Godly - by His Divine power and life and graces. That's the supreme blessing of Holy Communion, although there are others which are very important. (T:3779)

Christ's eternal self-offering.

Christ longs for us to realise that at every Mass we take part in something Heavenly, holy and exalted. We should remind ourselves that God is love: a triune love which is beyond our comprehension yet which we know to be blissful, unending, and generous and fruitful. We know that Christ's loving self-offering to the Father, in the Spirit, is eternal, and that it is being shown out, on earth, in the Holy Sacrifice of the Mass. And that's why we can reflect, with awe and wonder, that there is no greater act of worship on earth than the Holy Sacrifice of the Mass.

The reason why the praise which is offered in the Mass is so powerful and exalted is that it is Christ's own praise, offered from our midst. We can say that at every celebration of the Mass we participate - more fully than at any other time - in the eternal act of praise and love which takes place within the Godhead: within the 'heart' of the Holy Trinity. (T:4270)

A pledge of eternal glory.

It's as though the Mass is the 'moment' at which we can leap most surely, in the Spirit, into Christ's perpetual loving prayer to the Father which takes place in Eternity. We can be helped to realise that this is true, if we look back for a moment to Christ's life on earth, and to the reason why Christ instituted the Holy Eucharist.

When He was doing His Father's Will on earth, whatever the cost, Christ was living out in the flesh, for our sakes, the very self-giving love which He shows towards the Father in Heaven. He especially showed out that eternal love by loving His Father's Will even when this led Him through an unjust trial, to the Cross. So each person who makes himself one with Christ today in the living memorial of the Cross - by sincere participation in the Mass - can be sure that he is one with Christ in Christ's eternal self-offering in the inner life of the Holy Trinity.

That is why we say that the Holy Eucharist is a pledge of eternal glory as well as a sacrifice for sin. Whoever belongs to Christ, and participates in the Mass, and receives Christ worthily in Holy Communion, has a foretaste of the union and communion which we can enjoy for all Eternity, if we remain faithful. (Also T:4270) *(See illustration 26)*

One great act of love.

Through God's self-revelation in Christ our Saviour we have grown in understanding of the Godhead. We know that everything God does is one great act of love. We cannot see God's love for God, in God, in Eternity. Yet the unending love of the Three Divine Persons is the very love which caused Christ to descend to earth to live amongst us, to die for us, and to rise from the grave, in order to draw us into the life and love of the Godhead. Through the Holy Sacrifice of the Mass that same love is now made ours to offer to the Father.

As we gather with the priest, by whose hands we offer Christ's praise to the Father, in the Spirit, we offer a love and homage worthy of the Father. We offer Christ's love: Christ's unique and perfect sacrifice; and in doing so we increase our union with the Father. It's as if we are drawn upwards towards the almighty Father Who is love's origin and source. (Also T:4270)

With solemn dignity.

Though God delights in every loving glance towards Him by one of His children, He also delights in the formal prayers which we might 'borrow' from the Sacred Liturgy for use in private prayer. For example, He is deeply honoured by a sincere recital of the Trisagion: "Holy God. Holy and mighty One, Holy and Immortal One." As we pronounce the phrases which are long-treasured in the Church we join our voices to the voices of the thousands who praise God in Heaven with solemn dignity as well as gladness. We send into Heaven, thus, the very message of Heaven, where all the Saints and holy Angels adore and praise God in extraordinary joy and glory. (T:4478 and T:4504)

The fruit of the sacrifice.

God our Father wants everyone to be taught five important truths about the Mass. First, He wants us all to understand that at this 'living memorial' of Christ's Passion and Death we are present to the very same sacrifice as that once offered by Christ on Calvary. Secondly, He wants us to believe that Christ died for our sins. Thirdly, He wants us to realise that by offering this sacrifice of the altar we offer Christ's sacrifice for our own sins. Fourthly, it's only if we are fully 'in communion' with the Church through which the Holy Sacrifice is offered that we can offer it completely as our own - at the hands of the priest. Only in such a state are we truly fully part of God's priestly People; and we are plainly not 'in full communion' if we no longer believe in the truths of the Faith, or if we have not yet confessed our mortal sins, or if we have left the Catholic Church to join another body of worshippers, or if we have chosen to marry 'outside' the Church - or have in any serious way set ourselves against Christ and His Church. Fifthly, however, the Lord wants us to understand that Holy Communion is the 'fruit' of the sacrifice, for those whose sins are forgiven.

The Mass is not merely a 'Holy Communion' service; nor is it merely a special family meal. If children are not taught the whole truth about the Mass, they won't learn how to unite themselves with Christ in His offering of the Holy Sacrifice; nor will they belong to a generation which offers a Mass for a special intention. (T:4518)

TEACHING OUR CHILDREN

The next generation.

It is the Will of God that we pass on to our children the all-important details of the Faith, and so keep them from emulating those of our ancestors who betrayed or deserted Christ and His Church. It is not only our privilege but our duty to teach the next generation.

We can convey our own faith and fervour to our children by teaching them and by setting a good example. We can also help them by speaking joyfully about the lessons we have learned from present and past teachers of the Faith, by mentioning with joy the lives and examples of the Saints, by teaching them about Christ's triumphs in every age, and by sharing something about our own knowledge and experience of His love and mercy. (T:1259B)

Choosing our words with care.

We should speak with care at all times about sacred ceremonies and objects but especially when instructing children. 'Good' language about things to do with our Faith will encourage good behaviour and so will reinforce good teaching about reverence in worship.

The Communion wafer which has been consecrated is best described to little children as "The Host", or "the Sacred Host," or "the Body of Christ," and not merely as "the bread." These children will soon be encouraged to kneel and to adore Christ, when they see the Blessed Sacrament on the altar. They will be confused if they are asked to worship or to genuflect to something which has been spoken of merely as "the bread". Yet they will readily kneel and adore if they are told that Christ is Really Present: that 'the Host' is His Body - risen, entire and 'disguised'. If "the bread" is the name used in a casual fashion for what has become His Sacred Body and Blood after the Consecration, they will be less easily led, later, to an understanding of the Holy Sacrifice. The 'meal' aspect will be at the forefront of their minds. It's our duty to help them to understand, using appropriate words, that the Mass is first of all a sacrifice to God. Although the Rite of Communion is essential to the Mass it is incomprehensible without the whole Eucharistic prayer and the Eucharistic Sacrifice. (T:2291A)

Our duty to speak.

The unruliness and noisiness of some of the children in church today is due to ignorance rather than malice. Yet it's our duty to speak gently to those children, if they are nearby. If we don't do so, some of them might never be told about reverent worship and about God's holiness. (T:2485)

The sacredness of the building.

We should pity the parents who allow great ignorance in their children; for example, those parents who permit their children to shout their way from back to front of the church without a single gesture of reverence towards Christ, showing no respect for those who are praying. It's a cause for shame that many Catholic children today give no thought to the sacredness of the church building, or to Christ's Presence in the tabernacle. (T:2976)

How to behave in holy places.

It is not appropriate that people call loudly to one another the length of the church, except in an emergency, or that children be allowed to shriek and run about or to jump up and down the sanctuary steps. Christ loved to comfort and feed little children. He wants them to be close to Him. But He also wants parents to teach them how to pray, and how to behave in holy places, and how to act during the Sacred Mysteries. (T:3064)

Apathy and discourtesy.

Christ wants us to realise that for a whole generation there has often been a lack of instruction about reverent behaviour in church and at prayer. This has led to the apathy, ignorance and discourtesy commonly demonstrated in His Presence today, in our churches. (T:3332)

Taken to a quiet place.

Christ is not honoured where children are loud and boisterous in church rather than prayerful and reverent. His love for them is inextinguishable. He delights in their trusting and happy hearts. Yet He wants them to be taught how to behave at holy ceremonies and in holy places. He knows that children can be trained to be quiet, or can be taken to a quiet place which has been set aside for distressed or noisy children, or even taken outside, if they won't behave. (T:3348)

By the hill of Calvary.

If we want to explain the Mass in visual terms, whether to children or to adults, we can say that, at every Mass, it's as though the small hill of Calvary appears through the ground at our feet. At every Mass, it's as though we are standing by the Cross on which Christ died for our sins. We are offering, in our day, the very sacrifice which Christ once offered from the Cross on Calvary, as His Holy Mother stood close by. Yet we are offering it in a different manner: a sacramental manner. (T:3557)

Our living Lord.

It's important that children be told that the Mass is a memorial of the saving work of Christ on Calvary - and of His Resurrection and Ascension. We must also say that it's a living memorial, not a mere remembrance, and that this is because Christ is alive and is Really Present amongst us, sacramentally, and remains amongst us in the Blessed Sacrament of the tabernacle.

We should explain the meaning of words such as sacrifice, sacrament and tabernacle; then we can go on to explain that since we couldn't be with Christ when He died on the Cross nearly two thousand years ago we can be with Him now, as He offers that same sacrifice at the hands of the priest. If we say this, children will be given more insight, and will develop a greater sense of awe and gratitude, than if they are merely told that the Mass is a community celebration or a sacred meal.

It will also delight them to hear that if we receive Christ in Holy Communion with love and devotion we can be made holy - by His Divine power and life and graces. (T:3779)

The First Commandment.

In handing on the Faith to Catholic children, we can be glad to know that there is scarcely a Catholic child who hasn't learned that we should care for our neighbour and help the poor and the sick. But few have been offered as clear an idea of how to fulfil their duties towards God, as required by the First Commandment. (T:4172)

Christ's explanation.

Christ wants us to help our children to understand the real meaning of the Mass. He asks us to explain the Mass to little children just as we explain other things to children: by telling a true story - and by using appropriate language, to offer something as fascinating as a bed-time story.

The 'story' will have a beginning, which is 'God', and an end - which is ourselves at Mass today; and this story will have not just truth, but also excitement, and a Hero, and drama and sadness, and then joy.

The story should also relate to them, through what we say about sinfulness, and Church membership, and the privileges given to 'children of God'. We should include, in our story, that Jesus commanded His followers to "Do this" - 'this' being a solemn remembrance of what He's done, and the making-Present of Jesus Christ amongst us, sacramentally.

We should show that to go to Mass is an awesome privilege as well as our duty.

We should explain that the Mass, as well as being a sacrifice, which we'll explain a little later on, is a special, holy ritual feast which first took place within a ritual Passover meal. It is not an informal community meal.

We must say that it is so holy that we have special gestures and words. And special behaviour is required of us, behaviour which is reverent, respectful, prayerful and sometimes silent. That is why we do not chatter, race about, shout to our friends or play games in church. We pray to God, and do what the Church asks of us throughout the Mass. Then we leave quietly when the Mass has finished and when we have finished our prayers. (T:4844)

Lessons for children.

Christ delights in seeing the zeal and the love of those priests who make great efforts to teach children about the Mass, and to make them and their parents welcome. He is thrilled whenever His priests encourage parents to play their part in handing on the Faith. Yet there are times when, through a desire to help parents, or to show zeal about the childrens' participation, a kind-hearted priest asks dozens of little children to sit in the sanctuary during the Mass. In Christ's sight this is neither good nor useful for the children, nor helpful for the parents and other Mass-goers.

The words of Christ in the Gospel about allowing the children to come to Him are misinterpreted where they are seen as indicating that children need not learn how to participate with solemnity in the solemn worship of the Church. Christ cherished the children who came to Him in His earthly life; yet He would not have been happy to see them run all over the Temple precincts, ignorant of how to behave in a house of prayer.

Today, He fervently welcomes children who come to receive Him in Holy Communion. Yet He likes them to be taught how to genuflect, how to kneel, and how to process in church, as well as how to trust in His love. Where children become accustomed to sitting idly around the church, neither standing for the Gospel nor kneeling for the Consecration, they are not being helped and educated in worship in the way the Lord desires. (P.U.T:16)

Humility and purification.

It's important that children are taught not only about God's great love for us all, but also about His astounding beauty, majesty, glory and power. They should also learn that God wants to share His glory with us, because He is immensely generous and kind. But they deserve to hear the whole truth, which is that no-one can share it who hasn't some humility, or who hasn't undergone some purification. That truth is not much taught to Catholics today; and Christ wants even children to hear it.

Christ sees that courageous priests and teachers and parents who speak about humility and purification are not proposing what some would label a 'stern' doctrine; rather, they are telling the simple truth both about human nature, which is sinful or inclined to sin, and about Divine nature, which is holy. (T:4999)

The Lord's throne-room.

It's a matter of great concern to Christ that many children have not been taught how to conduct themselves in church. Some have no idea of how to act with courtesy and reverence, and how to make reverent gestures, and how to act and speak quietly, if they need to speak to parents or other people before, during or after the Sacred Liturgy.

Christ invites us to teach the children that the church is like a 'throne room' of the Lord; so no-one should behave in it with less courtesy and respect than is usual in the throne room of an earthly monarch. (T:5015)

Lacking love and humility.

It is plain, in Christ's sight, that those who are lacking in reverence today, towards Him, are often lacking both love and humility.

Though it is right that we be aware of our dignity as God's family, it is a grievous thing, in the Lord's sight, that Christian children today are taught more about self-esteem than humility, and that many Catholic parents and teachers look with disdain upon the penitential practises of Saints of past ages. Many scorn the humble phrases which the Saints have used in prayer, and describe the reverent gestures used by the Saints in prayer as being unnecessary or old-fashioned. (T:5020)

Sacrifice and sacrament.

Children need to be taught that the Mass is both sacrifice and sacrament: both a solemn, living memorial of Christ's Passion and Death, and a joyful sacred meal for the family of God. Christ asks us to consider this question: If children don't learn that Christ came to earth to die for our sins, to save us, and to lead us to Heaven, how can they be grateful to Him? How can they be so grateful that they show their gratitude by leading holy lives as well as by sincerely welcoming Christ in Holy Communion?

It's only too easy to 'reduce' the content of the Faith, when we teach children. If, for example, we give the impression that the Mass is simply a happy family meal in church at which we thank God our Creator for our beautiful planet, and for Jesus His Son Who came to earth to show us how to be kind, they receive a gravely inadequate version of the Catholic Faith.

Even children need to recognise Mankind's need of the help of God - so marvellously given through the Incarnation.   Even children need to hear about the Cross and the empty tomb - as well as about healings and parables - and to hear about the sacrifice of the altar as well as about the Blessed Sacrament which we receive in Holy Communion.   We should be eager to share these important truths of the Faith, but in a language that children can understand. (T:5024)

FEASTS AND MEMORIALS

Special feast-days and anniversaries.

Christ likes to see us celebrate and enjoy special feast-days and anniversaries. There are days for mourning, as well. Through the Church, He gives us time to reflect on everything which the human heart needs to ponder. Christ refreshes and encourages us with His joy and light, especially on feast-days. This is how He enables us to endure the more difficult parts of our earthly 'journey'. (T:186)

Celebrating each festival.

We should be glad to celebrate feast days, anniversaries and special occasions, which are reminders of Christ's love for us.

On every such occasion, when we pray with sincerity and devotion, Christ adorns our souls as havens of His mercies and graces, as He too celebrates and enjoys the festival. (T:567)

Gratitude towards Our Lady.

We should be glad to honour Our Lady and to celebrate her feast days. Christ wants us all to realise that we can prove our love for Him by loving the holy Mother whom He reveres. (T:741)

Helped by the prayers of the Saints.

We should have faith in the Church's teaching about how greatly we are helped by the prayers of the Saints. We honour them by our requests for help. It's as though they jostle for the privilege of helping us.

They are delighted whenever we thank and honour them as Christ desires. They like us to confide in them and to ask their assistance; furthermore, they have every sympathy for us in our struggles; and they understand our temptations. (T:812)

The Saints' delight in our greetings.

We should unite our prayers to the prayers of the priest, during the Holy Sacrifice. With him, we can remember and name the Saints who now live with Christ in Heaven. They are thrilled to be remembered and named by us during our holy celebration; and they are touched and grateful for all God's graces and joys and for their friendship with ourselves who are Christ's friends on earth. (T:958)

To decorate the church.

We can imitate the Holy Angels, who make fervent preparations for the great feasts, for example, the Feast of the Nativity. They are present in the sanctuary, bearing heavy garlands of leaves with which to decorate the church in honour of Christ and His holy Mother and Saint Joseph. (T:1040B)

With beautiful garlands.

We should imitate the fervour of the citizens of Heaven. They decorate the sanctuary of the church with beautiful garlands. They adorn the Lady Chapel too, as all Heaven prepares to celebrate the feast of the Assumption of Christ's Holy Mother. (T:1171)

The Mysteries of Christ's life.

If we transcend our limited ideas about the Mass, and about Christ's Presence amongst us, we'll find that the reality - known by a pure and vigorous faith - is more marvellous than we have ever realised. We'll understand the astonishing truth: that, during the Holy Sacrifice, we are present, here in this church, to the whole life of Jesus Christ, Who is Present with us! We are present to the Mystery of His holy Incarnation, to His life, His healings, and His teaching, and to His Death, Resurrection and Ascension - and more.

We need to ponder the significance of Christ's Real Presence. He is both God and man, and has come amongst us in order to offer His Holy Sacrifice for the glory of the Father, and to feed us on His Sacred Body and Blood. Yet there is no end to the blessings to be reaped from His Presence. Just as Christ is 'entirely' with us, sacramentally, during the Holy Sacrifice, so we can share, mysteriously, in His entire life! Truly, in these Holy Mysteries of the Church - as we kneel in Christ's Presence - and through the sacred feasts and seasons, we touch Christ in a thousand different and life-giving ways. (T:1330) *(See illustration 22)*

Feasts and seasons.

We should realise the marvel of the depth of our friendship with

31. CHRIST OUR HIGH PRIEST.

When the moment arrives for us to receive Christ in Holy Communion, we pause to say: "Lord: I am not worthy to receive you …" Christ our High Priest is Really Present. He is majestic and holy, yet also compassionate and tender. OIL-L:375. *("Look, I am standing at the door, knocking. If one of you hears me calling and opens the door, I will come in to share his meal, side by side with him." Rev 3:20).*

32. AT THE MERE TOUCH OF HIS HAND.

By a mere 'touch' in Holy Communion, Christ can deliver us from turmoil and fear. In all sorts of ways, He is at work to remind us that we are His beloved friends, immensely precious to Him. OIL-M:864. *("Now you are able to appear before him holy, pure and blameless - as long as you persevere and stand firm on the solid base of the faith, never letting yourself drift away…" Col 1:22-23).*

33. LITTLE SINS FALL LIKE ASHES.

Our little sins fall like ashes, as Christ draws each one of us towards Heaven, through our union with Him in Holy Communion. OIL-M:158. (*"In making these gifts, he has given us the guarantee of something very great and wonderful to come: ... you will be able to share the divine nature and to escape corruption in a world that is sunk in vice." 2 Pet 1:4*).

34. LEANING ON CHRIST'S HEART.

Though we don't yet see the face of Christ, we meet Christ in Holy Communion in real intimacy and joy. It's as though we can put aside all our fears and distractions in order to lean on His heart. OIL-M:154. *("Come to me, all you who labour and are overburdened, and I will give you rest. Shoulder my yoke and learn from me, for I am gentle and humble in heart." Mt 11:28-29).*

35. SHARING THE LIFE OF THE HOLY TRINITY.

When we draw close to Christ in Holy Communion, the Father and the Holy Spirit are not absent. Rather, in our loving union with Christ we are drawn further into the life of the Holy Trinity, to be embraced, consoled and transformed. OIL-S:1794C. *("Anyone who is joined to the Lord is one spirit with him." 1 Co 6:17).*

36. A BLESSING FROM GOD, THROUGH HIS CHURCH.
Christ Himself blesses, helps and sustains us - with the Father and
the Holy Spirit - through the blessing we receive from the priest.
OIL-S:1259. *(To you all then, who are God's beloved in Rome, called
to be saints, may God our Father and the Lord Jesus Christ send grace
and peace." Rm 1:7).*

Christ, and the marvel of our intimate union with Him through the Sacred Liturgy. We are not limited to story and speech in our friendship with Christ. We can be with Him: united to Him in a special way according to the feast or season in the Church. For example, after Christmas, at Epiphany, we can rejoice in being close to 'Jesus-now-shown-out' in His Epiphany. He is here, now Present with us at the altar. He is here, the same Person Who received visitors in His infancy. We who are truly close to our Divine Saviour, by our presence with Him now, during the Holy Sacrifice, are present also to the Person Who is held in Mary's arms, as she shows Him to those who have searched for Him in His infancy. So it is, also, with all the events of His life.

By our presence beside Christ, here at the Holy Sacrifice, where He is Really Present with us, we are touched by the grace of all of His life's Mysteries. It's as if those Mysteries are unravelling before us as feast follows upon feast. (T:1388)

Joining in our celebrations.

We should share in Christ's joy and glory, on His feast days. We can remind ourselves of the sheer delight which is now being shown by the Saints and the holy Angels as they too celebrate Christ's Real Presence in the Blessed Sacrament, on the feast of His Sacred Body and Blood, also known as Corpus Christi. (T:1442)

The Feast of the Holy Rosary.

We shouldn't be perturbed by the small number of companions at the Holy Sacrifice of the Mass. Many holy Angels are with us in church to celebrate, for example, our Mother's feast day - the feast of "Our Lady of the Rosary" - no matter how few of us have been able to attend.

The church is especially crowded near the sanctuary. The holy Angels cluster about the altar, in order to adore Christ and to honour His beloved Mother. (T:1485)

Our Lady and Saint Joseph.

Our devotion to Christ gives Him greater delight if it embraces everyone He loves so dearly. Whenever He comes in glory to the altar, at the Consecration, as His holy Angels bow low in adoration, He delights in our greeting. He also delights in hearing us thank His Mother and Saint Joseph for their kindness to Him during His life on earth. Whenever we honour them, we honour Christ. (T:1842)

Rewarded for their faithfulness.

It's important that we love and honour the Saints, especially on their feast-days. In the glory of Heaven, the Saints delight in the honour and thanks which they receive from their friends on earth through the words of the Mass. Their delight stems from the knowledge that it's the Will of the Father that they are rewarded in this way for their faithfulness in earthly life. There is great joy amongst them as we, who comprise the Church on earth, remember them and celebrate their triumphs.

Whenever the Church on earth marks a special occasion, there is a celebration in Heaven, with special honour bestowed upon the Saint involved in that special event. It's as if a great and gleeful party is held at which even the most humble of Saints can delight in the joyful congratulations which are offered by Heavenly friends as well as by friends on earth. (T:1870)

Christ's close relations.

It's important to remember that Christ our incarnate God loves all His relations. He loves to see us made joyful; and He delights in being close to people who love Him - for example, ourselves, and the Saints in Heaven. He celebrates the feast of All Saints with especial gladness. (T:2045)

Expressions of love for Christ.

We touch Christ's heart profoundly by our devotions, as we gather together on 'Good Friday' in grateful remembrance of His sufferings. He delights in our expressions of love and contrition. (T:2172)

Special treats.

We should look forward with confidence to each celebration of a feast-day. We should all expect to enjoy them, just as happy children expect to enjoy each special treat which has been arranged by loving parents.

All who love and thank Christ's Mother can make her feast-days their own. (T:2498)

Through Mary.

We are right to turn to the Father in Christ's name, to offer special thanks on the feast day of the Annunciation. It is through Mary that Christ has come to us to offer us salvation; so we should pray that other people will learn more about her role. Mary is the holy, ever-Virgin Mother of Christ, the Son of God; and so her great part in the plan of salvation should be recognised and celebrated by all 'children of God', and never minimised. (T:2568)

Celebration in Heaven.

Every feast-day we celebrate is being celebrated also by the Saints of Heaven. (T:2746)

Our Lady of Sorrows.

Christ is deeply touched by our grateful reflections on His Passion and by our words of gratitude to Mary - 'Our Lady of Sorrows' - who bravely and compassionately stood beside Him as He died to save us. (T:2997)

The feast of the Holy Trinity.

Christ is true man: risen and glorified; yet He is also true God, and therefore equal in majesty to the almighty, invisible Father, and to the Holy Spirit. That's why we should celebrate with gladness, each year, the feast of the Holy Trinity, even if we don't yet understand the depths of this holy Mystery. This is a day of especial joy for Christ. He shares His own glory with His friends by setting each of those souls on fire during the Mass or during Exposition of the Blessed Sacrament, making souls radiant with His Divine and holy light. (T:3067) G.H.T.

Music, in honour of Our Lady.

Our Blessed Lady is the greatest of all Saints; and we should never forget that she is very close to us. Sometimes she appears in church, to stand besides us, and to listen to the anthem which is being sung in her honour - for example, the 'Salve Regina,' after Holy Communion, on the feast of All Saints. (T:3297)

Eight special days.

We should remember that each of the days in the Octave of a great feast is like the feast itself, in Heaven and in Heaven's sight. So we should believe that God gives special joys and graces to each person who celebrates the feast with contrition, renewed joy, and gratitude during those eight special days. (T:3416)

Christ never forgets.

We need never be downcast, if we find that a special feast-day or anniversary which is important to us has been overlooked by the priest, or by the sacristan or by our own relations. Christ never forgets. Even when there are no special prayers, flowers or greetings, we can be sure that, in Heaven, Christ and His Mother, and all the Saints and Angels, are remembering and celebrating this Wedding Anniversary, or Ordination Anniversary - or whatever happy and holy event has caused us to praise and thank God. (T:4897)

THE YEARLY CYCLE

Christ: the same yesterday, today and forever.

We should rejoice that we can meet Christ in the sanctuary, and that when we do so we meet the Saviour Who gives us more than His Real and glorious Presence. Whenever Christ draws us close to Himself, in and through the Mass, He enables us to touch and 'meet' every aspect of His life: the life of the Person Who is both God and man.

It's because Christ's Divine nature is perfect and unchanging that we can reach out to Him - at every meeting - confident of being able to explore, in prayer and through the Liturgy, every mystery, event and aspiration of His life. Through the Holy Mass - in and through His Real Presence here - Christ makes present to us every age and incident of His life on earth, as well as sharing with us the graces and the glory of His Divine life and love. (T:1641)

THE END OF TIME

At the end of time.

We should rejoice in our privileged place as we praise and adore the Father with the whole Church, in and through Christ. Christ has drawn together many people - ourselves amongst them -

gathering us in His name before the Father, during the Sacred Liturgy, making us one People, ready for the eternal 'gathering' when, at the end of time, His victory will be revealed. (T:1326)

Every thought revealed.

We gain great benefits from having made a good preparation for Mass. If we are sorry for our sins, and are willing to reveal to Christ our every thought and yearning, we allow Him to change us. And if we continue to change, we need have no fear on the Great Day at the end of time, when every thought will be revealed.

If we wisely reveal our hearts and lives to Christ, today, in sincere prayer, we shall be preparing for the day of Judgement. On that day, God will reveal the wisdom of His plans and purposes. He will reveal our hidden motives, our secret acts, and hidden evils - though not our forgiven sins, which have all been 'banished'. So the more fully we reveal to Christ, today, all that is shameful and unworthy of a child of God, then the quicker can He lead us into a life of simplicity, purity and peace. (T:1623)

PRAYER

Calm, elegant behaviour.

We should all worship with great reverence, out of love for Christ. It's only right that we kneel and bow with a holy courtesy. Christ asks us to remember that calm, solemn and elegant behaviour, with gentle gestures and dignified movements, is supremely fitting for the celebration of the Holy Mysteries. This is because our worship in the Sacred Liturgy mirrors the accompanying worship of the Church Triumphant, whose Saints and Angels join us in the sanctuary.

We need to remember to Whom we address our prayers. It is not fitting that we worship with minds and hearts alone. If weak people like ourselves are careless in bodily posture, or lazy or distracted in our communal gestures, we are led to be careless or distracted in our minds; and then we fail to pay Christ the honour which is due to His majesty. (T:36A)

Our champion and intercessor.

In public and private prayer, we should pray with confidence as we pray in Christ's name. It's as though every prayer we offer to the Father is 'vouched for' by Christ.

We who are united to Christ by love and obedience offer our prayers with His authority and love. He is our champion and intercessor. It's as if Christ stands beside each one of us and says to the Father - as though to a King - "Accept the message of this person, My own friend, as though it were issuing from My own lips." If we pray in spirit and in truth through Christ our Lord it is impossible that the Father should fail to hear us. (T:51B)

With attentive hearts.

It's important that we pay attention to what we hear in church. Our hearts should echo every prayer of the Mass. (T:129)

Side by side with Christ.

For perfect participation in the Mass, we can place ourselves as if side-by-side with Christ in prayer, and pray to the Father with sincere, trusting and fervent hearts. In order to offer Christ perfectly to the Father in the Holy Sacrifice and in our whole lives, we should be Christ's images, as if holding out our arms in love and offering, as each of us says, with Christ: "Here I am, obedient to death!" (T:408)

One with Christ.

We should offer ourselves to the Father with Christ, as we gather before the altar, close to our Saviour.

As we turn in prayer to the Father we share in Christ's dazzling radiance, His obedient self-offering, and His confidence that He is heard. His prayer pierces Heaven as does no-one else's; and so our prayers reach Heaven if they are united to His. (T:493 and T:494)

A fire of glory.

We should remember to pray with fervour and sincerity. When we cluster joyfully before the altar, we can be certain that the prayer we pray together, with and through Christ, rises up powerfully to Heaven, like a great fire of glory. (T:819)

With trust and humility.

We need to trust in Christ, as we pray. Trusting confidence in Him, combined with humility, will unite us more surely with His Holy Sacrifice than any fine words or humble postures (T:856)

From within our frailty.

We should believe that the prayers we pray in union with Christ are powerfully effective. Through our contrite hearts, and Christ's prayer to the Father, we can offer a prayer of infinite power and glory from within our frailty. (T:921)

Focused on the altar.

During the Mass, Christ is urging us all: "Pay attention to the altar." What He means is that we should pay attention to the words and prayers which the priest offers on our behalf; and we should unite our hearts to Christ's self-offering. (T:966)

In truth and faith.

Whoever wants to offer God worthy praise and thanks should believe that no purer, greater prayer can be made in honour of the Father than a self-offering, in utter truth and faith, united to Christ's own offering of Calvary and altar. (T:1019C)

The most powerful prayer.

We should aim to live in unceasing union with Christ, so that His prayer and ours will be 'one prayer' to the Father.

The prayers which Christ offers through His Church are always heard and granted. We can rely on the prayers offered from our altar during the Mass for the salvation of all who freely unite themselves to their Saviour, and for unity and faith within the Catholic Church.

The Holy Sacrifice of the Mass is the most powerful prayer for every good intention. There, at the altar, Christ offers Divine praise, infinite thanks, perfect reparation and perfect petitions. (T:1020)

Each Guardian Angel.

We can be encouraged in prayer by the knowledge that our holy Angel stands reverently beside each of us as we pray 'in Christ', whatever type of prayer we offer in Christ's name. These Angels are beside us as we make sincere acts of faith in Christ, for example, during our sincere recitation of the Creed, during the Mass.

Each Guardian Angel is overjoyed to see Christ praised. Also, when Christ is praised, the Saints in Heaven are overjoyed at the sight, and are full of admiration for us who turn to Him in trustful prayer.

We should never forget the presence of our holy Angels. Our prayers will become more careful, reverent and unhurried if we remember not only the Lord to Whom we offer praise and thanks, but also the holy Angels beside us who witness our every word and gesture. (T:1524)

Infinitely-worthy prayers.

We need to unite our prayers with Christ's, during the Holy Sacrifice. In our presence, He offers to the Father perfect praise, perfect thanksgiving for all that is good, perfect reparation for sins, and infinitely powerful pleas for Mankind. Christ wants us to be comforted by the knowledge that those of us who accept unavoidable suffering most patiently are the most fully united with His sacrifice on behalf of Mankind, and therefore with His Divine and infinitely-worthy reparation. (T:1565)

To cause confusion.

We must be aware of the work of the Evil One who is trying to darken our lives and to draw souls away from trust in God, whether he is working to achieve this directly or indirectly. Though we ourselves are responsible for much of our slow progress towards union with God, the Evil One most certainly tries to do harm. He tries to spoil each new stage of our prayer, to cause confusion, to besmirch pure friendships, to implant unworthy thoughts, to make us quail in self-doubt, and to change anything in our lives which is good or holy.

Truly, the Evil One is at work, close-by. He makes constant efforts to 'muddy the waters' in every peaceful and grace-filled heart. But if we remain aware of his tactics we can act vigorously to halt his evil work. We can cling ever more fervently to God our Father through our mortifications, reflections, prayers, and good works; and then our lives - like clear pools which reflect the sunlight - will reflect the Father's glory. (T:1823)

A closer resemblance.

We should always strive to be more charitable and more prayerful. We can think about the work of a tailor who is asked to make a perfect copy of a garment. Just as his new piece of work must 'match' the original garment in every detail, so we who wish to offer Christ's perfect sacrifice 'perfectly', or wholeheartedly, should try to 'match' and resemble Christ as closely as possible.

We imitate Him most surely, during the Holy Mass, by 'matching' our prayers to His in the following ways. First, our praise of the Father should be as wholehearted and sincere as Christ s praise. Secondly, our thanks to our Father should be as sincere and lavish as Christ's own thanks. Thirdly, our prayer of reparation and sorrow-for-sin should be as heart-felt as Christ's, but with this difference: that He suffered for our sins, whereas we bewail our own sinfulness. Fourthly, our petitions during the Mass, as well as at other times, should be made with a 'Christ-like' purity of intention, and with a desire to 'match' Christ's own burning desire to see the Church strengthened, people everywhere helped, and the Father glorified. (T:1961)

To ensure salvation.

Everyone should pray. The merest 'whisper' of faith from the heart of a needy person who turns to God in prayer can ensure salvation. (T:2220)

An act of trust and submission.

God our Father delights in our prayerful words. He counts every phrase of the Creed a tribute. He counts every phrase of the 'Our Father' an act of trust and submission. He counts every phrase of the 'Hail Mary' a humble salutation, and every phrase of the 'Glory Be' an act of veneration. He counts every moment's meditation on the Passion and Death of Christ His Son a loving and fruitful occupation. Whoever truly loves Christ, the Son of

God, touches the Father's heart. (T:2534)

Worthwhile occupations.

Because the first Commandment is about love for God, we can be certain that our adoration and worship, and our spiritual communion with Christ, are more worthwhile activities than any other occupation, provided that we don't neglect obvious duties towards our neighbour in order to spend time in prayer. (T:2787)

To be single-minded.

We can learn from people in the world: lessons about motivation, and training. If we want to be single-minded in trying to achieve our aim, which is to reach the heart of the Godhead, we can learn a lesson from those who are ambitious, and who have learned the importance of concentration, regular practice - and even suitable clothing and posture.

Some of us are willing to go to endless trouble to dress and speak in appropriate ways for a special family party, or for a meeting with someone influential at work. Yet we don't make a fraction of the same effort in order to show respect for God, and gratitude for His perpetual loving-kindness. (T:3143)

One with Christ.

We make progress in the spiritual life when we realise that we offer Christ's sacrifice to the Father most perfectly when our hearts' desires are the same as Christ's heart's desires.

It's important that we unite our works and sufferings to Christ's offering. Yet when we can truly say that our desires are the same as His, we can be sure that we are one with Him in His unique offering. And those desires are that every person see the truth about Christ: that everyone come to believe in His teachings, to receive the sacraments, to give up sin, and to live in holiness and peace, loving and serving God and one's neighbour. (T:3684)

Love for the Church.

All Catholics should believe the truth and be willing to profess it: that the Catholic Church is for everyone, and that all who belong to it have sacred duties and obligations as well as immense gifts and privileges.

Whoever wants to offer the Holy Sacrifice most worthily will be praying, with Christ, that the Church will continue to preach and to grow, and to share, from its fullness, "the means of salvation". Each of us can pray for the other desires of Christ's heart, also mentioned in the Mass, such as special help for the Clergy, and for the Faithful Departed; and each of us can delight in giving glory to the Father and honour to His Saints and holy Angels. (Also T:3684)

Thousands of joyful voices.

We should pray every prayer at Mass with gladness and sincerity, for example: "Holy Holy, Holy Lord, God of power and might, Heaven and earth are full of your glory". As we pray these words, the thousands of Saints of Heaven, with all the Angels - and all the Holy Souls - are united with us in gladness and awe and celebration. With one voice, we are offering praise to God the Father Who, though unseen, draws us towards Himself by His holiness and power and beauty. (T:4532B)

At the 'edge' of Heaven.

By every act of love for God and every expression of gratitude it's as if we take a surer and more peaceful part in the worship of Heaven. It's as if, by prayer, we are at the 'edge' of Heaven, united in prayer with all the Saints and holy Angels who gaze upon the Holy Trinity. Even now, from our places on earth, we have a share in that holy worship, through our union with Christ, and our willingness to devote time to Him in prayer, as we unite ourselves with Christ in praise of the Father.

By our every effort to love God more, we enable Him to draw us closer to His heart, in the embrace of His Holy Spirit. (T:4710)

DISTRACTIONS

The majesty of Christ's sacrifice.

We should keep on praying during the Holy Mass, even when the words of the priest are almost inaudible because of the shouts of babies and little children. Nothing can detract from the majesty and dignity of Christ's tremendous sacrifice which is offered on the altar during our celebration. (T:957A)

Day-dreaming before the sanctuary.

When we are tired, and when our whole intention has been to pray sincere prayers, but we find ourselves day-dreaming before the sanctuary, we can be sure that Christ, Who is love incarnate, doesn't mind. He already knows about the things we do out of love for Him, and He knows our frailty, as well. (T:2991)

Over-active thoughts.

It's true that we can lessen the likelihood of having distractions during the Mass if we arrive in good time, and make a prayerful preparation; yet we can be sure of Christ's love, whatever our state. He looks with sympathy and compassion upon those of us whose thoughts are over-active because of recent and demanding work done for Him just before we arrive in church. (T:5008)

OUR ATTITUDE

Our privileged place.

It's easy for us to forget how privileged we are in being permitted to pray before Christ, amidst the Angels of Heaven. (T:54)

With a firm will.

We mustn't give in to the temptation to think that faith depends upon fluctuating feelings or sensations.

We can turn to Christ and to His Saints in prayer and praise, with a firm will, no matter what state our emotions are in, and even if we see no glimmer of 'light' in our souls.   Our prayers are valuable. Truly, God exists, and He hears us. (T:76)

Through the Spirit.

We should let our hearts be touched by the thought of the true Fatherhood of God. The fatherhood of men is a pale reflection of the reality. Our Heavenly Father created us. He sustains us in His love, together with Christ our Redeemer, and with Their loving Spirit. They are one God, always 'at work' to help us.

We should recognise the work of the Holy Spirit. It is through the Spirit that Christ embraces all who revere His Presence during the Holy Sacrifice of the Mass. (T:87)

Dependent on Christ.

We should unite our hearts and minds to the priest's intentions, at Mass. He is calling out on behalf of Christ's Body, the Church, which is gathered together before the altar. So we should always remember that we are dependent on Christ: on the holy sacrificial prayer which He offers on our behalf, through our priest. We should be praying to God with gratitude, instead of entertaining discontented thoughts about the length of the Mass, or grumbling to ourselves about our hardships. (T:113 and T:114)

Peace, purity and perfection.

We should pray fervently during the Mass, asking for the virtues we need and desire. Through Christ, we can obtain the peace, purity and perfection we long for. We can place our trust in Him and accept His blessings, which pour down upon us as we pray during the Holy Sacrifice: blessings brought to us through the Holy Spirit. (T:163)

Our pains and sacrifices.

We should unite all our pains and sacrifices to Christ's great offering, now that He has come amongst us in the Holy Sacrifice of the Mass. He is Really Present, robed as a priest, as He stands before us in the sanctuary. (T:545)

Towards union with Christ.

We should remember what Christ is doing for us, as He urges us to praise the Father with Him, through the Holy Sacrifice of the Mass. Christ is leading us towards union with Himself even in our earthly life, and towards eventual bliss with Him in Heaven! (T:754)

In sincere thanksgiving.

We need to go to Mass with an attitude of sincere thanksgiving to God for His goodness. If we are thankful, we can share the joy of the holy Angels who are thrilled by Christ's love for us all, and awed by the humility He demonstrated at His Incarnation. (T:794)

Pure intentions.

We should act, move and speak with reverence, during the Mass, in honour of Christ; yet we should never let attention to the external aspects of our public worship become more important than the pure and powerful intentions of our souls. (T:856)

Brothers and sisters of the Saints.

We should rely on Christ if we want to persevere on the way to His Kingdom. Christ can give us all the graces we need, to help us to persevere as far as Heaven. By His grace, we have already been made His children - brothers and sisters of the Saints, and friends of the holy Angels. That's how much He loves us: even people like ourselves who are so sinful and inadequate. (T:922)

The perfection of this worship.

However flawed are our voices or actions at Mass, we should recognise the perfection of the worship in which we take part. The whole Church of earth, Heaven and Purgatory praises the Father. That's why we can be certain that the praise of the Father which is offered by the Saints and the holy Angels, through Christ, in our presence, during the Holy Sacrifice, is as joyful, glorious and majestic as the praise which is offered eternally in Heaven! It is perfect because it is offered by Christ our God Who has come amongst us through His sacramental Presence. (T:1156B)

Wholehearted participation.

We must take part worthily in the Holy Mass, and so join in Christ's saving work. No-one offers Christ's sacrifice to the Father wholeheartedly who does less than Christ, that is, who is unwilling to offer his own life to the Father - in union with Christ - in the Father's service. (T:1271)

Christ's atoning work.

It's important that we acknowledge Christ's atoning work: His Passion, Death, Resurrection and Ascension. We can all be certain, about Christ and about Heaven, that without His Death we could not enter; and it's during the Holy Mass that we can acknowledge His saving work. (T:1432)

Christ's sacrifice, ours.

We should hold nothing back in our self-offering to God, in our everyday work and in our worship. Whoever offers himself to the Father and is wholly united to Christ the Redeemer, and dedicates to Christ all his desires and hopes, with his life and his energy, praises the Father 'perfectly'. By living 'in Christ' he is able to offer Christ's perfect prayer of praise, at Mass, as if it is his own! Such is the marvel of true union.

Christ's sacrificial praise, rising up to the Father from the altar, in the power of the Holy Spirit, is like a Divine fire which is burning before us: a triple flame which leaps upwards to Heaven. And our praise reaches Heaven, amidst these 'flames', because of Christ's power, our love, and our union with Christ. (T:1506)

The power of humility.

We should treasure humility. When we have placed all our trust in God, and not in ourselves, we are blessed with the love of the Father, the wisdom of the Spirit, and the sweetness of Jesus Christ, the Son of God, our Saviour.

The person who lives in humility has more power than Archimedes had with his fulcrum and lever. Through humility, we increase the strength of our union with Christ, and therefore we come to share His power. That's how we can work with Him to change the world: by His power, not through our own schemes, and our frailty.

We should cling to the knowledge that the grace of Christ, at work in a weak person, is more powerful than any merely human effort. (T:1718)

Complaints and disobedience.

We need to reflect on how willing we are to be obedient to Christ's plans at all times. Many of us grumble about what He asks us to do, even about tremendously important things such as regular attendance at Mass. (T:1933)

Christ, on the Cross.

We should celebrate the Sacred Mysteries with solemnity and gratitude. Christ is praying to the Father on our behalf Christ is Present with us at the Consecration in a special way. In His sacramental Presence, and through His perfect self-offering to the Father at the hands of the priest, He is achieving the work of our salvation.

It's as though His Cross has been planted at the centre of the sanctuary, with Christ hanging upon it. And Christ Who is Present amongst us offers, today, the very same Sacrifice as that which He offered long ago during His Passion. It is a self-offering to the Father which is now complete, perfect, loving, obedient and infinitely worthy. He offered it then, in obedience to the Father's Will; and He offers it today from our altar. (T:2009)

A true union.

We need to strive even more fervently to unite ourselves, wholly, to the perfect offering which Christ makes to the Father during the Mass. And we do this with special fervour and sincerity as the priest is saying, of Christ, "Through Him, with Him, and in Him, in the unity of the Holy Spirit, all glory and honour is yours, almighty Father, for ever and ever."

We can make the Holy Sacrifice more 'fully' our own in several ways. The first way is by having a sincere intention: a sincere longing for all that our Saviour is longing for. If this is true of us, our requests of the Father will be made wholeheartedly and will be the same as Christ's requests: for grace, perseverance and salvation for ourselves, with pleas for help for the entire Church, both for living and departed members. If we are truly united with Christ, we will offer, with Him, sincere praise of the Father, sincere thanks for everything that is good, with a sincere expression of horror-of-sin: whether this expression be implicit, because of our contrite hearts, or made explicit, in words. (T:2087)

A weight of loneliness.

We shall grow in admiration for Christ if we realise what a crushing weight of loneliness He has suffered for our sakes - even at the Last Supper, when He was with His close friends. No-one who was there had any real idea of what Christ was determined to undergo for us all, to offer us the hope of salvation.

That's one of the reasons why we ought to worship Him with both solemnity and awe, when we are present at this living memorial of His Passion, Death, Resurrection and Ascension. (T:2583)

A living sacrifice.

At its heart, the Holy Sacrifice consists of the offering from our altar of the Sacred Body and Blood of Christ our God Who is Really Present amongst us after the Consecration. We should therefore approach this living sacrifice in a worthy manner: with fitting solemnity, and gratitude. (T:3057)

Each time, a perfect offering.

We must never imagine that a particular celebration of Mass has been a 'failure', perhaps because the priest couldn't be heard, or we who attended were few in number, or our responses poor.

Although we should hope to be better prepared or better instructed, we can be certain, provided that the priest is validly-ordained and celebrates a valid Mass, that Christ's infinitely-worthy sacrifice has been offered from the altar, to the glory of God and the benefit of the whole Church, and the joy of Heaven.

The Holy Sacrifice of Christ is a perfect offering, no matter how lukewarm the faith and love of the lay-persons who participate in the Mass or of the priest at whose hands it is offered. Yet the degree of attention and love with which the Mass is offered is not insignificant. (T:4761)

Honoured by our love.

God the Father is honoured by Christ's offering in every valid Mass, no matter how badly it is celebrated; yet the Father is honoured more if He is honoured not only by His Son's perfect sacrifice but also by the love and reverence of those of us in the Church who offer it; and the following illustration explains this further.

We can imagine that a priest is receiving gifts from two of his parishioners and that the parcels he receives look identical - and indeed, the contents prove to be identical, when he has opened both parcels. He has received a perfect gift from each parishioner, yet it's plain to all the onlookers that the priest has been honoured more by the person who handed him a gift with gladness and a warm smile than by the person who - sullen and resentful - threw a box at him, unwilling to take the trouble to place it respectfully before him on the table.

Thus it is when Christ's friends attend Mass. If we really love Christ (and the Father and the Holy Spirit) we take care about preparation, participation and thanksgiving; and the Father (and the Son and the Holy Spirit) are honoured by our love as well as by the perfect sacrifice of Christ which we offer. (Also T:4761)

SPECIAL INTENTIONS

The most powerful prayer.

We should remember that during the offering of the Holy Sacrifice Christ asks the Father - on behalf of His brothers and sisters - for many gifts, all of which are granted. So the best and most effective prayer for an earthly friend is for the Holy Sacrifice to be offered for that person's intentions. We do this by asking a priest to offer Mass for this intention. The best and most powerful prayer for a departed soul -'best' because it is prayed by Christ - is the Holy Sacrifice, offered to the Father as a plea for pardon and salvation. (T:1020)

Offered in thanksgiving.

It is a wonderful act of faith to arrange for a Mass to be offered in thanksgiving for a special occasion. Whatever Christ wants for this person shall be achieved, because Christ himself is here. It's as if Christ is holding out His arms to the Father in prayer. Christ is praying our petition for us, at the 'per ipsum', as we are offering Christ and His sacrifice and His glory to the Father in praise of the Father's glory. And as we put our trust in Christ, the Father grants our petition, for Christ's sake. (T:2689)

Help in their purification.

The Faithful Departed are powerfully assisted by our fervent and prayerful efforts to help them in their purification. The prayers and Masses we offer do indeed enable them to enter Heaven more swiftly than if we had not helped them. (T:2799)

The gratitude of the Angels.

We need to remember that the sanctuary is full of holy Angels: tall and slender and still, gathered to adore our Saviour. They are witnesses to our worship, as well as participants; and they hold in special esteem those of us who love them, honour their presence - and even think so highly of them as to have a Mass offered in thanksgiving to God for their existence and for their love. (T:4002)

With His Infinite love.

In specially arranging to have a Mass offered in thanksgiving to God, we do something both praiseworthy and wise. It's as though we're saying to the Father: 'My desire to thank You for this gift or joy is so great that I've arranged for Jesus Himself, with His infinite love, to thank You on my behalf! (T:4006)

TRUE ECUMENISM

Not yet 'one in Christ'.

There is an abyss which is deep, but not wide, between ourselves and our spiritual brothers and sisters who love Christ but who are not in full communion with the Catholic Church.

Christ asks us to do what we indeed want to do, which is to welcome them with joy into our hearts and lives. Yet we cannot please Him by pretending that we are wholly 'one in Christ' with them: nor should we be reluctant to stretch out a hand, to help them to step across the gulf. In everything, we must act and speak in truth and love. (T:318)

Ignorant of the Mass.

We must work and pray with the hope of seeing all who love Christ eventually gathered about Christ during the Holy Sacrifice. Many devout Christians pray to the Father in Christ's name but pray oblivious to the source of the power of their prayer 'in Christ'. That source is Christ's Holy Sacrifice, which is re-presented during the Holy Mass. It's as if the other Christians' worship of the Father is 'lit' by the light which shines from Christ's prayers and Christ's Presence, at the altar, at the Holy Sacrifice of the Mass.

Christ asks us to consider a Christian who praises the Father in Christ's name, yet who is ignorant of the Mass, or so misguided that he thinks that he is right to ignore the Catholic Church and the Holy Sacrifice of the altar. This Christian is nevertheless praising the Father through Christ's offering in the one, true Sacrifice of Calvary and altar, even if he doesn't yet realise it. (T:1597)

A devout remembrance.

Catholics should understand that there is a mountainous difference between the Holy Sacrifice of the Mass and a devout remembrance by other Christians of the 'Last Supper'. No comparison can be made, so vast is the difference, between someone being present to a supremely-important event, and someone else - far away - entertaining grateful and prayerful thoughts about that event, no matter how devout and loving those thoughts might be.

Christ wants us all to go to the 'heart' of the Mass, in understanding. He wants us all to see that the whole value of the Mass stems from His Real Presence in the Blessed Sacrament, and from His perfection, that is, from the infinite worth of a Divine Person being offered in sacrifice to the Father. It should be a cause for great gratitude on our part, that the act to which we are present at the Holy Mass - Christ's sacrifice - is of Divine worth; and, therefore, it is effective. It makes effective, in our lives, the graces won for us by Christ on Calvary. That is why we should treasure the Mass, and not carelessly equate it with the services of other Christians. (T:1668)

From the pulpit.

It is the responsibility of the Catholic Clergy to preach the homily during the Mass; and no Catholic Bishop, priest or deacon should allow a non-Catholic minister - or any lay person - to take his place. It is not unknown for non-Catholics to speak in a misguided way about the Eucharist and 'intercommunion'; and even to suggest that it matters little to which church we belong, as long as we have faith in Christ. Though such comments might be aired in conversations, they should not be offered to Catholics during the Mass when they deserve to hear truth from the pulpit, and not private opinions. (T:2423)

A plain memorial, or the sacrifice of Christ.

Christ wants us to know and love truth: and that includes the truth about the Holy Sacrifice of the Mass. This truth includes knowing what the Mass is. It also includes knowing what can be lacking in other non-Catholic ceremonies which also have the title 'Eucharist', but where previous generations have abolished or undermined the Mass, or where the ministers lack valid orders.

That's why Christ invites us to reflect, respectfully and fearlessly, upon the prayers and actions of good people who meet together to enact a plain memorial of Christ's Passion.

The sincere prayers of such devout people delight Christ, honour the Father, draw other souls to love Christ more surely, and stir up gratitude at what He has done for sinners. However, no such act of remembrance - however devout - is to be confused with the Holy Mass, at which the Sacrifice of Calvary is re-presented.

Wherever Christ offers His Holy Sacrifice today - through His priest, His prayer, His Spirit, His Presence and His offering - the infinite blessings of that redeeming act flow outwards upon us who take part and upon those for whom we pray, as we pray in union with our Saviour. Through the Holy Sacrifice of the Mass, sinners are forgiven, and departed souls are purified. Furthermore - besides and beyond other marvels - the Father in Heaven receives perfect praise and thanks from upon earth, from His Son, our Divine Lord and Saviour, Who is Really Present amongst us in a sacramental manner. And because we 'belong' to Christ that praise is ours to offer as our own! (T:2444)

The Catholic Church.

No other marvel on earth can compare with the Mass. There's an overwhelming difference between the Catholic celebration of the Holy Mysteries and the sincere worship of God by other Christians who are outside the visible Catholic Church and who do not have Mass because their Clergy lack valid priestly orders. Catholics should not deny this difference, even though it's plain that everyone who has been made a true 'child of God' by Baptism - whatever communion he belongs to - worships 'in and through Christ'.

The Catholic Church was founded by Christ Himself and still worships in a way which is in accordance with His wishes, as do those Churches which have valid orders but which are not in full communion. That's the truth which the Church is bound to proclaim, by her words and actions, whilst respecting sincere people who have not heard her teachings or who cannot agree with her doctrines. (Also T:2444)

Sincere homage to God.

Many good Christians, through no fault of their own, don't know about or recognise Christ's One Holy Catholic Church. They worship together bound in love for one another and for Christ their Lord, yet they offer sacred worship according to the style devised for them by people who disliked much of what comprises Catholic faith and worship. It's true that the aim of these good people today is to pray in a reverent manner worthy of the Holy Trinity. As they pray "Holy, Holy, Holy Lord", it's as though the bells of Heaven ring out in praise of God, and in joy that Christians offer sincere homage to God, with beautiful music in His honour. Yet the memorial of Christ's death, devoutly recalled by such participants, is not the 'living memorial' which Catholics rightly call the Holy Sacrifice of the Mass and which is celebrated by the Catholic Church, by the Eastern Churches, and by some other Christians.

Where the Mass takes place, in all its glory, it is being celebrated in and through the Real Presence of Christ the King, Whose holy Mother is beside Him. And as this true re-presentation of Christ's saving work takes place - a living memorial of His Passion and Death, Resurrection and Ascension - the whole Church of earth and Heaven and Purgatory is united in this act. She is united with her Saviour, as the holy Angels look on. And in the radiant light of Divine splendour, the Son of God offers to God the Father, in the power of God the Holy Spirit, the unique sacrifice which has reunited Mankind with the Godhead. In doing so, Christ offers praise which is uniquely and infinitely precious and glorious. (Also T:2444)

A marked difference.

In order to minimise misunderstanding, Catholics ought not to take a prominent part in the 'Eucharists' of those who are not in communion with the Catholic Church. Many Catholics don't realise that there's a marked difference between the celebration of the Holy Mysteries in the Catholic Church and the sincere worship which is offered to God by those of His children who are outside the one, visible Church which Christ founded and who don't celebrate Mass. Truly, many of those good people worship 'in' and 'through' Christ, His Son; yet if their priests lack valid orders, they do not offer, as from a Catholic altar, the Holy Sacrifice once offered from the Cross. Catholics who receive 'Communion' in such services are disobeying the one true Church, founded upon the Apostles - the Church of which they are privileged to be members. (Also T:2444)

With admirable gratitude.

It is our duty, as followers of Christ, to 'speak the truth' with love. And so, as we look at other communities, we can praise their fervour yet lament what is lacking in their state, or their celebrations. It is obvious that some are enacting a devout memorial of Christ's death. They also remember Christ's Resurrection, and thank the Father for all that His Son has done for them; and their gratitude is admirable. Yet they are not saved by their participation in those prayers. They are not present to the sacrament of their salvation. Nor do they feast upon the sacrificial food, which is Christ Himself - the Holy Eucharist - although it's true that many believe that they do so. Indeed, they might be making what we call a spiritual communion. (Also T:2444)

Good intentions.

Christ sees that very many Christians live 'outside' His visible and united Catholic Church and celebrate a memorial of the Last Supper, in a service at which there is neither a validly-ordained priest, nor a saving sacrifice, nor food from heaven. Their salvation is not through their 'Eucharist', although they can achieve salvation through baptism and an active faith in Christ, and through good intentions, as they serve and praise God in what they believe to be the right and best-possible way.

People from amongst such congregations who do achieve salvation will find, to their astonishment, that they have been saved through their faith in Christ and through the Holy Sacrifice of the Mass - at which they have rarely or never been present, perhaps through no fault of their own. They will recognise its significance, at last - with astonishment and perhaps remorse.

At last, they will see that whereas only a handful of Christ's followers could be present at Christ's bloody offering on Calvary, everyone who believes in Christ and who accepts His invitation to enter the Catholic Church can be present at the Holy Sacrifice of the Mass, and can be saved through it, since it's the very same sacrifice as that which was offered from the Cross. They will understand at last, with awe and wonder, that our loving Father has ensured that Calvary's Victim is Really Present, in every Mass, to offer His perfect oblation and to intercede for sinners. They will therefore see how tragic it is that so many people, in every age, fail to believe in or to enter Christ's one, true Church. (Also T 2444)

Christ's perfect self-offering.

We should treasure the truth about the Mass: that the sacrifice of Calvary is re-presented, today, though in a different manner, a sacramental manner. The power of this celebration is astonishing. It is by a devout participation at this Holy Sacrifice of the altar that we who believe in Christ and in His saving work can demonstrate our faith, and can stand beside Christ as He pleads for our salvation. We are caught up in the whole Paschal Mystery: in Christ's perfect self-offering for sinners. (Also T:2444)

Not validly-ordained.

It is right and fitting that Christians work and worship together in appropriate ways; yet some events take place which confuse some Catholics and lead other Catholics astray. At such events, many good-hearted but misguided men call themselves Catholic, and even robe, adorn and label themselves as Catholic priests and Bishops, even though they are neither Catholic nor validly-ordained. Some of them even robe and 'elevate' in the same way the women whom, mistakenly, they believe have been ordained to the ministerial Priesthood. And some of these men and women who think of themselves as being Catholic priests are saddened by

Catholic regulations which ban 'parallel Eucharists', and regular 'intercommunion'.

Many of these true children of God are baptised, and generous in God's service and generous towards their needy neighbours. Yet there are great wounds - causes for sadness - at the heart of the life of numerous Christian communities. For example, most of them lack valid orders; and this lack is not a minor matter. It means that their ministers have neither the priestly authority to preach, nor the priestly power to change bread and wine into the Sacred Body and Blood of Christ, nor the power to forgive sins, to bless, to confirm, to ordain, or to anoint the Faithful.

That's one reason why it is not fitting that non-Catholics preach in a Catholic church during the Sacred Liturgy. That's why they ought not to hope to 'concelebrate' with Catholic priests, or even conduct what are called 'parallel Eucharists'. That's why it's unwise of us to install 'shared tabernacles' in shared churches - or to encourage other practises inappropriate between people who are not yet 'in full communion'. (T:2522)

Refraining from judgement.

It is God the Father Who wishes everyone to turn to Him and to His Son - and Who invites us all to receive the sacraments of the Church. Yet none of us can judge the thoughts or the state-of-soul of people who are not members of the Church and who therefore don't attend the Holy Sacrifice and who don't 'touch' Calvary in the manner made possible by God. God knows the thoughts and desires of those who don't appear to know Him in this way; and He can see which person has taken steps towards Him, through a direct prompting of the Spirit, or through the influence and faith of one of Christ's true friends. (T:2570)

Christian invitation.

All who love the Church can see that it's a matter of great concern that many Catholics don't ask for Confirmation. And therefore we cannot dismiss as unimportant the fact that many other Christians don't complete their Christian initiation, because their priests' orders are invalid, or because, in some communities, sacraments after Baptism are seen as unimportant. (T:4108)

Unorthodox opinions.

Christ sees it as a serious matter that some priests, and some of the laity who volunteer to help in the Church and who become active in ecumenical work and worship, do not believe in all of the Church's teachings. Catholics cannot be said to be acting as true representatives of the Catholic Church if they make plain their dislike of Church doctrine and discipline. They are neither just nor wise if, in the groups they influence or steer, they air their unorthodox personal opinions, or disobediently take part in 'intercommunion.' (T:4172)

Conflicting assertions.

Christ asks us all to beware of shrugging aside the truths which He revealed to us at the cost of His life. For example, where there is a careless attitude in Ecumenism, there is sometimes found a careless attitude to other Faiths, even the view that conflicting assertions about God can be reconciled in a new synthesis.

Every Catholic should believe that God looks with infinite love upon every individual - of every faith or none. Yet it's because of that love that God wants everyone to recognise what is true and what is false, amongst the ideas cherished by human beings. And so the Church proclaims in every age the Good News about Christ's saving work. She invites everyone to believe that God the Father sent His own Son into the world to save sinners. Jesus Christ the Son of God is at work today, through His Church, reconciling sinners with the Father, and sharing His Divine life with us through sharing His Spirit: the Spirit of holiness. It is He, the Holy Spirit, Who can transform weak creatures like ourselves and enable us to persevere in holiness until God calls us to share His life in Heaven. And that is why well-instructed Catholics who believe in the teachings of Christ's Church and who meet Christ in His Word and in the sacraments, work to share the Faith with other people, as well as to engage in charitable dialogue about our common hopes and problems.

The Church speaks the truth when she tells us that there are seeds of truth and goodness in other faiths; yet since the Christian Faith consists of God's unique self-revelation in and through Jesus Christ His Son, we must not imagine that the world's other faiths provide equally-safe and equally-worthy parallel ways to God. (Also T:4172)

A changed attitude to Mission.

Christ asks us to recognise that imprecise or mistaken opinions about Ecumenical and Inter-faith work lead inevitably to a changed and even apathetic attitude to Mission.

Some Catholics have suggested that it's impertinent of us to invite other people to turn to Christ, to accept the truths of the Faith, and to change their lives. Some Catholics even entertain the idea that people should be allowed to remain indefinitely at a stage of 'pre-evangelisation'. They wrongly suggest that it is cruel to expect people to reject aspects of their own culture in order to embrace the Catholic Faith. Yet the Church is, by its very nature, missionary.

The very purpose of the Church is to preach the truth in order to save souls. She also heals, feeds, educates and consoles suffering human beings. Yet the first aim of this Divine institution is to bring people to share the riches of life 'in the Spirit': to have their sins forgiven, and to achieve union with God now and for all Eternity, in and through Jesus Christ. (Also T:4172)

Only one Saviour.

There are Catholics who even suggest that Christ is not the unique Saviour. Some perhaps don't realise that what they say is not only false but dangerous. By implication, they suggest that people have no need, for salvation, of Christ's saving death on the Cross, Christ's Resurrection, or Christ's Church, and her sacraments. By implication, they brush aside Christ's warning that we have no life in us if we don't eat the 'living bread come down from Heaven': the Holy Eucharist which is the living memorial of Christ's saving work and the necessary Food for the journey to Heaven (Also: T:4172)

Mistakes to avoid.

If Catholics are well-instructed in the Faith they will know how to act in every situation, whether in social life or in worship And so Catholics should be taught how to behave during the services of other Christians as well as how to behave at Mass. We all deserve to be well-instructed, for example, about why we mustn't receive 'Holy Communion' (as it is called) elsewhere. Furthermore, it can be misleading if Catholic priests preach at the ordination of other Christians.

We do not genuflect to tabernacles in Anglican churches because a 'priest' who is not validly-ordained has not changed bread and wine into Christ's Sacred Body and Blood. We mustn't feel obliged to copy everyone in everything for fear of seeming uncharitable or judgmental. We act charitably if we are truthful, and if we are obedient to Christ Who teaches us and guides us through our Bishops. (T:4493)

Widely-differing beliefs.

Though Catholics are right to welcome and honour non-Catholic visitors who attend Mass, it is not necessary, nor is it just, to give them greater outward honour during the Sacred Liturgy than is accorded to a communicant member of the Catholic Church. A faithful Catholic who has a 'mustard seed' of true faith and who can participate fully in the Mass, as Christ wishes, is more worthy of an honoured place than another Christian with his great 'plant' of sincerity. The reason is that the Catholic, through being in full communion with the one, true Church, can exercise his lay-priestly role. He is truly one with Christ and the Church at the offering of the Holy Sacrifice - unlike a Christian visitor who has a different understanding of 'Church.'

Perhaps that visitor doesn't believe in some of the great truths of faith and morals. Perhaps he doesn't listen to and obey the Pope and the Catholic Bishops. He might never ask the Saints - whom Catholics honour at every Mass - to intercede for him. Perhaps he disbelieves in the Angels who throng the sanctuary, and would never ask for their prayers. He might think it impossible that Christ is really and substantially Present after the Consecration and would not be willing to kneel or genuflect in adoration before the Sacred Host. We cannot know exactly what he believes, however. We only know that he is not Catholic. So even if he were honestly to declare that he believes in the Holy Trinity, respects the Pope, believes in a strong moral code, and loves Our Lady and the Saints and Angels, his faith is plainly not strong enough to have led him into membership of the Catholic Church. Or he believes that he is a Catholic when the Catholic Church sees that he is not. So his faith does not match the faith of the simplest faithful Catholic: a person whose faith in Christ has either led him into the Church or - if he was a cradle Catholic - has kept him in it.

So the faithful Catholic is a full member of Christ's priestly People, in a way which is not true of someone who, though he might be an admirable person, and even a leader of thousands of Christians, has not yet recognised or entered Christ's one, true Church. (T:4494)

Christians together.

For all sorts of reasons, it is plainly true that when Catholics wish to host a prayer-gathering with other Christians it is not always appropriate to celebrate Mass. Reverent and delightful prayer-services can be devised in which Christians with widely-differing beliefs can take part with little concern about ceremonial or leadership. (Also T:4494)

The simple faithful.

At a celebration of Mass in a Catholic church or Cathedral it is not appropriate to usher non-Catholic ministers to the sanctuary whilst faithful Catholics have not enough places made available to them, but have to sit where they can see little, and strain to hear the words of the Liturgy.

It is not just, that non-Catholic ministers are sometimes placed around the altar, throughout the Holy Sacrifice of the Mass, when many are neither confirmed, nor 'in communion' with Catholics. It is not just, that at the heart of the Mass, when Christ is made sacramentally Present at the Consecration, Catholics who look towards the altar to adore Christ, should see other Christians sitting around the altar, some of whom are embarrassed at not wanting to genuflect, and others uncomfortable at being placed at the very centre of a rite which they neither approve of nor understand. Nor is it just that those people have a place of honour whilst many of the Catholic laity have been unable to find a seat, or have not been able to get into the building. (Also T:4494)

Making a statement.

Every visitor to our church deserves respect; yet Christ noted the widow who 'put in everything she had,' at the Temple. Christ sees that any 'ordinary' Catholic who believes in the truths of the Faith, tries to practise them, and goes regularly and gratefully to Mass and the sacraments is more worthy of honour - having put 'all he has' into such a demonstration of trust in God - than any non-Catholic ecumenically-minded participant in our worship, no matter how eminent the visitor might be in public life or in his own community.

He may well be virtuous, and sincere in his beliefs. But in showing that he has not come into visible and full communion with the Catholic Church, he makes a statement about his faith, though God alone can see his heart. He shows, either that he does not agree with some of our major teachings, or that he is ignorant of them, or has misinterpreted them, or thinks it unimportant that we disagree on certain topics, or is unsure what he believes; or perhaps he would even like to be Catholic but thinks the cost too high.

Although, in God's sight, he is worthy of a warm welcome in church, and respect for whatever office he might hold in his own community, he is spiritually unable to take part in the Sacred Liturgy as fully as a faithful Catholic who is in a state of grace. That's the reason why, in God's sight, it is the faithful practising Catholic who deserves a sure place at the Liturgical celebration. (Also T:4494)

6.   CERTAIN TASKS.

MASTER OF CEREMONIES

A self-less attitude.

Christ looks on with admiration as a particular priest 'hovers' attentively near his Bishop, during the Sacred Liturgy, ready and eager to be of service. Whoever serves in such a selfless manner brings joy to Christ, and joy to all who delight in seeing the Sacred Mysteries celebrated in a reverent and well-ordered manner. We too can please Christ if we adopt such a selfless attitude towards Him, our Saviour, not just in the Liturgy but in everyday life.

If we imitate that priest's attitude we'll be ready to welcome Christ's Will for us, simply because it is the Will of our friend and God - no matter what it might involve, nor whether it brings us pain or pleasure. (T:2495)

SERVERS

The sacred vessels.

It is the Will of Christ that the sacred vessels we use during the Mass be handled with reverence, and that especial care be taken in the placing and handling of vessels which might still contain particles of the Sacred Host or traces of Christ's Precious Blood. (T:2291A)

Carelessness.

It is particularly unfitting that - against the advice of Holy Scripture and the custom of the Church - some women enter the sanctuary with their long hair unrestrained.   It is not God's Will that female altar servers or Extraordinary Ministers of the Eucharist move about the sanctuary with long hair flowing freely. It is not appropriate.   (T:2395 and T:2423)

Vanity in the sanctuary.

Although some priests make use of the current, special permission to allow girls and women to act as servers Christ wants these servers to realise that there is no place for vanity in the sanctuary. Some of them are not suitably prepared to serve at the altar - if their long hair is hanging loosely about their faces and shoulders. This is not only inappropriate, but also dangerous, because of the lighted candles which are carried about and which are placed on the altar. Long hair should be tied back. (T:2518)

Courageous priests.

Christ wants it to be known that those of His priests who instruct servers should be brave and forthright in telling girls and women about the modest clothing and demeanour which are appropriate for the sanctuary, just as they tell boys and men about why they should have clean nails, and appropriate foot-wear. (Also T:2518)

Noise and haste.

Everyone who approaches the holy altar, or passes it, or who enters the sanctuary, should behave with modesty and reverence, and without rushing about or disturbing the prayerful silence in church. (T:3065)

Unthinking worldliness.

The Church has decreed that with the permission of the Bishop a priest may invite girls to serve at the altar; yet it's a cause for alarm that serious drawbacks can arise when older girls or women are serving. Christ invites those who regulate the Sacred Liturgy to consider things in the following way: The Sacred Mysteries are so holy, and give such glory to God, that they should be celebrated in a manner wholly reverent, and wholly appropriate for sacred rites. Those in charge should minimise the possibility of the rites being conducted with unseemly or unnecessary 'risks'.

For example, it would not be fair to encourage a person who is very weak, and unsteady on his feet, to carry the book of the Gospels for the length of the church; nor is it right to ask someone wholly unintelligible to attempt a Scripture reading. This is not cruelty but commonsense in arranging ritual worship. On the same grounds, it is not wise to allow young women to serve at the altar if they routinely decorate their hair in startling ways, or wear garish make-up or high heels. These are ways in which, perhaps unthinkingly, women introduce worldliness into the sanctuary, and distract attention from the altar.

For the same reason, it is not wise to invite girls and women to act as servers and thus to wear a special garment, if they would therefore be required to dress and undress in or near a sacristy where priests and male servers robe and disrobe for Mass. Nor is it appropriate that a sacristy become a place where girls and women busy themselves with hairstyles and cosmetics before and after Mass. (T:4851)

Like stagehands.

It is not appropriate for servers to strip off their servers' garments the moment they have processed through the church, and then to rush about the sanctuary clad in scruffy sportswear, moving items about and blowing out candles carelessly, like stagehands in a hurry to change the scenery before the next act. They act as if, when Mass has ended, the sanctuary is no longer a sacred place with a Holy Presence.

Servers should act with dignity and thoughtfulness whether in church or in the sacristy. The sacristy is not a place for boisterous behaviour when the Mass has ended, but a place in which to prepare for Mass in a prayerful manner and to return to after Mass still in a prayerful frame of mind. Much of the noise which some servers make in the sacristy echoes round the church itself, and disturbs those who have remained in church to pray.

Everything done for the glory of God in or near the sanctuary should be done with dignity and reverence, whether during the Mass, before it or after it. It remains the sacred place where the Holy Sacrifice is offered, even between those times when we celebrate the Sacred Liturgy. (P.U.T:16)

EXTRAORDINARY MINISTERS OF THE EUCHARIST

Abuses and mistakes.

There are many devout lay-persons who respond with love and reverence to the request that they assist their priest in distributing Holy Communion to some of the people in the Parish, both in church and in the homes of the sick who cannot attend Mass. Yet there are mistakes made, and various abuses of this privilege.

Some priests lack the courage to instruct their parishioners in modes of dress and behaviour which are appropriate for the church and the sanctuary. Other priests have absorbed the current view that it's 'un-Christian' to tell anyone what to do, or to offer helpful criticism. Yet Christ Himself, and His Apostles, didn't hesitate to lead people towards right behaviour; and Christ asks His Clergy today not to shrug off their responsibilities. (P.U.T:17)

The duty of the Clergy.

It's the duty of the Clergy to encourage their parishioners to behave well in church, and so they should ask all who serve, read, or otherwise minister in the sanctuary to clothe themselves modestly and to act in a suitable manner.

Christ asks us to remember that a good mother asks her children to wash their hands before a meal. A good science teacher tells his pupils to wear goggles during a scientific experiment. A good priest tells us to approach God and His sanctuary with reverence and awe; and priests do wrong if they fail to 'speak the truth with love' to people who - by their appearance or conduct - act in slovenly, worldly, indecent, thoughtless or foolish ways in our churches. (P.U.T: 18).

A hall-way to Heaven.

Christ wants everyone to understand that the sanctuary is a very holy place. He wants everyone who ministers in the sanctuary to realise that every worldly display of jewellery, of heavy make-up, of naked limbs, or immodest clothing is unseemly and unfitting. We are right to value the human body - and to praise God for everything good we see, and everything beautiful. Yet the sanctuary is like a hallway which leads directly to Heaven. So we act there with a 'Heavenly' decorum and dignity. (T:2519)

A true sister-in-Christ.

Women who are given responsible work to do in parishes should not 'plague' priests with comments and perpetual jokes about 'womens' rights'. The best collaboration between lay-persons and priests is rooted in mutual respect, faith in Christ, and obedience to His Church. No true sister-in-Christ will usurp aspects of a priest's ministry, or make barbed comments, or defy his authority. (T:3031)

Vanity or ostentation.

It is the duty of the Clergy to ensure that their parishioners understand the Lord's wish: that those who minister in or by the sanctuary should not be ostentatious or worldly in appearance, and should avoid lavish use of lipstick and brilliant nail varnish, and immodest clothing. (T:3348)

CATECHISTS, PARENTS AND TEACHERS

Devoted to Christ.

In fulfilling their duties in the family of the Church, catechists, parents and teachers are directly or indirectly preparing people to take part in the Mass. The Holy Eucharist is at the heart of Catholic life; and so every person who encourages candidates, catechumens or pupils in holiness helps to prepare them to participate in a worthy manner in the Sacred Mysteries.

That's why we need to reflect, now and then, on whether we are really 'of one mind' with Christ as we work to hand on the truths of the Faith. True disciples of Christ are devoted to Him: wholehearted in love for Him, fervent in prayer, eager to learn from the Bishops chosen for us by Christ, faithful to the teachings of the Church, grateful for Christ's gifts, lavish with their time in His service, delighted by their Heavenly food, and faithful in interceding for Christ's People, the Church. (T:1720)

With unflagging zeal.

We should be full of zeal: wise, pure, charitable, unflagging zeal. Souls are endangered whenever faith is not taught, whenever disobedience is condoned, whenever eternal hopes are replaced by earthly goals, whenever proud souls mock the faith and the devotions of Christ's 'little ones', and whenever worship is tarnished: as when admiring attention is focused by worshippers not upon the Father but upon themselves and their lives. (T:1909)

A sincere and admirable intention.

Although Christ wants everyone to be better instructed about the sacraments, and urges us to share our knowledge with other people, if we are able, we needn't imagine that the shy, the inarticulate, the unlearned or the simple cannot participate 'fully' in the Mass.

All who 'pray the Mass' can pray it 'well' with even a little faith and a poor understanding, provided they share Christ's intention. Whoever hopes to grow in faith, but who wishes, meanwhile, to be sincere in offering Christ's Holy Sacrifice, will share Christ's 'attitude'. Each person will offer himself to God the Father in love and submission, in union with Christ, with the sincere and admirable intention of serving God, and of doing His Will in everything, until death.

In that degree of resemblance, in love, to Christ His Saviour, the devout, reverent and humble participant more than 'makes up' for what he might lack in learning and understanding. (T:2674)

Loyal to the teachings of the Church.

Christ invites the Clergy to take extra care, in choosing catechists to help them. Catechists should be of good standing in the Church, rooted in the community, and genuinely prayerful, as well as knowledgeable about the Catholic Faith. They should be loyal to Christ, to His Church, to the Church's teachings, to the sacraments - and also reverent in prayer. If any catechist does not believe the teachings of the Church, he cannot hand them on, as he ought, with joy and conviction. (T:2775)

Necessary changes.

Christ wants us to realise that changes are necessary in the way in which we teach people about the Mass, which is the greatest prayer. Christ Himself sees that the attitude of Catholics to the Mass, which is the holiest event on earth, has been drastically altered. Many teachers omit to teach that the Mass is more than a memorial meal. Many of them never teach that it is the sacramental re-presentation of Christ's unique sacrifice of Calvary, and of the whole Paschal Mystery by which we are offered salvation. It is a sacrifice offered by the priest, with and for the whole Church - living members and departed. Yet many Catholics aren't aware of these truths.

Many Catholics have never been told that the merits of the sacrifice of Calvary are applied to our souls through our sincere and prayerful participation in the sacrifice of the Mass. This is the very same sacrifice, now offered in a different - a sacramental - manner. Nor have they been told of their obligation to attend every Sunday and holy day of obligation; nor have their children - who often view the Mass primarily as a meal - learned how to behave during the Church's solemn and sacred rites. Few adults and children realise, therefore, that the Mass can be offered for the living and the dead, and for a special intention, on special occasions. (T:4172)

No real understanding.

It is a widespread problem, in Christ's sight, that the Mass is regarded primarily as a meal. Some Catholics have wrongly been told that 'bread and wine' are consumed, or that this is a time when people can show out their talents. Appropriate participation should be encouraged. Yet where people have no real understanding of the heart of the Mass, which is Christ's sacrificial offering, the focus of attention eventually becomes not Christ but those people who are present. And then dreadful changes take place.

Where it is not known, or it is forgotten, that at every Mass it's as though we stand at the foot of the Cross, there is less gratitude to Christ for what He has done for us. There is little awareness of His Presence. And where attention is drawn away from Christ, the degree of adoration and reverence diminishes, and there is a diminished sense of awe in receiving Holy Communion. There is also a growing disregard for Christ's sacramental Presence in the tabernacle, and the loss of awareness that the solemnly-consecrated church is a holy place. (Also T:4172)

The approach to prayer.

Christ asks us to realise that wherever the Faith is taught with a greater emphasis on human 'needs' than on the Will of God for us, there arises a novel attitude to private as well as liturgical prayer. He wants us to see what sort of attitude has developed, and how regrettable is the change.

Many Christians have been taught to see their time of prayer as primarily a time of self-help and relaxation in God's presence. The prime aim is to achieve peace and joy - rather than to give glory to God.

God loves to give peace and joy to people who trust in Him, and who rest trustingly in His presence. Yet it's a cause for concern where Christians look upon prayer as being mainly something therapeutic for themselves. Prayer is indeed helpful to ourselves. Our prayers of petition and intercession are very important for ourselves and the Church, and for the world. But prayer is supremely the means of giving glory to God through adoration, and through the asking of His Will, the acknowledgement of His goodness - with acts of humility and contrition.

There is an admirable desire on the part of Christian preachers and teachers to speak more frequently about God's love for us all, and to banish fear. Yet where people are not made aware of God's glory and majesty, and of our debt to Him, they are unlikely to give Him the profound homage which is His due. Christ sees that a generation has just come to adulthood which - with exceptions - rarely stands or kneels to pray, or scarcely prays at all in family groups or alone. And these are some of the reasons for the noise and irreverence today in Catholic Churches. (Also T:4172)

An authentic message.

Christ looks on with gladness wherever Catholics who believe the Faith and try to practise it also teach the Faith in its fullness without side-stepping its sterner doctrines or distorting the overall message. He is our God and Saviour, our guide and leader. And He asks us to remember that every good leader needs friends whom he can trust. He can be sure that they will carry out his wishes. He knows from experience that - unlike others - they won't distort any of the urgent, important messages which he sends out through them. And thus it is in the Church. Christ asks for His authentic, important and urgent message about sin and repentance, and salvation, to be accurately spread by the Clergy, and also by catechists, parents, teachers and theologians, indeed, by every active member of the Church. (Also T:4172)

Mission and catechesis.

Christ asks us to remember that we are privileged to be Catholic Christians, able to share Good News about Him. We should persevere in mission and catechesis, whether the truths of the Faith are greeted with gladness or dismay. Christ wants us to know, however, that some Catholics today offer a distorted message. He reminds us that sinful human beings are deeply in need of Truth as well as love.

Christ asks us to remember that Truth is unchanging even though the way in which it is expressed can vary. Furthermore, the Faith we profess is so marvellous - and so important for Mankind - that it should always be shared with gladness and received in gratitude. It is so simple that it can take root whenever people with willing hearts hear about it and accept it, and resolve that by God's grace they will practise it faithfully. Courageous people will even shoulder the Cross, for Christ's sake, confident that He will help them to persevere to the end. Yet Christ sees that some sincere enquirers today are offered a watered-down or distorted version of the Catholic Faith.

This is a tragedy wherever it occurs. And amongst the many reasons for it being so tragic is that it not only deprives individuals of the sure guidelines for the 'hard road' to holiness, and to true joy, it also lessens their awareness of their need of God's graces. It conveys to them little of the grandeur of God as well as His goodness. It can even mean that they are neither awed by God's holiness nor contrite because of their own sinfulness. And if they fail to see how marvellous is our membership of the 'communion of Saints' and how tremendous is our need of the sacraments they are unlikely to understand or to treasure the Mass. Yet the Mass is the summit and the source of the life of grace. Indeed, it is rightly called the 'sacrament of our salvation.' (Also T:4172)

Discontent and disloyalty.

Christ asks us to beware of being influenced wherever we meet a new and inaccurate version of the Faith: a version neither full nor faithful.

In the life of the Church today it is an admirable thing that so many Catholics are turning to Sacred Scripture. But special care is necessary in the use of lectionary-based programmes of Catechesis. Some of them omit important issues if little reference is made to modern teaching documents of the Church. Certain moral teachings can be glossed over or omitted which are not clearly delineated in Scripture but which have been clarified in the Tradition and the teaching of the Church.

Christ is glad and grateful that 'The Catechism of the Catholic Church' is available, for those who want to share the truths of the Faith - sure truths, well expressed. Yet He sees that it remains little-used where some of the contents are unacceptable to Catholics influenced by un-Catholic ideas. (Also T:4172)

The true Faith.

Christ asks us to remember that everyone in the Church who teaches the Faith has the duty of handing on the message once given through Christ and His Apostles.

It is a marvellously consoling message about how almighty God has intervened in the affairs of Mankind: because of His compassion and love. It tells us that the Father's love for Mankind is so great that He sent His Son to earth by the power of the Holy Spirit, to take flesh from Mary the Immaculate Virgin, and then to die for Mankind's sins. Thus did Christ the Son reconcile Mankind with the Father. Furthermore, Christ has revealed the Holy Trinity. He yearns to draw us all - through our Divine adoption - into the Communion of Saints, and to bring us in the end to the heart of the Holy Trinity, to live there in joy and love forever. And that is why Christ invites us all to repent and to be baptised, so that we can be transformed and share His life.

He has handed on this message and invitation, in every age since His Resurrection and Ascension to Heaven, through the one, holy Church which He founded and which is still one and holy today. Yet although He has proclaimed that He has come to give us life - abundant life - He has warned us that the gate to life is narrow, and the road hard. He asks us all to realise that we lie to ourselves and mislead others if we speak and act as if the road to Heaven is broad and easy. (Also T:4172)

The sure, safe way.

In the Gospel faithfully preached to us through the centuries, we have a thrilling message about an infinitely-loving Divine Saviour. It is a 'strong' message about rebellion and redemption, sin and forgiveness, and the Cross and the Resurrection. It speaks about loss-of-God and salvation, self-will and sanctity, and the danger of Hell as well as the hope of Heaven's glory. This is why Christ asks us to realise that the choices we make in everyday life can affect our eternal destiny. And He now reminds us - with truthfulness and love - that we are helpless without Him.

It's because Christ is truth and love that He asks His followers in each generation to count the cost, and to take up their cross. Yet the way He points out is a safe, sure way, which is clearly revealed through the ages by those Bishops who continue the work of the Apostles, together with the Pope who continues St. Peter's work. Christ has given certain men the authority to teach the truth about Himself and about His wishes, and to guide us on the way to Heaven.

If we really understand the reason for Christ's Incarnation we will see why His Church has always urged sinful people towards contrition, prayer and penance, as a prelude to the pure and holy life which each person will try to lead, and as means of remaining faithful on the journey. Each person who lives thus, guided by the Holy Spirit, will prove his love for God - and express gratitude for the Faith which he has received - by loving God and God's Will above everything.

In living to serve God and neighbour he can find the peace and joy for which human beings yearn. That peace is experienced because of the presence in such a soul of the Holy Spirit, indeed, of the Three Divine Persons - with Their gifts of faith, hope and charity, besides many more gifts and graces. (Also T:4172)

The example of the Saints.

Whoever is willing to learn from the example of the Saints will learn that our joy in living as true children of God is increased if we persevere in love through the inevitable trials and sufferings of earthly life, which we accept as purifications - in patience, by God's grace, in imitation of Christ in His terrible Passion. Then we can become more aware of the goodness of the Father Who sent Christ to earth by the Spirit's power, for our sakes - to redeem us. Christ stripped Himself of glory so that He could live amongst us. He shed His Blood for us. And now He feeds us and renews His Divine life in us by giving us His Holy Body and Blood in the Mass. The Holy Sacrifice is a living memorial of Christ's saving work on earth!

Today, as in every age, all who belong to Christ's Body, the Church - the Mystical Body - and who participate in Christ's sacrificial prayer and offering allow themselves to be drawn towards Heaven and towards the Father from Whom Christ came. That's the marvellous news that it's our duty to share, however unfashionable we are, in today's world, as we speak about sin and purification.

Christ asks us to reflect upon these things. He wants to help us to see what many Clergy and laity have already noticed: that there is a different message sometimes given out today. It is a message not in accord with the plain teaching of the Holy Father, the Pope, and the other Bishops. (Also T:4172)

'Death to sin'.

Christ asks all who wonder what sort of Gospel He wants to see preached to look to the Apostles to learn a great deal. The Apostles' love for their flocks caused them to yearn to bring people towards the true happiness which is found through holiness. The Apostles weren't afraid to speak about the grave, personal sins which everyone should abandon who wants to live a holy life 'in

Christ'; yet they provided an example of loving concern for sick, sinful or anxious people.

In their courageous witness the Apostles imitated Christ Who obeyed His Father's Will no matter what hardships had to be endured. They trusted in the Father's wisdom and love, and urged the Faithful to do the same, on the 'narrow way' to Heaven. They had the courage to lead people on a way of truth, faithfulness and love. They led people through death - 'death' to sin - to life, which is real spiritual health: through transformation to joy.

The Apostles spoke the truth about human sinfulness and Divine holiness, as we know from Sacred Scripture and the Sacred Tradition. They taught that it is not 'easy' to be saved. It is possible, for all who will strive to do what is right, and persevere to the end. A sure hope of salvation is given to all who come to God through Christ in humility, faith and gratitude, and who move 'upwards' through love towards holiness and peace. That's why Christ asks us to beware of a different 'Gospel' sometimes heard today. Whether through ignorance, pride or fear or blindness, or a desire not to be unpopular, some people try to steer us onto a new path. It is not the 'uphill' path to holiness and truth but a downhill path which leads away from true discipleship. (Also T:4172)

An incomplete presentation.

Some well-meaning Catholics teach a minimum, in matters of discipline and custom, and belief, in case it should 'drive people away.' Thus, good-hearted newcomers are left ignorant, and therefore unable to provide authentic instruction on the Faith for their own children and for others who question them.

Some Catholics who teach the Faith also teach that we mustn't worry if we disagree with Church teachings. They say, rightly, that we ought to follow our consciences as we journey through life. Yet they never speak of erroneous consciences. Nor do they explain that what is intrinsically evil remains an evil, and has evil consequences, even if a person has done evil in ignorance, with a good will.

Some Catholics routinely declare, "There are no easy answers" - forgetting, or disbelieving, that the Cathechism has a great number of simple truths within it. They fail to assure us that we can rely on the Church, and on the grace of God for guidance and for virtue if we sincerely wish to keep God's Commandments which are plainly taught by the Church.

Some Catholics, by their sincere but misguided efforts to bring peace-of-mind to sinful people, say that there's no need to worry about sins since God understands everything. They rightly speak about His mercy, yet without suggesting the need for repentance - or the joy it brings. And some even encourage the attitude that since God is endlessly loving towards us all, there's no need for us to sacrifice earthly happiness in order to keep the Commandments. Some people who teach the Faith say it is almost impossible to commit a mortal sin. They say little about the necessity of overcoming temptations and of persevering in the Faith until death. They even say that it is easy to be saved. (Also: T:4172)

An uncertain sound.

The Catholic Faith is true, coherent and exciting. So Christ asks us to consider the regrettable results of incomplete or unorthodox teaching. Plainly, children and adults have no clear 'picture' of their privileges and duties, as individuals. Yet there are further repercussions. Where an uncertain faith is preached, like the uncertain sound of a trumpet, family life is damaged, and vocations to the Priesthood decrease. And when there is a huge failure to transmit the Faith in the classroom and in parish catechesis, many people cease to practise the Faith, causing dismay and discouragement to those who have remained faithful.

37. CHRIST OUR LIGHT.

Even after Mass, Christ is with us in our church, in His glory: by His sacramental Presence in the tabernacle. He delights in our sincere thanks for His gifts, and He inspires us to share the Good News of His love. OIL-S:4384. *("You have made known the way of life to me, you will fill me with gladness through your presence." Ac 2:28).*

38. HOLY COMMUNION FOR THE SICK.

Holy Communion is brought to the sick and housebound members of the Church. Christ is Present 'whole and entire' as the Eucharistic Minister holds up the Sacred Host. Our Risen Lord shares His Body, Blood, Soul and Divinity. OIL-M:1038B. *("I am the living bread which has come down from Heaven. Anyone who eats this bread will live forever; and the bread that I shall give is my flesh, for the life of the world." Jn 6:51).*

39. THE FIRE OF CHRIST'S PRAISE.

With the eyes of faith we see the glory and holiness of Christ as a 'fire' of praise soars Heavenward to the Father from Christ in the Blessed Sacrament. We can kneel before the tabernacle or the altar, expressing our love and gratitude, allowing Christ to irradiate us with His graces. OIL-S:2138. *("He is the radiant light of God's glory and the perfect copy of his nature, sustaining the universe by his powerful command." Heb 1:3).*

40. CHRIST'S LIGHT, SHINING THROUGH US.
The greater is our willingness to love and serve God and our neighbour, the more powerfully does the grace of Christ pour through our lives upon other people. OIL-M:195. *("The life and death of each of us has its influence on others." Rm 14:7).*

41. LOVE FOR OUR NEIGHBOUR.

When we leave to take up our everyday business, when the Mass has ended, we must do everything in the name of Christ. We can bring Christ's truth and love to everyone we meet.   OIL-M:651. *("Just as I have loved you, you also must love one another. By this love you have for one another, everyone will know that you are my disciples." Jn 13:34-35).*

42. FOLLOWING CHRIST'S WAY.

If we surrender our lives to Christ and strive to do His Will in everything, whether as lay-persons or Clergy or religious, we help other people to follow the sure way to Heaven.   OIL-M:1184C. *("You were sanctified, and with your blood you bought men for God of every race, language, people and nation and made them a line of kings and priests, to serve our God and to rule the world." Rev 5:9-10).*

Christ's wish for all of our catechumens and candidates, and also Catholic children and adults, is that they all receive a rich and full presentation of the Catholic Faith, not a truncated or distorted version.

Christ has a simple question to put to everyone who sincerely wants to hand on the Catholic Faith - and who encounters the changed versions which are sometimes taught today. He invites each of us to think carefully about what we hear and read. He asks: "Would Saint Paul recognise what some people teach in this way - recognise it as the Gospel he preached? Would the other Apostles?" (Also T:4172)

True children of God.

Christ Who is love wants us to believe in His love for us. Truly, none of us can speak extravagantly enough about His immense love for each one of us; and yet that pure, burning, infinite love desires to see us brought to the knowledge of the truth: the truth about His holiness. And He wants us to know about the obedient and holy way of life into which we should enter if we wish to live as true 'children of God,' and so be made fit to enjoy Eternal Life in His Kingdom.

Christ asks all who claim to love truth to give a truthful answer to these questions: Do they sincerely believe all the truths of the Catholic Faith? Are they willing to explain and defend them? Are they determined to be loyal to the Church? (Also T:4172)

An authoritative and accurate statement.

Christ wants us to know that He is glad and grateful for the publication of the document 'Dominus Iesus'. He is glad that the Holy Father has spoken of it with approval.

In Christ's sight, it sets out very clearly these important truths of the Catholic Faith: that Christ has given to His one Church the

authority to teach, and that Christ is the only Saviour. (Also
T:4172)

7. SPECIAL CONCERNS.

MASS ATTENDANCE

Our need of God.

It's important that we remember that even in our weakness, we are precious to God. Knowledge of our weakness can lead us to trust in Him, whereas with self-sufficiency our souls are in danger. Whoever knowingly and willingly says "I do not need God or His Church or the sacraments" is lost, by his own choice - unless he repents before he dies. (T:1057A)

Christ, in mourning.

Christ longs for us all to love His Church and to listen to her teachings. It's as if He is mourning the behaviour of those of His own children who have mocked, betrayed or tried to destroy His one, true Church, whether in its buildings, in its teachings, or in its members.

Here in England, many of His people in the past have deserted Him, have desecrated His altars and - in our own time - have pierced His 'prophets' to the heart with the irreverence, pride, self-sufficiency and serious sins which damage souls and lead to disunity. His true prophets are those who - out of love for Him, and whatever the cost - continue to teach the Faith today, in its fullness. In doing so, they are removing the dusty layers of cynicism and neglect which veil Christ's eternal truths and His unchanging Will. (T:1140)

Grumbling and dissatisfaction.

Christ wants us to realise how shameful it is, that many 'children of God' constantly grumble and express dissatisfaction in God's service. He asks: which of us has the right to complain of our trials when He, our God, has descended from power and glory, to save us? He has shown us all how to bear pain and humiliation. He has set an example of patience, charity and forgiveness. Through the graces which He gives us in prayer, especially in the Mass, we can change our hearts and imitate His behaviour. (T:1586)

Ignorance and darkness.

Christ asks us to encourage one another to throw off the veils of ignorance and darkness, and to run frequently to the Holy Sacrifice of the Mass, where our human life and Christ's Divine life can 'meet' most perfectly. A faithful person who prays sincerely at that 'intersection' of human and Divine life will be helped there to see all things clearly, as if in Divine light. That's how each of us can be helped to change, and to become more 'Christ-like'. (T:1670)

Refusing His invitation.

Christ has invited each of us to join Him in praising the Father in the most perfect possible way: through the offering of the Holy Sacrifice to which we unite ourselves, and through obedience to Christ's Holy Will amidst everyday joys and trials.

It's true that we have free will; yet we are very foolish if we thrust aside Christ's invitation that we join in His work, be liberated from sin, and achieve union and salvation. We are heading for disaster if we refuse every sort of grace, whether knowingly or unknowingly, and spurn the merits of the sacrifice-for-sin which Christ offered on Calvary. (T:1734D)

Every town and village.

We should appreciate how privileged we are to be able to attend Mass so frequently. Its importance cannot be over-estimated. It benefits not only ourselves, and the special people for whom we pray - and the whole Church - but people in every town and village in this country. In London, Birmingham and Manchester, and all over the country, all sorts of people owe the graces which they can receive - if they are willing to accept them - to the merits of Christ's sacrifice, and to the fervent prayer which, on behalf of us all, He offers from the altar.

We can be certain, as we think about the Mass, and attend Mass, that Christ's sacrifice - with our sincere prayers - benefits the whole country. When Christ comes to our midst to offer His sacrifice to the Father, at the hands of our priest, it's as though Calvary has risen up from the heart of England. It's as if numerous towns and villages and great stretches of country-side lie spread out beneath Christ's Cross. Truly, the sacrifice which Christ once offered on Calvary is being offered now - in England, in our century - from our altar.

That's why the 'work' of prayer which we shoulder, daily, is powerfully effective. Whenever Christ offers His sacrificial prayer in our sanctuary, we who are united to Him in our hearts and wills, and by our presence before the altar, are co-operating with His work. With Him, we draw upon the people of our own time and country all sorts of Heavenly graces - and forgiveness. Our Heavenly Father lavishes His blessings upon our country, through the merits of Christ's self-oblation: a sacrifice once offered on Calvary and now re-presented on the altar. (T:1740C)

Faithful to the Mass.

We need to understand how simple is Christ's plan of salvation, and how simple is our part in it. The invitation which He is making to us, and to all people, is: "Be faithful to the Mass." By

His Holy Sacrifice, and by our union with Him - in a life of grace - as He pleads for us before the Father, we are given a sure hope of salvation, if we remain faithful until we die. Since the Divine Son is perfect, His offering is perfect.   Therefore we who unite ourselves with His perfect offering are redeemed by it!   (Also T:1740C)

Our willing participation.

We need to understand how crucial for us is our willing participation in the Holy Mysteries. We who are present, through the Mass, at the offering of Christ's sacrifice, and who are devoted to Christ and repentant, are willingly uniting ourselves with Him in the act which saves us from eternal death.

It's true that our willing attendance at the Holy Sacrifice of the Mass is important because faithfulness to the Tradition is important, as is Christian fellowship, hearing the Word of God in Sacred Scripture, and Holy Communion.   But such willing attendance is supremely important for us because, through our association with Christ's sacrifice, which is the redeeming act by which He conquered sin and opened Heaven, we too can hope to enter Heaven, when the Father calls us. (Also T:1740C)

Disastrous for our souls.

Christ sees that many people today have never been taught what a terrible thing it is if we 'children of God' no longer come to the place of sacrifice: if we no longer come before the holy altar to be present with Christ as He offers the sacrifice which can save us!

The ignorance - or malice or carelessness - which keeps so many people away from the sanctuary and altar can be disastrous for souls. Christ sees it as grievously sad that sinful people, in need of His help, reject Him, and His promises.

If we refuse to attend the Holy Sacrifice, we refuse to co-operate with the Work of Christ which could have saved us. We stay aloof from the church: from the sacred place in which stands the altar of sacrifice. Furthermore, we turn from the Church which is Christ's Body. We shun the Communion of faithful disciples who are all bound together in love: gathered as a blessed and holy People with Christ and His holy Mother. If we won't stand close to Christ at Mass we demonstrate the desire to do our own will rather than His Will; and His Will is still made plain by the Church, who is calling: "Be faithful to the Mass. Come to the Holy Sacrifice, to save your souls, and to reverence your Creator." (Also T:1740C)

Eternal loss of God.

It's important that we realise the truth: that in deliberately choosing to stay away from Mass, we don't just omit a few prayers which might have benefited our own souls. We also abandon the prayers we might have offered, with Christ, for this generation, this era, and for the souls of the departed. We turn our backs - perhaps without realising it - on the redeeming Work which, here in our day, Christ is offering for our salvation. We make plain our contempt of Him, showing our indifference to the sufferings which He bore for our sake on Calvary. We freely choose a different way from His, a way which leads to darkness, and towards the loss which is eternal doom. (Also T:1740C)

Touched by the grace of Christ.

If we are faithful, and brave, we will remind hesitant friends that we must never walk away from Christ! If we are fearful of serving Him - tempted to imagine that to live outside the circle of His friendship is to live in freedom - we can keep in touch with Christ and His Church, through going to Mass, even if we can't yet pluck up courage to be wholly committed to Him in every area of life.

If we are present at the offering of the Holy Sacrifice we are touched by the grace of Christ to some degree, even if we're still trying to follow our own path: not yet wholly surrendered to Christ's embrace, nor fed by His Heavenly food and wisdom, but worshipping at the 'edge' of His great light. When we still attend Mass, numerous blessings and graces enfold us, through proximity to Christ, the source of all good, and through proximity to those of His friends who are living 'in Christ'. Their prayers will help us. We powerfully influence one another by our prayers; and so we help to draw one another into the radiant light of Christ's life and friendship. (T:1770)

Estranged from his Creator.

Only by the grace of God can we remain faithful; and that's why we must never grow complacent in the service of Christ. Yet we must pity those who appear to be guilty of grave sin, and who refuse to repent, or who refuse to believe in Christ, or who believe and repent to a limited extent but allow pride to keep them from being reconciled. Christ can see the truth: that, of their own free will, many of them remain in the 'pit' which is estrangement from their Heavenly Father. People who refuse to leave their 'pit' risk being unable to enter Heaven. If that happens they will be surrounded, eternally, by people like themselves: people who are proud-hearted and rebellious.

We should be grateful to God, if we can recognise our own sinfulness. If we are spiritually blind we neither appreciate our dire need of salvation, nor look for help towards our Divine Redeemer, Who has sacrificed Himself to save us. (T:1784)

Eternal unhappiness.

Christ asks us to consider the consequences of prolonged rebellion. A deeply sinful person who refuses to believe in Christ is following a downward path; and this is because he is unwilling to turn to the Father to say: "Christ has borne the punishment for my sins." Without Divine help, won by Christ, he cannot emerge from the 'pit' of sinfulness; and the results can be disastrous.

If a sinful person does not repent before he dies, he remains trapped in his blindness, is estranged from his Creator, is unable to rise up to joy, and cannot receive the rewards of the forgiven. He is doomed to eternal unhappiness, is denied the company of holy and faithful souls, endures the presence of those who - like himself - are without faith, hope, or Divine charity, and remains with the 'God-less' for all Eternity. (Also T:1784)

On every Sunday and holy day.

We must help everyone to see what simple instructions Christ has given us. When He took bread and wine, for Consecration, on the night before He died, He asked His Apostles to "Do this" in memory of Him. He invited them to imitate His actions and to repeat His words so that they too could consecrate the bread and wine, and they too - through His Sacred Body and Blood - could offer His Holy Sacrifice. In our own day, and in every era, His intention remains the same. He invites His priests to do what was done by His Apostles; and He invites us all to take part in the Holy Sacrifice.

Since it is Christ Who is teaching us all through His holy Church, we must accept His Church's instruction that we all attend and offer the Holy Sacrifice on every Sunday and every holy day 'of obligation'. It is an instruction which should be obeyed by everyone who professes to love Christ. (T:1857)

Through our willing attendance.

Christ wants us to reflect upon what we are signifying through our willing attendance at Mass. We signify our acceptance of Christ's saving Work on our behalf, and our acceptance of the message which He gave from the Cross: the message by which He begs us all to live in loving obedience to the Father's Will. We signify our need of continued Divine help, and our need of life-giving food: Christ's Sacred Body and Blood. We signify our true communion with other people who adhere to Him, within His Church. And we signify our longing to have been present - had we lived many centuries ago - to stand beside His Mother Mary, as she stood beside the Cross.

When a member of the Church refuses to participate in the Holy Sacrifice this indicates either a distressing and dangerous ignorance of its true significance, or a weak faith, or a refusal to remain united to Christ in a state of self-sacrificing love and obedience before the Father. (T:1961)

To love and serve God.

Christ sees today that, of all the Catholics who attend Mass regularly, many rarely reflect upon their need of God's graces. Yet God our Father has a great plan for Mankind. He invites us all to make our way towards the eternal joy that can never be taken away from us.

Our Blessed Lady consented to play her part in God's plan; and through her consent Christ our Saviour came on earth amongst us. Now, God our Father is inviting each one of us to take part in His plan. Innumerable gifts are being offered to us, today, if we will accept them; and highly worthwhile tasks are offered to us - if we will consent to undertake them.

Everyone who is born on earth is invited to co-operate with God, to fulfil God's plans. To love and serve God is the purpose of our existence. He wants to purify us all, to set us free from sin, to change us, and to make us upright and beautiful. That's what He wants for all the people He has created - if we'll give our consent. So it's plain that we're not merely selfish but foolish, if we say to God, "I will not join in Your plan," or "I will disregard Your wishes;" or "I will ignore the reason for my existence. I will amuse myself as I please. I will not serve You;" or even, "I can be a good Catholic without going to Mass." (T:2074)

Only if we consent.

Truly, Christ died for all. By His Death and Resurrection He made salvation possible for everyone; yet if we hope to be saved we must give our consent. This is the meaning of freedom: that needy and sinful people like ourselves can only be saved when we freely accept our need of salvation, and when we turn, therefore, to the only Saviour. Our God and Father is good; never, therefore, would He snatch away the freedom which is His gift to everyone who lives on earth. Yet the consequences of freely choosing to abandon God and goodness are horrendous.

If we wish to be saved - to be reconciled with Christ, and kept faithful - we must 'run' to Christ. We must place ourselves close to Him by our bodily presence at the offering of His Holy Sacrifice, or by our hearts' sincere intention if, for special reasons, we cannot 'reach' Him at Mass.

It's by our willing union with Christ, today, that we who have become His brothers and sisters through Baptism continue to receive His gifts and graces. We need to continue our willing union with Him, daily and hourly. Part of that life of union consists of associating ourselves, at Mass, with His prayer for our salvation as He speaks to the Father on behalf of all people. (T:2095)

Mutual encouragement.

We must encourage one another towards holiness. When we meet people who have stayed away from the Holy Sacrifice perhaps because of ignorance or lack of faith or spiritual blindness, we mustn't judge them, but we must encourage them to attend. With a little help, some of them might see how marvellous is Christ's holy offering from our sanctuary: from the altar of sacrifice.

With a little encouragement, they would open their eyes to the crucial redemptive Work which is re-presented here: a Work which is a free gift for those who are willing to unite themselves to it and so to allow themselves to be redeemed. (T:2203)

An immense barrier.

Christ wants us to understand that a calamity occurred when human beings first rebelled against God. Through sin, it's as if a separation was made of Mankind from the Godhead. It seemed as if an immense barrier covered the skies from top to bottom, to separate earth from Heaven. It was a barrier so complete and firm that only Christ, by His death on the Cross, has made it possible for us to reach out and touch God the Father in the hope of sharing Eternal Life. It was as if, in Christ's Passion, His Cross was like a sword which pierced the veil. It tore apart the fabric, to make a way through, for all who would trust in Christ. This is a way through which we can rise up by His Spirit's power to touch the Father, and so to enter Heaven's bliss. Hence the true significance of the Holy Sacrifice of the Mass.

We who live in times far removed from Christ's earthly life-time have only one 'place' to which we can go to be at Calvary, where our way to God was achieved. That 'place' is near an altar where one of our priests is offering the Holy Sacrifice once offered from the Cross. (T:2570)

Trust in Christ.

We need to come together for Mass because we need Christ, and we need the fruits of His unique sacrifice. Only by remaining 'in' Him until we die can we remain 'in' the Father and the Father's love, after death: saved by Christ the Redeemer in Whom we have put our trust. (T:2772)

Our free choices.

It's a kindness to help people to understand the importance of prayer, and Mass attendance. Everyone remains free to move towards the Father, in earthly life, by obeying His Son, and so to move swiftly away from sin - or to live in sin and blindness. (T:2801)

Refusing to pray the prayers.

Truly, we need to attend Mass, if this is possible: if we are not kept away by illness, travel or care for the sick or infants, for example. At Mass, we pray: "Give us peace in this life, save us from final damnation ... approve our offering ... let it become for us the body and blood of Jesus Christ your only Son, our Lord ... Do not consider what we truly deserve, but grant us your forgiveness ...". Therefore it's plain that we need to pray such prayers not once but regularly, and that we need to attend Mass if possible.

The Church is right to ask us to attend on Sundays, and on holy days of obligation, and to encourage even more frequent attendance. She does so not only to increase the praise of God from our world. She does so in order to keep us from danger, since each Catholic who refuses to attend, as a faithful member of the Church should attend, is refusing to pray the prayers by which we ask God for salvation. (T:4784)

Given with love.

We need the Holy Eucharist - our Holy Communion - in order to receive 'life', as Jesus says in the Gospels. We don't deserve such a share in Divine life. It is not a reward for good behaviour. It's a gift of love, given by God Who loves us - just as He has given us the Incarnate Christ from love and has created the Universe from love.

The intimate union with Jesus which we can achieve by Holy Communion is God's chosen way of preparing us for life in Heaven, if we are willing. This is why Christ's Church explains that all members of the Church should attend Mass on Sundays and holy days and should also - if we are in a state of grace - receive Christ in Holy Communion. We can say "No" to this gift; yet we shall be responsible for the terrible consequences of trying to live without God. Whoever remains forever without God, Who is the source of all joy and all that is good, will find himself having to endure the unendurable, by his own free choice. (P.U.T: 19)

The importance of the Mass.

Our trust in Christ, and our regular devotion to Him in the Mass, and the prayers we offer through Him at Mass, can keep us devoted and trusting not just in everyday trials but also in our approach to death.

Sincere followers of Christ, when they come to die, long to meet death with grace and courage, in the hope of Heaven. None of us is worthy to share God's life; yet we believe that God offers salvation as a free gift to those who believe in Him and in His Son Jesus Christ, who died to save us. That's why our regular attendance at Mass and our habitual reverence for Christ, and our trust in His promises, can prepare us to face death with confidence. If we have believed in Christ to the extent that we have become members of His Church, and have tried to live in contrition, humility and love, and if we have offered to God the Father, for our sins, Christ's saving sacrifice - which is re-presented at every Mass - we have good reason to be hopeful.

In such circumstances, we have good reason to believe that we have been washed clean in the Precious Blood of Christ which, with Christ's Sacred Body, and in union with the whole Church, we have offered for our sins, from our altar. We have been marvellously nourished by Christ's Sacred Body and Blood in Holy Communion: by the spiritual food which gives life. We have good reason to hope, therefore, that having had our sins forgiven, and possessing the 'life' which Christ offered us, God the Father will take us swiftly, when we die, to His heart in Heaven.

Such is the importance of the Mass, and of our sincere participation in it. (T:5133)

GESTURES

Body and spirit.

We are body and soul; and we have been made for union with God, in body and soul, when we are transformed and glorified. And so even now we should worship with our bodies and souls. We can use body and soul in God's service and in the service of our neighbour. Hence the Lord's delight on seeing our sincere gestures of reverence towards Him as well as on hearing sincere words from our lips and sincere cries from our hearts. (T:58)

Reverent genuflections.

Though we shouldn't interrupt the Sacred Liturgy with extravagant, private expressions of devotion, we should never be afraid to show our love towards God at appropriate times through sweet phrases, or holy gestures: for example, in our personal prayers of preparation and thanksgiving, and in our reverent bearing in prayer, and in the way we genuflect or bow to demonstrate love or adoration. (T:2925)

Reverent gestures.

Members of the laity who have not yet begun to follow the rubrics in various gestures, such as making the sign of the Cross before the Gospel, and bowing during the Creed at the mention of Christ's holy Incarnation, will please and honour Christ if they do so. (T:3046)

Submission and admiration.

Even though God sometimes holds us in prayer as a Father holds a little baby on His lap, as we rest silently in prayer before Him, in mutual delight, we must remain aware of His holiness and our frailty. We still need to bow and kneel before the Lord - especially in church, which is a 'house of prayer' - if we want to express our submission and admiration. (T:3399)

Our Father's delight in us.

We can pray to God in any place, and whether we are lying down or sitting upright; but He is touched by our reverence whenever we kneel to pray to Him. (T:3908)

SPEECH

'Artificial' voices.

It is plainly right that priests and lay-people should be taught how to enunciate their words with care, since it's the wish of Christ and His Church that all who participate in the Mass are helped to know and understand what is happening. Yet by over-scrupulous efforts to achieve clear diction, some people develop voices which are so artificial as to distract the listeners from the meaning of the words of the Liturgy instead of helping them to understand them. (P.U.T: 20)

Different languages.

Christ invites us all to realise that His Father is honoured equally by people who pray sincere prayers in Latin, and those who pray sincere prayers in any other language. It is not right that those who prefer Latin look disparagingly at people who prefer other languages; and nor is it right that people who prefer to use the vernacular dismiss Latin-enthusiasts as being 'old-fashioned' or 'pre-conciliar'. The Church permits the use of both Latin and other languages in various circumstances or with certain permissions. (P.U.T: 21)

Underlying problems.

People who look upon the Liturgy as Christ looks upon it can see that disagreements between Catholics about language occasionally serve as unspoken expressions of disagreement about more serious matters.

Christ's suggestion, for all who want to celebrate the Mass in a way which is worthy of Heaven, and beneficial for the participants, is that we should ask ourselves: "What is God like - almighty God Whom I worship in and through these Sacred Mysteries? How does a mature 'child of God' act in God's house of prayer, amongst the holy Angels and in the Presence of Christ?"

Christ asks us to realise that very many changes have accompanied the increased use of the vernacular: some unnecessary or unwise, and some refreshing. But some of the most unfortunate changes have contributed to the decline in Mass-going. (P.U.T: 22)

Of greater importance.

Our time would be better spent, in Christ's sight, ensuring the provision of sound teaching about the Mass and the other sacraments than in discussing whether the most suitable language for the liturgy is Latin or the vernacular.

Where there is sound teaching about the nature of God, about the wonder of the Incarnation, about the duties of Catholics, and about the laws and precepts of the Church, there is usually found great gratitude for the Catholic Faith, dignified behaviour in church during the Sacred Mysteries, and great awe and love before Christ in the tabernacle - no matter what language is used for the prayers. (P.U.T: 23)

CLOTHING

In a reverent manner.

There's no need for us to feel self-conscious about acting in a reverent manner towards Christ. He delights in our reverent worship, as some of us women veil our hair in His Presence, to please Him. We should rejoice that we are willing to honour Him in this way. Far from being a "little thing", such conformity to Scripture and to the custom of the Church is something great, in His sight. (T:1530A)

Veiling our hair.

If we think about the essence of prayer, we know that we please Christ if we have a 'contrite heart'. And if we love His Will, we further delight Him. We know, too, that we are wise to kneel in Christ's honour, to bow in reverence before Him, and to honour His Saints and holy Angels with appropriate and reverent greetings. We please him by such efforts; yet something is lacking. Our worship is more nearly perfect when women cover their hair during the Holy Mysteries.

We women please Christ if we accept His invitation to veil our hair during the Mass, and wherever Christ is Present in the Blessed Sacrament; though we mustn't imagine that this particular question of dress is a matter of good or evil. It is a matter of wanting to honour Christ perfectly and being willing to do what is necessary to achieve perfection.

Christ is always at work, leading us towards perfection in prayer, if we are willing, since reverent worship is supremely important. Yet the reverence with which we women honour Him in prayer can be deepened even further if we are willing to risk a little mockery in order to do what is fitting. It is Christ's wish that - where it is possible - we wear appropriate clothing, during the celebration of the Holy Mysteries, if we wish to offer Him perfect homage. (Also T:1530A)

Greater respect for Christ's Divinity.

We women can ask ourselves: "Are we willing to pay as much honour to Christ exteriorly as interiorly?" Although we might have reverent hearts, and although our gestures in worship might be as reverent as we can make them, our clothing is not always appropriate for a perfect participation in the Sacred Liturgy. In every century of the Church's worship, Christ's 'daughters' have covered their hair when they have prayed in church; and we can choose, even today, to be faithful to His wishes, as recorded and handed on for every generation.

In this comparatively minor matter many women sheepishly and wrongly followed other people, when in the past they abandoned this practice of covering their hair in church. We show a greater respect for Christ's Divinity if we accept this invitation to veil our hair whenever Christ is Present in the Blessed Sacrament. This pleases Him and also helps us to grow in holiness. Every act of self-conquest in this matter is also an admirable act of humility. (Also T:1530A)

In accordance with the Tradition.

If we do what is right, during the Liturgy, there's no need to imagine that we are being 'singular' in worship, or causing division. If we honour God, who is divided?

By our obedient and reverent worship we do not 'cause' division. We give glory to the Father. If other people are critical, they themselves cause division in the community, from uncharity towards women whose apparently 'novel' behaviour is not a novelty at all. Rather, it is in accordance with the traditions handed on, cherished and accepted in every age of Christian history and on every continent.

We mustn't worry about what others think or say, as we try to be obedient to Christ, faithful to the ordinary and customary way of approaching Him in public prayer.

Anyone who feels 'provoked' to anger by our modest clothing or who thinks us old-fashioned is not of one mind with the Saviour through Whom we offer praise to our Heavenly Father. (Also T:1530A)

The reverence due to His Divinity.

Christ is deeply moved whenever someone sacrifices her own will in order to please Him by acting with the reverence which is due to His Divinity. He sees that in some parts of the world few women are faithful to the customs of the Church in this matter.

We must never forget that He is thrilled by the efforts of those of His children who 'conquer' themselves, and who do difficult things in order to fulfil His wishes. He delights in the love which drives us to overcome our fear of humiliation or criticism from other people. (T:2010)

Objects of curiosity.

Christ delights in seeing women cover their hair, for the offering of the Holy Sacrifice. He delights in the love which drives us to obey Him even in a strange church - when we're away from home - where we feel foolish, and we are objects of curiosity. He is powerful enough to banish the pain in our hearts and minds, or to help us to bear it. (T:2046)

Immodest clothing.

No woman should wear immodest clothing. Yet it's a greater cause for sadness if women are immodestly clothed in church, or in the sanctuary during the Mass - though many have never received good advice on this subject. (T:2291A)

Inappropriate fashions.

Christ wants us to think about the sort of clothing which is appropriate for people who appear in the sanctuary during the celebration of the Holy Mysteries. Some women are not appropriately clothed at present.

Although no woman should go anywhere in public immodestly-clothed, it is particularly unfitting that women appear in the sanctuary wearing immodest clothing - examples of which are common today. Nor is it right that - against God's wishes, as made plain in Holy Scripture and in the traditions of the Church - women enter and move around the sanctuary with long hair carelessly displayed, unrestrained, and more suited to a bedroom than a church. (T:2395)

Humiliation and pity.

Christ our Saviour, Who looks upon us from the heights of glory, loves to reward us for our sacrifices, for example, when we women cover our hair, in His honour, in church, and do this out of respect for His Divinity. It pleases Him enormously that we are willing to honour His Real Presence in the Blessed Sacrament, in this way, and that we are even willing, for His sake, to appear to be old-fashioned.

Christ knows and understands everything, including the fact that some sufferings - whether brief or prolonged - are harder to bear than others. Humiliation, pity, exasperation or enforced loneliness are hard to bear with patience. Christ knows that greater love and courage can be needed to bear these things willingly - in imitation of Him and out of love for Him - than to bear physical pain. (T:2506)

A consecrated church.

Christ is pleased if women consider their simple duty towards Him and then act in obedience to His wishes. We are right to veil our hair whenever we're in a Catholic Church for prayer, whether or not the Blessed Sacrament has been briefly transferred elsewhere. A consecrated church is a very holy place. So Christ delights in seeing our willingness to undertake a fitting act of reverence for Him and His sanctuary. In the same way - if this is practicable - we can do this whenever we receive Him in Holy Communion at home, or in hospital. (T:2585)

In small ways, and great.

Christ is delighted when we accept and obey His wishes in great things - and in small. He is delighted, for example, when a woman veils her hair in church, for love of Him, or obeys Him by not seeking to be an ordained priest, or by not seeking to preach from the pulpit during the Liturgy. The Father looks with gratitude upon everyone who honours and obeys His Son. (T:3177)

Wearing a mantilla.

Christ wants us to know that He is touched to the heart by little 'offerings', when we offer the sacrifice of being conspicuous, or looking foolish or 'old-fashioned,' as we women veil our hair in obedience to His wishes. In putting on a scarf or hat or mantilla, we women give a powerful witness to the reverence which is due to Christ at every celebration of the Mass. (T:3216)

DANCE

A poor understanding.

Christ looks on with joy whenever we make new efforts to beautify the Sacred Liturgy, or make it more reverent. Yet Clergy and teachers show that they have a poor understanding of the Holy Sacrifice if they encourage people to take part in inappropriate dancing displays in church - even 'designing' such displays to take place during the most solemn parts of the Mass.

When girls or young women dance in or near the sanctuary, perhaps attempting to illustrate a 'theme' of Christ's Paschal Work, but wearing immodest clothing, they distract worshippers from prayer. They draw attention to human achievements instead of the Work of Christ. They cause offence by their near-nakedness. They show their ignorance of the Sacred Tradition, and - though they might be blameless, because ill-advised by other people - they diminish the dignity of the gathering.

Christ and His Mother look with love upon every participant in the Mass; but they are not honoured by such innovations. Rather, they look with pity upon those who haven't yet been taught to participate in the Holy Mysteries in an appropriate manner. (P.U.T: 24)

A solemn memorial.

Some people mistakenly believe that dance-troupes can play a valid and worthwhile part in the Mass by giving a short display just before or after the Consecration - or at other parts of the Mass. Yet such displays give no honour to Christ. They are highly inappropriate at Mass; and this has been made plain by the

Church authorities.

It is true that a gentle, rhythmic procession to the altar is permitted in countries where such things are part of everyday life. To move to music in a procession in a stately and dignified way is a normal part of life in certain cultures. Yet things are different in Europe. Christ sees that some who take part in so-called 'liturgical dancing' perform with good intentions. He also sees how, in their ignorance, they wrongly imagine that the solemn memorial of His Passion, Death and Resurrection can be suitably 'adorned' by an interlude of dance in which scantily-clad girls or women leap about right next to, or even within, the sanctuary. (P.U.T:25)

CHANGES

Private likes and dislikes.

We mustn't give in to the temptation to criticise changes in liturgical style. If we notice a legitimate but unappealing alteration to do with the Mass we shouldn't be despondent. Certain new ways of doing things facilitate the offering of the sacrifice which Christ Himself offers from our altar.

It's important to be generous-minded, as we ponder private likes and dislikes in comparatively minor liturgical matters. Our Heavenly Father wants us to remember that it's the Will of God that we accept the teaching and discipline of the Church. (T:1510)

Recollected and prayerful.

We must encourage people to be faithful and to trust that God still guides His Church. None of us need despair about change and confusion in the Mass. The 'heart' of the Mass remains the same, century after century. The great act of sacrifice is effective in every circumstance because it is Christ's great act; and so it is effective even where the manner of its celebration is unworthy. That's why we can all participate sincerely, whatever superficial changes occur.

Whatever style of Mass we attend, we can do good and worthwhile things. If we are devout and faithful friends of Christ we can turn to the Father through Christ. We can be recollected and prayerful. We can gaze towards the altar. We can imitate faithful people of every past century of Christian history by uniting our hearts to Christ's great self-offering, during the Mass: a self-offering so glorious and effective that all who know about it and who sincerely love Christ yearn to be present. (T:1804)

Christ's own action.

We must be faithful and obedient: loyal to the Church founded upon Peter and the other Apostles. How unwise we are if we turn away from Christ because of discord or disappointment. Yet others, too, are unwise, in His sight. Those people in the Church who make any emphasis, change or addition which causes the great 'heart' of the Liturgy to be minimised or overlooked are unwise: even sinful. Christ looks with pity upon those who - through ignorance or disobedience - are discouraging or scornful about the reverence and the honour which we should offer to God at the central act of the Holy Sacrifice.

Many people today see the Mass as merely a family meal, and know or care little about Christ's own action during the Holy Mass, about the act of offering which makes possible our salvation. (Also T:1804)

Our lowly places.

Each of us 'ordinary' worshippers should value our lowly places within Christ's Church, as we continue to pray regularly, yet seem to make little contribution to the outward life of the community, through force of circumstances. Prayer and faithfulness, however, are supremely important, in community life.

We should never forget that Christ sees and understands everything. He sees clearly that many who appreciate a profoundly reverent celebration of the sacraments, with straightforward reminders of the truths of the Catholic Faith, are sometimes pushed aside on the great pilgrimage of the Church. Christ sees that ordinary people - simple, faithful people who have no special gifts - are sometimes pitied or overlooked. There are those who care more for fashions in spirituality and for the good opinion of their colleagues than for the simple customs of the lowly and the inarticulate who are so precious to Christ, and who themselves form part of the Sacred Tradition. (T:1947)

DISOBEDIENCE OR COMPLAINT

Foolish additions.

Whenever the Sacred Liturgy is distorted by foolish, unworthy, or strange events or additions, we shouldn't feel obliged to join in those parts, or to praise such things. (T:781)

Following the rubrics.

It's God's Will that we imitate His Son by our love and obedience: and that includes obedience to the Church, to the Sacred Tradition. So we should see the Sacred Liturgy as something precious handed down to us, and the rubrics as wise instructions - not to be carelessly ignored. (T:939)

In loving obedience.

Christ invites us all to be obedient to His wishes, though He wants none of us to imagine that we can 'win' His good opinion by our behaviour. He loves us, even while we are sinners. Nor does He want frightened people to imagine that we can win extra 'approval' from Him by a merely outward show of obedience or devotion. He is delighted, however, when we love Him so much that we freely choose to keep His Commandments and also to obey the precepts, rules and customs of His Church. (T:1484)

In freedom.

Christ has a 'picture' to show us, to illustrate the clear relationship between the observance of rules and the experience of freedom. He asks us to imagine that, in the fork of a branch of a tree, a nest is balanced. A little chick sits contentedly within it, trustfully opening its beak for the Mother bird who has just arrived with some food. The nest has been built from hundreds of little pieces of straw and twigs, carefully placed and inter-woven. And so it's plain that just as a bird's nest perched on a branch might be made up of hundreds of little 'twigs' and bits of straw, so the Church's rules and laws and recommendations can be seen as the twigs which form a 'nest'. Only upon a firm, safe, purpose-built foundation - in utter freedom and security - can a mother bird safely and in a leisurely way feed her chicks, whom she loves. And thus it is with God and the soul. In that sort of security and intimacy God and the soul can communicate in a true union of love, unhindered by laws, although laws have provided the foundation for that relationship to develop as it ought.

We in the Church can remember that no 'chick' can be fed if he doesn't admit his need. He cannot be fed if he refuses to wait patiently for food. He'll be unable to receive food if he attempts to destroy the nest in which he sits. He will be quite unprotected, if he chooses the 'freedom' of flailing feebly around on the ground below, half-starved and easy prey for any passing attacker. Similarly, someone who hopes to enjoy a close relationship with Christ and hopes to be fed by Him as by a loving mother, should reflect upon the meaning of freedom.

Christ is love incarnate. It is therefore impossible that He force us to love Him, or force us to receive His gifts. Yet how can someone be fed by Christ if that person - like a chick who refuses to sit in its nest - refuses to meet Christ in prayer or in the sacraments? How can Christ teach people who scorn the Commandments, and the other sure teachings proposed by the Church in faithfulness to Christ Who guides her? It is through obedience to Christ and His Church that we can find the greatest joy and freedom. (Also T:1484)

Complaining or campaigning.

Some members of the Church disagree with the Church's teaching about a male Priesthood - even though it was recently affirmed by the Holy Father, the Pope. Some complain or campaign, nevertheless, hoping to achieve their aim, which is the 'Ordination' of women. Yet though they might imagine that their cause is just, they neither please God nor help the Church, by their protests.

It's important that Catholic preachers and teachers state as often as is necessary that it is not the Will of God that women be priests. They should share the good news that, in the Catholic Church, many women are already at work for Christ, though not as priests, but in womanly ways. They are at work in intimate conversation, domestic affection, hard thinking and frank talk. They also act as balm and salve to wounded souls. These women are at work in the midst of the great throng of Christ's People: some women in highly responsible positions as Professors, teachers and catechists, or spiritual guides or retreat-givers, and some unnoticed and apparently unrewarded. But they are all kindly and caring amidst crowds, amidst bustle and noise. They all honour Christ and please Him, as they do His work. These women act with kindly authority, sure of their role, comforting struggling people. They are not priests, but they are most certainly helping their fellow-travellers during the journey to glory.

Many of these women are good 'mothers' of souls, as they urge souls towards the priest: towards the shepherd of souls who sits at one side of the road to Heaven, ready to listen, to judge, and to forgive, acting 'in persona Christi.' Even if the priest is a weak man, he is someone chosen by God, strengthened, and elevated and clothed in authority.

Faithful women such as these can be seen as true 'mothers' of souls, as they usher wounded people to the place of the soul's re-birth, the place of Reconciliation, where Christ, the Great Director of souls, forgives sins through His priest. Christ thus prepares the souls of His People for a further stage of the journey which has already begun - and for the destination, which is Heaven. (T:1554)

Rudeness and disobedience.

Christ wants us all to know that whoever spreads malicious gossip about the Clergy, or proclaims that the constant teaching of the Church is wrong, or is seriously disobedient to those whom Christ has placed in authority in His Church, or who wilfully commits serious sin of any sort, is like someone who deliberately cuts his own body or inflicts some other harm upon it. It's plain that if we behave like that we're extremely foolish, because in acting thus we endanger our own spiritual lives. (T:2831)

Hurting Christ's Body.

If we are members of the Body of Christ we must respect the whole Body. We hear, in the Scripture reading, that "The church is his body," and "He its head." Yet Christ sees that there are many in the Church who strike at that Body by mocking His chosen teachers, by mocking the Holy Father and other Clergy, or by denying some of the truths of the Catholic Faith.

Those who mislead the Faithful by such mockery or denial are taking a sword to wound Christ, and also to wound themselves, who themselves are parts of Christ's Body. (T:2860)

Un-likeness to God.

Whatever vocation each of us follows in the Church, we must beware of doing or saying anything which works against our particular vocation. By any sort of unfaithfulness on our part, or disobedience, we not only set a bad example; we show an un-likeness to God Who is always faithful and loyal and - as shown in Christ's life - obedient. (T:3365)

Sincere prayers.

Christ invites us all to be sincere and trusting when we approach Him in prayer. Yet He asks us to ponder this question: How sincere are our prayers to Him, in private prayer, or at Mass, if we speak loving words to Him yet ignore, in everyday life, His chosen teachers?

Christ loves everyone - whether we are good-hearted or rebellious, misguided or heroic in charity. He asks us to believe that His love for us is infinitely-great and always compassionate. Yet He can see at every moment the hearts of those who declare their love for Him whilst at the same time they refuse to listen to Him as He guides them through the Bishops - including the Pope - to whom He has given His authority. He sees that some Catholics praise the Father whilst calling 'unjust' the Father's laws and Commandments; and some praise the Holy Spirit Whose guidance they spurn as they prefer a personal interpretation of the Church's teaching to the plain truths on faith and morals which Christ offers through those who obey and serve His cause. (T:4172)

To speak the truth.

Where there is conflict amongst Church members about aspects of the Sacred Liturgy, it's important that all concerned try to look upon each situation from God's 'point of view.' Then it can be plainly seen that He asks us all to act with charity towards one another, to speak the truth about what we know to be right or wrong, to accept the teaching and discipline of the Church, for the sake of harmony - and to be faithful to the sacraments, and to prayer, and to the wise promptings of the Holy Spirit Who is always at work to help us. (T:5051)

By loving obedience.

Whoever is tempted to disregard the rubrics here and there, to fulfil his own preferences, is perhaps encouraging his parishioners to cast an over-critical eye upon many other aspects of the sacred rites. Furthermore, he is indirectly making things difficult for fellow-Catholics who are trying to persuade children or new Church members to respect the rubrics and to respect the practices and customs of the Church. Heaven is made glad by our loving obedience to the Church, even in little matters. (T:5062)

APATHY

Our Lord and God.

Christ longs for us all to understand that He Who comes to the sanctuary is our Lord and God. Though He is true man - one who attracts by His gentleness and humility - He is also true God: Creator and Redeemer, majestic in His glory. That's why, if we really love Him, we should greet Him with mixed delight and awe.

He sees that there are people who are almost enraptured at the sight of the majestic beauties of Creation, on seeing films of the movement of the planets in the vast distances of space, or when travelling to the Grand Canyon or to huge deserts or mountains or waterfalls. Yet they aren't aware that the origin of all power, beauty and wisdom is Present amongst them during the Holy

Mass.

Christ sees that many people are overwhelmed with warmth and delight when they hear happy news about human relationships. They weep for joy on seeing a mother welcome home the beloved son who was thought to have died in a war. But these same people scarcely give a thought to the supremely-triumphant drama which is represented before them weekly and even daily in the sanctuary.

Our Lord and God is here, in every celebration of the Mass. Christ is here: the one Who came to earth for our sakes, suffered to save us, and emerged triumphant from the tomb after torture and death. He has promised to give everlasting life and bliss to all who put their trust in Him and persevere to the end. He is here amongst us at the bidding of His priest and through the power of the Holy Spirit; and yet Christ meets apathy and indifference! (T:3067)

Ignorance and discourtesy.

Very few children genuflect as they pass before the altar and tabernacle. Christ sees the plain truth: that for a whole generation there has been a widespread lack of instruction about reverent behaviour in church and at prayer. This is what has led to the apathy, ignorance and discourtesy which is so often demonstrated in Christ's Presence, before, during, and after the Mass.

We who love one another hesitate to appear critical of one another. But there is an urgent need for us to open one another's eyes to the irreverence which Christ witnesses daily, in His Church. (T:3332)

IRREVERENCE

Something awesome.

We must always be reverent before the altar. It is an altar of sacrifice. Something awesome and holy takes place there at every Mass. There, Christ's Precious Blood - the Blood of the Covenant - is offered to the Father, in our presence. (T:253)

Christ's glorious Presence.

We ought always to act with reverence in church. It's as if Christ our High Priest stands before us, after the Consecration. He is robed as a priest, and is radiant with joy. A halo encircles His head. He stretches out His arms in welcome and in triumph, as His glorious Presence fills the sanctuary. (T:550)

Setting a bad example.

We should offer the Holy Sacrifice with reverence. If we fail to do so, we prove our ignorance, or apathy, or carelessness or lack of faith - and we set a bad example. (T:553)

Just like the holy Angels.

We should imitate the holy Angels who are aware of the privilege of being close to Christ in the Blessed Sacrament. They venerate Him. They are eager to adore Him wherever the Sacred Host is placed, whether in the pyx, the tabernacle or the altar. They live to serve and adore Christ - just as we should, if our love for Him is sincere. (T:825)

High and holy worship.

At every Mass, frail creatures like ourselves, who have been made glorious by the grace of Christ, are privileged to take part in the staggeringly high, holy and joyful worship of Heaven itself. This is possible only because of the eternal offering which Christ makes on our behalf to the Father. This is why reverence is called for, and careful preparation. (T:860) *(See illustration 13)*

Christ's Precious Blood.

We should pray with deep reverence, at the Holy Sacrifice of the Mass. When Christ was nailed to the Cross, long ago, His Precious Blood poured from His wounded feet, down upon the earth, as if to spread across the whole globe. It is through His Blood, shed for us, that our sins have been forgiven. So we are right to pray with heart-felt gratitude as Christ offers His perfect prayer and perfect sacrifice to the Father, on our behalf and in our presence. (T:1419B)

A union of hearts.

We should imitate the reverence of the holy Angels. Whenever the Holy Sacrifice is offered on the altar, they bow down before Christ, our Lord and Creator. We too can express our reverence at that moment; indeed, we're already doing so if we are kneeling throughout the Eucharistic Prayer. But we act with the greatest reverence towards Christ if we are firmly uniting our hearts to the sacrificial prayer which Christ offers to the Father through our priest. And when the priest prays out loud, speaking of Christ, saying: "Through Him, with Him, in Him, in the unity of the Holy Spirit, all glory and honour is yours, Almighty Father, for ever and ever", we can add our fervent "Amen". (T:1443)

Christ amongst us.

No matter how distressed we are by the noise or irreverence in church during the Mass, it's important to keep in mind what is really important. Christ is amongst us! So we should rejoice in His Presence, and in His love. If we turn our hearts towards Him, we allow Him to help us to overcome our impatience. (T:1679)

Good habits.

We needn't worry about being a little bit distracted when we make reverent gestures towards Christ, for example, if we genuflect before the Blessed Sacrament even though our minds are elsewhere. Good habits are admirable; and we honour Christ by our reverent way of acting, even if we're not perfectly recollected.

We can imagine that a school-teacher in past times would have been delighted to see a child pausing in the central aisle in order to make a respectful curtsey before her - from habit - after entering the classroom. Even if the child were plainly distracted by thoughts of the work she was about to do, the teacher would have been pleased by the gesture. In the same way, Christ delights in reverent gestures, even whey they are absent-minded. We honour Him least if, because of carelessness or ignorance, we refrain from paying Him reverent homage. (T:1780)

Good news.

The greatest and most sincere reverence is shown towards Christ by those who not only behave in a dignified way in church but who also believe in Christ's love, and are grateful that He once came to earth to live amongst us and even sacrificed Himself on our behalf.

Truly, Christ died on the Cross because of the sins of Mankind. He has made it possible for people of every generation to be reconciled with the Creator from Whom they have been grievously estranged. We were all in dire need of salvation; and Christ, alone, was fit to plead for us, His brothers and sisters. He, alone, has been able to offer sufficient and perfect reparation to our Heavenly Father for the sins of the whole human race. And the Good News which His Church has never ceased to proclaim is that everyone who believes in Christ can emerge from the 'pit' of sinfulness and 'estrangement-from-God'. We can even find a place on earth - our church, with its altar and tabernacle - where, in a sacramental manner, Christ is Really and substantially Present! Whoever really believes this, and is genuinely grateful, will act towards Christ with unfailing reverence. (T:1784)

With less reverence than Christ.

Christ suggests today, that if we are growing careless in church, we might ponder the fact that He Himself, in His earthly life, offered praise to the Father with reverence and humility, even kneeling to pray. He doesn't ask us to kneel all the time; but He wants us to think about our attitude. How do sinful people like ourselves dare to offer praise and thanksgiving to God our Father with less reverence than Christ? (T:1861)

The Communion of Saints.

Christ wants us to realise that the consecrated building in which we gather together for Mass is a holy place where we are all praying amongst the holy Angels. We offer praise to our Father in Heaven by the offering of the Holy Sacrifice: in Christ's Presence, and by His Spirit's power. This liturgical worship has succeeded the solemn praise once offered in the Temple of Jerusalem; and it is no less holy. It is Christ's perfect praise, offered in our presence; and that is why nothing should mar the celebration, neither irreverent or careless behaviour, nor undignified words and actions, and immodest clothing: all unsuitable for the 'Communion of Saints!' (T:1920)

Appropriate clothing.

Christian modesty should be fostered by all who love Christ. Modesty is to be encouraged in every way of life; but those who minister in the church or sanctuary have an additional obligation to wear clothing which is suitable for the solemn celebration of the Holy Mysteries. Unless people are so poor that a change of clothing is a luxury, those who arrange the Liturgy should suggest that scanty or dishevelled clothing which is suitable for a beach holiday - or for a sportsfield or for a stage - is scarcely suitable for the sanctuary. (Also T:1920)

Outweighing our faults.

Christ is delighted whenever someone makes a devout gesture of reverence towards the Blessed Sacrament and thus towards Him, in an era when many people are careless or irreverent. He is pleased if we are not ashamed to adore Him profoundly, no matter who is watching. Even a little scrap of sincere devotion far outweighs our little faults, especially when we have risked or borne humiliation in order to honour Christ. (T:1967)

Beauty, order and peace.

Christ's attitude is always one of love and welcome, when He comes to the altar. Yet He delights especially in coming to the altar in a church where He is greeted with a reverent welcome which is worthy of His Divinity. He is thrilled to be welcomed amidst beauty, order and peace, by obedient people who have looked forward with joyful yearning to His sacramental Presence. (T:2029B)

Christ's anguish.

We should generally avoid looking at people who are acting irreverently in church, and try to refrain from mental criticism or judgements. We please Christ by praying sincere prayers for them, just as we pray for everyone else who is here in the church with us, at Mass. Yet Christ is glad that we yearn to see Him honoured and adored. He wants us to realise that a great anguish gripped His heart, during His earthly life, at every sign of irreverence towards holy things or towards the Holy One: His Father. (T:2243A)

Disturbing the holy Angels.

It's important that we remember that our church is 'holy ground'. It is a place for worship. Christ our Saviour is Really Present in the tabernacle. His holy Angels adore him, day and night. Like spears of light, they are motionless yet prayerful, here in this holy place where the Holy Sacrifice is offered from the altar. It is by 'disturbing' these hundreds of holy Angels who stand guarding the church, and by caring little about the continuing worship of fellow-Catholics, that those of us who rush about in church or speak in a noisy manner are doing wrong. (T:2310)

Christ amongst His friends.

We should remember Christ's dual nature: the fact that He is both God and man. By His Divine Will and power, He is Present in the Blessed Sacrament, delighting in our reverent praises. He is touched to the heart by our genuine love. Yet very frequently, where Christ has come to be with us, in His sacramental Presence, He meets indifference or unbelief.

Such is the depth of Christ's humility that He permits this shameful behaviour. But how much He loves to be amongst people who love Him. He delights in being amongst His friends in every reverent gathering. (T:2410)

Children running riot.

It is not God's Will that children be allowed to run riot in a holy place as their parents or attendants sit by, ignorant or careless.

Christ would like to hear the Clergy speak up bravely about the reverence which is due to Him at all times, and which is especially appropriate in His own 'house of prayer' where He is Really

Present.

It's true that Christ's heart is blissful now, in Heaven's glory. Yet it's as though He could weep, just as He once wept over Jerusalem, at the irreverence He sees so widespread today. (T:2423)

Little children can be taught.

Few of us are willing to speak frankly about the need for reverence in God's 'house of prayer;' yet even little children can be taught to be reverent and prayerful.

It might even be our duty to speak to our parish priest about noisy children - yet only in general terms, and not in order to criticise individuals. Rather, we can keep him informed so that he can encourage everyone to respect God's house. (T:2430)

Respect for God.

Wonderful advice is given, today, about the respect which is due to people of all ages and all races; yet how few voices are heard which ask for respect for God in His sanctuary: a place which has been consecrated and made holy, for sacred worship. Very few people are willing to speak about the reverence which is due to Christ Who is sacramentally Present in the tabernacle. (Also T:2430)

A good beginning.

We should long to see Christ being offered the reverent attention and worship which is due to Him: worship also due to the Father and the Holy Spirit. Everyone who thinks about faith in the Holy Trinity, and then reverence, should be aware that reverence starts 'here.' It's here in church, and by encouragement in outward forms of good behaviour, that people who have come to pray and to offer the Holy Sacrifice can be prepared for an inward change of heart. (T:2485)

Reverence in other places.

People who know about Christ's glorious and Real Presence in church, and who delight in it, and who therefore recognise a Catholic church as being a holy place, will act here in a reverent and prayerful way. Furthermore, there is some hope that they'll be reverent and prayerful when they leave the building and meet the sacred in other places: whether through people or places, or journeys of pilgrimage, or through relics or holy pictures, or symbols.

A Catholic who has somehow remained ignorant of Christ's Presence in our church, however, and who is ignorant of the importance of both the tabernacle and the altar, and who is ignorant, too, of the fact that the whole building has been consecrated, is unlikely to act as he or she ought to act. People who are irreverent, careless, unloving or thoughtless in church are unlikely to treat with reverence the holy things or people or places they encounter outside the 'house of God.' (Also T:2485)

Participating in Heaven's 'song'.

When Christ the Son of God is Really Present amongst us in sacramental form, the praise which He offers in our presence from the sanctuary is the very same as the praise He offers to the Father eternally, in Heaven: watched by the Saints and holy Angels.

People who believe in Christ's Presence and therefore understand something of the majesty and dignity of the praise which soars Heavenward from this holy place, will also understand how to behave. They will know why preparations are required of all who want to take part with humility, and why reverence and order are required during the Sacred Liturgy. If we believe in Christ's praise and delight in it we are grateful that He has allowed sinful people like ourselves to come into His Presence and to participate in

Heaven's eternal 'song'. (T:2530)

Close to the Holy of Holies.

If we witness carelessness or disrespect in church we should remember that Christ was outraged in the Temple precincts, not only at the shabby treatment of the poor, but also at the disrespect being shown so close to the Holy of Holies.

His desire to see reverent and charitable behaviour is not less today. He especially wants to see it in the heart of His own 'house': in the church building, where His people stand so close to the tabernacle, yet where many are entirely forgetful of His holiness and Divine majesty.

It's true that some of the ill-trained children and loudly-chattering adults are acting in a disrespectful way through no fault of their own but through ignorance. Yet their irreverence shouldn't be overlooked by those whose task it is to encourage both reverent Liturgy and charitable behaviour in the 'house of God'. (T:2608)

Growth in holiness.

Christ wants us to realise that if we want to grow in holiness we should worship with awe and reverence as well as gratitude and trust. (T:2779)

Noise or confusion.

Where people are trained to act with reverence - even though their faith might be weak and their sense of awe very feeble - there is some hope that an increasing faith within that soul will not be 'stopped' in its growth. It is hard for faith to grow in a soul, however, when there is noise, irreverence or confusion - all things easily sustained where that person is outwardly loud, irreverent or undisciplined in worship. Hence the importance both of good instruction and good example. (T:3064)

Awesomely beautiful or good.

Many of us fail to show due reverence to Christ in prayer. Few of us act as if we are approaching someone Who, though wholly loving and gentle, is clothed in infinite majesty and glory.

Because we sometimes lack faith in the glory of the Godhead we fail to show either delight or awe: things which arise in the 'normal' human heart at the sight of everything known to be awesomely beautiful or good. Christ sees a great need, today, for everyone to be made aware of the majesty of the Godhead - and to be reminded that Christ Who comes to the altar is true God: our Creator and Redeemer. (T:3067)

Respect for each 'temple'.

In order to bring about change, Christ wants us to 'see' what He sees. In this era, when many hearts and minds are coarsened, and when even many of us in Christ's Church have little respect for the 'temples' of our bodies - which are temples of the Holy Spirit - we sometimes sin against such 'temples' by our thoughtless or unchaste behaviour. So it's almost inevitable that there's little respect for another sort of 'temple': for a holy place such as a church, which has been consecrated for solemn worship, and where Christ is Really Present in the Blessed Sacrament. (T:3150)

Careless and bored gestures.

Christ sees a 'wound' at the heart of Catholic worship today. He rarely sees the sort of awe and gladness which is described in the Scripture reading, in the first book of Maccabees, where "the whole people fell prostrate in adoration praising to the skies him who made things so successful. For eight days they celebrated the dedication of the altar, joyfully offering holocausts, communion sacrifices, and thanksgivings."

Christ sees that very few Catholics have a firm belief in His sacramental 'Real Presence'; and that's why few of us bother to acknowledge His Presence with gratitude and reverence. So He wants us to ask ourselves: "Which 'outsider', were he to visit some of our churches and witness the careless and bored gestures of so many Catholics, would believe what is proclaimed by everyone who teaches the Catholics Faith with conviction: that God lives among us, sacramentally?" Christ asks us to realise that this is a privilege so great that it causes wholehearted believers to worship in awe as well as joy. (T:3327)

A novel attitude.

There has arisen amongst Catholics a novel attitude to prayer, when it is seen more as a time of relaxation than as a time in which we wholeheartedly offer our time and our attention to God.

It's true that God's love for us is total, and that He loves to share His joy and peace with us in prayer. But if we neglect to mention God's majesty and glory, as we speak of Him to our children, as we try to encourage them to pray, we allow a generation to come to adulthood with little idea that we should offer to God the honour and reverence which are His due. And when Catholics are not taught the importance of formal worship, and rarely stand or kneel to pray, there is inevitably noise and irreverence in Catholic churches. (T:4172)

Little relation to Heaven's worship.

It is true that the Lord sees our souls' good intentions - no matter how brief or fleeting. Yet He asks us to consider what relation to Heaven's worship can He see in the careless or random genuflections made by His own children? Very many of us, in our pitiable ignorance, stroll about chatting in His 'house of prayer', careless of the Presence in the tabernacle, and careless of the need of other people to pray in peace before the God Who is all-holy as well as all-love.

Many people don't realise that, for God's children, the joy of prayer increases as the bond of love between God and creature is made stronger by every expression and act of love. (T:4728)

Signifying our beliefs.

We need to recognise the importance of the signs we use, in Church life. For example, Christ is made Present at the Consecration under the appearance of food, to signify that He wants us to receive Him as our spiritual food. Likewise, when a priest genuflects after the Consecration, he signifies - by that act of adoration - his belief that it is no longer bread on the altar, but Jesus Christ, sacramentally Present. In the same sense, other people in church make an equally eloquent statement of 'belief' by their inappropriate behaviour.

Those who rarely genuflect, or who gossip loudly in church and disturb people who are praying, signify their attitude. They 'show out', by their 'signs', either gross ignorance of how Christians should behave in God's 'house', or little respect for God, Whom they fail to honour in ways recommended by our Bishops through the ages. They show disrespect for the 'house of prayer' which is just as sacred as the Temple which Jesus was horrified to see dishonoured by the traders.

Christ was angered not simply by the way in which the poor pilgrims were treated, but also by the lack of reverence for God's 'house'. That was His attitude, even though He knew that the days of worship in the Temple were numbered because the Romans were going to destroy it. (T:5041)

Reverence and decorum.

Christ wants us all to remember that we pray in church amongst the holy Angels; indeed, there are so many Angels in the church that it's as if they fill the spaces between all the people present.

How much more willing we would be, to act in church with the reverence and decorum worthy of 'God's house', if we remembered what holy company we have, during our prayers. (T:5101)

NOISE

Permitting riotous behaviour.

Many of us are at fault during noisy and irreverent worship, whether we are the irritating or the irritated. If we complain and grumble about noises and distractions we are not fully immersed in prayer; but if by our silence we permit riotous behaviour we are ignorant or careless about the solemn celebration of the Holy Mysteries. (T:457A)

Disturbing the holy Angels.

If we are noisy in church we are disturbing the holy Angels who - in their hundreds, like spears of brilliant light - throng the church interior, and adore Christ, day and night, in the Blessed Sacrament. (T:2310)

Every Mass, a triumph.

We mustn't become despondent about the inappropriate or irreverent things we see and hear in church. The Mass is a wonderful act in which we can always rejoice, however great the noise and irreverence around us. Every Mass is a triumph and a cause for rejoicing, whatever the circumstances, because we celebrate the whole Paschal Mystery at each Mass: the whole saving Work of Christ, through which Mankind and the Father were reconciled. Yet we should encourage everyone to be reverent, since every Mass is a solemn memorial celebration of the sacrifice once offered by Christ from the Cross. That sacrifice is re-presented now to make it effective in our lives. Through it, we offer homage and glory to the Father, in the power of the Spirit.

At every Mass we offer to the Father, at the hands of the priest, the body which was once nailed to the Cross, and the blood which was poured out for our salvation. This is the blood of the new Covenant. So although we celebrate Christ's wonderful Resurrection from the dead, and His Ascension, we offer a living sacrifice in reparation for our sins. No-one should treat the whole Mass as being merely a light-hearted event at which the community is bonded together and God is praised. (T:3057)

Loud gossip in church.

It is important that, with gentle dignity, we who are members of one Body demonstrate our love for one another and greet one another. Yet parents who, at the end of the Mass, chatter and gossip loudly about everyday affairs in front of the Lady Chapel or the sanctuary, when they could talk elsewhere and allow some peace for those who wish to pray, set a poor example to their children. (T:3064)

Attention fixed on God.

It is supremely important that we have charitable hearts, if we want to resemble Christ, and please Him. So it's best that we all make gentle efforts to keep our attention fixed on God, amidst distractions. Yet it's also essential that, when appropriate, the Clergy teach the importance of reverence in church.

Christ loves to hear the sincere prayers of gratitude and praise which we offer to Him from amidst the 'Babel' of noises and conversations in the church. He would like to see hundreds of people turning to Him with joy, in the silence of their hearts, both before and after Mass, instead of gossiping about worldly matters. (T:3418)

Straight after Mass.

If we really believed in Christ's Real Presence we would never sit loudly chatting and gossiping in church straight after Mass as if in a cinema or café, ignoring the presence of Christ and His holy Angels.

We must never forget that Christ now lives in majesty and glory - which is the glory, also, of the Father and of the Holy Spirit: and Christ is Really Present in the tabernacle that we see before us.

We cannot see Christ; but it is Christ our God - the living God, Who is one with the Father and the Holy Spirit - Who is Present in the tabernacle   It is plain, therefore, that only someone who is grossly ignorant of Christ's Presence, or who doesn't believe in it, or who is spiritually so blind or insensitive that he barely remembers that Presence, can routinely gossip at length near the sanctuary, oblivious to those who are praying. (T:3916)

Very noisy children.

Very noisy children should be persuaded to be quiet, or helped to be quiet by an interesting book, or taken to a 'cry-room', or carried outside the church until they have agreed to behave well.

Those who pander to aggressive children not only disrupt the prayers of their neighbours; they also fail to give children the training which is necessary if those children are to learn respect for their neighbours and respect for God in His house of prayer.

Christ sees that because of lack of courage, or sentimentality, in dealing with such children, some parents and priests allow the peace of our churches to be disturbed to such an extent that hardly anyone is shocked when children chew gum in church, roll around the floor in boredom, and play 'catch' around the pews. Even their parents stand in front of the sanctuary, loudly discussing holidays and football results, instead of kneeling in gladness and awe before Christ Who honours us by His infinitely-holy Presence. (P.U.T:26)

With tact and kindliness.

Many priests have expressed the opinion that they don't comment on the bad behaviour of children or the unacceptable level of noise in church because it will drive people away. But though tact and kindliness are called for, rather than stern denunciations, a priest is failing in his duty and showing lack of respect for Christ his God if he refuses to teach or remind people how to behave in this 'house of prayer'. Also, he shows lack of respect for those members of the Church who are trying to prepare for or participate in the Sacred Liturgy. (P.U.T:27)

Simplicity and patience.

Christ spoke in simplicity and patience about the need of His disciples to eat His flesh and drink His blood. He didn't try to restrain people who listened with disgust and then walked away. And so, today, He wants His priests to speak the simple truth at all times, both about the sacramental life and about our behaviour in church. Christ asks them to say, for example, that it's the duty of adults and children to behave in church in a peaceful and prayerful manner, both before and after receiving the sacrament of Christ's Sacred Body and Blood. And whoever walks away, offended at having received good advice about good behaviour, from someone with authority to teach, is responsible for his own alienation. (P.U.T: 28)

Loud conversations.

It should be a cause for repentance amongst parents, teachers, and even priests, that so many of them have failed to teach children how to behave in church.

Children can be well-rehearsed for the Liturgy on special

43. DUTY IS LIKE A GOLDEN THREAD.

Our everyday duties are like a golden string left to us by the Lord. If we fulfil them faithfully and lovingly, we can be sure of doing God's Will, and we can move forward steadily towards the light of Heaven. OIL-M:1445. (*"Whatever your work is, put your heart into it as if it were for the Lord and not for men, knowing that the Lord will repay you by making you his heirs."* *Col 3:23-24*).

44. IN A CHASM OF LONELINESS.

We can find Christ in the Holy Eucharist, no matter how obscure our lives, how isolated our community. We trust that if we stand firm, we shall one day reign with Him. OIL-M:1501. *("You should be living holy and saintly lives while you wait and long for the Day of God to come ... the new heavens and new earth, the place where righteousness will be at home." 2 Pet 3:11-13).*

45. CHRIST, AMONGST HIS PEOPLE.

We can be certain that Christ is keeping His promise of remaining amongst us. He is present in the Church through the Scriptures, through his ordained ministers, through the community of the faithful, and supremely through the Sacrament of His Body and Blood. OIL-M:1327. *("And know that I am with you always; yes, to the end of time." Mt 28:20).*

46. CHRIST, THE BRIDGE TO HEAVEN.

Christ alone has bridged the gulf between earth and Heaven. By His Passion, Death, Resurrection and Ascension, He has made a sure path to the Godhead for all those who believe in Him. OIL-M:81. *("I am the Way, the Truth and the Life. No one can come to the Father except through me. If you know me, you know my Father too." Jn 14:6-7).*

47. THE SOULS OF THE JUST.

If we remain faithful, and die 'in Christ,' we shall certainly reach Heaven, whether straight after death, or after a necessary purification. OIL-M:691. *("If the Spirit of him who raised Jesus from the dead is living in you, then he ... will give life to your own mortal bodies." Rm 8:11).*

48. THE GLORY AND THE GATHERING.

Those who love Christ are united with Him and with each other - whether they live on earth, in Purgatory, or in Heaven. Whenever we kneel in prayer we join the worship of this 'Communion of Saints.' We long to share in the eternal fulfilment of Heaven, united with one another in love with the Father, the Son, and the Holy Spirit. OIL-M:42A. *(" His servants will worship him, they will see him face to face ... they will not need lamplight or sunlight, because the Lord God will be shining on them." Rev 22:3-5).*

occasions when they recite the bidding prayers, and carry the gifts to the altar. But it's as though the children undo their good work when they erupt into loud conversations and laughter, unchecked by adults, at the very moment the Mass has ended. Even if the children are blameless, perhaps through lack of instruction, they show irreverence in a sacred place, disturb the Angels, and disrupt the prayers of those who are still praying in thanksgiving for their Holy Communion. (T:5012)

Next to the sanctuary.

It is especially to be regretted that parents and even catechists set a bad example by gossiping amongst the children, right next to the sanctuary.

Christ loves children, as all Christians know. It's because He loves them that He wants them to be taught - for their greater happiness and for the Father's glory - how to genuflect after leaving their places in church, and how to leave the building quietly, in order to talk outside with their parents and friends. (Also T:5012)

The simple truth.

It's important that we are all reminded about reverent behaviour in church. Christ looks on joyfully when responsible people speak with firmness, yet also with charity, to state the simple truth about the Church's teaching and discipline. He admires the courage with which they fulfil His Will, even as they risk being labelled as 'hardliners' or even Pharisees - in an age when obedience is not seen as a virtue. (T:5016)

Heaven's point of view.

It is true that many of those people who act in irreverent or foolish ways in church are good-hearted and kind: simply ignorant of how to behave in God's house. Yet Christ wants to see us all understand the truth about what sort of behaviour is worthy of Him and what isn't appropriate. That's why He invites us to look at the situation today as if from Heaven's point of view.

He wants us to consider what all Heaven sees, of our worship. If it were possible for Saints and Angels to be surprised they would be astonished, as they look into some of our Catholic churches, to hear the shrieks and the shouted conversations, before and after Mass, and to see little evidence of any interest being taken in Christ's sacramental Presence in the tabernacle. Rather, there is jovial uproar, just as at closing time in a pub; and this is in what the Church has always called our 'house of prayer'. (T:5115)

SACRILEGE

A pool of darkness.

It is very important that we're in a state of grace if we plan to approach Christ our God, to receive Him in Holy Communion.

Whenever someone who is not in a state of grace approaches and receives Christ into his soul in Holy Communion it's as though he is inviting Christ to enter a pool of darkness. But when Christ is received by willing souls who have allowed His Holy Spirit to do His purifying work, Christ enters souls which have been changed into places of light and beauty. Such souls are worthy of Him; and He can enter them in Holy Communion as joyfully as a King Who enters a bright room in a beautiful palace. (T:2412)

Blind or impenitent.

We are Christ's dear friends; and He loves to be close to us in Holy Communion. This 'banquet' of Christ is a foretaste of the banquet in which we all hope to share, in Heaven. Yet Christ asks each of us to realise that anyone who has committed a serious sin and yet expects to join in the 'banquet' in church without having made a good confession is like a reckless, returning son who says: "I'm returning home, but I've done nothing wrong." Or perhaps he says: "I haven't been away," or even: "I'm back; and I've been using time well."

Christ sees that whoever speaks in the first manner is blind, or simply denies his sinfulness. By the second, he lies about his sin; and by the third, he shows himself to be impenitent.

Each of us should realise that there is no light, but only darkness in our souls, if we have kept them 'tight-shut' through wilful blindness or denial, or lying or impenitence about serious sin. Christ wants us to realise that no-one in such a state is right to choose a seat at Christ's bright and beautiful banquet, to eat his fill. (T:2559)

Darkness and rebellion.

Christ wants us to realise that when someone has knowingly rebelled against Him, and has not repented, yet chooses to receive Christ in Holy Communion, that person is unable to benefit from Christ's Presence. This is not through lack of generosity in Christ but through the attitude of the person who receives Him unworthily.

It's as if, in that state of darkness and rebellion, such a person is refusing to let the grace of Christ enter. It's as if he has shut the 'door' of his own soul. By remaining determined to continue in his sins, it's as if he is fighting to remain imprisoned within his own will so that he can continue to pursue his own plans instead of God's Will. (T:4885)

Grievous disharmony.

When Jesus lived on earth, He suffered heartache on meeting

people who refused either to welcome Him or to listen to His teachings and His warnings. The disharmony between such souls and Christ's soul was painful for Christ. And that sort of disharmony exists today whenever someone persists in serious sin and then - with neither a moment's contrition nor a changed way of life - goes forward to receive Christ in Holy Communion. (T:4885)

Unrepentant or unprepared.

Christ wants us to consider what He sees so frequently today. Because of their ignorance or disrespect, many people in the Church who are unprepared or unrepentant come to Holy Communion to receive Christ. And He is our God, Who sees everything. He sees that such people are unaware of His immense holiness!

People who are ignorant and therefore unprepared for Holy Communion - perhaps through no fault of their own - don't realise that they are approaching our Divine Saviour Whose holiness is as great as the Presence in the Holy of Holies in Jerusalem. Indeed, His glory is the very glory - the Shekinah - once seen in the Holy of Holies. In Christ's sight, however, some of these unprepared people are blameless. It is the unrepentant who are in far greater need of help. Very sinful people who approach Christ and who are blind to their grave sins are also blind to Christ's immense purity and glory. They show no honour towards Christ as they step forward to receive Him; and they receive no benefit from their sacrilegious Communions. (T:5041)

Grave sins.

Christ sees that few of us receive reminders about those sins which are most prevalent today, and which damage souls and even wreck family life. Christ knows that we are frequently reminded by the Clergy about the dangers of 'consumerism,' or of lack of care of the environment - or lack of respect for the handicapped.

Yet He sees that far fewer priests and Bishops speak out bravely to remind us about the evils most common today in 'ordinary' life, for example, about ambitious mothers - or fathers - neglecting their children or their ageing parents.

Christ sees that few of the Clergy speak out as bravely as they ought, to warn that it is gravely immoral for a man and a woman to live together as man and wife before they marry, or for any couple to use contraceptives, or for persons of the same gender to have a sexual relationship, or for a spouse in a valid marriage to desert his or her spouse, except in a case of extraordinary risk or danger. It is gravely immoral for any spouse who is in a valid marriage yet who has undergone a civil divorce to undergo a 're-marriage' outside the Church. It is gravely sinful for a woman to have an abortion - or for any person to encourage, promote or assist at an abortion, or for anyone to consent to fertility treatments condemned by the Church, such as those which involve the creation and 'disposal' of human embryos. These are some of the sins which the Lord asks the Clergy to mention, and which He asks people to repent of and to confess. We cannot receive Him in Holy Communion and imagine that serious sin doesn't matter.

Since we are all sinners, we mustn't be foolish enough to judge the consciences of people who claim that they have 'clear' consciences about some of the behaviour described above, and who sincerely believe that the Church is wrong in her teaching. Yet all who, by their teaching or preaching, help to form consciences can ask people to do all they can, through prayer and study, to avoid having an 'erroneous conscience'. They can point out that only a very determined and bold person would look at the teachings of Holy Scripture and the Catechism, and of solemn Councils, and at the words of Popes and Saints through centuries of consistent teaching on such subjects, and yet say: "They were mistaken. I know I'm right." (Also T:5041)

Right and wrong.

It's true that some Catholics have been taught little about sin and virtue. It's also true that some people of good-will, who are mired in a situation of grave sin, come for Holy Communion sorry for their sad state and determined to go to Confession as soon as possible. Yet others step forward not caring that they haven't confessed their grave sins, indeed, not yet having decided to give up sin. Or they are full of the pride which causes some people, who have made no effort to examine the reasons for the Church's moral teachings, to prefer their own opinions about right and wrong to the sure teaching which Christ gives in every age, through the one Church.

Every 'apostle' in the Church today should be teaching the truth about right and wrong, so that we can all repent of our sins and allow Christ to sanctify us by His Spirit dwelling within us, and to feed us on our journey to Heaven with the 'food of Angels' - His Sacred Body and Blood, in Holy Communion. (Also T:5041)

A great stain.

To help us to think about serious sin, and Holy Communion, Christ asks us to picture a woman who is appalled that someone has spilled a drink over her wedding dress, just before her wedding ceremony. She would go to endless trouble to make sure that she didn't have to walk towards the altar to be married, with everyone able to see the great stain across her gown. Yet Christ sees that few people take as much care to remove the great 'stains' from their souls - which Christ can see - as they approach the altar to receive Him in Holy Communion.

Christ's love for each person is infinitely tender; yet it would be better if those of us who are in a shameful state were to change - by Confession - into 'clean garments'. That's how we can be made ready not only to receive Christ in the Blessed Sacrament, but also to meet Him joyfully when He calls us to come 'home' to

Heaven. (T:5066)

In a state of grace.

We should all be determined to remain in a 'state of grace': to be good friends of Christ, and free from serious sin. This is important not just so that we can receive Christ worthily in Holy Communion, but also so that we can face death with trust and hope.

When Christ looks at a soul who is in a state of grace, He sees a fire burning: a 'fire' which is the light and love of the Holy Spirit Who dwells within such a soul, transforming it. This is the state which all of us ought to desire, since it's only in a state of grace that we can enjoy an eternal joyful communion with other graceful souls, and also relish forever the joy of knowing God's love.

God loves everyone, all the time; yet people who are alienated from Him don't experience and enjoy His tender concern. Instead - if they know about Him - they spend their lives misinterpreting His holy presence and His powerful concern. They suppose that He is merciless and cruel. (T:5104)

Alive 'in Christ'.

It's supremely important that we do all we can - by God's grace - to remain in a state of grace. It's only in such a state that we can enter Heaven - or Purgatory - when we die. If we are 'alive in Christ' when we die, we can live in Him forever. But if we are 'dead to Christ' when we die, if the Spirit's 'fire' in us has been extinguished by self-will, or has never been set alight, we cannot enter Heaven or Purgatory. This is not because God is unloving, which is impossible. It's because we cannot 'bear' the joy and glory of Heaven unless we have been transformed in and through Christ.

Death is the dividing line. After death it is impossible for people who are not in communion with Christ, or with His 'Communion of Saints', to start or to renew such communion. Those who have permanently rejected 'life in Christ' have therefore rejected the eternal bliss and perfection and joyful communion which they might have found through a grateful response to His invitation. (Also T:5104)

Our state-of-soul.

Truth is always true. What the Church has always taught is true today, and is important for us all to know: that salvation is possible in and through Jesus Christ, and that it matters enormously how we live, and what state-of-soul we are in at the moment of our death. (Also T:5104)

Not reconciled with God.

It's supremely important that we all come to know God in and through Jesus Christ, and that we are made ready for Heaven. Christ wants us all to be reconciled through Him with the Father, to enjoy His love, and to lead good lives.

God our Father is never cruel or unjust, and so He is inviting us all to receive His forgiveness and to share His life. Yet we are free to choose whether to say 'yes' or 'no'; and if we refuse to repent and to draw close to Him, we cannot be saved.

Just as a person who isn't sorry for his serious sins and hasn't bothered to confess them can draw no benefit from making a sacrilegious Communion, so a person who is not reconciled with God, and then dies, cannot share God's life and love. It is impossible. Just as oil and water cannot mix, so a soul which through its own fault is lacking the 'fire' of charity - which is the Holy Spirit dwelling within it - cannot joyfully enter God's fiery love and life, at death, since it is unlike God. 'Like' must meet 'like' if union is to be achieved between frail human beings and their all-holy Creator. (Also T:5104)

God of majesty and glory.

The Lord wants us all to realise that, in every age of history, a person who has begun to believe in the majesty of God has instinctively knelt before God, awed by His holiness. And though God's infinite love for us has been revealed, through the prophets, and then most fully in and through His Son Jesus Christ, God's holiness is no less great than His love. Hence the need, in our day, for us to replace irreverence, carelessness and sacrilege with adoration and respect.

God the almighty Father Whom we praise and honour in the Sacred Mysteries of the Church is infinitely merciful and compassionate. He is a gentle Father; yet at the same 'time' He is like an almighty Fire, now wreathed in majesty. His is a majesty and glory so great that, clearly seen, they would destroy us if we were unprepared. His wisdom is greater than anything we can imagine. His glorious presence is overwhelming for those who meet Him in the prayer of union or in Eternity. His voice, if heard, would shake the whole building in which we gather, to pray. His purity is so pure and exquisite that we would weep for shame if we suddenly saw, close to Him, our filthiness. Yet His love is so true and holy that if we realised its depth we would die of love or shame or fear, overwhelmed by His goodness. This is the God - the only God - who sent Christ to us, from love: Christ who possesses the Divine nature, but Who has assumed our human nature too, to live and die amongst us, to save us. And God our almighty Father asks us yet again, through this book, to show profound reverence towards Christ, true God, Who remains amongst us in the Most Holy Sacrament of the altar and the tabernacle.

It's because such deep reverence is rarely shown today that the Lord has asked for many reminders of Christ's teaching to be put in this book, to help us all in our behaviour. (T:5190)

Our need of purification.

God is so holy that we cannot live with Him in Eternity unless we have been purified of all sin and made perfect: made fit also to be with the Saints and holy Angels who already live 'in' Him. Sin is so horrible that it is worthwhile for us even to sacrifice our lives rather than to sin. We can take as our models the martyrs of the Church, such as Saint Charles Lwanga. Yet many Catholics have forgotten how horrible sin is, or haven't been told about sin, and the fact that Jesus died for our sins. Many Catholics routinely receive Holy Communion today who are precious to God, as His creatures, yet whose ways of life, and failure to repent, would horrify the Apostles.

Christ wants us all to 'see' what He sees. Many Catholics make unworthy or sacrilegious Communions. Many people are so badly instructed that they don't know that the Mass is the saving sacrifice of Christ, re-presented in our sanctuary. Many children have not been taught how to behave in the 'house of God', in the Presence of Christ in the Blessed Sacrament. Many priests are blithely unconcerned about noise and irreverence in church. Other priests who are saddened by poor behaviour lack the courage to speak out. They wrongly imagine that it would be wrong of them to 'risk driving people away' by truthful speech about our duties towards God. Out of all these attitudes comes what Christ sees today: the current disgraceful noise and irreverence in church, all the more dreadful, in His sight, for being so widespread, accepted, and unrecognised as disgraceful. (Also T:5190)

Repentance and renewal.

A further reason for current blindness is that when many people are immersed together in a particular situation it is rare for any of them to see what it really looks like.

Christ sees that there has been a gradual 'slide', in the Church, away from reverence for God. Now people have become used to assuring one another that all is well, and that the Lord is happy to see us all acting informally in church, with 'tolerance' Yet the true state of things today is seen more clearly by some converts. These people have never lost the sense of awe and wonder which first arose in their hearts when they discovered the truth about the awesome nature of God, and about His awesome gift to us of His Son. They see that this gift is given not just at the Incarnation, but also in the Holy Sacrifice of the Mass. So the Lord is once again asking us all to repent, to renew our spiritual lives, and to praise and serve Him with hearts full of reverence and awe, as well as gratitude and joy. (Also T:5190)

8. THE CHURCH BUILDING

A HOUSE OF PRAYER

The holiness of Christ.

We are right to prepare a special place - a house of prayer - for the celebration of the Holy Mysteries. Yet whether we celebrate the Mass in a small room or a great Cathedral, the sacrifice which Christ offers through His priest is powerful, holy, glorious and awesome. It is holy because of the holiness of Christ, the Divine Victim, not because we meet in one sort of building rather than another. (T:858)

Drastic re-ordering.

Christ delights in the love which causes us to care for our church buildings and even to bring about changes in vestments, décor, architecture and music which are appropriate for particular times and places. At the same time He wants us to remember the importance in our churches of paintings and sculptures, so that we have visual reminders of Gospel truths, with symbolism, colour and decorative motifs. He wants us to value the various traditional devotions by which we preface, adorn or end our liturgies. That's why He looks on with no gladness at the efforts of some people to over-simplify the Sacred Liturgy. He takes no delight in the plans of those who want to strip the Liturgy of the exterior beauty long-treasured and encouraged by the Church.

Christ is honoured by the exquisite vestments used by the Clergy.

He is pleased to see painted or sculpted or stained glass images of the Saints and of Biblical themes. He wants us to retain our visual reminders of the story of His Passion and Death, and to value our Crucifixes, and our 'Stations of the Cross'. He is deeply touched by our reverent and courtly genuflections and other gestures. (P.U.T:17)

Special clothes and decorations.

In Christ's sight, we have a right to see Christian symbolism portrayed through Christian art, as well as through the actions of the priest and the materials he uses, such as water, oil, wine and bread.

Christ asks us to realise that people who want to strip the Liturgy of its material beauty are like those who would proclaim - about a silver wedding celebration or a similar worldly event - that we have no need of special clothes or special decorations, provided we educate the guests about the meaning of the event and take part in a wholehearted manner. Yet to over-simplify is not to act according to the plan conceived by God Himself.

He has given Mankind beauty, colour, and imagination, with extraordinary materials, and skill in art and crafts and music. He Himself first encouraged us to decorate His holy places when He instructed the Chosen People about sacred places and spaces, and about worship.

Some customs and traditions can be discarded or changed, over the centuries. Yet we can never accurately call 'out-moded' our desire to give the best of everything to God: both the most perfect preparation of our hearts, to praise Him, and also the most beautiful adornment of our 'house of prayer'. Thus, we honour God Who is almighty and all-holy; and it is more plainly seen that the Sacred Liturgy in which we take part is one with the infinitely-beautiful eternal 'Liturgy' of Heaven. (P.U.T: 30)

ART

Devotion to Christ.

Christ is deeply honoured and delighted when we venerate His image, whether He is portrayed on a crucifix or in other sorts of images or sculptures in the church. He is deeply touched by our devotion to Him in His Passion, shown out, for example when we pray in church in front of the 'Stations of the Cross.' (T:836)

Worthy of God's majesty.

We are right to adorn and beautify God's 'house of prayer,' and to ensure that the Holy Mysteries which are celebrated before us are 'clothed' in elegant, beautiful and dignified outward signs which are worthy of God's majesty. Yet whether our surroundings are simple or ornate, we can be sure that the celebration we share with hundreds of our brothers and sisters 'in Christ' still resembles - at its heart - the gathering of Christ and His Apostles, when they sang together for the Passover. Then, as now, Christ is Really Present in the midst of the gathering.

How simple and glorious is Christ's plan, and our joyful response. Truly, our Lord is Really Present now with His present disciples! (T:1048)

Tasteless surroundings.

We should fix our hearts and our attention on things which are really important, as we pray in church before the Mass begins. Christ's Real Presence can strengthen and console us in every Catholic Church, no matter how crude or tasteless might be the decorations we encounter.

We mustn't give in to despondency when we visit other Catholic churches and dislike the style of the 'art-work' or decorations which surround us. It's true that Christ delights in the beauty which is lavished upon many of the sanctuaries from which He offers His Holy Sacrifice. Such beauty in churches and chapels honours His Divinity; yet He rejoices in every effort which devout people have made to decorate His churches in His honour. Our heart's true joy should stem from the knowledge of His love for us, and from His Presence in the Blessed Sacrament; so if we see ugly or upsetting things around us we mustn't let such things distract us from our prayers. (T:1531)

Unworthy surroundings.

We should hope to see our churches beautifully adorned in Christ's honour; yet we should believe that His glory blots out all that is unworthy in our surroundings. We can comfort ourselves with the knowledge that we are surrounded by awesomely-beautiful companions, since the holy Angels are with us. We can be sure that the holy Angels - who are always attentive and glorious - are welcoming Christ in the sanctuary during the Eucharistic prayer. (Also T:1531)

The veneration of holy images.

Christ delights in seeing us venerate Christian images. All honour which is paid to His Mother's image, for example, is accepted as paid to her whose image it is. And so it is with other worthy images: with images of Christ our Lord, and images of other holy people. (T:1535)

By images, and prayerful gestures.

Christ and His Church know that faith, love, and sacrifice are nurtured and proclaimed by sight and by symbols: a visual 'language'. Through our quiet reflection upon images of faith, and by our prayerful gestures, our bodies and souls are stilled in recollection; and our hearts and minds are led more easily to prayer.

We give glory and homage to God through the beauty of holy places, whether humble or majestic: in elegant buildings, with beautiful language, music and clothing. Yet we should always remember the purpose of the Holy Sacrifice. We must never forget what lies at the 'summit': we are present to the very act through which is 'worked' our Redemption. (T:1804)

Angels, decorating the church.

There is a glorious sight in church, on special occasions. The holy Angels are here within the church. They are very busy, preparing the church for a special Mass. They decorate the interior with garlands of leaves and roses: such is Heaven's delight as it 'waits' to see God glorified by a special event. (T:2270A)

A place of prayer.

It is the Holy Spirit Who has inspired His faithful children to build, adorn and dedicate each special building which is rightly known as a 'house of God'. It is only fitting that we have a place of prayer where the living Church gathers to offer the Holy Sacrifice. (T:2746)

The usefulness of holy images.

Christ knows our nature; indeed, He shares it; and He Who is the living image of the Father knows that images can be useful for us in prayer, when we use them as helpful if temporary aids to prayer and meditation, and not as idols.

We can use visible images in order to learn how to pray to the invisible Father; though this will be a temporary measure. The important thing is that by learning how to pay attention, and yet learning how to look as if 'through' an image, towards God Whom the image represents, we learn to aim our burning 'darts' of prayer towards Heaven. By the use of visual aids, we are being trained for true prayer. (T:3143)

Behind the altar.

Christ invites people involved in church design to realise that we will be less inclined to think of worship as tedious if we are inspired to awe by a beautiful sight behind and around the holy altar. Both children and adults can be helped by seeing holy images which evoke wonder, or provide reminders of the truths of the Catholic Faith.

Whoever enters a Catholic church and sees not a brick wall beyond the altar but a representation of something of Heaven's glory, is helped to raise his heart and mind to God. Prayer is easier, initially. His thoughts are more easily fastened on Heavenly realities. His heart is stirred by the beauty, his soul awe-struck by the glimpse of glory - and his body is therefore gladly 'given' to reverent worship, by stance, gestures, bows, and genuflections and elegant movements. All who worship thus, in unity, inspire one another to greater reverence. From this will stem other good things, such as the realisation of the importance of appropriate clothing for this holy place, hushed and respectful conversation if necessary, respect for the continuing prayer of other worshippers, and a clear distinction between the sacred space and the adjoining rooms where people chat, and hold sales and social functions. (T:3176)

Worthy of the Holy Trinity.

Some people say that Christ instituted the Eucharist at a simple supper - and that austere churches and simple furnishings are therefore best for us today. But the Liturgy we celebrate in church is aptly called the Sacred Liturgy. It is the Holy Spirit Who has inspired Christian people, from early times, to build and adorn places of worship which are worthy of the Holy Trinity - and of the Real Presence of Christ.

There is a place for austerity, for those who have been called by God to lead simple lives in austere monasteries, for example. Yet the 'ordinary' Faithful in parish churches benefit from immersion in the beauty of religious images, sacred symbols and ornamentation. That's why Christ is delighted whenever He sees people arranging for a worthy painting or sculpture to adorn a sanctuary wall, for example.

He invites us to picture a church which has been embellished in a way which honours Him. He asks us to picture a brilliantly-lit rear sanctuary wall. Behind the altar is a tabernacle, at head height - surrounded by a huge painting or relief, with an Angel pictured on each side. And Christ is pleased to see - painted higher on that same wall - an image of Himself and His Holy Mother, as huge figures, in glory, with something indicated of the glory of the other Saints who share His life in Heaven. He wants us to realise that if we decorate our churches in this way, everything is made more bright and glorious so that as we enter the church we are led towards the 'heart' of the church: towards the altar. Yet we have a glorious Presence nearby and a glorious image above; and in such circumstances, our thoughts are more easily 'channelled' towards the hope of Heaven. (Also T:3176)

In a dusty corner.

Christ looks on with compassion when some of His faithful friends come to church to praise Him and to honour His Saints, yet find that ancient statues of the Saints have been placed together in a dark and dusty corner lest they mar the 'severe beauty' of the reordered church interior. Yet ordinary Catholics who live 'in the world' shouldn't have to worship week by week in austere monastic surroundings.

If we must cope, in everyday life, with a million bright and disturbing worldly images we should be able to find, in our local church, images which can 'redress the balance.' We need to see visual reminders of the Creation story, of the Chosen People with their Prophets and Patriarchs. We need to see pictures of the Gospel stories which inspire us, the Saviour Who guides and feeds us - and the Passion He endured because He loves us. We need reminders of the Saints who love to befriend us, especially the Virgin Mother who loves to pray for us, and the holy Angels who guard us. We need reminders of the Heaven which awaits us. That is why as much care should be taken in commissioning appropriate pictures and statues as in making decisions about the walls, seats and lighting. (P.U.T:31)

Love for Our Lady.

No Catholic church is complete unless there is an image which serves as a reminder that we should thank God for Our Lady. Christ's Ever-Virgin Mother is our mother too, in the spiritual life: and so we like to see an image which reminds us of her love, just as people in everyday life like to share photographs of their loved ones, when the opportunity arises. If nothing is seen representing the Blessed Virgin Mary this indicates that some of us in the Church have little love for her. It shows that we have little delight in her continuing existence, her presence in Heaven, her love for her spiritual children, her powerful prayers, or her privileges and her feast-days. (T:3370)

A catechism in pictures.

Those of us who have heard of Saints Cyril and Methodius know that they preached to the Slavs many centuries ago, and that they "preached to them in their own language." The Lord wants us to understand what needs 'preaching' today, to us who need Him and who need His Church. He sees that many of us need our own 'language': the language of pictures - as well as words.

By means of images, millions of people in the world today receive and welcome information about worldly topics; and many who watch pop-videos, films, television, news-bulletins and picture-advertisements, and many more types of picture-information, rarely read a paragraph of text. Therefore some people will welcome information received through pictures, about the Catholic Faith and the spiritual life, which they wouldn't otherwise welcome or absorb.

Other people in the Church today mistakenly believe that we are all literate, and have no need of paintings, as in earlier times. Yet Christ wants us to realise that there's a greater need than ever before for a 'catechism-in-pictures' which should contain images about the various stages of the spiritual life, and about prayer - and also about the Godhead: the Most Holy Trinity. (T:4335)

Fitting ornamentation.

Here, in our church, 'God lives among men'. Yet we receive little help to believe this if Christ's sacramental Presence in our churches - His substantial Presence - is not fittingly acknowledged or is ignored.

The Holy Eucharist is the means by which we can receive from God the grace to persevere in faith; and it's also the source of the holiness which Christ holds out to every contrite soul who approaches Him. That's what we must continue to tell people who don't yet value the Mass, or Holy Communion, or the Blessed Sacrament reserved in the tabernacle.

All who are involved in the design and placement of tabernacles should reflect upon the nature of Him Who is Present with us sacramentally even when the Mass has ended. Christ is God-made-man. He is truly human, yet also a Divine Person: God with us. No-one, therefore, should be afraid of using fitting ornamentation, illumination and veneration in the placement and care of tabernacles for the Blessed Sacrament.

Christ takes special delight in seeing us provide worthy settings for this most holy of all the sacraments, in seeing us make a good preparation to receive Him in Holy Communion, and in seeing us approach Him with reverence and gladness. (T:4544)

MUSIC

Rejoicing in Our Lady's virtues.

We should continue to rejoice in Our Lady's virtues and in the rewards which Christ has showered upon her. She listens with delight to our singing whenever we are joining together, offering hymns in church in her honour.

We shouldn't imagine that our flawed or feeble efforts to praise God and to honour Christ's Mother are unworthy of them, or unappreciated. In Heaven, Mary delights in hearing Christ praised for His goodness towards her. Also - although it's true that Mary has no 'need' of our songs and anthems - she listens with unfeigned joy, just as when a good mother at a birthday party listens while her little children laboriously sing a special composition, out of love for her. (T:1466)

The Holy Mother of God.

We are not wrong to sing 'Marian' hymns and anthems during the Mass. Christ is always delighted to see His Mother honoured, and to hear us praise the virtues and privileges in which she has been clothed by the Father. The holy Angels too delight in hearing her honoured. They keep silent in her honour whenever an anthem is sung by our choir about her God-given role and her wonderful example. (T:2641)

Bad lyrics.

We honour God by the sincerity of our praises, and also by the beauty of the music through which we sometimes praise Him. Yet the words we use in the Sacred Liturgy are of even greater significance than the music; and so those who choose the words and music for use in our churches - whether Mass settings, hymns, or anthems - must take care not to use lyrics which contain untruths. For example, we shouldn't be asked to sing pieces which proclaim that we receive 'bread and wine' when we receive Holy Communion. Nor is it advisable that we routinely sing 'hymns' or anthems which contain neither thanks nor praises, and which nowhere mention God or His Church. (P.U.T:32)

Inappropriate behaviour.

It is not unknown, towards the end of a happy celebration in church, for people to keep applauding at inappropriate times, or even to cheer certain announcements, or to persuade the organist to play frivolous tunes as soon as the Mass has ended. These ways of behaving are wholly inappropriate for God's 'house of prayer,' which is a place of joy but not of worldliness. (P.U.T:33)

A quiet part of the building.

Christ and His Saints and holy Angels delight in the chants and melodies offered by devout choirs and congregations; yet Christ is not honoured when His sanctuary is used as a stage for the singing of worldly songs by worldly people, many of whom are unaware of the sacredness of the building.

Christ delights in the concern of those who, out of love for Him, decide to remove the Sacred Host from the tabernacle before a concert, to place it in a quiet part of the building. Yet it's not His wish that such non-sacred events are allowed in the church in the first place. We scarcely witness to the sacredness of our church if the Blessed Sacrament has to be moved in this way. We scarcely demonstrate proper reverence towards Christ our God if we treat His sacramental Presence as inconvenient because people want to socialise and sing. (P.U.T:34)

Sacred or secular.

It's very important that we treat each Catholic church building as a 'house of God.' The church is a holy place, consecrated for solemn worship. We shouldn't act, on various occasions, as if it's 'only' a concert hall, or a meeting place for secular gatherings.

Catholics who remove the Blessed Sacrament from the tabernacle for a while so that they can treat the church as merely a meeting place are as unwise as Catholics who would empty a beautiful and sacred reliquary box in order to use it as a sandwich tin, for an afternoon, during a parish picnic. (T:5287)

A sacred place.

It is inconvenient for parishioners to manage without a church hall, should they lack one. But when a church is used merely as a hall for an event or entertainment, those who enter it can unlearn, in an evening, what priests and teachers and parents should have worked for years to instil.

We should all have learned the special ways of showing reverence for God in a sacred place, with special respect towards the altar and the tabernacle. Once 'un-learned', such reverence is not easily learned again. Furthermore, our attitude to Christ is not wholly adoring and grateful if we move the Blessed Sacrament out of our church so that we can behave for a few hours, in His own house, in an unprayerful manner. (Also P.U.T:35)

THE SANCTUARY

A holy place.

We must remember what Christ has done for us, by rescuing us from sin. It's important that we make new efforts to be worthy of His friendship, and to be worthy of the life we now lead, as we receive Christ in Holy Communion. The sanctuary and the altar which we see before us are holy. They are so holy that it's as though a trench separates them from the body of the church - a trench which is full of flames. Divine light is shining down upon the whole area; and the fire which is leaping upwards from the trench around that area represents the purification which is necessary before anyone should think of approaching, whether to serve in the sanctuary or to receive Christ in Holy Communion.

If we intend to step towards the altar we ought to prepare ourselves. We should welcome the purification which God can achieve in us through our penance, prayer and Reconciliation, when we have decided to give up sin, by God's power, and to aim for holiness. (T:1630) *(See illustration 14)*

Inappropriate behaviour.

The sanctuary is a holy place; yet even priests sometimes fail to behave there in a manner appropriate for the place of sacrifice. We should all be glad and grateful if our priests are good-humoured and cheerful. Yet priests are not being very wise if they keep trying to 'lighten the atmosphere" in church by frequent wisecracks, and by unnecessary and jocular interpretations of the Liturgy. (T:3348)

The place where Heaven and earth meet.

Christ asks us to remember that the sanctuary is a very holy place. We will be more likely to act with reverence in and around the sanctuary if we realise that the place where the priest stands - at the altar - is the place where Heaven and earth meet, in and through Christ. (T:3510).

THE SACRED VESSELS

Like dirty dishes.

The sacred vessels which are used at Mass are indeed sacred: holy. So unless this is unavoidable, it's not appropriate for the sacred vessels to be left unpurified after Holy Communion, merely being put at one side like so many dirty dishes to be washed up after a meal. Nor is it appropriate that these vessels, which might still contain Christ's Sacred Body and Blood, be carried out casually to the sacristy for purification by Eucharistic ministers who are encumbered by handbags. (P.U.T:36)

THE CRUCIFIX

Opposition and hardship.

Baptised Christians like ourselves deserve to see a crucifix, as we gaze towards the sanctuary. If we sometimes enter the church, worrying about opposition and hardship, we can glance at the Cross, and at Christ's wounded body, to see our incarnate God made helpless: in freely-chosen love and obedience, in faithfulness to the Father's Will and to duty.

Here is the place, therefore, to ponder our own attitudes, relationships, and duties. In every perplexing situation we can glance at the Cross to be reminded of the lengths to which Christ went to save us and to bring us, with Him, to our true home in Heaven. (T:1676B)

By which Christ redeemed us.

The Lord asks us to remember that wherever there is a 'Crucifixion' scene, as a fitting sculpture or painting on the wall of the sanctuary, it gives Him glory. This is because it helps everyone present to keep in mind the act by which Christ redeemed us. It also reminds us of the sacrificial nature of the Mass for which we have gathered together.

Yet there's something more to consider. Christ wants us to realise how glad He is when a work of art, by its colour, composition and tone - a work of art which depicts some aspect of His Paschal Work - beautifies an otherwise bare wall. (T:2769).

SHRINES

Heavenly friends.

Christ loves to welcome us to His holy places: to every church or shrine. The shrine of a Christian Saint is like a doorway to Heaven; and we should treasure our friendship with the Saints as well as with Christ.

We are right to seek the help of the Saints. They are waiting to help us; and by our prayer near the Lady Chapel, or at the tomb of a Saint, or in some other special area, it's as if a 'door' to Heaven has opened. Many holy friends look joyfully towards us, from Heaven. They are longing to hear our prayers. (T:1680)

Consecration or custom.

We should cherish holy places. Wherever the Church has made a shrine because of a consecration, or relics, or a martyrdom, or custom, we can kneel in prayer, confident of receiving special graces as we renew our spiritual union with Heavenly friends.

At every holy shrine where our God is honoured - whether honoured directly, or honoured through our love for His Saints and His holy Angels - it's as though the Saints are jostling for the privilege of hearing and greeting us, their earthly friends. The Saints are radiant in the light of God's glory; and it's as if they usher to the front of the holy company the Saint whose name we invoke as we make our special request.

We should share with other people the marvellous news that Christ rewards us for our faith, courage and determination. Great joys and graces await everyone who makes even a little pilgrimage to one of the Church's sacred shrines in order to seek Christ's special help and to give Him glory. (Also T:1680)

The need to be recollected.

Just before the Mass begins we need to be recollected, so that we can assist at the offering in a whole-hearted manner. So although we are right to delight in and benefit from the special shrines and chapels in church, since they assist us in our prayers and cause us to be drawn closer to Heaven and to Christ, we should see them principally as aids to devotion outside the time of Mass. (T:2204)

BEAUTY

Worthy of Christ's Divinity.

Christ wants us all to know how deeply touched He is by a sincere welcome. We should realise how happy Christ is, when He appears by the altar in glory, at the Consecration, to be greeted in the church and sanctuary with great love, and with solemn and heartfelt veneration, befitting His Divinity. He is honoured by the careful preparations. He is honoured that candles are held aloft by kneeling servers. He is honoured by the incense, by the order and beauty which surround Him, and by the hushed, reverent and prayerful silence. (T:1493)

Reverent genuflections.

Christ take especial delight in being with His People wherever there is great love for Him, wherever things are beautiful, in His honour, and wherever there is peace and order in our worship, with reverent gestures and genuflections: all offered because of genuine love for Him, and in honour of His Divinity. (T:2745)

With beauty and order.

The liturgy should be celebrated with awe and reverence, amidst beauty and order, to give fitting honour to the Father. (T 3064)

Gratitude towards Christ .

At the time of Christ's Incarnation, He 'leaped down' from Heaven to an apparently ordinary everyday life. The Son of God, through Whom the whole Universe was made, was content to live amongst us for many years in poverty and obscurity. Going about in His public ministry, He endured the mockery, coldness, and arguments of those who hated Him, as well as the misunderstanding of His friends - and eventually desertion. For our sakes, He endured torture and death, before His glorious Resurrection and Ascension. It should be the aim of every sincere Christian, therefore, to show perpetual gratitude towards Christ for His loving-kindness - and to thank the Father of glory Who sent Him, and the Spirit by Whose power and love Christ was made man. And we can express that gratitude and thanks especially-well at every Mass.

Here in church, today, in this everyday setting, Christ our incarnate God leaps down, we can say, to be with us sacramentally in our ordinary way of life. And just as it's highly appropriate that we greet Him with reverence, gratitude and delight, so it's also appropriate that we beautify the church buildings and its furnishings, and, in doing so, provide a hint of Heaven's glory.

Christ is Heaven's glorious King. Nearly two thousand years ago He left behind His glory, for our sakes. And it's as though the Church through the ages, in the celebration of the Sacred Mysteries, has tried to make up to Christ for what was lacking for Him when He once lived on earth in ordinary surroundings. (T:3487)

From Saint Paul's Letter to the Colossians.

"Since you have been brought back to true life with Christ, you must look for the things that are in heaven, where Christ is, sitting at God's right hand. Let your thoughts be on heavenly things, not on the things that are on the earth, because you have died, and now the life you have is hidden with Christ in God. But when Christ is revealed - and he is your life - you too will be revealed in all your glory with him.

That is why you must kill everything in you that belongs only to earthly life: fornication, impurity, guilty passion, evil desires and especially greed, which is the same thing as worshipping a false god; all this is the sort of behaviour that makes God angry. And it is the way in which you used to live when you were surrounded by people doing the same thing, but now you, of all people, must give all these things up: getting angry, being bad-tempered, spitefulness, abusive language and dirty talk; and never tell each other lies. You have stripped off your old behaviour with your old self, and you have put on a new self which will progress towards true knowledge the more it is renewed in the image of its creator; and in that image there is no room for distinction between Greek and Jew, between the circumcised or the uncircumcised, or between the barbarian and Scythian, slave and free man. There is only Christ: he is everything and he is in everything.

You are God's chosen race, his saints; he loves you, and you should be clothed in sincere compassion, in kindness and humility, gentleness and patience. Bear with one another; forgive each other as soon as a quarrel begins. The Lord has forgiven you; now you must do the same. Over all these clothes, to keep them together and complete them, put on love. And may the peace of Christ reign in your hearts, because it is for this that you were called together as parts of one body. Always be thankful." (Colossians 3:1-15).

What is Radiant Light?

Radiant Light is a small movement within the Roman Catholic Church which seeks to encourage people to grow in faith and to share their faith with others. The movement was founded by Elizabeth Wang - a Catholic housewife, mother and artist - in obedience to the wishes of Christ, Who is 'the radiant light of God's Glory' (Heb 1:3). She has received many teachings and visions from him to renew the Church, and over the last few years she has been writing, painting and talking about them. These teachings are simply reminders of the constant teaching of the Church.

Radiant Light is also a small non-profit-making company which publishes the works of Elizabeth Wang and organises various events about the Catholic Faith. It has wide trading objects, together with two specific aims which are:

'For the glory of God the Most Holy Trinity, for the honour of the Blessed Virgin Mary, and out of love for the Catholic Church and loyalty to the Pope and the Bishops in communion with him.

(1) to advance the Roman Catholic religion
(2) to promote the works of Elizabeth Wang

Please write to the Harpenden address below if you would like to be put on the mailing list.

If you would like to help support the work of Radiant Light, please send a UK cheque to **Radiant Light, 25 Rothamsted Avenue, Harpenden, Herts, AL5 2DN., U.K.** Cheques must be made payable to 'Radiant Light'. Thank you.

Company No. 3701357 (Company limited by guarantee and not having a share capital).

Visit the Radiant Light web-site at:
www.radiantlight.org.uk

Book Orders and Distribution.

Radiant Light books, videos, postcards and posters are available from St. Pauls book shop next to Westminster Cathedral, London:

St. Pauls
(By Westminster Cathedral)
Morpeth Terrace
Victoria
London SW1P 1EP
United Kingdom.

Tel: 020 7828 5582
Fax: 020 7828 3329

email: bookshop@stpauls.org.uk
order on-line at: www.stpauls.org.uk

Mail-Order: If you would like to order Radiant Light works through the post, St Pauls has a very efficient *mail-order service*, which will send your order throughout the UK and anywhere in the world. Please telephone St Pauls and ask them how you may order Radiant Light books. *But please do not send money or orders until you have been in touch with them.*